International Human Resource Management

PEARSON

We work with leading authors to develop the strongest
educational materials in business and management bringing cutting-edge
thinking and best learning practice to a global market.

Under a range of well-known imprints, including Financial Times Prentice Hall,
we craft high-quality print and electronic publications which help readers to
understand and apply their content, whether studying or at work.

To find out more about the complete range of our publishing, please visit us
on the World Wide Web at:
www.pearsoned.co.uk.

Second Edition

International Human Resource Management

Globalization, National Systems and Multinational Companies

Tony Edwards and Chris Rees

Financial Times
Prentice Hall
is an imprint of

Harlow, England • London • New York • Boston • San Francisco • Toronto
Sydney • Singapore • Hong Kong • Tokyo • Seoul • Taipei • New Delhi
Cape Town • Madrid • Mexico City • Amsterdam • Munich • Paris • Milan

Pearson Education Limited
Edinburgh Gate
Harlow
Essex CM20 2JE
England

and Associated Companies throughout the world

Visit us on the World Wide Web at:
www.pearsoned.co.uk

First published 2006
Second edition published 2011

© Pearson Education Limited 2011

ISBN: 978-0-273-71612-9

British Library Cataloguing-in-Publication Data
A catalogue record for this book is available from the British Library

Library of Congress Cataloging-in-Publication Data
Rees, Chris, 1966-
    International human resource management : Globalization, National Systems and Multinational
Companies / Chris Rees and Tony Edwards. -- 2nd ed.
        p. cm.
    Rev. ed. of: International human resource management : globalization, national systems and multinational
companies / Tony Edwards and Chris Rees. 2006.
    Tony Edwards name appeared first in earlier ed.
    Includes bibliographical references and index.
    ISBN 978-0-273-71612-9 (pbk. : alk. paper)
    1. International business enterprises--Personnel management.   I.   Edwards, Tony, 1968-   II.   Edwards,
Tony, 1968- International human resource management.   III.   Title.
HF5549.5.E45E38 2011
658.3--dc22   2010032985

10 9 8 7 6 5 4 3 2 1
14 13 12 11 10

Typeset in 9/13 Stone Serif by 75
Printed by Ashford Colour Press Ltd., Gosport

Brief contents

Contents

8 HR in cross-border mergers and acquisitions   139

Tony Edwards and Chris Rees

Part 2 THE MANAGEMENT OF INTERNATIONAL HRM

9 International management development   163

Jean Woodall

10 Recruitment and selection of international managers   184

Fiona Moore

Phil Almond

Reader in International and Comparative HRM, De Montfort University.

Phil has published widely on issues relating to HR and employment relations in multinational corporations, including editing, with his colleague Professor Anthony Ferner, the Oxford University Press volume *American Multinationals in Europe*. He also has active research interests in the area of comparative employment relations and comparative methodology. He is currently leading an ESRC-financed, cross-national study concerning the relations between multinationals and sub-national governance actors, and their effects on human resources and labour markets in the UK, Canada, Ireland and Spain.

Stephen Bach

Professor of Employment Relations, King's College London.

Stephen's principal research activities relate to public service HRM and changing workforce roles. His research interests include: international migration of health professionals; new ways of working in the public services; human resource management in the health sector; public–private partnerships and the future of public service trade unions. His books include *Employment Relations and the Health Service* (Routledge, 2004) and he is editor of *Managing Human Resources* (Blackwell, 2005). Stephen has provided policy advice to a wide range of organizations including the International Labour Organization, Organization of Economic Cooperation and Development and World Health Organization.

Virginia Doellgast

Lecturer in Employment Relations and Organisational Behaviour, London School of Economics.

Virginia's research interests are in the areas of comparative employment relations and human resource management, with a focus on Europe and the US. She recently completed a comparative study on the restructuring of frontline service jobs in the US and German telecommunications industries and an international research project on human resource management in the global call centre industry. Virginia is currently Principal Investigator on an ESRC-funded project examining the employment effects of organizational restructuring in the European telecommunications industry.

Tony Edwards

Professor of Comparative Management, King's College London.

Tony's research focuses on the management of labour in multinational companies, including the diffusion of practices across countries, the influence of the domestic business system on international HR policies and the management of human resources during and after international mergers and acquisitions. This work has been published in journals such as *Journal of Management Studies, British Journal of Industrial Relations, Industrial Relations* and *Human Relations*. Tony is currently engaged in a large project examining employment practice in multinationals in nine countries, and is Principal Investigator on an ESRC grant that is leading the international programme of collaboration.

Howard Gospel

Professor of Management and Senior Research Fellow, King's College London.

Howard is also an Associate Fellow of the Said Business School, University of Oxford, and of the Centre for Economic Performance, London School of Economics. His research interests are employer labour policy, corporate governance and labour management, employee voice systems, and skill formation and training, all with a comparative perspective.

Enda Hannon

Senior Lecturer in Employment Relations and Employment Law, Kingston University.

Enda's research interests are focused on examining the drivers of job quality in low-wage, low-skill sectors, and the comparative political economy of employment and skills. His PhD research, undertaken at Warwick Business School, examined prospects for employment upgrading for production operatives in the British and Irish dairy processing industries. He is currently undertaking an ESRC-funded project on knowledge-intensive firms in the British and Irish pharmaceutical and software sectors.

Fiona Moore

Lecturer in International HRM, Royal Holloway, University of London.

Fiona is an industrial anthropologist who received her D Phil from the University of Oxford. Her research focuses on identity in MNCs, and she has conducted studies on the use of ethnic identity as a strategic resource by German expatriates in London, identity among workers and managers at an automobile plant, and the social adjustment of Korean labour migrants in London. She is currently researching hybrid identities among Anglo-Chinese managers. Her publications include *Transnational Business Cultures* (Ashgate, 2005) and *Professional Identities: Policy and Practice in Business and Bureaucracy* with Shirley Ardener (Berghahn, 2007).

Chris Rees

Senior Lecturer in Employment Relations, Royal Holloway, University of London.

Chris has research interests broadly around the sociology of work and employment in comparative perspective. He is currently engaged in projects on (i) the cross-border transfer of employment practices and (ii) trade union responses to CSR in MNCs. He has published in various journals (incl. *Organization Studies, Work Employment and*

Society, European Journal of Industrial Relations, Human Resource Management Journal, and *Employee Relations*). He has a PhD and MA in Industrial Relations from the University of Warwick, and a BSc in Sociology from the University of Bristol.

Sanjiv Sachdev

Principal Lecturer in Employment Relations, Kingston University.

In recent years Sanjiv's research has focused on employment relations aspects of public service reform, currently in relation to the UK prison service. He has been consulted by the National Audit Office in this area. He has written for the *Guardian,* various practitioner publications, and had work published by the think tank, Catalyst, and the Institute of Employment Rights.

Adam Smale

Assistant Professor, Department of Management, University of Vaasa.

Adam's research interests lie in HRM, electronic HRM and knowledge transfer in multinational firms. His work in these areas has been published in, for example, *International Business Review, Journal of World Business, International Journal of Human Resource Management* and *Human Resource Management Journal.* He is currently involved in a large-scale project on global talent management amongst 12 Nordic multinationals. He received his MA from Kingston University and his PhD from the University of Vaasa.

Guy Vernon

Lecturer in HRM, University of Southampton.

Guy's research concerns international and comparative people management and the linkage between people management and employee and business outcomes, and has been published in the *European Journal of Industrial Relations, Economic and Industrial Democracy* and *Employee Relations.* His research on reward has centred upon the implications of cross-national comparative variation in the significance and nature of collective bargaining for pay structures and systems. Guy is also co-author (with Chris Brewster and Paul Sparrow) of the 2007 second edition of the Chartered Institute of Personnel and Development text *International Human Resource Management.*

Jean Woodall

Dean of Westminster Business School, University of Westminster.

Jean has written or edited eight books, including *New Frontiers in HRD* co-edited with Monica Lee and Jim Stewart (Routledge, 2004), and *Ethical Issues in Contemporary Human Resource Development* with Diana Winstanley (Palgrave, 2000). She has published on a wide range of topics in the field of human resource development including career management for women, work-related management development, professional learning, and ethics and HRD, as well as on public sector management, and HR outsourcing. Her most recent research is on the development of part-time lecturers in higher education. Jean is a former editor-in-chief of the journal *Human Resource Development International*.

Miao Zhang

Principal Lecturer in International HRM, Kingston University.

Miao's research interests centre on HRM in MNCs and comparative HRM. Her recent work focuses on HR strategies and practices within emerging economies. She is currently engaged in examining innovation and the diffusion of employment practices in Chinese multinationals operating in different countries, and is also leading a collaboration on innovation and social networks in different work organizations with Tsinghua University in China. Miao's work has been published in various journals, including the *International Journal of Human Resource Management* and *Employee Relations*.

Acknowledgements

We are grateful to the following for permission to reproduce copyright material:

Figures

Figure 2.6 adapted from 'The external wealth of nations mark II: revised and extended estimates of foreign assets and liabilities, 1970–2004', *Journal of International Economics*, 73, 223-250 (Lane, P. and Milesi-Ferretti, G.M. 2007)

In some instances we have been unable to trace the owners of copyright material, and we would appreciate any information that would enable us to do so.

Tables

Table 3.1 from 'Disappearing Taxes or the "Race to the Middle"? Fiscal Policy in the OECD' in L. Weiss (ed.) *States in the Global Economy: Bringing Institutions Back In* (Hobson, J. 2003), Cambridge University Press

Chapter 1

Introduction

Tony Edwards and Chris Rees

This book is about the management of international human resources and employment relations within multinational companies (MNCs). It aims to be distinctive in both its structure and content. In this introductory chapter we firstly outline the broad approach of the book, in terms of how it compares to other similar texts in the field. We then indicate the key analytical themes that run throughout the book, before providing an overview of the content through a brief summary of each chapter.

There is a growing number of introductory texts in the fields of international HRM and international/comparative employment relations. In broad terms, these can be broken down into three types. First are those which are structured along national lines, with individual chapters on different countries and comparisons between them being for the most part largely implicit, other than in the introduction and conclusion sections. Examples are the collections edited by Kamoche *et al*. (2004) on HRM in Africa, and Budhwar (2004) on HRM in Asia-Pacific, as well as those by Bamber *et al*. (2004) and Ferner and Hyman (1998) that focus on national systems of industrial relations, and that by Morley *et al*. (2006) which adopts a regional and national approach (together with some thematic chapters in the second half). While these books provide very detailed explanations of distinctive national patterns, they are not designed to cover the broader field of international HRM in any detail, and so tend not to be suitable as core texts on such courses. Second are those books with a predominantly international business (IB) focus which attempt to cover many different aspects of corporate strategy and focus on international HR issues in certain dedicated chapters. Good examples here are Lassere (2007), Morrison (2009), Parker (1998) and Rugman and Collinson (2009). These books provide a lot of useful material on such issues as the strategies and structures of multinational companies, and the economic context within which such firms operate, but like the first category they are also not designed explicitly for international HRM courses, and tend not to explore HR issues in any particular depth. Third are those books which take a more thematic approach, with chapters on particular areas of international HR policy, most commonly pay and reward, training and development, recruitment and selection, and so on. Well known examples include Brewster *et al*. (2007), Dowling *et al*. (2008), Harzing and Van Ruysseveldt (2004) and Tayeb (2005).

It is this third approach which our book most closely resembles, and there are three further distinctions we would make within this category. First, some of these books focus primarily upon the management of those (mainly senior) staff who travel frequently between countries. Good examples are Brewster and Harris (1999) and Scullion and Collings (2006). We see this area as one part of international HRM, an important one undoubtedly, but not the only one. Thus our focus is wider, incorporating the study of both managerial and non-managerial employees. A second distinction is between approaches to understanding international HRM that focus on national cultures as a key explanatory factor and those that explore the importance of institutional and historical context in more detail. The first of these is the one that is most widely used in international HRM research more generally, and features very strongly in some of the textbooks, such as Jackson (2002) and Tayeb (2005). While not disregarding culture, we stress the benefits of understanding how economic and social activity is shaped by institutions at the national and international level. Consequently, we seek to adopt an approach that is primarily institutional, but which incorporates an appreciation of how values and attitudes differ across borders. A third distinction is between books written by just one or two people and edited collections involving a large number of contributors. The first of these, of which Hollinshead (2010), Perkins and Shortland (2006) and Tayeb (2005) are examples, has the advantage that the writing style is more likely to be consistent throughout. However, this does requires the author(s) to write about all areas of international HRM, including those where they perhaps do not have particular research expertise. In contrast, edited collections, exemplified by Harzing and van Ruysseveldt (2004) and Ozbilgin (2005), have the advantage of drawing upon expertise from a range of subject specialists, and yet consequently run the risk of losing some coherence and overall thread of argument. We have chosen a mid-way position in this respect, writing Part One of the book largely ourselves and then drawing on input from experts in particular areas in Part Two.

The rationale for this split is that Part One establishes a solid conceptual and analytical framework for understanding the context for international HRM, and Part Two consists of the application of these ideas to particular areas of international HR practice. In order to provide further coherence throughout the book, we have also highlighted six distinct themes, established at the planning stages as dilemmas or dichotomies with which we would want all the contributors to wrestle. These themes are referenced at different points throughout the text, and serve to emphasize that the book does not seek to offer 'one best way' blueprint solutions for international HR practitioners, but rather aims to take a balanced and critical stance towards the formation and execution of HR policy in MNCs, and to locate management action firmly within its economic and societal context. The six themes are as follows:

Globalization versus embeddedness

The most obvious theme of the book concerns globalization. The book begins by reviewing the hotly contested debates concerning the extent to which globalization is really novel on the one hand or has historical precedents on the other. In developing the limitations to globalization, we show how economic activity is embedded in distinctive arrangements at local level. Having set out the main aspects of the globalization debate, this becomes a theme running throughout the rest of the book.

Cultures versus institutions

If economic activity is embedded in distinctive arrangements at national level, then we need to consider how we might think about the nature of embeddedness. We contrast the culturalist approach, widely adopted in international HRM research, with various types of institutionalism. The strengths and limitations of each of these are assessed. On balance, we tend towards a more sympathetic treatment of institutionalism and offer a sharp critique of (some aspects of) the culturalist perspective. We also discuss attempts to combine the two, and address debates concerning how managers within MNCs perceive and respond to varying institutional contexts.

Choices versus constraints

While actors within MNCs unquestionably have scope to choose how they operate and what strategies to pursue, these choices are far from being unconstrained. The nature of these constraints to a large extent follows from the second point; if firms are embedded in distinctive cultures and institutions then they are to some extent governed by the requirements that these present. However, we can also see institutions as facilitating certain courses of action – in other words, they are resources as well as constraints – and actors in senior positions in MNCs have some scope to choose where to operate and which policies to pursue.

Integration versus differentiation

As we have said, the book focuses on the multinational company, and the fourth theme relates to a key aspect of the strategies of MNCs. A familiar idea in the field is to contrast the pressures to integrate a firm's operations across borders (arising from the opportunities to realise synergies in different countries, for instance) with the pressures to differentiate these operations (that stem from ongoing distinctiveness in national contexts). We develop this in a number of respects, including the ways in which MNCs balance these pressures across regions and divisions. The issue of regionalization (both as an MNC strategy and as a feature of the comparative context for international business) is one that features at a number of points in the book.

Standardization versus segmentation

A less familiar dilemma in international HRM research is the issue of the form of integration that firms pursue. One way of integrating operations across countries is to set up operating units that replicate the functions that are carried out in other countries, which we refer to as standardization, while another is to separate out various parts of the production process so that each is concentrated in a particular location, which we term segmentation. Profoundly different implications for how MNCs manage their international workforces flow from each of these, and there are also a range of interme-diate positions. We develop these arguments explicitly in Chapters 5 and 6 and they feature in a number of other chapters as well.

Collaboration versus contestation

It is understandable that a central concern in much international HRM research is on how MNCs can arrive at collaborative ways of working across borders. Clearly, though, many of these processes are subject to contestation. That is, the preferences and strate-gies of various groups within firms differ from one another, and individuals and groups will use whatever sources of power are at their disposal to advance and defend their own interests. This is true for the globalization process in general, and for the way that MNCs manage their international workforces in particular; and while all organizations are characterised by political struggles between different groups of actors, this is espe-cially the case for large, complex MNCs that cross national divides.

As mentioned, the book is arranged in two sections. Each contains seven chapters. Part One of the book (Chapters 2–8) attempts to address in a coherent way a wide range of the debates and issues which set the context for understanding international HRM practice.

In Chapter 2 we critically examine the concept of globalization, outlining the main arguments on either side of the so-called 'globalization debate'. We stress how interna-tional HRM activity needs to be understood not only in terms of globalization, but also as subject to a variety of pressures from other levels of analysis – namely the regional, the national and the organizational. We are interested here in the ways in which fac-tors at all four of these levels combine in differing ways to influence IHRM strategy and practice in MNCs. Chapter 3 examines the role of national differences in international HRM more closely, contrasting cultural and institutional approaches, and considering theoretical attempts to synthesize the two into a more all-embracing understanding of 'national effects'. It also outlines recent ideas about how to more adequately explain the interaction between what managers do within organizations and the other three 'external' levels of analysis – the national, the regional and the global. In Chapter 4, Phil Almond builds on this by looking at specific ways in which employment systems differ on a national and regional basis, and considers the issue of whether countries can usefully be grouped together. He then looks at how the cross-national differences high-lighted might affect decisions on HRM issues in international context. These three chapters, taken together, provide a solid introduction to key aspects of the context within which international HRM is conducted.

The next four chapters focus on aspects of MNCs that impact more directly upon international HRM activity. Chapter 5 reviews the variety of explanations concerning why firms internationalize, and the alternative strategies and structures that MNCs can pursue. It considers how we understand and define the multinational company, and the role of MNCs in globalization, examining processes of expansion in particular. It is clear that MNC managements operate with only partial knowledge of different business systems and national environments, and so the alignment of appropriate strategies and structures is crucial, as is the question of how to transfer knowledge across borders and between business units; hence, the chapter looks in detail at strategy making, and stresses the importance of micro-politics and organizational power relations as key drivers and shapers of the actual practice of strategy. We note here that despite the often strong arguments that competitive advantage comes through operationalizing a truly 'transnational' strategy, in practice this is often extremely difficult as companies remain embedded in distinct national contexts, something we highlight with a discussion of the so-called 'country-of-origin effect'. In Chapter 6, Adam Smale proceeds to tackle the issue of the key drivers of global HRM integration in multinational corporations. He presents the arguments concerning why MNCs are inclined to pursue more extensive integration (as opposed to differentiation) in the future, and identifies the range of mechanisms through which MNCs can facilitate the global integration of their HRM practices. The chapter also critically evaluates when the global integration of HRM can be regarded as having been accomplished. Chapter 7 outlines a number of aspects of the diffusion of HR practices across borders within MNCs. We see that national systems provide both opportunities for and constraints upon this process, and we again stress the political dynamics involved in diffusion, and how these informal processes are as important an explanatory factor as more formal structures. Chapter 8 considers the issue of cross-border mergers and acquisitions (M&As), highlighting again the distinct influence of 'national effects', in particular the nationality of the parent firm and the ways that HR issues are handled differently in different host environments. We also see here the highly political and contested nature of change, illustrated by key questions at various stages of the merger process (e.g. how to populate senior management positions, where to locate head offices, and where cost-cutting should have the biggest impact).

Having established a solid conceptual and contextual foundation, the focus of the book then moves in Part Two (Chapters 9–15) to examine substantive HR issues within an international context.

We begin this section with two chapters examining aspects of the management of international staff, namely how they are developed for international assignments (Chapter 9) and how they are recruited and selected (Chapter 10). In Chapter 9 Jean Woodall stresses the importance of understanding the context of management assignments and the role of the individual manager in organizational learning. She discusses the particular attributes necessary for success in this area and outlines some of the initiatives that MNCs can profitably take, such as cross-cultural awareness training and multicultural team building. The impact of both global and local pressures is also apparent in Chapter 10 by Fiona Moore, where she stresses their influence upon recruitment and selection processes. She gives particular attention to the argument that the rise of international managers is creating a distinct group, a 'global elite', from whom MNCs can recruit. She concludes that this is something of a myth, as managers are never truly 'rootless', and those on assignments often stay in countries where they have been successful, such that processes of globalization again encourage divergence as much as they do convergence. The key lesson for practitioners is the need to keep in mind the specific set of circumstances surrounding each assignment.

The issue of pay and reward is addressed in Chapter 11, and that of employee representation in Chapter 12. In Chapter 11, Guy Vernon outlines the variety of different national contexts that companies face when developing international reward strategies, the factors which explain this cross-national variation, and how these factors impact upon the degree of genuine 'strategic choice' that managers have. National settings are again seen to provide constraints upon as well as opportunities for innovation in management strategy, and whilst no simple 'one best way' prescriptions are available, HR nevertheless has a crucial role to play in the assessment of national patterns and the development of considered pay arrangements. The area of employee representation is one where managers in MNCs increasingly need to take strategic decisions regarding their approach. In Chapter 12, Enda Hannon considers national variety in forms of employee representation, and explains some of the approaches that companies are taking. He argues that although there is an increasing significance to international developments, implementation still remains largely the responsibility of managers at a local national level.

The final three chapters consider topics that have rapidly moved up the hierarchy of issues that MNCs seek to address. The first of these is international corporate social responsibility (CSR). In Chapter 13, Sanjiv Sachdev takes a critical look at what companies actually do in the name of CSR, and assesses the debate over regulation versus voluntarism. He stresses the important role that HR professionals can play in this area of policy, one which is often seen as no more than a 'corporate gloss' and yet has the potential to have a significant impact. In Chapter 14, Stephen Bach tackles the issue of migration. He examines trends in international migration and its causes, the main impact that migration has, particularly in terms of who benefits and who loses, and assesses the human resource management challenges that arise from employing a more diverse workforce. Finally, in Chapter 15, Virginia Doellgast and Howard Gospel consider the issue of outsourcing at the international level. They begin by providing background on trends in outsourcing and then discuss the HRM issues and choices associated with it. A theme of the chapter is the ways in which national institutions affect the costs and benefits of different strategic choices by firms, as well as the particular challenges MNCs face as they seek to manage outsourcing contracts across national borders.

We seek throughout the book to establish relevant theoretical and conceptual material and to supplement this by reviewing the empirical evidence. In order to allow students to further relate this to organizational contexts, we illustrate some of the key issues with case studies in Chapters 5 to 15, and provide review questions and suggestions for further reading in all chapters. The idea for the book came from our experience of teaching final-year under-graduate and master's students over a number of years at different institutions. We were constantly telling students that there was no 'one best book' in the area, but rather a number of useful texts which they would need to consult. While we would certainly not claim our book to be 'the best', we hope to have provided a research-informed text which will be considered as an integrated and thorough contribution to the field.

References

Bamber, G.J., Lansbury, R.D. and Wailes, N. (eds) (2004) *International and Comparative Employment Relations* (4th edition), London: Sage.

Brewster, C. and Harris, H. (1999) *International HRM: Contemporary Issues in Europe*, London: Routledge.

Brewster, C., Sparrow, P. and Vernon, G. (2007) *International Human Resource Management*, London: CIPD.

Budhwar, P.S. (ed.) (2004) *Managing Human Resources in Asia-Pacific*, London: Routledge.

Dowling, P., Festing, M. and Engle, A. (2008) *International Human Resource Management: Managing People in a Multinational Context* (5th edition), London: Thompson.

Ferner, A. and Hyman, R. (eds) (1998) *Changing Industrial Relations in Europe*, Oxford: Blackwell.

Harzing, A.-W. and Van Ruysseveldt, J. (eds) (2004) *International Human Resource Management* (2nd edition), London: Sage.

Hollinshead, G. (2010) *International and Comparative Human Resource Management*, Maidenhead: McGraw-Hill.

Jackson, T. (2002) *International HRM: A Cross-Cultural Approach*, London: Sage.

Kamoche, K., Debrah, Y., Horwitz, F. and Muuka, G.N. (eds) (2004) *Managing Human Resources in Africa*, London: Routledge.

Lassere, P. (2007) *Global Strategic Management* (2nd edition), Basingstoke: Palgrave.

Morley, M., Gunnigle, P. and Collings, D. (eds) (2006) *Global Industrial Relations*, London: Routledge.

Morrison, J. (2009) *International Business: Challenges in a Changing World*, Basingstoke: Palgrave.

Ozbilgin, M. (ed.) (2005) *International Human Resource Management: Theory and Practice*, Basingstoke: Palgrave.

Parker, B. (1998) *Globalization and Business Practice: Managing Across Boundaries*, London: Sage.

Perkins, S. and Shortland, S. (2006) *Strategic International Human Resource Management*, London: Kogan Page.

Rugman, A. and Collinson, S. (2009) *International Business* (5th edition), Harlow: Pearson.

Scullion, H. and Collings, D. (eds) (2006) *Global Staffing*, London: Routledge.

Tayeb, M. (2005) *International Human Resource Management: A Multinational Company Perspective*, Oxford: OUP.

Part 1

THE CONTEXT FOR INTERNATIONAL HRM

Chapter 2

Globalization and multinational companies

Chris Rees and Tony Edwards

Key aims

The aims of this chapter are to:

- introduce and critically evaluate the concept of globalization;
- consider the role of the multinational company (MNC) as central to the analysis of international HRM;
- examine the dynamic relationship between MNCs and states;
- introduce four interdependent levels of analysis for understanding management action in MNCs: the organizational, the national, the regional and the global.

Introduction

The rhetoric of globalization is seemingly all-pervasive. Politicians and journalists frequently stress the demands of the global economy in narrowing domestic policy options, the perceived requirement to be global has come to dominate popular discourse in the field of international management, and the concept has also been embraced by academics, with the number of articles and books featuring globalization in the title now running into the thousands. Globalization also generates heated debate across the political and ideological spectrum. As Dicken (2007) notes, probably the largest body of opinion consists of what might be called the 'hyper-globalists', either on the political right (the neo-liberal 'pro-globalizers') or on the political left (the so-called 'anti-globalization movement'). In both cases national states tend to be seen as no longer significant political actors or meaningful economic units, and consumer tastes are assumed to be homogenised and satisfied through the provision of standardized global products, created by global corporations with no allegiance to place or community. In this way globalization is consistently portrayed as the most powerful force for change in the modern world economy.

However, despite the pervasiveness of the concept, Scholte observes that 'much discussion of globalization is steeped in oversimplification, exaggeration and wishful thinking. In spite of a deluge of publications on the subject, analyses of globalization tend on the whole to remain conceptually inexact, empirically thin, historically ill-informed, economically and/or culturally illiterate, normatively shallow, and politically naïve' (2005: 1). Not only are most existing formulations of the term ambiguous or inconsistent, but debate is often mired in polarized exchanges. On one side are those who exuberantly proclaim that the greater part of social life is determined by global processes in which national cultures, national economies and national borders are dissolving. This group, as described above, are known as the 'strong globalists' or 'hyper-globalists', and would include, for example, Bhagwati (2007), Giddens (2002), Korten (2001) and Wolf (2004). On the other side, another set of observers question the extent of change in the international economy, and argue that many aspects of the globalization argument are either exaggerated or not unprecedented. Writers such as Doremus *et al.* (1998), Guillen (2001), Hirst *et al.* (2009), MacGillivray (2006) and Zysman (1996) would be placed in this camp.

We examine these competing positions in this chapter, and advance a more balanced assessment of what is really happening in the name of globalization, and what implications these trends have for the nature of international management. We also look briefly at the role of MNCs as key players in processes of globalization, and consider how their actions are related to particular features of their 'home' and 'host' national locations, and in particular to the actions of states. This leads to a consideration of the complex interrelationship between organization-level strategies in MNCs, national and regional contexts, and forces of globalization, and hence to the outline of a broad four-way conceptual framework for analysing international HRM.

The globalization thesis: core propositions

At the heart of the 'strong' globalization thesis is the notion of a rapid and recent process of economic globalization. A truly global economy is claimed to have emerged, or to be in the process of emerging, in which distinct national economies and, therefore, strategies of national economic management, are increasingly irrelevant. The world economy has internationalized in its basic dynamics, is dominated by uncontrollable market forces, and has as its principal economic actors and major agents of change truly 'transnational' corporations that owe allegiance to no nation state and locate wherever on the globe market advantage dictates. As Scholte notes, management gurus such as Ohmae (1995) and Naisbitt (1994) have 'created best sellers with their praises of a 'borderless world' ... [and] much of the business press has heralded 'the stateless enterprise' that maximizes efficiency and profits by operating freely across a global field' (2005: 17). Likewise advertisers, journalists, politicians and what Scholte calls 'others prone to hyperbole' (2005: 17) have celebrated the present as a thoroughly globalized world. Relatedly, social theorists commonly talk of a new global order, one facet of which is the claim that companies have become increasingly 'de-nationalised' from their local origins (Castells 2009; Sklair 2002; Wolf 2004). These general arguments set a context within which attention is drawn to a number of key economic trends:

● national and regional economies are becoming dominated by a new global system of economic co-ordination and control, in which competition and strategic choices are organized at the global level;

- national and international firms are becoming subordinated to transnational firms that differ significantly from them and are accountable only to global capital markets;
- the ability of nation states to regulate economic activities is rapidly declining, and global markets increasingly dominate national economic policies;
- national economic policies, forms of economic organization and managerial practices are converging to the most efficient ones as a result of global competition.

There are some developments in the global economy that appear, at first sight, to be commensurate with this picture. The last half century or so has witnessed a growth in trade that is faster than economic growth, meaning a higher proportion of goods and services are subject to the pressures of international competition (see Figure 2.1). Moreover, the last three decades have witnessed a sharp growth in investments by MNCs, captured in levels of foreign direct investment (see Figure 2.2). Whilst a number of different strands to this 'globalization thesis' can be identified, what they have in common, as Child (2002) outlines, is a lack of sensitivity to particular nations or regions as special contexts, referring instead to 'universal rationales'. This universalism is seen to arise from ubiquitous economic and technological forces, and predicts an increasing 'convergence' between modes of organization as countries develop similar economic and political systems, accelerated by the process of globalization. Child thus describes these perspectives as 'low-context' insofar as they 'do not grant national context any analytical significance over and above the characteristics that happen to characterize a country at any point in its development' (2002: 28).

Technological change is often seen as one of the most important contributory factors within this view of globalization. Countless authors have stressed the relationship between globalization and technological revolutions in transport, communications and

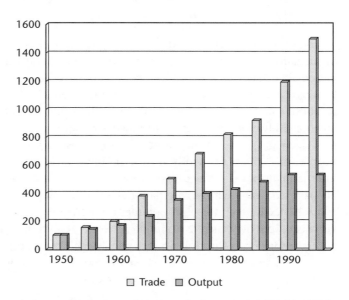

Figure 2.1 **Trends in world trade and output** (indices equal 100 in 1950)
Source: Hirst and Thompson (2009: 70)

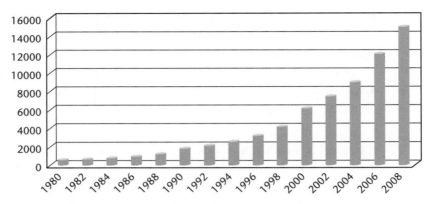

Figure 2.2 The growth in the stock of foreign direct investment ($billions)
Source: UN (2009)

data processing. Information and communications technologies are seen to offer ground-breaking new ways of handling information, which in turn have implications for the design of effective organizations. As Scholte notes, these developments have changed what is produced and how it is produced, and 'many observers have in this light characterised the global economy as an information, knowledge, post-industrial, network or service economy' (2005: 23). However, as Dicken observes,

> it is all too easy to be seduced by the notion that ... technological change is linear and predictable ... [when in fact] technology is not independent or autonomous... Technological change...is a socially and institutionally embedded process... Technology should be seen as, essentially, an enabling or a facilitating agent...while not making particular outcomes inevitable. (2007: 73, 74)

Although the argument that the cross-national spread of very similar technologies across organizations brings similar consequences almost certainly oversimplifies the picture, it is undeniable that technological developments have brought about important changes in transport and communications. The transformation of electronic and telephonic communications means that the speed and cost of transmitting information across borders have fallen sharply, something that is immediately apparent from the growth of the internet (see Figure 2.3). The fall in real terms in the cost of international travel has meant that people travel more frequently for the purposes of tourism. The reduction in the cost of international travel coupled with the reduction of barriers to migration in areas like the EU have led to a growth in international migration (see Figure 2.4).

Allied to the technological argument is a frequent assumption of psychological universalism, in which there is an implicit view that all human beings share common needs and motivations. It thus follows that the design of work organization, as well as managerial control and reward systems, should treat this as a major exigency. As Child observes, these ideas are well established in the study of organizations and management:

> For the past 100 years, from scientific management through to contemporary industrial and social psychology, there has been a search for a generally applicable theory

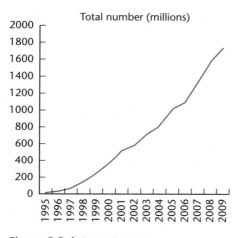
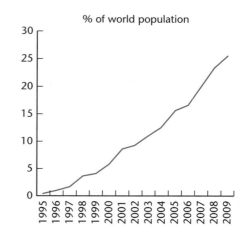

Figure 2.3 Internet usage
Source: www.internetworldstats.com

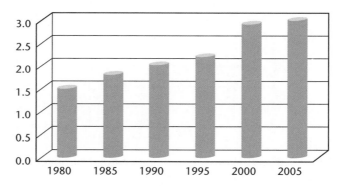

Figure 2.4 Stock of international migrants (% world population)
Source: various, including Guillen (2001); Wolf (2004)

of motivation at work...While these psychological theories differ in detail, they take individuals or groups as their focus, more or less in isolation from their cultural and social context. Thus people are regarded as essentially the same everywhere...The assumption of universal human needs has importantly informed the analysis of utility that underlies much economic theory. (2002: 31–32)

Once again, however, fundamental criticisms can be advanced of these arguments (Child 2002: 32). Psychological universalism may be a plausible notion when considering basic human needs, such as food and security, but it is highly questionable when addressing so-called 'higher-order' needs that are of a cognitive rather than material nature, such as esteem and self-actualization, since these are expressed primarily through social norms and are thus subject to cultural definition.

A further strand of argument within the convergence thesis is to do with political universalism. The fall of the Berlin Wall and Iron Curtain led many to believe that more and more countries were converging on the model of society found in much of Western Europe and North America. This view was most famously expressed in Fukuyama's (1992) book *The End of History and the Last Man*, in which he argued that ever larger parts of the world were converging on liberal democracy and free-market capitalism, such that there was no other form of society that we could expect to emerge as superior. Hence, for Fukuyama, this convergence represented the 'end of history'. However, the implication that social, political and economic systems are converging on a single model has been severely criticized. Although certain aspects such as the financial system have in some respects become highly globalized (see Figures 2.5 and 2.6), several major societal systems can still be discerned, and these constitute major divides across the globe, such that any general pattern of convergence is therefore limited. We explore the nature of these national differences more fully in the next two chapters.

Despite the evident weaknesses in the arguments concerning technological, psychological and political universalism, their prevalence has set a context in which *economic*

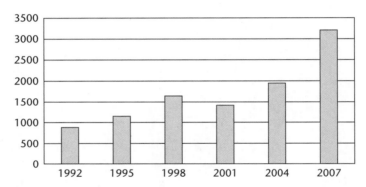

Figure 2.5 Global foreign exchange market turnover Daily averages in billions of US dollars at April 2007 exchange rates
Source: Bank for International Settlements

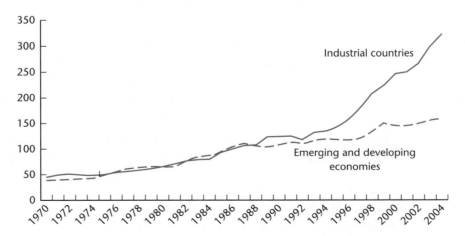

Figure 2.6 Net foreign assets (Ratio of sum of foreign assets and liabilities to GDP)
Source: Lane and Milesi-Ferretti (2007)

explanations of globalization have taken place. Much of the globalization thesis draws from classical economic theory, which purports to explain the formal organization of economic activities by firms as an economically rational response to market conditions. The convergence aspect to the argument is that 'free-market' economics will eventually prevail in all societies and present a common context for management. As such, 'national conditions tend to be treated as constraints on the effective operation of the market system' (Child 2002: 30).

There are many powerful advocates of the benefits to governments of encouraging economic globalization, primarily through programmes of deregulation and privatization. The most prominent newspapers and magazines that focus on economics, such as *The Economist* and *The Wall Street Journal,* extol the virtues of such an approach. Likewise many influential think tanks and policy institutes, such as the Organization for Economic Co-operation and Development (OECD), praise non-intervention by governments, liberalization, transparency and freedom of capital movements. Moreover, the dominant philosophy in international economic institutions such as the World Trade Organization (WTO) and the International Monetary Fund (IMF) is similarly pro-market forces and anti-government intervention. Globalization, in this view, will produce most benefits if companies and consumers are left to their own devices.

The globalization thesis: a critique

The strong globalization and convergence thesis, as outlined above, has attracted a range of critics. The principal objection is that close examination of the relevant data undermines many of the central claims about the extent and novelty of what is occurring in the name of globalization. From a sceptics viewpoint much of what is said about the global economy is mythical. Purportedly global companies in fact remain deeply embedded in their respective 'home' countries, and their actions are thoroughly enmeshed in the logic of inter-state relations (Almond and Ferner 2006; Geppert and Mayer 2006).

Although there are undoubtedly global*izing* forces at work, this does not mean that we live in a fully global*ized* world economy. Some countries (like the US) and some regions (like Western Europe) have generally experienced more globalization than others (like Mongolia or Sub-Saharan Africa). Likewise urban centres have on the whole accumulated more global connections than rural areas. Global relations have also tended to fall unevenly across different age groups, classes, cultures, genders and races. Authors such as Hirst *et al.* (2009), Doremus *et al.* (1998), Huntingdon (2002) and Stiglitz (2002) have made a series of points which throw a quite different light on the nature of the international economy.

Firstly, it is argued that the newness of the current situation has been grossly exaggerated. The world economy was actually more open and integrated in the half century prior to the First World War (1870–1914) than it is today, when 'trade, investment and, especially, population migration flowed in increasingly large volumes between countries' (Dicken 2007: 7). As Scholte observes, whilst many imply that globalization is a recent development, it is in fact 'a recurrent trend that has appeared at several previous junctures in the history of the modern states-system' (2005: 19). In proportional terms, levels of trade, permanent migration and investment between countries were as high, if not higher, in the late nineteenth century as they were in the run up to 2000 (Hirst *et al.* 2009).

The openness of the international economy from 1870 to 1914 shows up most starkly when we examine patterns of migration. The nineteenth century witnessed the biggest migration in history as 60 million Europeans moved to the Americas, 60 per cent going to the US. In the latter quarter of the twentieth century the overall numbers of people migrating (on a legal basis at least) were lower than they had been 100 years earlier. As Figure 2.4 shows, while the stock of international migrants has doubled in the last quarter of a century or so, it is still the case that only 3 per cent of the world's population reside in a country that is not their original one (and see Chapter 14). This is largely because of clampdowns on immigration by the developed economies in general and the US in particular. Even in the European Union, where freedom of movement across borders has removed formal obstacles to migration, levels of migration as a percentage of the population are actually very low.

In other respects, the international economy is today more open and integrated, but the change again looks less than dramatic when viewed in historical perspective. A good illustration of this is trade. Trade volumes increased remarkably quickly in the nineteenth century, so much so that in 1914 they stood at 45 times their value in 1780, but the two World Wars and the Great Depression of the early 1930s markedly reduced international trade. The growth since 1945 should be seen to some extent as a recovery from these effects. If the contemporary period is compared with the period before the First World War, trade volume has clearly risen but its growth looks less spectacular: whereas cross-border trade was 18 per cent of global GDP in 1914, it was 25 per cent in 2000 (Legrain 2002: 108). Figure 2.7 illustrates this point by showing changes in exports across four points in time during the twentieth century for four countries.

The capital mobility which is occurring in the current period is also yet to produce a massive shift of investment and employment from the advanced to the developing countries. The world economy is thus far from being truly 'global'. Rather, trade, investment and financial flows remain heavily concentrated in the so-called 'triad' of

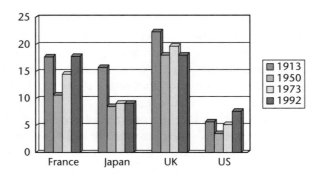

Figure 2.7 **Exports as a proportion of GDP**
Source: Hirst and Thompson (1999: 63)

Europe, Asia Pacific and North America, and this dominance seems set to continue (Rugman 2005). Moreover, companies are not becoming 'footloose' global players, but in large part remain rooted in one of the three regions of the triad. The developed economies combined account for around 84 per cent of outward foreign direct investment (FDI) and also receive just over 68 per cent of inward FDI (UN 2009). When one considers the greater population of the developing countries, this concentration appears even more remarkable. Africa, with a population of around one billion, receives just 3.4 per cent of total FDI, and India, again with a population of nearly one billion, receives just 0.8 per cent. Even China, which has witnessed a massive increase in FDI, receives only around 2.5 per cent of the total (more if Hong Kong is included) but accounts for over 20 per cent of the world's population. In other words, there is severe inequality in terms of who receives and benefits from FDI.

Finally, genuinely 'transnational' companies also appear to be relatively rare. Most companies are based nationally and trade *multi*nationally on the strength of national location of assets, production and sales, and there seems to be no strong tendency towards the growth of truly transnational companies (Morgan *et al.* 2005). Even among the largest 100 MNCs in the world, which are those that we might expect to be the most globally oriented, the evidence points to the strong roots that these firms have in their original national base (see Figure 2.8). The UN conducts an analysis of this group of firms, looking at the proportion of their assets, sales and employment that is located abroad. The 'Transnationality Index', which is an average of these three ratios, shows that while this is steadily increasing (see Chapter 5), most of these firms still have strong links to their original home country. We know from other sources that most MNCs retain very strong linkages with the financial system in their country of origin and fill most senior managerial positions from the home base (Almond and Ferner 2006; Boxall and Purcell 2008). The weak development of globally oriented firms is consistent with a continuing *internationalizing* economy, but much less so with a rapidly *globalizing* economy. MNCs still rely on their home base as the centre for their economic activities, despite all the speculation about globalization.

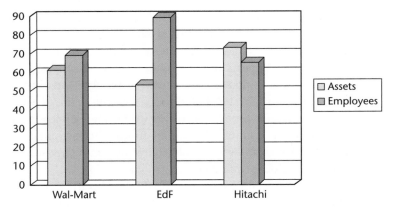

Figure 2.8 **The concentration of three MNCs in their country of origin** (% of total)
Source: UN (2009)

Economic globalization: a balanced assessment

As we have outlined above, the more measured accounts of globalization stress the uneven incidence of globalizing processes among countries, classes and other social groupings. As Scholte puts it, 'Globalization is indeed a distinctive and important development in contemporary world history. However its scale and consequences need to be carefully measured and qualified' (2005: 18–19). In terms of economic globalization, while it is unquestionably the case that trade and FDI have grown rapidly in the last 50 years, and especially so in the last 25 years, their overall levels are still quite small when compared with domestic output and income. Moreover, many sectors are dominated by purely national or sub-national level organizations and, hence, are relatively free from the pressures of globalization. Those activities conducted by the state in most countries, such as education and health provision, are examples, as are many private services.

A key implication of these qualifications to the 'globalization thesis' is that the forces for convergence in national forms of economic organization in general, and the organization of firms in particular, are not as great as is commonly implied. National differences remain significant. Moreover, societies with different institutional arrangements will continue to develop and reproduce varied systems of economic organization, with different economic and social capabilities in particular industries and sectors (Sorge 2005; Streeck and Thelen 2005). In this sense, economic mechanisms do not operate in isolation from their societal context, as some versions of economic theory suggest. As Whitley puts it, there is no 'systematic rationality governing economic activities that lies beyond, and separate from, any specific set of social arrangements' (2000: 5).

One of the key developments that *has* undoubtedly occurred is the internationalization of financial markets. Over the last 20 years, the barriers to transferring money from one country to another have greatly reduced. Exchange controls – the mechanisms that governments use to restrict flows of money into and out of their countries – have fallen out of fashion, frowned upon by bodies like the IMF. Accompanying these shifts in government policy have been technological developments that have greatly reduced the cost and time involved in transferring money across borders. The result has been an explosion in the movements of 'hot money' across the globe, with the pattern of movement being driven by the available returns. The *daily* turnover in global foreign exchange markets is now estimated at well over $3 trillion, more than 100 times the amount traded 30 years ago (see Figures 2.5 and 2.6).

International trade has also increased sharply. During the post-war period trade has grown consistently faster than national output in the developed economies, as a result of which a higher proportion of the goods and services that are bought and sold are produced in one country and sold in another. In fact, many goods and services are produced through integrated global 'chains' of firms across a number of different countries (Gereffi *et al.* 2005; Lane 2008).

A more nuanced analysis of globalization would distinguish between the quantitative linkages between countries and the growth of these linkages on the one hand, and the qualitative nature of these linkages on the other. In relation to the former, an implicit view which is commonly adopted is that the last quarter of the twentieth century witnessed a step change in the *pace of growth in the linkages between countries*: trade and foreign direct investment increased sharply; financial markets were deregulated and subsequently became highly internationalized; information exchange across borders became dramatically quicker and cheaper, and so on. It is this definition which underpins much of the work that is commonly characterized as the 'strong globalization thesis'. In relation to the latter, globalization has been perceived as a process in which there is a growth in the *functional integration of national economies*. Those who define globalization in this way commonly argue that the ties between countries are becoming stronger. For instance, whereas simple trading linkages often unravel in the event of a war or trade dispute, and hence can be seen as shallow linkages, the growth of FDI and international subcontracting has produced global production chains that are deeply embedded in the workings of the international economy. Dicken sees this as an important distinction in identifying what is novel in the contemporary period:

> Most important have been the changes in both the *where* and the *how* of the material production, distribution and consumption of goods and services (including, in particular, finance)...There has been a huge transformation in the *nature* and the *degree* of interconnection in the world economy and, especially, in the *speed* with which such connectivity occurs, involving both a *stretching* and an *intensification* of economic relationships...We live in a world in which *deep integration,* organised primarily within and between geographically extensive and complex *transnational production networks,* and through a diversity of mechanisms, is increasingly the norm. (2007: 7)

There is no doubt the new world economy is qualitatively different from the past, and yet few multinational enterprises are truly global, and most trade, investment and networks take place within the three main triadic blocks (Europe, North America, Asia Pacific). At a macro-level some economists, notably Rugman (2005), have convincingly demonstrated that most economic flows are in fact regional. He also notes the success of regional and bilateral trade agreements, as compared to global, multilateral initiatives.

Even in those aspects of economic activity where globalization is most prevalent, it should not be assumed that this only leads to greater homogeneity, convergence and uniformity across countries. Globalization does not have a consistent social impact, but rather causes greater change in some national systems than others, depending on the nature of the phenomena in question. Moreover, idealized 'global' procedures and practices are usually transformed considerably when they are introduced into domestic economies (Ferner *et al.* 2006; Smith *et al.* 2008). Convergence is thus always tempered by divergence. As Child expresses it:

> Paradoxically, at the same time as transactional boundaries weaken, there is an increased awareness of cultural differences and a growing celebration of cultural diversity...Globalization may therefore be stimulating divergent as well as convergent developments in organization. On the one hand it facilitates a centralized standardization of organizational practices and products; on the other it promotes local identities which encourage decentralized organizational responses. (2002: 46–7)

Globalization and multinational companies

Without doubt one of the most notable features of the international economy is the growing spread and influence of MNCs. We have seen how these firms are commonly portrayed as 'stateless' economic actors, behaving qualitatively differently from more nationally based competitors (Bartlett and Ghoshal 2002). Moreover, together with the expansion of international trade and growth of international capital markets, the increasing power of MNCs has been linked to the emergence of a so-called 'borderless world' in which national boundaries, and the states controlling them, have less economic significance than the decisions of transnational business elites and financial markets (Bhagwati 2007; Giddens 2002). This process is in turn seen as diminishing the significance of national and regional forms of economic organization, in favour of a new cross-national form of capitalism that is in the process of replacing them through superior efficiency. While this latter claim may often be exaggerated, there is no doubt that, more than any other single institution, the MNC is seen as the primary shaper of the global economy. As Dicken notes:

> the global economy is shaped by the TNC through its decisions to invest, or not to invest, in particular geographical locations. It is shaped, too, by the resulting flows – of materials, components, finished products, technological and organizational expertise, finance – between its geographically dispersed operations. (2007: 107)

It is beyond question that the scale of economic activity controlled by MNCs has grown sharply in the last 20 years or so. The United Nations Centre on Transnational Corporations estimates that there are around 61,000 multinationals in the world controlling around 900,000 subsidiaries. These firms make annual sales of $19 trillion and directly employ around 54 million people. The stock of FDI controlled by MNCs increased steeply from $560 billion in 1980 to $14.9 trillion in 2008 (UN 2009; see Figure 2.2). This was driven mainly by the sharp growth in cross-border mergers and acquisitions, which rapidly increased the extent to which many MNCs are spread across countries.

However, it is not simply the scale of MNCs and the resources they control that is significant. There are also important developments in the way these firms structure themselves, and the strategies they pursue. This issue is considered in depth in Chapter 5, but it is worth noting here some of the claims regarding the implications of globalization for corporate structures and strategies. For instance, according to Bartlett and Ghoshal (2002), the new economic environment is creating the need for a new type of organization – the *transnational* organization – which recognizes new resources and capabilities, captures them and then leverages the advantages on a worldwide scale. Although the extent to which many MNCs can be characterized as truly transnational can be disputed, as we will see, there are many examples of MNCs moving towards a greater geographic dispersion of business activities.

One of the implications of this trend for human resource management is the emergence of a highly flexible cadre of international managers, capable of implementing the very complex strategies involved. The 'transnational solution' predicts that instead of having careers that are driven by vertical moves up the organizational hierarchy, the focus will shift to managing lateral moves aimed at broadening and sharpening experience (Moore 2005). The way in which managers are allocated to assignments and temporary projects will become more cross-functional, cross-business and cross-geography. We deal with the development of international managers in more detail later in the book, looking specifically at career management and internationalization in Chapter 9, and at how senior managers are recruited and selected in Chapter 10.

As Dicken notes, the precise manner in which the MNC organizes and configures its production networks arises from a number of interrelated influences, notably its specific history and geography, including characteristics derived from its home country embeddedness, as well as its cultural and administrative heritage in the form of practices built up over a period of time, together with the nature and complexity of the industry environment (competition, technology, regulatory structures etc). As such, 'TNCs continue to reflect many of the basic characteristics of the home country environments in which they remain strongly embedded' (Dicken 2007: 107).

Indeed, while some of the actions of MNCs may lead to common processes across countries, in other respects they take advantage of national differences and, therefore, are actively *reproducing* nationally distinct practices. There remain important national differences in the attractiveness of locations for investment and other business activity, and MNCs try to reap benefits from the specific 'locational advantages' associated with each system in which they operate. These advantages are not just those associated with the cost of labour, but extend to capturing a body of knowledge and skills within a local workforce, access to markets, and the ability to tap into a cluster of successful firms in a particular industry and region (Belanger *et al.* 1999). In Chapters 3 and 4 we consider in more detail the literature on national systems of innovation, production regimes and national business systems. This literature points to real differences in the way countries have traditionally gone about their innovative activity and established their typical business environment, and how business is conducted therein. Moreover, companies need national legal and commercial policy provisions to protect their investments and their products from being copied, and are therefore dependent upon national regulations (Loveridge 2006). These various constraints prevent MNCs from being entirely 'stateless'.

Insofar as MNCs seek advantages from both their home and host locations, they can be seen as 'political actors', using power to shape the conditions under which they conduct their productive activities (Edwards *et al.* 2006; Ferner *et al.* 2005; Kristensen and Zeitlin 2005). In this process, employment arrangements are rarely transferred unaltered from the MNC home country. As Belanger and Edwards (2006) observe, all kinds of hybrid arrangements exist, reflecting differences of national regulatory regime, particular labour market circumstances, and different degrees to which head offices wish to impose standard models. As such they note that 'the power to transfer practices is thus highly contingent' (2006: 27). We explore the issue of the transfer of organisational practices across borders in more detail in Chapter 7.

This political view encourages us to see some of the tensions in the way that MNCs do business. They operate across many national regimes and are subject to different government policies, and they gain some power as a result, as in the capacity to threaten to shift production to other countries. But 'they also lose to the extent that they have to deal with differing regimes and absorb the transactions costs of doing so' (Belanger and Edwards 2006: 29). A similar dilemma exists in terms of their internal relations. On the one hand, MNCs can deploy influence over their subsidiaries in ways less available to domestic firms, notably through 'coercive comparisons' between sites in different countries (Coller 1996, Rohlfer 2007), and yet 'they also face particular problems of integrating operations from contrasting institutional and cultural contexts...[and as such] have to mobilize around political projects rather than simply having their own way' (Belanger and Edwards 2006: 28).

These tensions reflect a broader paradox in the nature of human resource management, and the reality of relations of power, control and consent between managements and employees in capitalist work organisations. Firms compete with each other, and must encourage the notion of competitiveness and continuous upgrading. They must, furthermore, reward highly motivated and talented employees, and encourage internal *competition* between employees, if they are to enhance external competitiveness. Yet, firms are complex organizations that rely, too, on employees *co-operating* with each other, and they need employees to work together for the overall objectives of the firm and not simply their individual objectives (which have the potential to be disruptive). Hence, there exists what has been termed a 'structured antagonism' between management and labour at the heart of the capitalist employment relationship. This antagonism cannot be 'managed away'; rather, new management initiatives will re-cast the balance between compliance and consent, but where that balance lies – i.e. the 'frontier of control' – is always negotiated (Edwards 1986). The work process is thus a social relationship, in which cooperation and conflict are jointly created. Hence, as Hyman (1987: 42) neatly expresses it, 'solutions to the problem of discipline aggravate the problem of consent, and vice-versa'. This same logic holds when we consider the political dimension within MNCs, where tensions emerge from the nature of management and, in particular, from the scope for employee resistance to central control. As Belanger and Edwards put it,

> TNCs ... must not only bargain with states and with their own managers but also secure a degree of consent from their employees. This process...has its own dynamics entailing a continuing bargain around control and consent...TNCs ... have resources, such as threats to shift production and the fact that labour, traditionally organized at national level, has found it hard to establish a direct voice at global level...Yet they also have to deal with employees with their own material and cultural resources, and these resources can be deployed in distinct ways. (2006: 31)

The strategies and structures of MNCs are thus dependent upon both 'home' and 'host' contexts. The notion of 'country-of-origin effects' refers to the characteristics of the institutions and business system of the country from which the corporation grew up, the *home* country, which may shape its policies and behavious in *host* countries. In reality, MNCs constantly oscillate between centralization and decentralization, and this balance is always negotiated (Morgan *et al.* 2001). There is continued diversity of organizational architectures, and a persistence of hybrid structures and practices (Ferner *et al.* 2006). The nature of strategy-making in MNCs, and in particular the problems of global integration of human resource management, are explored more fully in Chapters 5 and 6.

MNCs and the state

As we noted above, one of the central claims of the 'hyper-globalizers' is that we live in a borderless world where states no longer matter. A combination of the revolutionary technologies of transportation and communications and the increasing power of MNCs has, it is argued, shifted economic power out of the control of nation states. However, this is clearly a misleading view. While some of the state's capabilities are being reduced, and while there may be some 'hollowing out' of the state, the process is not a simple one of uniform decline on all fronts. Rather, the 'death of the nation state' has been greatly exaggerated. Managerial and systems transfers between companies and even subsidiaries are complex (Bjorkman and Lervik 2007), and talk of simple organizational convergence is so far exaggerated, although the trends are significant. National and local factors (government, culture, education, R&D, human resource policies, and so on) continue to be important (Thelen 2005). The potential for divergence and internationally hybrid systems remains. As Dicken observes,

> the national state, the major 'container' within which distinctive practices develop ... helps to 'produce' particular kinds of firms...Links...exist between the ownership-specific advantages of firms and the location-specific characteristics of the firm's home country. It is this link which helps to explain the different characteristics of TNCs from different source nations. (2007: 127)

To illustrate this point, Dicken refers to the examples of the large domestic market and high level of technological sophistication of the US domestic economy, which have helped produce the distinctive characteristics of US MNCs, and also the lack of natural resources and strong role of government in technological and industrial affairs that help explain attributes of Japanese MNCs, at least in their earlier development.

In general terms, MNCs need states to provide the infrastructural basis for their continued existence: both physical infrastructure in the form of the built environment and also social infrastructure in the form of legal protection of private property, institutional mechanisms to provide a continuous supply of educated workers etc. In particular, states have the potential to determine two factors of crucial importance to MNCs: (i) the terms on which they may have access to markets and/or resources; and (ii) the rules of operation with which they must comply when operating within a specific national territory.

It is often said that the major difference between HRM in the US and Europe is the degree to which it is influenced and determined by state regulations. Companies in Europe generally have a narrower scope of 'strategic choice' in this respect than those in the US. In Europe there is greater regulation of recruitment and dismissal, more formalization of educational certification, and quasi-legal aspects to industrial relations frameworks – including legislative requirements on pay, forms of employment contract, health and safety, hours of work, as well as rights to trade union representation and requirements to operate consultation or co-determination arrangements (Gold 2009; and see Chapter 12). EU member states also seek to regulate the labour market from which organisations draw their pool of employees, e.g. through various interventions in education, life-long learning and tax incentives. In this way states shape and influence business strategy and organization, and reflect distinctive 'ways of doing things', where particular institutions and practices are 'bundled together' (Weiss 2003). Moreover, nation states remain important not only in determining the competitiveness and characteristics of national economies, but in negotiating and structuring the shape of the international economy (O'Brien and Williams 2007). The largest MNCs are powerful organizations, but their power in relation to most governments has been exaggerated, and the size of their revenues in relation to national GDPs has often been calculated on a misleading basis. While MNCs do have specific advantages from their international operations, they also gain from locational advantages and the cooperation of national governments. It is not only the state, of course, but a combination of features of home and host environments, which shape and influence the nature of MNC operations. As Dicken suggests, MNCs and 'national effects' are thus interdependent. In his words,

> TNCs are 'produced' through an intricate process of embedding, in which the cognitive, social, political and economic characteristics of the national *home* base continue to play a dominant part...But...the very fact that TNCs are transnational – that they operate in a diversity of economic, social, cultural and political environments – means that they will, inevitably, [also] take on some of the characteristics of their host environments. (2007: 133)

Conclusions

Our discussion of the 'globalization thesis' and consideration of its weaknesses has highlighted the continuing importance of the national dimension, and the focus on the role of the MNC as a 'political actor' has stressed how companies and countries operate in a mutually constitutive way. In the next chapter we take these issues further to consider the various ways in which 'national effects' can be conceptualized and understood in terms of their impact upon management action.

If we are interested in the complex interrelationships between processes of globalization, national systems and companies, then this already provides us with three distinct levels of analysis for interpreting and understanding international human resource management strategies and practices. Considering the impact or implications of global economic trends first, we might in broad terms call this the *global effect*. While some strands of this argument are exaggerated or difficult to substantiate, there remains enough of substance to argue that genuinely global influences on management action are significant: unquestionably, developments in IT mean that ideas and technologies are spread around the globe more quickly than ever before; large chunks of the world that were until recently closed off from the international economy are rapidly becoming integrated into it; and many sectors that had hitherto been subject to close regulation and ownership restrictions have been liberalized and, subsequently, internationalized. Moreover, a key feature of globalization has been the growth of MNCs, and the chains of production and service provision that they control, while a set of international regulations and a nascent 'transnational elite' is emerging partly as a consequence of the activities of MNCs.

While some of the growing connections and linkages between national economies warrant the term global, others should more accurately be described as regionally focused. Thus a second level of analysis we can distinguish is a *regional effect*. As noted above, the dominant patterns of trade and FDI tend to be within three key regions of the world, namely North America, Western Europe and Asia Pacific. The major flows of international economic activity are either between these three 'triad' regions, or within one of them. There is also evidence that many MNCs operate principally at the 'sub-global' level, rather than at either a purely global or local level, both in terms of their formal structure and their orientation (Arrowsmith and Marginson 2006).

Although these global and regional trends are important, we have seen that they have not fully eroded nationally distinct influences on MNCs. In terms of the role of states or national systems in different countries, we can call this third level of analysis the *national effect*. This refers to the distinctive differences between business systems and the role of national institutions (financial, educational and governmental). We know that despite pressures for change, and notwithstanding the recent global economic crisis, financial systems continue to differ markedly across countries. Some national financial systems, such as those in operation in the US and the UK, are characterized by arms-length and fluid relations between senior managers in firms and shareholders, and by an active 'market for corporate control' in the form of takeovers. In contrast, the dominant features of other financial systems, such as those in Germany and Sweden, are of close and stable relations between managers and owners, and considerable continuity in ownership patterns. The interrelationships between the institutional and cultural aspects of countries' economies combine to form nationally distinct 'business systems' (concepts we explore more fully in the following two chapters). While global and regional effects may challenge some aspects of national distinctiveness, and lead to changes in important respects, the national level remains highly significant.

Finally, in addition to the global, regional and national, we can distinguish the *organization effect*. The nature of the three effects already discussed may set parameters within which organizations operate, but they do not completely determine strategies and practices at company level. There are a range of contingent factors that allow managers to devise courses of action that may differ from those of their competitors, and some of these relate to the way that MNCs are structured. For instance, MNCs that are organized around highly standardized or integrated production systems across borders are those that are most likely to be influenced by the pressures of globalization and regionalization into engaging in the transfer of practices across borders; in contrast, those that are a collection of disparate operations with little in common across countries are much less likely to do so. However, contingent factors at company level are not simply to do with formal structures, but also include power relations between actors at different levels within the organization. That is, corporate strategies are in part the result of political activity within the MNC. Therefore, the organization effect is crucial in mediating the influences that arise from the global, regional and national context.

In this book we are interested in the complex interaction between these four sets of effects. As we have seen in this chapter, much recent economic and political discourse overplays the extent and impact of *global* economic forces. At the same time, the popular business strategy and HRM literature can likewise tend to overplay the *organization* effect, in terms of exaggerating the degree of 'strategic choice' or scope for action that individual managers have to successfully introduce their preferred strategies. We do not share this populist view of managers as all-powerful strategic 'change agents', but rather we argue that management actions and policies are best understood in light of the constraints and opportunities provided by operating in particular contexts. Since much of the literature addressing these contexts is concerned with the implications of national differences, it is to a more detailed consideration of this aspect that we now turn.

Review questions

1 What is meant by economic globalization, and what evidence exists to show that it is taking place?

2 What are the major arguments advanced by those who question the so-called 'strong globalization thesis'?

3 To what extent can multinational companies usefully be described as 'political actors'?

4 How far do you feel it is helpful to distinguish between different 'levels of analysis' (i.e. global, regional, national and organizational) in understanding international HRM? Why might these distinctions be considered ultimately misleading?

Further reading

1 Dicken, P. (2007) *Global Shift: Mapping the Changing Contours of the World Economy* (5th edition), London: Sage.

Summarizes the various theories informing the globalization debate, and provides a comprehensive and informed discussion of the complex interrelationships between national level factors, multinational companies and changing technologies.

2 Hirst, P., Thompson, G. and Bromley, S. (2009) *Globalization in Question: The International Economy and the Possibilities of Governance* (3rd edition), Cambridge: Polity Press.

Discusses a wide range of issues concerning international political economy, and presents a vast array of data and evidence to undermine the arguments of those who see globalization as new and pervasive.

3 Ferner, A., Quintanilla, J. and Sanchez-Runde, C. (eds) (2006) *Multinationals, Institutions and the Construction of Transnational Practices,* Basingstoke: Macmillan.

An edited collection containing a series of well-informed research papers addressing the complex relationship between MNCs and national contexts, many utilizing a 'political economy' perspective.

4 Whitley, R. (2000) *Divergent Capitalisms: The Social Structuring and Change of Business Systems,* Oxford: Oxford University Press.

Remains one of the most comprehensive and scholarly attempts to describe and explain differences in economic organization between market economies, based on the notion of distinctive 'national business systems'.

References

Almond, P. and Ferner, A. (2006) *American Multinationals in Europe: Managing Employment Relations Across National Borders,* Oxford: Oxford University Press.

Arrowsmith, J. and Marginson, P. (2006) 'The European cross-border dimension to collective bargaining in multinational companies', *European Journal of Industrial Relations,* 12(3), 245–66.

Bartlett, C. and S. Ghoshal (2002) *Managing Across Borders: The Transnational Solution* (3rd edition), Boston: Harvard Business School Press.

Belanger, J., Berggren, C., Bjorkman, T. and Kohler, C. (eds) (1999) *Being Local Worldwide: ABB and the Challenge of Global Management,* Ithaca, NY and London: Cornell University Press.

Belanger, J. and Edwards, P.K. (2006) 'Towards a Political Economy Framework: TNCs as National and Global Players', in Ferner, A., Quintanilla, J., and Sanchez-Runde, C. (eds) *Multinationals, Institutions and the Construction of Transnational Practices,* Basingstoke: Macmillan.

Bhagwati, J. (2007) *In Defence of Globalization,* Oxford: Oxford University Press.

Bjorkman, I. and Lervik, J. (2007) 'Transferring HR practices within multinational corporations', *Human Resource Management Journal,* 17(4), 320–35.

Boxall, P. and Purcell, J. (2008) *Strategy and Human Resource Management* (2nd edition), Basingstoke: Macmillan.

Castells, M. (2009) *The Rise of the Network Society: v. 1: The Information Age: Economy, Society, and Culture* (2nd edition), Chichester: Wiley.

Child, J. (2002) 'Theorizing About Organization Cross-Nationally', in M. Warner and P. Joynt (eds) *Managing Across Cultures: Issues and Perspectives,* London: Thompson.

Coller, X. (1996) 'Managing flexibility in the food industry: a cross-national comparative case study in European MNCs', *European Journal of Industrial Relations,* 2(2), 153–72.

Dicken, P. (2007) *Global Shift: Mapping the Changing Contours of the World Economy* (5th edition), London: Sage.

Doremus, P., Keller, W., Pauly, L. and Reich, S. (1998) *The Myth of the Global Corporation,* Princeton: Princeton University Press.

Edwards, P.K. (1986) *Conflict At Work: A Materialist Analysis of Workplace Relations,* Oxford: Blackwell.

Edwards, T., Coller, X., Ortiz, L., Rees, C. and Wortmann, M. (2006) 'National industrial relations systems and cross-border restructuring: evidence from a merger in the pharmaceuticals sector', *European Journal of Industrial Relations,* 12(1), 69–87.

Ferner, A., Almond, P. and Colling, T. (2005) 'Institutional theory and the cross-national transfer of employment policy: the case of "workforce diversity" in US multinationals', *Journal of International Business Studies,* 46, 304–21.

Ferner, A., Quintanilla, J., and Sanchez-Runde, C. (eds) (2006) *Multinationals, Institutions and the Construction of Transnational Practices,* Basingstoke: Macmillan.

Fukuyama, F. (1992) *The End of History and the Last Man,* New York: Penguin.

Geppert, M. and Mayer, M. (eds) (2006) *Global, National and Local Practices in Multinational Companies,* London: Palgrave.

Gereffi, G., Humphrey, J. and Sturgeon, T. (2005) 'The governance of global value chains', *Review of International Political Economy,* 12, 78–104.

Giddens, A. (2002) *Runaway World: How Globalisation is Reshaping Our Lives,* London: Profile Books.

Gold, M. (ed.) (2009) *Employment Policy in the European Union: Origins, Themes and Prospects,* Basingstoke: Macmillan.

Guillen, M. (2001) 'Is globalization civilising, destructive or feeble?: a critique of five key debates in the social science literature', *Annual Review of Sociology*, 27, 235–60.

Hirst, P., Thompson, G. and Bromley, S. (2009) *Globalization in Question* (3rd edition), Cambridge: Polity.

Huntingdon, S. (2002) *The Clash of Civilizations: And the Remaking of World Order*, New York: Free Press.

Hyman, R. (1987) 'Strategy or structure?: capital, labour and control', *Work, Employment and Society*, 1(1), 25–55.

Korten, D.C. (2001) *When Corporations Rule the World* (2nd edition), West Hartford, CT: Kumarian Press.

Kristensen, P.H. and Zeitlin, J. (2005) *Local Players in Global Games: The Strategic Constitution of a Multinational Corporation*, Oxford: Oxford University Press.

Lane, C. (2008) 'National capitalisms and global production networks: an analysis of their interaction in two global industries', *Socio-Economic Review*, 6, 227–60.

Lane, P. and Milesi-Ferretti, G.M. (2007) 'The external wealth of nations mark II: revised and extended estimates of foreign assets and liabilities, 1970–2004', *Journal of International Economics*, 73, 223–50.

Legrain, P. (2002) *Open World: The Truth About Globalisation*, London: Abacus.

Loveridge, R. (2006) Embedding The Multinational Enterprise: The Micro-Processes of Institutionalization in Developing Economies, in Geppert, M. and Mayer, M. (eds) *Global, National and Local Practices in Multinational Companies*, London: Palgrave.

MacGillivray, A. (2006) *A Brief History of Globalization*, New York: Carroll and Graff.

Moore, F. (2005) *Transnational Business Cultures: Life and Work in a Multinational Corporation*, Aldershot: Ashgate.

Morgan, G., Kristensen, P. H., and Whitley, R. (eds) (2001) *The Multinational Firm: Organizing Across Institutional and National Divides*, Oxford: Oxford University Press.

Morgan, G., Whitley, R. and Moen, E. (eds.) (2005) *Changing Capitalisms?: Internationalisation, Institutional Change and Systems of Economic Organization*, Oxford: Oxford University Press.

Naisbitt, J. (1994) *Global Paradox: The Bigger the World Economy, the More Powerful its Smallest Players*, London: Brealey.

O'Brien, R. and Williams, M. (2007) *Global Political Economy: Evolution and Dynamics* (2nd edition), Basingstoke: Macmillan.

Ohmae, K. (ed.) (1995) *The Evolving Global Economy: Making Sense of the New World Order*, Boston, MA: Harvard Business Review Press.

Rohlfer, S. (2007) 'The Different Faces of Benchmarking: Structural Limits to Benchmarking and the Implications for Human Resource Management', *Warwick Papers in Industrial Relations*, No.83, Coventry: Industrial Relations Research Unit.

Rugman, A. (2005) *The Regional Multinationals*, Cambridge: Cambridge University Press.

Scholte, J.A. (2005) *Globalization: A Critical Introduction* (2nd edition), Basingstoke: Macmillan.

Sklair, L. (2002) *Globalization: Capitalism and Its Alternatives* (3rd edition), Oxford: Oxford University Press.

Smith, C., McSweeney, B. and Fitzgerald, R. (eds) (2008) *Remaking Management: Between Global and Local*, Cambridge, Cambridge University Press.

Sorge, A. (2005) *The Global and The Local: Understanding the Dialectics of Business Systems*, Oxford: Oxford University Press.

Stiglitz, J. (2002) *Globalization and its Discontents*, New York: Norton and Co.

Streeck, W. and Thelen, K. (eds) (2005) *Beyond Continuity: Institutional Change in Advanced Political Economies*, Oxford: Oxford University Press.

Thelen, K. (2005) *How Institutions Evolve: The Political Economy of Skills in Germany, Britain, the United States and Japan,* Cambridge: Cambridge University Press.

UN (2009) *World Investment Report 2009: Transnational Corporations, Agricultural Production and Development,* New York and Geneva: United Nations.

Weiss, L. (2003) *States in the Global Economy: Bringing Domestic Institutions Back In,* Cambridge: CUP.

Whitley, R. (2000) *Divergent Capitalisms: The Social Structuring and Change of Business Systems,* Oxford: OUP.

Wolf, M. (2004) *Why Globalization Works: The Case for the Global Market Economy,* New Haven: Yale University Press.

Zysman, J. (1996) 'The myth of a "global" economy: enduring national foundations and emerging regional realities', *New Political Economy,* 1(2), 157–84.

Chapter 3

Cultures, institutions and management

Chris Rees and Tony Edwards

Key aims

The aims of this chapter are to:

- examine the implications of national cultural differences for management action;
- consider in more depth the institutional bases of national business systems;
- outline theoretical approaches which attempt to combine or synthesize these different approaches;
- explore in more detail the four-way analytical framework for interpreting international HRM in MNCs.

Introduction

We concluded from the review of the 'globalization thesis' in Chapter 2 that increasing managerial control of economic activities in MNCs has not led to a 'borderless world' in which the decisions of transnational business elites are detached from the influence of nation states. Recent patterns of internationalization have certainly generated important changes in the characteristics of the international economy, and in the strategies of leading firms in most economies, but this has not meant that national systems have lost their influence. The internationalization strategies of MNCs can bring about significant changes in their *home* business system, but they only tend to do so under a set of particular circumstances. They can also impact upon *host* business systems, although here their influence is always mediated by local institutions and agencies, and the more cohesive and resilient these are, the less the system is likely to change as a result of foreign firms developing a significant presence (Morgan *et al.* 2005; Whitley 2000).

Whilst globalization is undoubtedly an important aspect of economic activity, it is less significant in its scale and consequences than some enthusiasts claim (Scholte 2005). Further, the ways in which the international management coordination of economic activities is developing reflect established patterns of economic organization and competition at national level, such that these structure any emergent properties of a new transnational business system (Dicken 2007). This chapter attempts to specify more clearly the dimensions of these established patterns through an examination of the nature of national differences in business systems in general and patterns of HRM more particularly. It is important for organizational analysis to be comparative, and so we need to have the tools to explain patterns of similarity and difference, of convergence and divergence.

We structure the discussion in terms of the two major analytical categories which are most often utilized to explain the importance of the national dimension. These are, first, *cultural* theories and, second, *institutional* theories. Both of these can be classed as 'high-context' approaches, in that they both focus on national level factors, as opposed to global factors, when accounting for differences between organizations, and further they expect these national differences to persist over time regardless of economic globalization. We consider the institutional approach as the more rigorous and useful of the two, and so devote more space to reviewing recent developments in this area. This leads to a deeper consideration of the four levels of analysis which were outlined briefly at the end of Chapter 2 (the organizational, national, regional and global), and the chapter ends with an outline of some recent theories and ideas that help incorporate these into an integrated framework, and thus aid our understanding of international HRM in MNCs.

Cultural perspectives

Cultural perspectives place the low-context theories outlined in the previous chapter into what are considered to be their appropriate cultural context. Economic utilities, personal motivations and the ways information is interpreted and used are seen to be strongly influenced by national cultures. Cultural values are considered to be deep-seated and enduring, varying systematically between societies, and conditioning what is acceptable organizational practice. These arguments continue to have a pervasive influence in management thinking and discourse. As Child observes:

> the cultural perspective has for some time provided the dominant paradigm in comparative studies of organization ... Attention to culture has an intuitive appeal to practising managers, for whom it serves as a convenient reference for the many frustrating difficulties they can experience when working with people from other countries, the source of which they do not fully comprehend. (2002: 33)

As Thompson and McHugh similarly observe, it is

> not difficult to see the basis of the appeal of cultural relativism...[since it] trades on recognisable, if somewhat stereotypical, national characteristics...[and] normatively the approach has obvious and useful applications in terms of training to make managers more sensitive to trading partners and to local cultural conditions. (2009: 75)

From this perspective, national culture is said to impact organizations by selecting and framing the particular sets of organizational values and norms that managers perceive as being consistent with basic assumptions developed within their countries – as a product of national patterns of early childhood, formative experiences and education, language, religion and geography. Differences in national culture affect organizations in many ways, and are widely seen as central to international HRM (Schneider and Barsoux 2003). They may influence attitudes in international negotiations, which themselves may determine the outcome of investments, trade and ownership within organizations. They may also create assumptions about appropriate pay systems and the importance of distributive justice, the role of centralization and hierarchies within organizational structures, the extent to which the manager–subordinate relationship facilitates effective performance management, and attitudes towards job and career mobility.

The problem of adequately defining and measuring national culture continues to be one of the key challenges confronting cross-cultural research. Unfortunately, a great variety of different approaches has been used, and there is little agreement regarding any definitive scale suitable for measuring cultural differences among nations. However, there is fairly convincing evidence that values *do* differ, and a popular method for making comparisons focuses on the concept of a 'value system'. This is what Hofstede (2001) attempted.

In Hofstede's work culture is firmly equated with nationality. Nationality is seen as having central symbolic value to citizens, creating shared ideas, values and meanings transmitted through family and community. National character and national culture are thus treated as indivisible. Hofstede defines culture as the 'collective programming of the mind' which distinguishes the members of one group or category of people from another, and in a landmark study he analysed survey data from 116,000 employees of IBM in more than 40 different countries. He initially identified four, later five, basic dimensions to express differences between national cultures:

1 *Power distance*. This refers to the extent to which people in a particular culture accept and expect that power in institutions and organizations is, and should be, distributed unequally.
2 *Uncertainty avoidance*. This indicates the extent to which people in a culture feel nervous or threatened by uncertainty and ambiguity, and hence create institutions and rules to try to avoid them.
3 *Individualism/collectivism*. In an individualist culture people tend to look after their own interests and those of their immediate family, whereas in a collectivist culture there is a tighter social framework in which each person respects the group to which he or she belongs.
4 *Masculinity/femininity*. In a masculine culture the dominant values are said to be ambition, assertiveness, performance, and the acquisition of money and material objects, whereas in a so-called feminine culture values such as the quality of life, maintaining personal relationships, and care for the weak and the environment are emphasized.
5 *Time orientation*. Originally termed 'Confucian dynamism', this relates to the time horizons that people in different cultures are oriented towards, with some looking several years ahead in deciding upon particular courses of action whilst others are more geared to the shorter term.

The model that Hofstede subsequently developed categorizes 40 nations into distinct cultural clusters according to their rank scores on each of these five dimensions, and on this basis he draws various lessons for management theory and practice. As Thompson and McHugh (2009) point out, in their own terms these lessons are fairly logical. Leadership in a collectivist society will indeed tend towards the group rather than the individual. If there is low power distance, schemes for employee participation are more likely to flourish. Self-actualization will tend to be more of a motivator in highly individualist societies than in those where 'keeping face' within group relationships is a prime social requirement. Certainly the culturalist perspective has one immediate and important implication for our understanding of international HRM. That is, if national cultures vary across a number of important dimensions, those differences suggest that models and theories of management may have a limited applicability to countries outside of the 'culture cluster' within which they were originally developed. Thus, Thompson and McHugh (2009) describe as 'admirable' the 'progressive intent' in Hofstede, namely to question the transferability of textbook – read US – management models to very different circumstances.

As Sparrow and Hiltrop (1994) have observed, MNCs will vary in the extent to which they recognize national cultural diversity. If managers believe the impact of national culture to be minimal, as in the case of the *parochial* organization, the general approach will be to ignore differences in employee values, norms and preferences. On the other hand, if managers view all other ways of doing things as inferior, as in the *ethnocentric* organization, their policy will be to minimize the impact of cultural diversity by, for example, recruiting a homogenous workforce. The tendency to hold one's own way as being the best is, of course, often reinforced by stereotypes of other cultures and nationalities. Finally, if managers recognize both cultural diversity as well as its potentially positive impacts, as in the case of the *synergistic* organization, the human resource policy will tend to place greater emphasis upon the creation of a truly international workforce, using similarities and differences among the nationalities to create new forms of management and organization.

Differences in national culture are also important in terms of HRM because of their potential impact on *organizational* culture. Both managers and researchers frequently point to the importance of organizational culture as a source of competitive advantage and as one of the key strategic 'levers' available to managers in order to create and maintain employee commitment. But, as Sparrow and Hiltrop remark, it is often too easily assumed that

> the creation of a strong organizational culture erases or moderates the influence of national culture...[and] that the values of employees working for the same organization – even if they come from different countries – are more similar than different. However, the evidence suggests that our national culture is so deeply ingrained in us that...it cannot easily be erased by any external force [such as a company culture]. (1994: 77)

Thus, it is unlikely that even truly *transnational* organizations, as described in the previous chapter, will find it easy to move 'beyond nationality' in terms of employee attitudes and values.

The culturalist approach has become very popular in international HRM research, representing the mainstream of the subject. Writers have used national culture as a way of explaining why MNCs of various national origins adopt different HRM practices. For example, Ngo *et al.* (1998) examined the effect of the country of origin of US, UK and Japanese MNCs in Hong Kong. On the basis of marked differences between the MNCs according to their nationality, and further marked differences within a sample of local firms, they argue that a number of aspects of the home country culture influence the nature of HR practices in the foreign MNCs. The culturalist approach has also been used extensively to explain the way in which MNCs adapt to *host* country cultures. An illustration of this is Tayeb's research on a US multinational in Scotland, in which she argues that the parent company's global approach had to be adapted to several aspects of the local culture (Tayeb 2005).

However, the nature of Hofstede's data, and the methods employed to analyse them, have been the subject of considerable controversy. McSweeney (2002), for instance, argues that Hofstede's study suffers from a number of important weaknesses, such as the assumption of cultural homogeneity within a country, and the difficulty of generalizing for a national culture on the basis of sometimes quite small samples of one occupational group in one company. More broadly, fundamental problems remain with the way the concept of national culture is conceptualized and applied. Is culture all pervasive, as Hofstede has argued, taking primacy over other factors in terms of predictive power? If so, the comparative study of organization across cultural boundaries employing concepts derived from only *one* culture becomes hazardous in terms of validity criteria. As Child puts it, if meanings vary in different societies then 'this questions the equivalence between cultures of any comparative concept and its operational measurement. Universalistic concepts and their standardized measurement of the kind that cross-cultural scholars like Hofstede have employed become suspect on the basis of this argument' (2002: 33).

Child notes, moreover, that we still do not have an adequate theory of the relevance of culture for organization, and asks: which organizational features are shaped by culture?; how are they so influenced?; and what is the significance of culture *vis-à-vis* economic, technological and political factors? In addition, it is a common assumption in much of the culturalist literature that national differences can simply be expressed in cultural terms, and that the 'nation' can be used as the unit of analysis for culture, but this is highly questionable (Moore and Rees 2008). First, almost all countries, but particularly large ones, are characterized by considerable cultural heterogeneity. That is, there are wide variations *within* countries according to regions, social classes, ethnic groups, and so on (McSweeney 2009). The US is a prime example, classified by Hofstede as a single cultural unit and yet clearly constituted by a hugely varied array of cultural groups. Second, as Ferner (2000) puts it, a key problem with culturalist approaches is that they actually *explain* relatively little, and tend to simply raise further questions: how, for example, did particular values and attitudes come to characterize a particular country?; and, crucially, how can we account for change over time in these values and attitudes?

While Hofstede's study is widely considered to be the classic contribution to the culturalist canon, others have advanced similar arguments using different methodological approaches. One of the best known examples is Trompenaars and Hampden-Turner (1997). They use a more sensitive device than Hofstede – namely, scenarios containing ethical and practical dilemmas put to over 15,000 managers at their own seminars – and on this basis they identify patterns of responses that reflect different systems of values. Seven 'cultures of capitalism' are outlined, based on national cultures, and the underlying argument remains similar to Hofstede's, namely that every culture is held to have a tacit dimension rooted in a subconscious set of beliefs that form the bedrock of national identity. However, Thompson and McHugh again point to the major flaw in this approach, namely that

> the patterns attributed to national mindsets can and do change...societies or sectors within them can become more centralised and autocratic as the result of political changes, management fashions or power struggles. (2009: 76)

By locating attitudes within a largely unvarying national character, cultural relativists tend to produce overly static descriptions that exaggerate the durability of values and practices. As such, many of Hofstede's pronouncements look particularly dated. Thompson and McHugh refer to the example of the former Communist countries. Most of them indeed manifested high power distance, collectivism and uncertainty avoidance, but this is 'hardly surprising given the nature of their shared command economy and centralised party-state apparatus' (2009: 75). However, Russia and other ex-Eastern bloc countries are now experiencing rampant individualism and uncertainty following the collapse of the old solidaristic social norms, but 'there is no evidence...that this reflects or is driven by changes in national mindsets' (2009: 75).

Although Thompson and McHugh acknowledge that a focus on national culture can serve as a useful antidote to explanations that over-emphasize economic and techno-logical convergence, they argue that 'such benefits come at a price' (2009: 75), and that 'culture is a slippery concept that can be applied with misleading results' (2009: 77). The problem is that 'such perspectives pick up on cultural differences and then believe they have explained them' (2009: 75). In fact it is not at all clear that, say, finance-driven short-termism in a particular economy derives either from cultural/mental models in general, or Anglo-Saxon ones in particular. It is equally possible to argue that this kind of individualism, with associated high levels of bankruptcy and takeovers, is 'an outcome, not of a mental model, but of specific historical and contemporary institutional arrangements in Anglo-American political economies' (2009: 75). This highlights how weaknesses in the culturalist approach point to the need to address more fully the crucial role of institutions in structuring economic activity.

Institutional perspectives

Institutionalist theories provide the means for correcting some of the problems associated with the ideas of the cultural relativists. Here the emphasis is on normative adaptation and the 'cultural rules' to which organisations conform, but these rules are now understood as 'social rules embodied in *institutional processes* more than mental constructs carried about in people's heads' (Thompson and McHugh 2009: 77). These perspectives emphasize that management and business have different institutional foundations across countries. Key institutions are the state, the legal system, the financial system and the family. Considered in combination, such institutions constitute the distinctive social organization of a country and its economy (Hall and Soskice 2001; Whitley 2000). In the context of debates about globalization raised in the previous chapter, Whitley sums up the importance of national institutions as follows:

> Cross-border economic flows and coordination processes depend overwhelmingly on national state legal systems, enforcement mechanisms, and institutional arrangements to manage risks and uncertainty sufficiently to enable strategic decisions to be made. Internationalization, then, remains highly interdependent with national agencies' and institutions' structures and actions. As a result, its effects on established systems of economic organization and firms are greatly guided and limited by variations in these national institutions. (2000: 122)

In stressing the historical 'embeddedness' of social structures and processes, the institutionalist perspective carries two particularly significant implications for the cross-national analysis of organizations. First, institutions are likely to be 'sticky' in the face of economic and technological change, in the sense that they are relatively slow to change. Second, social organization influences a country's ability to efficiently undertake certain kinds of production or other economic activity. National institutions such as education systems and the structure of social relations can, through their impact on the degree of ascription or achievement in the society, impact on the ability of a country to base its economic wealth creation on innovation rather than, say, mass production. Institutionalists therefore argue that the conditions of economic survival through specialization around national strengths tend to preserve *nationally distinctive patterns* of organization, even within an open and globalized economy. One illustration of this is that levels of taxation continue to differ markedly between countries. As Figure 3.1 shows, despite periodic fluctuations, the differentials in taxation levels were still greater at the end of the 1990s than they were in the 1960s.

We can immediately see a number of obvious ways in which national institutions help shape and determine international HRM practices. The role of the state, financial

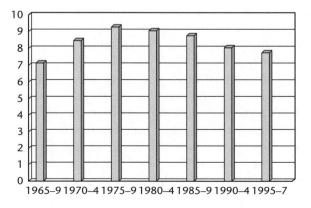

Figure 3.1 National differentials in tax regimes (standard deviations)
Source: Hobson (2003)

systems, national systems of education and training, and labour relations systems combine to form a dominant 'logic of action' in each country, and these will guide management practice. The social, legislative and welfare context influences many areas, such as: recruitment and dismissal; the formalization of educational qualifications; aspects of industrial relations, pay, and health and safety; the working environment; the nature of the employment contract; levels of co-determination and consultation, and so on (Sparrow and Hiltrop 1994: 52–59). Moreover, as we indicated in Chapter 2, a major difference between HRM in the US and Europe, and indeed between European countries, is the degree to which HRM is influenced and determined by state regulations. Differential national labour legislation reflects established political traditions concerning the extent to which employee rights should curtail the autonomy of managers to respond to pressures in ways they deem appropriate. Generally speaking, legislation affording employees consultation and negotiation rights is stronger in Europe than in the US, although there is considerable variation within Europe between, for example, the relatively deregulated UK and the more regulated countries such as Germany and Sweden. The role of factors such as state direction and family ownership in East Asian economies also figures prominently in institutionalist accounts.

A central concept within the institutionalist approach is that of the 'business system'. This concept ties together in a coherent way the historical, cultural and institutional processes that shape national or regional economies. It enables a focus on the way in which state, financial, industrial relations and other systems combine together to influence organizational practices. Whitley (2000) makes a useful distinction between 'background' institutions (e.g. family, education) that structure general social patterns and norms, and 'proximate' institutions (e.g. labour market systems) that constitute the more immediate business environment. This approach has a great deal in common with broader institutionalist perspectives in sociology (Powell and DiMaggio 1991; Scott 2001), and in particular with the 'societal effects' approach of Maurice and Sorge (2000). Their research showed that work organization patterns differ markedly due to nationally specific institutional logics that produce stable organizational and employment patterns. In particular the national ownership of firms facilitates the absorption of practices, ideas and culture from those institutions. Such logics are particularly located in education, training, labour market and industrial relations structures. This helps to explain, for instance, why salary structures, career patterns, management and authority relations vary among closely matched French, German and British firms (Lane 1989).

The institutionalist perspective also stresses the principle of 'functional equivalence', which has a direct relevance for understanding the transfer of HRM practices in MNCs (something we discuss in more depth in Chapter 5). This principle states that although business practices may differ from one firm to another, and from one nation to another, they are not automatically inferior or superior to each other. Firms and nations may practise what are in effect functional equivalents, which, although different, produce better results in specific strategic, market, institutional or national contexts (Gamble 2003; Kostova 1999). In other words, the purpose and effects of similar phenomena will vary according to circumstances and context, something which challenges any easy notion of universal 'best practices' in management.

As noted in the previous chapter, these national differences are not static character-istics that act only to constrain management action. Rather, MNCs will seek opportuni-ties and advantages from national differences. They will look for particular comparative and competitive strengths in 'locational advantages' associated with national or region-al production, innovation and business systems. Commonly, apparently minor advan-tages associated with a specific part of their overall production process are decisive in location decisions, as MNCs create complex international divisions of labour based on locational specialization, forming what Gereffi *et al.* (2005) have termed 'global com-modity chains'. One illustration of a region that has attracted MNCs is the Jaeren dis-trict of Norway, which has developed a cluster of firms engaged in the production of advanced industrial robots. A leading local firm, Trallfa Robot, was taken over by the Swiss-Swedish MNC ABB in the late 1980s, creating ABB Flexible Automation. Prior to the acquisition, ABB produced most of its robots for the European car makers in Vasteras in Sweden, but instead of restructuring by closing down the Jaeren plant and moving production to Sweden, ABB increased capacity and employment in its Norwegian subsidiary in order to capture the externalities available in the local area, namely the pool of skilled labour and the existence of specialist suppliers. In this way the presence of ABB has *strengthened* the local innovative and business system, rather than undermined it (Belanger *et al.* 1999). A quite different situation is that of the Bangalore region of India which has been the recipient of much investment by European and US companies in call centres and information processing centres. An example was the decision by British Telecom in 2003 to transfer many of its call centres from the UK to India. In this instance, the company was motivated primarily by the availability of computer-literate, English-speaking staff who could be employed at a fraction of the cost of their UK counterparts.

National models of capitalism

What the institutionalist perspective helps us to see above all is that the macro-struc-tures of the global economy 'continue to be manifested in specific configurations in specific places...In other words, they...are *territorially embedded*. There are *varieties of capitalism,* not one single universal form' (Dicken 2007: 11). A number of detailed stud-ies have examined the processes by which particular systems of economic co-ordination and control developed their distinctive features in different countries, and how contextual – especially institutional – factors might account for these. Consequently, theorists have identified the presence of a number of 'ideal types' of capitalist organisa-tion. An established two-way distinction, as made for example by Hall and Soskice (2001), is between liberal market economies (LMEs) – such as the US, Britain, Australia, Canada, New Zealand, and Ireland – and co-ordinated market economies (CMEs) – which include Germany, Japan, the Netherlands, Sweden, Finland and Austria. In liberal economies the market plays the dominant role in co-ordinating economic behaviour, and the state remains an arm's-length enforcer of contracts. LMEs are thus character-ized by short-term oriented company finance, deregulated labour markets, general edu-cation, and strong inter-company competition. In co-ordinated economies, by contrast, economic behaviour is strategically co-ordinated to a larger extent through non-market mechanisms. CMEs are thus characterized by long-term industrial finance, co-operative industrial relations, high levels of vocational training, and co-operation in technology and standard setting across companies.

While this dual categorization is common, others have developed more varied models. Coates (2005), for example, has described *three* models. In market-led capitalisms (e.g. US, UK) accumulation decisions are largely left to private companies in open financial markets. In contrast, state-led capitalisms (e.g. Japan, South Korea) combine the market and political dominance of private capital with state direction of growth decisions through administrative and banking structures. Finally, negotiated or consensual capitalisms (e.g. Sweden, Germany) may have less direct state regulation of capital accumulation, but management of the economy and enterprise is filtered through co-ordination arrangements in which labour as well as capital has influence and rights. Amable (2003) utilizes distinctive 'institutional domains' to generate his typology: product market competition, labour market institutions, finance and corporate governance, social protection and the welfare state, and the education and training system. Grouping capitalist economies based on their similarities (using cluster analysis) in these institutional domains generates *five* models of capitalism: a market-based model, a social-democratic model, a continental European model, a Mediterranean model, and an Asian model.

The notion of distinct national systems or 'varieties of capitalism' began to gain considerable currency in the 1980s, when significant differences were noted between the excellent economic performance of Germany and Japan, and the (relative) industrial decline of Britain and the US. These differences were attributed by many to the distinct institutional arrangements of German and Japanese capitalism. The remarkable competitiveness of these ostensibly more organized or 'co-ordinated' economies, where the market played a lesser role, was seen in their ability to mobilize collective inputs and long-term commitments. So, the varieties of capitalism approach not only suggests that national economies are characterized by distinct institutional configurations that generate a particular systemic 'logic' of economic action, but, crucially, that these logics will infer *comparative institutional advantage,* insofar as different institutional arrangements have distinct strengths and weaknesses for different kinds of economic activity (Deeg and Jackson 2008). Moreover, it implies a theory of institutional *path dependence.* Contrary to notions of convergence on a single model of 'best practice', common pressures may be refracted through different sets of institutions, thus leading to different sorts of problems and calling forth distinct solutions. In sum, the institutionalist approach looks at economic activity as being socially embedded within institutional contexts, and compares these contexts across different scales, such as sectors, regions and, especially, nations (Hancke *et al.* 2007).

National systems and MNCs

In different ways, both the culturalist and institutionalist perspectives outlined above stress the strength and influence of national systems. However, it has been argued that such 'high context' approaches may prioritise the stability of cultural or structural conditions to the neglect of human agency and individual 'strategic choice' (Crouch 2005). In this sense, HRM and management in general might be seen as over-determined by these contextual factors, with explanations giving insufficient attention to the role of individuals in changing or amending their context. This counter-argument reminds us of the importance of bargaining, choice and agency, and of firms as influential actors in the shaping of their business contexts. The precise influence of institutions and cultures is not linear, but is open to bargaining and decision-making within the firm (Amable and Palombarini 2009). Moreover, firms themselves are not passive recipients of broader economic, social or political trends, but active participants in shaping these trends. Further theoretical and empirical progress thus requires 'the ability to generate a more dynamic theory of institutional change' (Jackson and Deeg 2006: 7). Even the more rigorous institutionalist perspective has frequently been based on 'comparative statics' and an emphasis on institutional stability, such that the role of power and politics has been relatively neglected. However, this deficiency is now being addressed, and

> there is a growing recognition that the institutional environment does not mechanically determine organisational forms...There are still choices within constraints, and embeddedness still has to be enacted. (Thompson and McHugh 2009: 79)

There are various ideas currently gaining ground which seek to grasp the complex interplay between the organizational, the national, the regional and the global, and to provide the conceptual tools for understanding the dynamics of the relationship between them. Much of this work is inspired by a desire to move beyond what are increasingly seen as rather sterile debates around 'national effects'. Research emphasizing the importance of national and societal influences certainly serves as a necessary corrective to simplistic arguments about the pressures for universalism and global convergence, as we argued in the previous chapter. However, a common feature of research into the development of HRM in MNCs and its transfer across borders to host countries is to assume that national business systems are cultural or institutional 'givens', and so play down the scope for, and importance of, internal disputes and conflicts within MNCs.

Viewing the MNC as operating within a 'transnational social space' is one way of emphasizing the interdependent connections between the organization and both regional and global effects (Morgan *et al.* 2005; Williams and Geppert 2006). Here MNCs are considered as distinct from national firms insofar as they create organizational boundaries that cross national and institutional contexts, and in doing so senior managers seek to impose order on what are distinctive institutional settings. Practices and procedures that work routinely in one national context can become problematic in different national contexts, each of which has distinctive 'rules of the game' as to how economic activities and firms are to be co-ordinated. One consequence of this is that the MNC constitutes an inherently disordered or, at the very least, segmented 'social space'. As Morgan *et al.* (2003) argue, corporate-level managers will attempt to order this 'transnational social space' in many ways. The creation of common policies and procedures, and the application of formal means of monitoring and accounting for performance, are bureaucratic ways through which order is instilled, while the creation of common organizational cultures is another way in which control may be sustained. This influence from the centre will frequently be challenged by other groups of actors within the company, where they see their interests as being threatened by central control. Actors within subsidiaries control resources to which those at corporate level do not have access, such as knowledge of the local business context and other particular types of expertise. Thus, *power relations* are central to the internal workings of MNCs. As we have likewise argued elsewhere (Edwards *et al.* 2006; Rees and Edwards 2009), *extra-*firm institutions at the macro–level and *intra*-firm political processes at the micro–level are strongly interconnected.

The nature of these political processes, and the responses of organizational actors at a variety of levels within MNCs, vary markedly across firms. As Ferner and Edwards (1995) argue, various 'channels of influence' are likely to be found in different combinations across different types of MNC. For instance, the headquarters of MNCs that are highly integrated across borders are likely to rely heavily on formal authority relations to ensure that subsidiaries comply with their demands, whereas this type of influence is likely to be much weaker in MNCs with a more devolved or 'federal' structure. The internal workings of MNCs are a key part of what we identified in Chapter 2 as the *organization effect,* and the relations between groups of actors are one source of variation between MNCs in their responses to global, regional and national influences.

This draws our attention to what might broadly be called a 'political economy' perspective, which sees MNCs not as monolithic or apolitical organizations, but as complex coalitions of interests, as political systems with a clear focus on capital accumulation. In Kristensen and Zeitlin's (2005) study, the HQ of a British-owned MNC often lacked any clear strategic view and its approach tended to be shifting and uncertain, and the subsidiaries had substantial power resources. Their work emphasizes internal politics at organizational and workplace levels, and micro-social processes of argument, interpretation and compromise. Managers and employees within the MNC are seen as 'reflexive agents' who are able to resist, re-interpret and mediate corporate initiatives (Elger and Smith 2005). In terms of the relationship between organisations and national systems, this approach sees MNCs as 'rule makers' as well as 'rule takers' (Streeck and Thelen 2005), and as being constituted by a series of on-going tensions between competing social forces (managers, financiers, shareholders, suppliers, labour groups, etc.). As Ferner *et al.* (2006) argue, it stresses the complex micro-political dynamics inherent in any one MNC, and the way these interests are shaped by a particular combination of:

- the power of different levels or units, reflecting structural location in global value chains (those with a more strategic role have more power);
- the nature of national-institutional domains (subsidiary actors draw resources from the national-institutional framework in which they are embedded);
- the complex structure of the company (actors may define their interests at the level of the national subsidiary, the global function, regional territories, etc.).

What these kind of arguments try to capture is the fact that neither national systems nor MNCs are static features of the global economy, but rather they have a complex and interdependent relationship with each other, and understanding this is key to understanding how and why certain management strategies (including in the area of HRM) will take different forms, and lead to varying degrees of relative corporate and national economic success, in different national and corporate contexts. As Thompson and McHugh explain:

> Global capitalism remains a dynamic system in which different strategies are available to establishing competitive advantage for companies and countries. In that competitive struggle, forces of divergence and convergence are in continual tension. Within the new structural constraints, firms have some room to make strategic choices, selecting policies and solutions that can shape their environment. For transnational companies a key tension is reflected in the contradictory pressures to standardise their operations, products and services so as to maximise the scale and cost benefits of global integration, while at the same time attempting to serve the needs of specific markets. (2009: 86)

One of the reasons for complexity is that different facets of societal or corporate organisation will be subject to different pressures. For example, while firms may have discretionary powers to adopt common HR policies, industrial relations systems are the least likely to be internationally standardised because they are the most embedded in national institutional frameworks. Production and management systems, on the other hand, are subject much more directly to 'dominance effects' from perceived best practices and the need of MNCs to integrate their diverse activities and structures. In other words,

> it is not just the existence of a 'global mind-set' that determines the likely extent of integration, but the very real pressures to standardise that impinge more on some corporate activities and in some sectors than others. (Thompson and McHugh 2009: 87)

One further, and more developed, analytical schema for interpreting these complex relationships is the System–Society–Dominance (SSD) framework (Elger and Smith 2005; Smith and Meiksins 1995), which analyses the three-way tensions within international firms between: (i) *generic* features of capitalist social relations and structures — i.e. property rights, wage labour, competition, capital accumulation (system effects); (ii) *particular* forms of management and labour derived from where MNCs originate and their subsidiaries are located – i.e. the way enterprises are historically embedded and conditioned by distinctive institutional arrangements and cultural dispositions (society effects); and (iii) *standardizing* forces derived from dominant actors or global discourses — i.e. the process whereby 'lead societies', or sectors or firms, develop 'best practices' or global standards which are seen as dominant ideologies or logics and are subsequently emulated through processes of diffusion (dominance effects). This analytical framework advances our understanding insofar as it captures the 'triple determination of action' and hence 'the iterative and complex nature of change' (Smith *et al.* 2008: 12). Thompson and McHugh describe this as 'the most effective way of understanding the complex interplay of capitalist political economy, international 'best practices' and the continuing role of national states and employment systems' (2009: 71).

Institutional environments are thus far more complicated than previously conceived, and firms will experiment and shift their practices, tapping in to new possibilities and previous legacies. As Morgan (2007) argues, in order to investigate these processes it is necessary to take a processual, historical view of how institutions and organizations interact, and in doing so we see the mutual interaction of 'path dependency' effects with organizational innovations, and as such 'organizations, actors and institutions are engaged in a process of *co-constitution* ... where actors learn new ways of working and engage in reshaping institutions to facilitate that process' (2007: 142).

Conclusions

In this chapter we have seen that despite claims of growing convergence and the globalization of managerial structures and strategies, the ways in which economic activities are organized and controlled differ considerably between countries. We have outlined the two major theoretical approaches that seek to account for and explain these national differences, the first based around the notion of national cultures and the second giving more credence to institutional factors. Moreover we have stressed how these are related and interdependent.

We have argued that the concept of the 'national business system' – being comprised of interlocking sets of institutions and structures in different spheres of economic activity – is a useful way of conceptualizing these differences. Variations across business systems give rise to markedly differing management styles and employment practices. Moreover, we have argued that these systems are dynamic and evolve in response to external pressures. Firms, particularly large international ones, are active agents in this process, responding to the pressures of globalization and regionalization, and exerting a degree of influence over the nature of national-level institutions and cultures. In other words, there are interdependencies between the global and the local, between cultures and institutions, and between management actions and social structures.

One problem with the culturalist and institutionalist approaches is that they tend to give undue primacy to *national* factors, and consequently downplay the way these interact with *global*, *regional* and *organizational* factors. How can we more adequately relate 'national effects' to these other three levels of analysis? We have considered this question by drawing on recent ideas that have sought to move away from rigid analytical categories and towards a more 'holistic' conception of the interaction between these different levels. These have included the concept of 'transnational social space', the 'political economy' perspective, and the 'system–society–dominance' framework. Each of these provides a more helpful way of thinking about these issues than the populist management mantra of 'think global, act local'. The next chapter begins to explore in more detail the broad political economy perspective outlined above, in terms of the way the political dynamics within MNCs interact with national and regional institutions, and also draws out more explicitly the implications of this approach for international HRM practices.

Review questions

1 Why are some of the perspectives that emphasize the importance of national-level factors often described as 'high context', while those emphasizing global factors are described as 'low context'?

2 What are some of the main ways in which national cultures are said to impact upon organizations and management?

3 Consider some of the criticisms that are often made of the culturalist perspective. Do you think that the institutionalist emphasis on 'national business systems' offers a more fruitful approach to understanding national differences?

4 Referring to recent research studies, describe how a broadly 'political economy' approach might be applied to understanding the nature of management action in MNCs.

Further reading

1 Hofstede, G. (2001) *Culture's Consequences: Comparing Values, Behaviors, Institutions and Organisations Across Nations* (2nd edition), Thousand Oaks, CA: Sage.

Summarizes Hofstede's seminal study on culture and management, describing the way he constructed each of the cultural dimensions he refers to, and discussing subsequent studies that have drawn upon his ideas.

2 McSweeney, B. (2002) 'Hofstede's model of national cultural differences and their consequences: a triumph of faith – a failure of analysis', *Human Relations,* 55(1), 89–118.

A much-cited research paper which advances a strong and convincing critique both of Hofstede's work and also of the assumptions behind the broad culturalist approach.

3 Deeg, R. and Jackson, G. (2008) 'Comparing capitalisms: understanding institutional diversity and its implications for international business', *Journal of International Business Studies,* 39(4), 540–61.

Provides a detailed and scholarly overview of the literature on nationally distinctive models of capitalism, and considers their implications for managers in multinational companies.

4 Kristensen, P.H. and Zeitlin, J. (2005) *Local Players in Global Games: The Strategic Constitution of a Multinational Corporation,* Oxford: Oxford University Press.

A fascinating and insightful in-depth study of the HQ and three subsidiaries of a UK MNC, illuminating processes of internal politics, negotiation and resistance at multiple levels within the company.

References

Amable, B. (2003) *The Diversity of Modern Capitalism,* Oxford: OUP.

Amable, B. and Palombarini, S. (2009) 'A neorealist approach to institutional change and the diversity of capitalism', *Socio-Economic Review,* 7, 123–43.

Belanger, J., Berggren, C., Bjorkman, T. and Kohler, C. (eds) (1999) *Being Local Worldwide: ABB and the Challenge of Global Management,* Ithaca, NY and London: Cornell University Press.

Child, J. (2002) 'Theorizing About Organization Cross-Nationally' in Warner, M. and Joynt, P. (eds) *Managing Across Cultures: Issues and Perspectives,* London: Thompson.

Coates, D. (2005) *Varieties of Capitalism: Varieties of Approaches*, Basingstoke: Palgrave.

Crouch, C. (2005) *Capitalist Diversity and Change: Recombinant Governance and Institutional Entrepreneurs*, Oxford: Oxford University Press.

Deeg, R. and Jackson, G. (2008) 'Comparing capitalisms: understanding institutional diversity and its implications for international business', *Journal of International Business Studies*, 39(4), 540–61.

Dicken, P. (2007) *Global Shift: Mapping the Changing Contours of the World Economy* (5th edition), London: Sage.

Edwards, T., Coller, X., Ortiz, L., Rees, C. and Wortmann, M. (2006) 'National industrial relations systems and cross-border restructuring: evidence from a merger in the pharmaceuticals sector', *European Journal of Industrial Relations*, 12(1), 69–87.

Elger, T. and Smith, C. (2005) *Assembling Work: Remaking Factory Regimes in Japanese Multinational Companies in Britain*, Oxford: Oxford University Press.

Ferner, A. (2000) 'The Embeddedness of US Multinational Companies in the US Business System: Implications for HR/IR', *DMU Business School Occasional Papers*.

Ferner, A. and Edwards, P. (1995) 'Power and the diffusion of organizational change in multinational enterprises', *European Journal of Industrial Relations*, 1(2), 229–57.

Ferner, A., Quintanilla, J., and Sanchez-Runde, C. (eds) (2006) *Multinationals, Institutions and the Construction of Transnational Practices*, Basingstoke: Macmillan.

Gamble, J. (2003) 'Transferring business practices from the United Kingdom to China: the limits and potential for convergence', *International Journal of Human Resource Management*, 14(3), 369–87.

Gereffi, G., Humphrey, J. and Sturgeon, T. (2005) 'The governance of global value chains', *Review of International Political Economy*, 12, 78–104.

Hall, P. and Soskice, D. (2001) *Varieties of Capitalism: The Institutional Foundations of Comparative Advantage*, Oxford: Oxford University Press.

Hancke, B., Rhodes, M. and Thatcher, M. (eds) (2007) *Beyond Varieties of Capitalism: Conflict, Contradictions and Complementarities in the European Economy*, Oxford: Oxford University Press.

Hobson, J. (2003) 'Disappearing Taxes or the "Race to the Middle"? Fiscal Policy in the OECD' in L. Weiss (ed.) *States in the Global Economy: Bringing Institutions Back In*, Cambridge: Cambridge University Press.

Hofstede, G. (2001) *Culture's Consequences: Comparing Values, Behaviors, Institutions and Organisations Across Nations* (2nd edition), Thousand Oaks, CA: Sage.

Jackson, G. and Deeg, R. (2006) 'How Many Varieties of Capitalism? Comparing the Comparative Institutional Analyses of Capitalist Diversity', *Max Planck Institute Discussion Paper*, No. 06/2.

Kostova, T. (1999) 'Transnational transfer of strategic organizational practices: a contextual perspective', *Academy of Management Review*, 24(2), 308–24.

Kristensen, P.H. and Zeitlin, J. (2005) *Local Players in Global Games: The Strategic Constitution of a Multinational Corporation*, Oxford: Oxford University Press.

Lane, C. (1989) *Management and Labour in Europe: The Industrial Enterprise in Germany, Britain and France*, Aldershot: Edward Elgar.

Maurice, M. and Sorge, A. (2000) *Embedding Organizations*, Amsterdam: John Benjamins Publishing.

McSweeney, B. (2002) 'Hofstede's model of national cultural differences and their consequences: a triumph of faith – a failure of analysis', *Human Relations*, 55(1), 89–118.

McSweeney, B. (2009) 'Dynamic diversity: variety and variation within countries', *Organization Studies*, 30(9), 933–57.

Moore, F. and Rees, C. (2008) 'Culture against cohesion: global corporate strategy and employee diversity in the UK plant of a German MNC', *Employee Relations,* 30(2), 176–89.

Morgan, G. (2007) 'National business systems research: progress and prospects', *Scandinavian Journal of Management,* 23, 127–45.

Morgan, G., Kelly, B., Sharpe, D. and Whitley, R. (2003) 'Global managers and Japanese multinationals: internationalization and management in Japanese financial institutions', *International Journal of Human Resource Management,* 14(3), 398–408.

Morgan, G., Whitley, R. and Moen, E. (eds) (2005) *Changing Capitalisms?: Internationalisation, Institutional Change and Systems of Economic Organization,* Oxford: Oxford University Press.

Ngo, H., Turban, D., Lau, C. and Lui, S. (1998) 'Human resource practices and firm performance of MNCs: influence of country of origin', *International Journal of Human Resource Management,* 9(4), 632–52.

Powell, W. and DiMaggio, P. (1991) *The New Institutionalism in Organizational Analysis,* Chicago, IL: University of Chicago Press.

Rees, C. and Edwards, T. (2009) 'Management strategy and HR in international mergers: choice, constraint and pragmatism', *Human Resource Management Journal,* 19(1), 24–39.

Schneider, S. and Barsoux, J.-L. (2003) *Managing Across Cultures* (2nd edition), Harlow: Pearson.

Scholte, J.A. (2005) *Globalization: A Critical Introduction* (2nd edition), Basingstoke: Macmillan.

Scott, R. (2001) *Institutions and Organizations* (2nd edition), Thousand Oaks, CA: Sage.

Smith, C. and Meiksins, P. (1995) 'System, society and dominance effects in cross-national organisational analysis', *Work, Employment and Society,* 9(2), 241–68.

Smith, C., McSweeney, B. and Fitzgerald, R. (eds) (2008) *Remaking Management: Between Global and Local,* Cambridge, Cambridge University Press.

Sparrow, P. and Hiltrop, J.M. (1994) *European Human Resource Management in Transition,* Hemel Hempstead: Prentice Hall.

Streeck, W. and Thelen, K. (eds) (2005) *Beyond Continuity: Institutional Change in Advanced Political Economies,* Oxford: Oxford University Press.

Tayeb, M. (2005) *International Human Resource Management: A Multinational Company Perspective,* Oxford: OUP.

Thompson, P. and McHugh, D. (2009) *Work Organisations: A Critical Approach* (4th edition), Basingstoke: Macmillan.

Trompenaars, F. and Hampden-Turner, C. (1997) *Riding The Waves of Culture: Understanding Cultural Diversity in Business* (2nd edition), London: Nicholas Brealey.

Whitley, R. (2000) *Divergent Capitalisms: The Social Structuring and Change of Business Systems,* Oxford: Oxford University Press.

Williams, K. and Geppert, M. (2006) 'Employment Relations as a Resource in the Socio-political Construction of Transnational Social Spaces by Multinational Companies', in Geppert, M. and Mayer, M. (eds) *Global, National and Local Practices in Multinational Companies,* London: Palgrave.

Chapter 4

Nations, regions and international HRM

Phil Almond

Key aims

The aims of this chapter are to:

- look more critically at the institutionalist and 'varieties of capitalism' approaches, and consider their implications for international HRM;
- explain the impact of 'home' and 'host' country effects on MNC human resource practices;
- examine in more detail the nature of power relations within MNCs and the 'hybridization' of HRM policies in different national contexts;
- consider how national variations have changed in the recent period of global deregulation.

Introduction

The previous chapter explored ways in which management action is shaped by national culture and by national institutional systems. This chapter expands on this by looking in more detail at some specific ways in which employment systems differ on a national and regional basis, and whether particular sorts of countries can usefully be grouped together in this respect. It then looks at how these cross-national differences might affect human resource management decision-making in MNCs.

Types and numbers of national system

According to the United Nations, there were, at the time of writing, 192 different states in the world. Evidently, some of these states, such as the large, rich countries, have much more power over how their business and employment systems are run than others. Yet, this still leaves, potentially, a high number of different institutional systems for regulating business and employment, if the idea of 'national business systems' set out in the previous chapter is valid. Perhaps luckily for students and researchers though, the existence of nearly 200 states does not mean that there are nearly 200 radically different national ways of organising employment. While, obviously, no two states are identical, cross-national patterns do exist to some extent. Without prior knowledge, for instance, it should not be particularly surprising that the way business operates in Brazil is more similar to Argentina than either is to the Japanese system. For students, researchers or reflective practitioners, then, rather than simply collecting facts about every individual state which we might have an interest in, it might be useful to see what we can say about what *types* of national system actually exist. It may then be possible to reach some conclusions about how these different types of system are likely to shape the HRM policies and practices of MNCs that have their *home* in each type of system, and also how MNCs from abroad may need to adapt to such *host* country systems.

❱ Two varieties of capitalism?

As outlined in the previous chapter, a large number of researchers have sought to compare national arrangements affecting business, work and employment (e.g. Maurice *et al.* 1986; Lane 1989; Whitley 1992). Among such writings, one very prominent work, and in terms of its classification of countries the simplest, is that of Hall and Soskice (2001), who argue that the way firms develop their core competencies is shaped by national social arrangements in a number of areas. The national arrangements they emphasize are:

- national industrial relations and pay setting arrangements;
- vocational training and education;
- corporate governance, particularly whether national systems lead to firms mainly obtaining capital for investment from long-termist (banks) or short-termist (the equity market) providers;
- patterns of inter-firm relations: the extent to which relations with suppliers, or other firms in the same sector, are collaborative or competitive;
- 'intra-firm' relations, i.e. issues relating to achieving the co-operation of workers. This would include, among other things, prevalent patterns of worker participation in decision-making over work organization, teamworking, and other similar practices.

Hall and Soskice (2001) hold that these different 'spheres' are closely interrelated, and are likely to be 'coherent' in any relatively successful national economy. So, while there are, in theory, for example, lots of different ways a national society might organize vocational training (c.f. Noble 1997), only a limited number of these are likely to work well in any specific country, given the functional need for a country's vocational training and education system to 'fit' with the nature of its industrial relations system, corporate governance system, etc. To take an example commonly used by institutionalist researchers, it is more difficult for firms to try to base competitive advantage on high-trust relations with employees if the financial system they operate under pushes them towards making workers redundant in reaction to relatively small short-term fluctuations in profitability, as has increasingly been the case in countries where stock markets are an important source of corporate finance.

If we accept the broad argument that elements of national economic systems must (and do) 'cohere' with each other, this has important practical, as well as theoretical, implications: it would mean that it is often difficult, and sometimes counterproductive, for firms and states to try to copy elements of employment policy from successful cases overseas, given wider differences in national business systems. Maurice *et al.*'s (1986) illustration of the unsuccesful attempt to transpose elements of the successful German training system to France is a case in point.

Hall and Soskice concentrate most of their work on two ways in which the various elements of a national system of capitalism can cohere: the liberal market economy (LME) and the co-ordinated market economy (CME). Although they sometimes claim that these are theoretically-derived ideal types, rather than being based on real economies, for the present chapter at least it is much simpler to think of an LME as being best represented by the US, and a CME by Germany. They do not claim that these are the *only* ways in which the different elements of national systems can cohere, but they do argue that the most successful developed economies tend to approximate to one or the other, with national economies that fall between the two poles having inferior economic performance (c.f. Hall and Gingerich 2004). The basic differences between the two types, and their expected effects on human resource management, are presented, in stylised form, in Table 4.1.

The varieties of capitalism framework has several features which are useful to a discussion of international and comparative human resource management. First, in general terms, it provides an intellectual justification for the argument that there is more than one potentially successful way to run an advanced economy. There is no reason, following this argument, to expect that employment policies (or HR practices) should necessarily tend towards one dominant pattern, as has sometimes been assumed in the HRM literature on convergence. In other words, what is perfectly logical in the US may make little sense in Germany. This in itself offers a powerful corrective to some of the more naïve assumptions that HR practices throughout the world are likely to, or should, approximate to models of HRM developed in the US, or whichever other national model is currently fashionable. Second, the general argument here indirectly offers some clues as to how MNCs from different countries might behave. In particular, MNCs from liberal market economies are likely to change the nature of their operations more rapidly—and have less employment security for their workers, within a 'market-driven' organisational approach—than is the case for MNCs originating in CMEs. How national differences shape MNC behaviour is dealt with in more detail below.

The varieties of capitalism thesis has been criticized on a number of grounds, however. Among other things, there are disputes on some of the evidence used (Almond and Gonzalez 2006), and arguments about how well the supporting theory deals with change or sub-national variation (c.f. Crouch 2005, who argues that one of the most important recent growth poles of the American economy, Silicon Valley, does not mainly work as would be predicted by the LME model). More importantly for the present chapter, there are marked differences *within* each of the two groups (Jackson and Deeg 2008); German employment relations may have similar effects on competitiveness to those of Japan, but working in Germany is very different to working in Japan (Jacoby *et al.* 2005; Marsden 1999; Thelen and Kume 2006). Even more worryingly for our purposes, the LME/CME dichotomy leaves out most of the world's economies. First, Hall and Soskice, like nearly all authors in this area, specifically limit their analysis to

Table 4.1 Differences between national varieties of capitalism, and effects on HRM

	Liberal market economy (LME)	*Co-ordinated market economy (CME)*
Examples	UK, USA, Canada, Australia, other developed English-speaking economies	Germany, Japan, Scandinavian economies, Netherlands, Austria, Switzerland
Finance system	Equity-based, large stock markets. Easy for investors to switch assets–this leads to strong pressures for short-term profitability	Credit-based, i.e. important role for banks. These often take a direct role in corporate decision-making, through representation at board-level, etc., and take longer-term view of corporate success
Relations between firms	Competitive and contract-based, e.g. subcontracting tends to be based on price competition and be relatively low-trust	Collaborative, both in terms of creating institutional infrastructure (wage bargaining, training, etc.) and in terms of long-term, high-trust relations across the supply chains of large firms
Vocational training and education	General education provided by state. Vocational training systems unstable, as large firms prefer to develop their own systems rather than contribute to sectoral/occupational systems	Firms pool resources into highly developed vocational training systems, usually at sectoral level (not Japan)
Wage determination	Workplace or firm level	More centralized (sectoral or national level)
Employment relationship	'Hire and fire' principles lead to low-trust relationships between employers and employees. Reliance on numerical flexibility	Long-term, higher-trust relationships for core workers. Reliance on functional flexibility
Union organization	Primarily occupational	Primarily sectoral (not Japan)
Role of the state	To ensure 'free and fair' markets, but otherwise to intervene as little as possible	To establish framework by which authority can be delegated to corporate actors, e.g. employers' organizations and trade unions
HRM	Attempts to increase co-operation from employees historically made difficult by conflictive industrial relations, more recently by low levels of employment security creating difficulties in obtaining commitment Individualization of HR (individualized pay and career development, decline of trade unions)	More collectively oriented HRM (higher levels of collective employee involvement, greater prevalence of autonomous teams, less individualized pay)
Areas of competitive strength	Sectors involving radical innovation (IT, science)	Sectors involving incremental innovation (engineering)

Source: elaborated from Hall and Soskice (2001), in collaboration with Maria Gonzalez the core developed economies. This is not without justification, in that a conventional institutionalist analysis of national employment systems really requires both that most of the working population have employment contracts, and that the country has a relatively high degree of control over a fairly stable economic and social system. The latter condition means it is also difficult to reach firm conclusions on how well the transformation economies of central and Eastern Europe fit together as a group. Even within relatively stable Western economies, though, an important group of countries—France, Greece, Italy, Portugal, Spain, and, with somewhat less certainty Turkey—is largely ignored. Hall and Soskice (2001) do raise this group as a potential third variety (named 'Mediterranean' economies), but, partly because they see this type of economy as less stable and successful than either LMEs or CMEs, do not pay all that much attention to them. For our purposes, it is important to include this group (see Table 4.2), as

Table 4.2 **The 'Mediterranean' variety of capitalism**

	'Mediterranean' economy
Examples	France, Spain, Portugal, Greece, Italy, Turkey
Finance system	Traditionally credit-based, combined with important role for the state. Recent trend to increasing dependence on foreign (US) equity investors for largest firms.
Relations between firms	Sectors co-ordinated around large 'national champions', with traditionally high degree of state involvement in creating sectoral strategies.
Vocational training and education	More emphasis on intellectual than vocational education. Academic qualifications very important for career development.
Wage determination	Historically sectoral in principle (except Italy), but real pay levels often determined at workplace/firm level, often informally.
Employment relationship	High degree of employment security for core workers, but low-trust relationships, partly due to reliance on Taylorism.
Union organization	Primarily ideological.
Role of the state	To ensure economic development and to govern the employment relationship.
HRM	Hierarchical management and Taylorist production organization historically attempted to reduce the need for high degrees of co-operation from employees, while strict labour law reduced differences in HR practice between firms.
	More recently, leading firms have increasingly borrowed elements of American-style HRM, particularly for managers and other highly qualified workers.
Areas of competitive strength	Sectors with highly rationalized production.

Source: elaborated from Hall and Soskice (2001), in collaboration with Maria Gonzalez

Mediterranean economies have employment and human resource management patterns which, again at the level of generalization, are different to those of either CMEs or LMEs. It is also worth noting that the more organized parts of many Latin American economies tend to share at least some of these features (Schneider 2009).

▶ A 'European' system?

Other groupings of countries, drawn less from theoretical premises and more from the empirical realities of geography and politics, also have some degree of validity. For example, in the 1990s some authors (e.g. Brewster 1993) posited a 'European' model of HRM. This had more influence from the state and trade unions, and was generally more social-democratic, that the then-popular HRM models derived from American business school models. This has parallels with, and to a degree was inspired by, attempts to develop and define the 'European Social Model' by political and other social actors within the EU.

The extent to which it makes sense to talk of a 'European model' depends on the level of detail that is required. In very broad terms, there are some features affecting employment relations in the EU which lead to commonalities. These would include relatively generous welfare states, high levels of social and political acceptance of pluralism, and, on the whole, relatively high degrees of state regulation of the labour market. To some extent, the development of European-level regulation of work and employment from the 1990s also provides for some degree of convergence between member states, through regulations on health and safety, working time, worker participation, equality, etc. It should be remembered, however, that European-level regulation does not strongly affect the core features of employment regulation in most EU countries, whose own national systems tend to offer more guarantees of worker protection than those set out in European legislation (there are partial exceptions to this in the UK, Ireland and some of the former Warsaw Pact new member states). Also, as we have seen when looking at *Varieties of Capitalism,* there are members of the EU in each of the three broad varieties, with effects on the application of European-level policies (Gonzalez 2010). In summary, talking about a 'European model' may make some sense at a rhetorical level to observers from outside Europe, but tells us little about how European business systems work, and the considerable differences between them.

National business systems and HRM in MNCs

If the national business systems in which firms operate affect their business and human resource policies and practices, this still leaves open further questions as far as MNCs are concerned. MNCs, by definition, operate in more than one national business system. From a reading of national varieties of capitalism models, it is not immediately apparent whether it is likely to be business system effects from the firm's *home* country (country of origin effects) that are most important, or from the *host* country (country of operation effects). In some cases, country–of–origin effects are more likely in some areas: one example here might be a general long-termist versus short-termist orientation, depending on the degree to which patient capital is available. In other areas perhaps host country effects are more likely to be important: examples here might include areas subject to legal or collective regulation, such as minimum wages, union rights or maximum working hours, particularly if such regulation is tightly enforced.

To further complicate the issue, it is by no means inevitable that senior managers in MNCs necessarily want to impose a country of origin model in all cases (see, for example, Kahancová 2008), or, indeed, that host country managers and workers will always defend the host country model of management. Many of these complicating factors relate to the overall international management strategy of the firm (Fenton O'Creevy *et al.* 2008), and to issues of organizational form (e.g. Bartlett and Ghoshal 2002). These are covered in more detail in the following two chapters. The remainder of the current chapter, while accepting the insights of this literature, adopts a complementary perspective, looking at how features of the business systems under which MNCs operate translate into HR policy and practice (and sometimes, how they do not) in subsidiary operations. This requires insights into the (formal and informal) negotiation of policy and practice, as well as into more strategic decisions about standardization and segmentation.

▶ The negotiation of policies: collaboration and contestation in the MNC

The goal of this section is to move from a general understanding of how different types of national business systems tend to affect firm behaviour to the question of how MNCs manage human resources. In order to do this, we need first to answer the question 'what does an examination of HRM in a multinational firm have to take account of that the analysis of a domestic firm does not?'.

In order to answer this question, it is useful to re-visit some of the implicit assumptions of much of the general literature on HRM and employment relations. In particular the concept of the 'effort–reward bargain' (Boxall and Purcell 2008) should be borne in mind. In part, this is the idea that the employment relationship is an unequal relationship between the sellers and buyers of labour (the employer has more power than the employee as it is easier for the employer to find another employee than it is for the employee to find an alternative way of making ends meet). More importantly for our purposes, it is also the idea that, despite this power advantage, the outcome of the relationship is still uncertain for the employer: paying someone a wage does not guarantee that enough appropriate work will be done, this is a matter of management. In order to ensure that this will happen, it is widely agreed that the employer needs a combination of control and disciplinary mechanisms, alongside means of building consent, loyalty and of using workers' initiative in ways that are useful to the employer (Friedman 1977; Legge 1995). As argued in Chapter 2, human resource management always requires some degree of control of employees, but also some mechanisms by which to ensure that workers' initiative can be used (to deal with unforeseen problems, etc). Equally, no system of managerial control is perfect; workers always have at least some power to resist, to create informal strategies, and therefore to affect the outcomes of the bargain.

The dilemma between control and building commitment and initiative also applies to other sets of organizational relations. Most obviously, in organizations of any size it applies to the relations between the owners of capital and salaried managers. Again, financiers are more powerful than individual managers (they can, in the last resort, replace them), but they do not exercise full control over managers, and in any case need them to use their initiative. As the varieties of capitalism literature shows, the relations between owners and managers differ substantially across nations, with notable effects on human resource management. Finally, the management function itself is split between several levels, both in terms of hierarchy and in terms of function. Control dilemmas are clearly present here too: higher level managers have to decide whether to set policy tightly, or loosely, giving more autonomy to junior managers and supervisors, for example. Again, it is counterproductive for senior managers to seek always to maximize control over their juniors, both because the effort involved in monitoring would be very expensive, and because of the loss of initiative from subordinates.

All these different organisational actors are involved in structured, unequal power relations, all of which can only be 'resolved' satisfactorily by combining some element of direct control with some level of autonomy. Importantly, the precise mix between the two depends, among other things, on the social environment. The nature of the national business system is an important factor here: acceptable regimes of control and collaboration between shopfloor workers, supervisors, line managers, strategic decision makers and owners in Britain may be very abnormal, to the point of being unworkable, in Korea, and *vice versa*. This is partly because rules (laws, collective agreements, systems of corporate governance) are different, and partly because expectations (i.e. what each group of actors collectively sees as 'fair', 'equitable' or 'normal') may be different.

All the above sets of power relations, and their resultant control vs. autonomy decisions, exist in any domestic firm of sufficient size. In an MNC, though, they are of a greater order of complexity. This is because, from the subsidiary perspective, decision-making on management practices, including HRM, is normally partly performed by managers whose understandings of employment and management come from their experience in different national regimes. To take a simplified example, in a British subsidiary of, say, a Korean firm, HR policies are likely to reflect some sort of encounter between, at minimum, Korean and British managers, and British workers.

Of course, such encounters are, once again, unequal power relations (senior HQ managers ultimately have more power than subsidiary level managers). But, even more so than in a domestic firm, it is not possible for HQ managers to control tightly everything that happens in foreign subsidiaries, nor, in most cases, is it likely to be desirable to try to, due both to the costs involved and the loss of subsidiary initiative.

In reality, the extent to which MNCs attempt to reflect their domestic managerial assumptions and practices abroad is highly variable. Much of this variation is due to issues of market positioning and global management structure (Dunning and Lundan 2008; see also Chapter 6). However, there is substantial empirical evidence that the degree of centralisation in decision-making on personnel policies is also shaped by the nationality of the firm, with, for instance, firms from the US generally being more centralised than those from other countries (Ferner *et al.* 2004; 2010). As Chapter 5 will examine in more detail, there are also a variety of means by which control may be exercised. These vary from the extensive expatriation of home country managers (most prevalent among Japanese MNCs, c.f. Chung *et al.* 2006), through extensive bureaucratic controls. Alternatively, controls may mainly be in the form of targets: these may vary from what from an HRM perspective can be described as indirect (such as financial targets) to the very direct (e.g. diversity targets, see Ferner *et al.* 2005).

In spite of these variations, though, it is important always to remember that neither the choices and constraints affecting the MNC as a whole, nor those affecting the international HQ or the overseas subsidiary, can be understood adequately without bearing in mind the choices and constraints affecting multiple groups of actors at different levels of the organization, in different countries. HR policies in a given overseas subsidiary of an MNC are likely to be shaped, to some extent, by the general characteristics of both home and host business systems, as well as by business environmental factors. But how the resulting policies play through into the reality of subsidiary HRM will always be shaped by multiple ongoing processes of 'negotiation' and interpretation by sets of *actors* at different levels of the organisation, all of whom have their own ideas about appropriate means of management, which will inevitably have been formed in reaction to the social setting(s) they are used to.

This does not mean that subsidiary workers and managers will necessarily 'prefer' the HR regimes which predominate in their own national business system to those of the foreign MNC they may work for. In societies where relatively autocratic forms of management prevail, it is quite possible that at least some workers actively prefer the more participative management policies of some foreign MNCs (if, of course, the foreign MNC chooses to use such policies globally). Equally, it is possible that women in very patriarchal societies who seek career advancement may prefer to work for foreign MNCs with relatively active diversity policies. It is also possible for some larger MNCs to specifically seek to recruit workers abroad who are particularly likely to conform to values that fit within country-of-origin-derived corporate cultures: attempting to select workers whose attitudes and experiences are compatible with desired 'global' corporate cultures has been a major factor in recruitment in some greenfield plants, particularly in Japanese but also in some American MNCs. To the extent that this is successful, the rationality under which workers operate becomes 'hybridized': it is somewhat less capable of being read off from a characterization of the host employment system, but somewhat less 'foreign' from an HQ perspective.

If subsidiary shopfloor workers can be made to (partially) 'think foreign', then there is at least the potential for actors at all levels of the firm to begin to develop rationalities that are not exclusively those of their own nationality. In the case of subsidiary *managers,* the international employment system of the MNC often encourages this. The Italian research of Delmestri (2006) is instructive here in revealing the different identities of middle managers working for Anglo-Saxon and Italian firms, with the former developing far more 'LME' type opinions and mentalities: significantly, these differences remained even where the Italian firms concerned were themselves MNCs.

More centralized MNCs deliberately attempt to 'globalize' managers through programmes of inpatriation and other forms of international mobility of managers (see

Moore 2006 on the multiple identities and individual strategies of expatriates). Similarly, the creation of some form of international internal labour market at managerial level (Butler *et al.* 2006) may be used to develop, at least at the levels to which it applies, an 'internal institutional community' (Elger and Smith 2006: 68) which may challenge, or attempt to bypass, the standard managerial assumptions of host country national employment systems. More general programmes of the international management of corporate culture also attempt to change rationalities in this way: indeed, Bartlett and Ghoshal (2002) emphasize the central importance of 'normative control', specifically with regard to their most advanced form of international firm, the 'transnational'.

None of these policies will entirely erase host country rationalities. Nor, in most cases, do they probably seek to. Nonetheless, the terrain on which decisions are made, and co-ordination dilemmas resolved, is altered, to a greater or lesser extent. The argument may also hold in reverse, albeit to a lesser extent: for example, one would expect an expatriate manager to gain at least some empathy with the common assumptions, ideas about fairness, etc., in the country to which s/he was assigned. In some cases, 'upward' transfer of ideas goes much further than this: the MNC as a whole may seek to learn from policies in successful subsidiaries and apply them in other countries. This process, referred to as 'reverse diffusion' (Edwards 1998), is dealt with in detail in Chapter 7.

To summarize, it is commonly recognised that the international encounter between business systems that occurs within MNCs causes 'hybridization' of HR outcomes. This hybridization of outcomes is the result both of the meeting of the effects of different objective features of national business and employment systems (rules, etc.), and of a degree of hybridization of the rationalities of workers and managers across the international firm's employment system (i.e. how people at different levels of the organization, and in different places, think about what might be desirable and practical policies).

A schematic representation of how different business systems interact in an MNC is given in Figure 4.1. In reality, it is an over-simplification; it excludes, for example, potentially important non-national organizational levels such as product divisions and regional management structures (c.f. Wachter *et al.* 2006), as well as encounters between managers and workers from different host countries (Boussebaa 2009). Equally, the relative importance and influence of the different levels is subject to the precise hierarchical structure and relations of power within individual MNCs: in particular, some national subsidiaries (those in strategically important markets, and/or fulfilling key organizational functions) are likely to have more influence than others. Nonetheless, the double directionality of the arrows in Figure 4.1 illustrates the complex pattern of causality involved in shaping employment policies and practices within MNCs, and the multiple levels at which 'hybridisation' of both ideas and policies takes place. The fact that the various arrows point in both directions does not imply equality of influence. As already pointed out, the hierarchical nature of the power structure means that the downward flow is likely to be potentially more significant than the upward flow in most cases. The next section looks at how these flows work in practice.

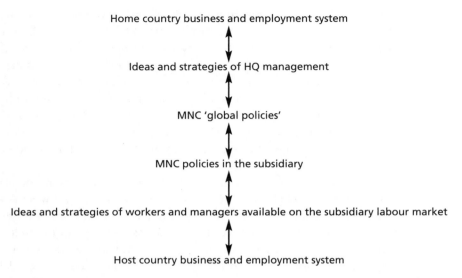

Figure 4.1 **Simplified representation of how national business systems shape MNC HR**

▶ The MNC as an international employment system

As Ferner *et al.* (2006: 6) point out, MNCs are far more than 'the micro-level product of competing...institutional influences from sector or NBS (national business system)'; they are 'powerful actors operating across institutional boundaries, with their own transnationally defined organisational logic, structure and strategy'. Their top decision-makers can decide the extent to which, and the elements of policy on which, they wish foreign subsidiaries to follow international rules and cultural tools. It is important, then, to remember that the extent to which top-level corporate decision-makers actually *want* the downward process to occur is itself variable.

It would certainly be a mistake to think that top country of origin managers necessarily believe that the human resource management situation that pertains in their home country operations is optimal (c.f. Sippola 2009 on Finnish MNCs' industrial relations approaches in the Baltic states). This applies even in dominant countries. For example, a number of large US MNCs that were forced by trade union organizing success to accept the traditionally conflictual HR model of unionized American firms remained strongly anti-union abroad (Colling *et al.* 2006). Equally, the low-trust employment regime, deriving from Taylorism, that has dominated US manufacturing, is far from an optimal background against which to introduce new forms of work organization, such as teamworking. In reality, the managerial policies that MNCs seek to export are often not the concrete country of origin practices, but rather managerial ideas and concepts; as Elger and Smith put it, a '"model of best practice", *formed within but emancipated from* specific national and corporate contexts' (2006: 57).

Second, even if top decision-makers want to create an international system based on learned ideas about best practice, those ideas may not entirely be those of the home country. In particular, some national systems are more popular among top international managers than others. Over the last two decades the dominant global human resource management model has essentially consisted of a 'lean' version of the American model of management, combined with some elements of work organization that are, in large part, a Western interpretation of Japanese production organization. Top managers in MNCs from other countries may well seek to create this dominant system worldwide, rather than export their own national model. This is an example of what the System–Society–Dominance (SSD) model, discussed in the previous chapter, would refer to as a 'dominance effect' (Smith and Meiksins 1995).

Third, top decision-makers may decide to use the existing differences between host country systems in a strategic manner. There may be good economic reasons to practice *strategic segmentation* of policies, which may involve a more or less conscious decision to stall, or at least be selective about, the downward flow in Figure 4.1, above. For example, a British firm with engineering operations in Germany may wish to exploit those elements of the host country system (see Table 4.1) which have given that country a competitive advantage in that sector, rather than standardising around a British model. Equally, as is well known, firms from rich countries operating in low-cost countries may well choose to minimize costs by avoiding the export of some of their more sophisticated management techniques.

In fact, this latter consideration does not only apply to developing countries. Within Britain, for example, Japanese MNCs show very mixed results in terms of the extent to which they attempt to replicate elements of the Japanese employment system. This is only partly because some of the main supporting elements of the employment system for large firms in Japan, such as high levels of employment security for core workers, are not present in the UK. Some 'Japanese' characteristics can be observed among some leading investors: the pay and grading system at Sony UK followed principles that would be recognizable in Japan; Japanese firms entering the UK from the 1980s sought to replicate the Japanese principle of company unionism by negotiating single-union deals with no-strike agreements; and considerable management effort and cost was expended on the recruitment of semi-skilled workers at firms such as Honda and Toyota (Hudson 1995). In other cases, though, particularly those researched by Elger and Smith (2005), there was very little evidence of the 'high road' elements of Japanese HRM. As these authors argue, this is not accidental, but rather represents the strategic use of elements of the HR patterns commonly used in supply chain firms in Japan (Dedoussis 1994), combined with a selective adaptation of host country practices, particularly those involving 'harsh conditions and union exclusion' (Elger and Smith 2005: 62; see also Milkman 1991 for Japanese MNCs in the US). What is happening in such cases does not represent an 'absence' of country of origin effects, but rather a strategic decision by senior actors within the MNC to segment its production and employment system, using, in this case, the light regulation of the host country system to create a division between 'core' and 'peripheral' workers, inspired by practice in Japan.

Management, ownership and country-of-origin effects

The varieties of capitalism literature, as introduced at the beginning of this chapter, basically explains national differences with regard to two dimensions. Firstly, it looks at how the effects of national institutions and historically developed cultural assumptions affect both the choices available to managers, and the ways in which managers and other actors think about these choices. As we have seen, when we look at MNCs, thinking about how these various effects might play out becomes much more complicated, as actors from different national systems, with different rules and different assumptions, meet. Second, the varieties of capitalism literature looks at the effects of different forms of corporate financing. In particular, it contrasts credit-based systems such as Germany where firms have tended to obtain finance through borrowing from banks over long time periods, with equity-based systems such as the US, where liquid stock markets have been much more important. Typically, these differences, which have their roots in processes of state formation and patterns of industrialization, are seen as having given rise to firms in 'coordinated market economies' such as Germany or Japan having access to 'patient' capital. In other words, those providing finance are more interested in long-term than short-term results. In return, they have an active say in how firms are run, whether through banks being represented on corporate boards, or through extensive cross-shareholdings as in Japan (Dore 1997). In 'liberal market economies' on the other hand, as shares can easily be bought and sold, investors have much shorter time horizons, and generally less interest in being actively involved in corporate decision-making. As Table 4.1 shows, this is important for human resource management as many elements of the business systems of co-ordinated market economies could not work if the pressure for maximizing short-term returns were as fierce as it has been in liberal economies. Equally, investors in liberal market economies would probably see the 'constraints' on rapid decision-making in co-ordinated economies (such as the difficulty of firing workers) as diluting firms' ability to take advantage of new opportunities.

With regard to this second dimension, the globalization of the last 30 years, particularly global financialization, has meant that we need to qualify this basic opposition in some important respects. First, liberal market economies such as the US and UK became *more* short-termist in their implications for those managing firms between the mid-1970s and the current period. In this period of financial deregulation, the owners of firms, particularly institutional shareholders such as pension funds, were able to increase their power over managers (O'Sullivan 2000). Many of the protections workers gained against managerial short-termism in the post-war era, through trade unions, legal regulation and an expanded welfare state, were eroded. These changes had direct impacts on the HR policies of, for example, US MNCs, with challenges to established career structures and increasingly 'hard' forms of performance management (Butler *et al.* 2006; Almond *et al.* 2006).

These changes did not only affect MNCs based in liberal economies. Globalizing firms from the more co-ordinated economies also needed to seek finance on international capital markets which are 'liberal' in nature. In such cases, it may have become more difficult to talk about MNCs having one simple nationality; if a German firm sought large proportions of its capital from American financial markets, the 'management' and 'ownership' parts of any country of origin effect may have begun to diverge. How much this would lead German managers to abandon 'German' ideas about management is unclear, particularly given the current global financial and economic crisis. It clearly makes sense, though, in examining possible national effects on what decisions specific MNCs make, to look at who are their owners as well as who are their managers. This may, in the longer term, also apply to American firms if these become financially dependent on Chinese or Middle-Eastern states. Equally, the proliferation in recent years of cross-border mergers and joint-ventures (see Chapter 8; Rees and Edwards 2009) also sometimes makes talking in terms of a home-host dichotomy more difficult.

Conclusions

In this chapter we have examined national differences in how capitalism and, therefore, human resource management, is organized, and the effects this has on HRM within MNCs. We have seen that there are a number of different ways in which countries have been grouped together, following similarities in how they organize business and employment relations. In particular, the chapter examined the differences between the two main models under which the main developed economies have been portrayed: the long-termist, high-trust model of the co-ordinated market economy, followed in different ways by Germany, Japan, and a number of smaller European economies; and the more market-based model of the liberal market economy, followed by English-speaking developed economies. We also looked at a third, 'Mediterranean' model, as well as more briefly looking at other possible groupings of countries.

In order to apply these models of national types of organization to MNCs, we have argued that it is necessary to look not only at national differences in rules, but also at how owners, managers and workers at different levels and places within the MNC get their ideas about what are appropriate forms of management, and how these are affected by differences in power. We also looked at why top decision-makers in the home country of MNCs may choose (or not choose) to apply elements of their 'home' business system abroad.

Finally, returning to the varieties of capitalism literature, we looked at how national differences may have changed in the recent period of globalized deregulation, and how changes, particularly to the ownership of MNCs, may have affected the choices made by their top managers.

Review questions

1 What are the main differences between the three 'varieties of capitalism' presented in this chapter?

2 Would you expect MNCs originating in a liberal market economy to have different policies to those originating in a coordinated market economy?

3 What is meant by the concept of 'hybridisation' of HRM policies in MNCs? Can you think of any likely examples of this process?

4 Does global deregulation mean that home and host country effects are becoming less important?

Further reading

1 Hall, P., and Soskice, D. (eds) (2001) *Varieties of Capitalism,* Oxford: Oxford University Press.

The introductory chapter to this book provides the theoretical framework behind much of the recent debate on cross-national differences in economic organisation and employment, and the division into two broad 'varieties' discussed in this chapter.

2 Morgan, G. and Kristensen, P. (2006) 'The contested space of multinationals: varieties of institutionalism, varieties of capitalism', *Human Relations,* 59(11), 1467–90.

A considered debate about how location in countries operating under different systems affects organisational 'micro-politics' and, therefore, the sorts of subsidiary policies pursued.

3 Edwards, T. and Kuruvilla, S. (2006) 'International HRM: national business systems, organizational politics and the international division of labour in MNCs', *International Journal of Human Resource Management,* 16(1), 1–21.

An alternative overview of many of the issues in the second part of this chapter, based on a critique of much research into international human resource management.

4 Jacoby, S., Nason, E. and Saguchi, K. (2005) 'The role of the senior HR executive in Japan and the United States: employment relations, corporate governance, and values', *Industrial Relations,* 44(2), 207–41.

A comparative examination of recent changes in the HR function in the US and Japan.

References

Almond, P. and Gonzalez, M. C. (2006) 'Varieties of capitalism: the importance of political and social choices', *Transfer,* 12(3), 407–25.

Almond, P., Muller-Camen, M., Collings, D. and Quintanilla, J. (2006) 'Pay and performance', in P. Almond and A. Ferner (eds), *American Multinationals in Europe.* Oxford: Oxford University Press.

Bartlett, C. and Ghoshal, S. (2002) *Managing Across Borders: The Transnational Solution* (3rd edition), Harvard Business School Press.

Boussebaa, M. (2009) 'Struggling to organize across national borders: the case of global resource management in professional service firms', *Human Relations,* 62(6), 829–50.

Boxall, P. and Purcell, J. (2008) *Strategy and Human Resource Management* (2nd edition), Basingstoke: Macmillan.

Brewster, C. (1993) 'Towards a "European" model of human resource management', *Journal of International Business Studies,* 26(1), 1–21.

Brewster, C. (1995) "Towards a 'European' Model of Human Resource Management", *Journal of International Business Studies,* 26(1) 1–21.

Butler, P., Collings, D., Peters, R. and Quintanilla, J. (2006) 'The Management of Managerial Careers', in Almond, P. and Ferner, A. (eds), *American Multinationals in Europe.* Oxford: Oxford University Press.

Chung, L.H., Gibbons, P. and Schoch, H. (2006). 'The management of information and managers in subsidiaries of multinational corporations', *British Journal of Management,* 17(2), 153–65.

Colling, T., Gunnigle, P., Quintanilla, J. and Tempel, A. (2006) 'Collective representation and participation', in Almond, P. and Ferner, A. (eds), *American Multinationals in Europe.* Oxford: Oxford University Press.

Crouch, C. (2005) *Capitalist Diversity and Change,* Oxford: Oxford University Press.

Dedoussis, V. (1994) 'The Core Workforce – Peripheral Workforce Dichotomy and the Transfer of Japanese Management Practices', in Campbell, N. and Burton, F. (eds) *Japanese Multinationals: Strategies and Management in the Global Kaisha,* London: Routledge.

Delmestri, G. (2006). 'Streams of inconsistent institutional influences: middle managers as carriers of multiple identities', *Human Relations,* 59(11), 1515–42.

Dore, R. (1997). 'The Distinctiveness of Japan', in Crouch, C. and Streeck, W. (eds) *Political Economy of Modern Capitalism,* London: Sage.

Dunning, J. and Lundan, S. (2008) 'Institutions and the OLI paradigm of the multinational enterprise', *Asia Pacific Journal of Management,* 25, 573–93.

Edwards, T. (1998) 'Multinationals, Labour management and the process of reverse diffusion', *International Journal of Human Resource Management,* 9(4), 696–709.

Elger, T. and Smith, C. (2005) *Assembling Work,* Oxford: OUP.

Elger, T. and Smith, C. (2006). 'Theorizing the Role of the International Subsidiary: Transplants: Hybrids and Branch-Plants Revisited', in Ferner, A. Quintanilla, J. and Sanchez-Runde, C. (eds) (2006) *Multinationals, Institutions and the Construction of Transnational Practices,* London: Palgrave.

Fenton O' Creevy, M., Gooderham, P. and Nordhaug, O. (2008) 'Human resource management in US subsidiaries in Europe and Australia: centralisation or autonomy?', *Journal of International Business Studies,* 39(1), 151–66.

Ferner, A., Almond, P., Clark, I., Colling, T., Edwards, T., Holden, L. and Muller-Camen, M. (2004) 'The dynamics of central control and subsidiary autonomy in the management of human resources: case study evidence from US MNCs in the UK', *Organization Studies,* 25(3), 363–91.

Ferner, A., Almond, P. and Colling, T. (2005) 'Institutional theory and the cross-national transfer of employment policy: the case of "workforce diversity" in US multinationals', *Journal of International Business Studies,* 46, 304–21.

Ferner, A., Quintanilla, J. and Sanchez-Runde, C. (eds) (2006) *Multinationals, Institutions and the Construction of Transnational Practices,* Basingstoke: Macmillan.

Ferner, A., Tregaskis, O., Edwards, P., Edwards, T. and Marginson, P. (2010) 'HRM structures and subsidiary discretion in foreign multinationals in the UK', *International Journal of Human Resource Management,* forthcoming.

Friedman, A. (1977) 'Responsible autonomy versus direct control over the labour process', *Capital and Class,* 1(1), 43–57.

Gonzalez, M.C. (2010) 'Workers' direct participation at the workplace and job quality in Europe', *Journal of European Social Policy,* 20, 2.

Hall, P. and D. Gingerich (2004) 'Varieties of Capitalism and Institutional Complementarities in the Macroeconomy: An Empirical Analysis', *MPIfG Discussion Paper,* 04/5, Cologne: MPIfG.

Hall, P. and Soskice, D. (eds) (2001) *Varieties of Capitalism,* Oxford: Oxford University Press.

Hudson R. (1995) "The Japanese, the European Market and the Automobile Industry in the United Kingdom" in Hudson, R. and Schamp, E. (eds) *Towards a New Map of Automobile Manufacturing in Europe? New Production Concepts and Spatial Restructuring,* Berlin: Springer, 63–91.

Jackson, G. and Deeg, R. (2008) 'Comparing capitalism: understanding institutional diversity and its implications for international business', *Journal of International Business Studies,* 39(4), 540–61.

Jacoby, S., Nason, E. and Saguchi, K. (2005) 'The role of the senior HR executive in Japan and the United States: employment relations, corporate governance, and values', *Industrial Relations,* 44(2), 207–41.

Kahancová, M. (2008) 'Embedding Multinationals in Post-Socialist Countries: Social Interaction and the Compatibility of Organizational Interests with Host-Country Institutions', *MPIfG Discussion Paper,* 08/11. Cologne: Max Planck Institute for the Study of Societies.

Lane, C. (1989) *Management and Labour in Europe,* Aldershot: Edward Elgar.

Legge, K. (1995) *Human Resource Management: Rhetorics and Realities,* London: Palgrave.

Marsden, D. (1999) *A Theory of Employment Systems,* Oxford: Oxford University Press.

Maurice, M., Sellier, F. and Sylvestre, J.-J. (1986) *The Social Foundations of Industrial Power,* Cambridge, MA: MIT Press.

Milkman, R. (1991) *Japan's California Factories,* Los Angeles: University of California.

Moore, F. (2006). 'Strategy, power and negotiation: social control and expatriate managers in a German multinational corporation', *International Journal of Human Resource Management,* 17(3), 399–413.

Noble, C. (1997) 'International Comparisons of Training Policies', *Human Resource Management Journal,* 7(1), 5–18.

O' Sullivan, M. (2000) *Contests for Corporate Control: Corporate Governance and Economic Performance in the United States and Germany,* Oxford: Oxford University Press.

Rees, C. and Edwards, T. (2009) 'Management strategy and HR in international mergers: choice, constraint and pragmatism', *Human Resource Management Journal,* 19(1), 24–39.

Schneider, B. (2009) 'Hierarchical market economies and varieties of capitalism in Latin America', *Journal of Latin American Studies,* 41, 553–75.

Sippola, M. (2009) 'The two faces of Nordic management? Nordic firms and their employee relations in the Baltic states', *International Journal of Human Resource Management,* 20(9), 1929–44.

Smith, C. and Meiksins, P. (1995) 'System, society and dominance effects in cross-national organisational analysis', *Work, Employment and Society,* 9(2), 241–68.

Thelen, K. and Kume, I. (1999) 'The rise of nonmarket training regimes: Germany and Japan compared', *Journal of Japanese Studies* 25(1), 33–64.

Thelen, K. and Kume, I. (2006) 'Coordination as a political problem in co-ordinated market economies', *Governance,* 19(1), 11–42.

Wachter, H., Peters, R., Ferner, A., Gunnigle, P. and Quintanilla, J. (2006) 'The Role of the International Personnel Function', in Almond, P. and Ferner, A. (eds), *American Multinationals in Europe,* Oxford: Oxford University Press.

Whitley, R. (ed.) (1992) *European Business Systems: Firms and Markets in their National Contexts,* London: Sage.

Chapter 5

International structure and strategy in MNCs

Tony Edwards and Chris Rees

Key aims

The aims of this chapter are to:
- consider alternative definitions of MNCs;
- be familiar with the main explanations for why firms expand into other countries;
- examine the extent to which firms have become globally dispersed;
- be familiar with the main influences on international strategy and some of the key work on various strategies that MNCs follow.

Introduction

The growth of MNCs is without doubt one of the driving forces of the process of internationalization. For Dicken (2007), they are the primary 'movers and shapers' of the contemporary global economy. MNCs dominate many industrial sectors, such as automotive, electronics and oil, while they are increasingly coming to dominate parts of the service sector as well, especially finance and telecommunications. The sheer scale of the operations of the largest multinationals gives them considerable influence over nation-states. Comparisons of the GDP of countries on the one hand and the 'value-added' created by MNCs (a better measure than sales which is more widely used) on the other show that 37 of the largest economic entities in the world are MNCs (Legrain 2002: 140). MNCs account for around two-thirds of international trade, and the stock of their foreign investments in 2007 was more than seven times its value in 1990 (UN 2008).

This chapter considers four issues. It begins by tackling the question of how to define a multinational company. At first sight this may seem to be a straightforward task, and indeed it is one that is often taken for granted in much academic work. However, as we will see, there are alternative definitions that one can use, with varying implications for how we view the impact of MNCs. The second part of the chapter explores the various factors that may motivate senior managers to expand the firm across national borders. Why would they seek to operate in more than one country? We will briefly consider the strengths and weaknesses of some of the explanations that have been advanced to explain this phenomenon. We will see that most of these take as their starting point the idea that there are inherent disadvantages in operating across countries and that, consequently, managers of a firm contemplating setting up foreign subsidiaries need something to enable them to overcome these difficulties. We contrast this conventional view with an examination of an alternative way of looking at the issue; namely, that operating internationally has significant advantages stemming from the power relations between such firms and nationally organized governments, institutions and associations. Building on this, the third issue we briefly consider is the extent to which MNCs have become 'global' in nature. If there are power advantages to be gained from a high geographical spread of activities, then might we expect MNCs to seek to become widely dispersed across countries, reducing their dependence on any one country? Competing perspectives on the globalization of the firm are reviewed and an assessment is made of the empirical underpinning of each. The final part of the chapter examines the nature of strategy and structure in MNCs. We review some of the best known typologies in this field, spelling out the varying strategies that firms pursue, the strengths and weaknesses of these and their implications for IHRM. We go on to investigate power relations between different groups of organizational actors within MNCs and the implications of the embeddedness of MNCs in their country of origin for strategy.

Defining a multinational company

What is a multinational company? Answering this question requires a consideration of the definition of a firm. The pioneering work here is that of Coase (1937), later developed by Williamson (1975), who argued that firms exist in order to avoid the 'transactions costs' involved in market exchange. These costs have a number of sources: the uncertainty associated with market transactions; the costs of acquiring knowledge from other agents; and the difficulty in devising complex contracts that cover every eventuality. Where these costs are significant, there will be an incentive for an economic agent to avoid them through setting up a firm to co-ordinate production, thereby substituting the hierarchy of the firm for the market. This line of analysis defines a firm as 'the means of co-ordinating production without using market exchange'. In other words, firms are defined in terms of the ownership of productive operations.

From this definition of the firm flows the most widely used definition of a multinational firm. The significance of transactions costs is likely to be even greater at the international than at the national level since firms will be faced with more uncertainty and higher search costs in obtaining information. Thus many economists have adopted the Coasian approach in defining a multinational as a firm in which the co-ordination of production without using market exchange takes the firm across national boundaries through foreign direct investment. The focus here is on legal ownership of operations in at least two countries as the defining feature of what constitutes a multinational (e.g. Buckley and Casson 1976). We term this the 'narrow' definition of a multinational.

A key aspect of the approach taken by Coase, Williamson and Buckley and Casson is the distinction between market and non-market transactions. However, some authors have questioned the significance of this distinction. For example, Cowling and Sugden (1987) have argued that this approach pays insufficient attention to the power relationship between one unit and another within a production chain, whether they are part of the same organization or connected through a market relation. They contend that in most production chains there is a 'centre of strategic decision making' that is able to exert a significant degree of control throughout the chain, regardless of whether units are legally owned or formally independent. What the Coasian definition misses, therefore, is the way in which a multinational can exert control over operations outside its formal, legal boundaries. For this reason, Cowling and Sugden define a multinational as 'the means of co-ordinating production from one centre of strategic decision-making where this co-ordination takes a firm across national boundaries' (1987: 12). The focus here is on the *control* of productive operations in at least two countries rather than the legal *ownership* of them. We call this the 'broad' definition.

The broad definition has the conceptual advantage over the narrow definition of capturing the wider impact a multinational has throughout the production chain. Some multinationals rely extensively on subcontracting and franchising to suppliers or retailers. Nike is an excellent example. In some ways, Nike is a very large firm, with enormous sales of $18.6 billion in 2008, yet, it only employs around 30,000 people. This very low level of employment is due to the fact that Nike subcontracts all of its manufacturing to formally independent suppliers mainly in Asia, where it is estimated that around half a million people depend on Nike for their employment. These subcontractors are only nominally independent: they produce to Nike specifications; they sell at prices determined by Nike; and in many cases they only produce for Nike. In addition, some HR practices within the subcontracted firms are determined by Nike, both directly through the firm's code of conduct (discussed in more detail in Chapter 13) that covers such issues as maximum working hours and conventions on overtime and indirectly through the cost constraints that Nike imposes on its subcontractors. Other firms in the textile sector use the practice of franchising to retail outlets, of which Benetton is a prime example. The company does not own any of its stores, but nonetheless exerts a high degree of control over them, determining the nature of the clothes they sell, the prices they charge and their layout. The narrow definition does not provide a conceptual tool for analysing the control that MNCs such as these exert throughout the production chain.

However, the broad definition is not so useful in assessing the legal obligations of MNCs. For instance, MNCs are generally not liable in law for environmental damage arising from the operations of subcontractors, nor are they responsible for cases of discrimination in employment that occur in their subcontractors. In analysing the responsibilities of firms in these respects, therefore, the narrow definition is the more appropriate. In addition, while MNCs exert some influence over HR matters in their subcontractors as we saw above, the degree of control is not as great as in the operations owned by multinationals. For instance, it is unheard of for MNCs to demand that their subcontractors establish performance management systems, but this is a common requirement that the HQs of MNCs impose on their own operations. A further reason to use the narrow definition in assessing the impact of MNCs is that it is much easier to operationalize. Generally, companies do not provide information on the numbers of people employed in subcontracted or franchised operations, nor is it easy to obtain information on their turnover or assets, making it difficult to use the broad definition to assess the scale of the operations that MNCs control. Consequently, most of the agencies that collect data on MNCs, such as the United Nations, use the narrow definition. Overall, then, the broad definition usefully highlights the importance of control of processes of production and service provision across borders, an issue that we return to at a number of points in the book, but in this chapter and in most of the rest of the book we are constrained into using the narrow definition. This is what we do unless we state otherwise.

The motivations for internationalization

We now turn to consider the various explanations that have been advanced to account for why firms internationalize, or, in other words, why MNCs exist. We start with explanations that have been advanced to explain the emergence of the first multinationals.

For many writers, the emergence of MNCs has been an entirely logical step in the development of international capitalism. The internationalization of capitalist economies is commonly seen as having progressed in three stages: from the circuit of commodity capital through trade; to the circuit of money capital through 'portfolio' investments; to the circuit of productive capital in the form of MNCs (see Dicken 2007). While international trade has a long history dating back several centuries, the other two circuits began to internationalize in the nineteenth century. Much of the investment by foreigners in productive activities abroad in the 1800s took the form of portfolio investment. This involved financial investors holding a stake in an enterprise but not assuming any responsibility for the management or operation of the company. In the case of the UK, much of this portfolio-type foreign investment was in infrastructure projects in parts of the British Empire (John *et al.* 1997: 18–19). A growing tendency during the nineteenth century, however, was for firms to be owned directly by foreign investors. Many of these were what has been termed 'free-standing companies' in that they were owned by individuals or institutions in one country but operated solely in another. This type of firm was not multinational in the sense that they did not own or control productive activities in more then one country. Corley (1994, cited in John *et al.* 1997) estimates that at the beginning of the First World War 55 per cent of Britain's outward investments were of the portfolio type and a further 35 per cent were in the form of free standing companies. The remaining 10 per cent were accounted for by foreign direct investment by the fledging group of MNCs.

One motivation for these firms to internationalize was the desire to secure a stable source of raw materials. Some firms sought to take direct control over the production of these raw materials in order to absorb the profit margin that would otherwise accrue to an independent producer and, perhaps more importantly, to prevent a rival from cornering the market. This explanation helps to account for the emergence of some of the earliest British multinationals, such as Cadbury and Dunlop. In some cases this type of foreign direct investment led to workers in the developing countries being highly dependent on MNCs, particularly where the foreign firm has control of a number of plantations, farms or mines. In this type of multinational there was relatively little central influence on employment practice in the subsidiaries; the firms tended to install an expatriate into running the subsidiary but the international HR department that is found in many MNCs today was almost entirely absent.

In the post-war period, many argued that the motivation for a firm to become multinational was not so much access to raw materials as access to a different factor of production, labour. In 1980 Frobel and his colleagues published a book entitled *The New International Division of Labour* that was concerned with developments in the manufacturing sector that were leading firms based in the 'core' economies of the advanced industrial states in Europe and North America to locate an increasing amount of production in the 'periphery' of the developing economies. In explaining the attractiveness to domestic firms in becoming multinationals, their focus was clearly on cost-minimization. They argued that three developments in the post-war period were making it easier and more attractive for firms to shift production away from the core to the periphery. First, improvements in transportation and communication made it cheaper and quicker to transport manufactured goods across the world. Second, changes in technology made it possible to de-link the production process so that it took place in disparate sites and could be performed by largely unskilled workers. Third, the growing pool of cheap and unprotected labour in urban areas in the developing countries provided a cheap and disposable workforce.

Taken together, these developments provided a strong incentive for firms in the core to become multinational. Frobel *et al.* (1980) predicted that FDI would increasingly flow to the periphery as firms took advantage of the wide differences in wages across countries. They argued that this gave rise to a 'new international division of labour' (NIDL) in which the routinized, low-skill operations of a firm such as assembly were located in the developing countries, while the more specialized, high-skill operations such as design, administration and marketing were retained in developed nations. Frobel *et al.* (1980) argued that the development of the NIDL resulted in greater exploitation of labour. Manual workers in the core economies faced the threat of job loss as production was shifted abroad, leading to higher levels of unemployment and/or less favourable terms and conditions. The prospects of workers in the developing countries were also bleak as the jobs brought to these areas were characterized by low pay and long hours. Moreover, the NIDL thesis predicted that the inflows of FDI would contribute little to the development of human capital in the developing countries since the jobs were largely low-skill in nature.

The NIDL concept has been severely criticised, however. In its simplest form, it does not take account of productivity differences between countries, which partially offset wage differentials. This is particularly important for MNCs in which the production process requires skilled workers. Moreover, in many industries labour costs are a small and declining proportion of total costs. Oman (1994, cited in Ferner 1997a) estimates that only 3 per cent of the costs of firms manufacturing semi-conductors are comprised of pay. The incentive to expand into areas of cheap labour is minimal for such firms. Perhaps the biggest failing of the NIDL is that it takes a one-dimensional approach to why firms invest abroad, focusing solely on cost-minimization. Consequently, it pays no attention to other factors besides cheap labour which are key determinants of MNCs' location decisions, such as access to markets. Because of these theoretical weaknesses, the NIDL could not explain the patterns of FDI in the post-war period; in contrast to the NIDL's prediction that FDI would be drawn to the developing nations exhibiting low wages, the dominant pattern is one of FDI being concentrated within the 'Triad' of major developed economies, primarily those in Europe and North America.

More recently, a similar but more sophisticated explanation for how companies internationalize has centred on the notion of 'chains' of operating units across countries. From this perspective, Gereffi *et al.* (2005) uses the term 'global value chains' to describe the way in which production processes are co-ordinated by one key player, which then structures the process that a product goes through from conception to consumption. For example, the production of Slazenger tennis balls is co-ordinated across nine different countries with firms in each country having a distinct role: the balls are designed by academics at Loughborough University in the UK; the clay is mined and transported from South Carolina in the US; the tins that contain the balls are manufactured in Indonesia; the balls themselves are produced in Bataan, a special economic zone in the Philippines; and so on (*Guardian* 2002). In this way, the various parts of the production process are 'delocated' from each other and, while these are carried out by nominally independent firms, they are actually closely controlled by the lead agent, Slazenger.

Where MNCs have grown in this way, HR matters tend to be seen as primarily local rather than global issues. For those operations that are subcontracted, this is primarily because the MNC tends to set only broad parameters for employment practice within which the suppliers must operate, as argued above. For those operations carried out within the confines of the multinational, HR matters are also decentralized because the operations carry out quite distinct functions, meaning that such issues as the skill and education levels of the workforce, the level of autonomy with which employees tend to work and the degree to which they are irreplaceable or substitutable all vary markedly. Thus, the 'delocation' of the production process is accompanied by a decentralization of the HR function.

By focusing on the interaction between geographical dispersion of operations on the one hand and the relative incentives of retaining work in-house or outsourcing it on the other, the notion of international chains of production represents an advance on the NIDL. In particular, it provides an explanation for why FDI remains concentrated in developed economies, with the growing international links with developing economies coming principally through arms-length trading relations. Arguably, however, even this more sophisticated approach pays insufficient attention to factors other than the costs or quality of labour in particular and production more generally. This points to the need to turn to explanations that focus on product market considerations.

In many cases it may be very difficult, sometimes impossible, for a firm to serve a market in one country through locating its operations in a different country. Firms serving a national market through exports may be at a disadvantage compared with local producers in that they are seen as foreign by consumers. This is particularly likely to be the case where consumers are patriotic in their preferences, seeking to buy from firms which employ workers in the country concerned and which contribute to the national economy. Governments, too, may be keen to buy products and services from firms which operate in their country in order to promote employment and growth.

Thus, firms may expand into a country to overcome this disadvantage. As well as it being advantageous to have a local presence for this reason, firms may also benefit from having a local presence because this gives them employees in the local environment who are well placed to understand the market concerned. Thus, the local presence helps the firm generate expertise in the product market that would be difficult to obtain through exporting. Having a local presence can also help firms to avoid tariffs or quotas which sometimes face firms relying on exports. This has been a particular motivation for Japanese firms setting up in the EU. In some industries, moreover, it may be imperative that firms have a local presence. This is the case where the immediacy of consumption demands that firms locate their production or service provision operations in the market, as is the case in hotels and catering for instance.

Where access to markets is the motivation for a firm to become a multinational, the implication for their role as employers is that the jobs they bring to a host nation will not be as insecure as proponents of the NIDL predict. The ability of a multinational to relocate in search of cheaper labour will be constrained by the need to maintain an operating presence in the market. Indeed, such MNCs might seek to adapt to local employment practices and to 'be viewed as "good employers" locally, leading them to provide better pay and conditions than the local average' (Marginson 1994: 70). In this scenario, the HR function will have an active role in ensuring that the package of terms and conditions, and the quality of working life more generally, are seen as favourable, at least compared with local norms.

It is clear, therefore, that 'market seeking' investments will be a major motivation for firms to become multinationals. This factor helps generate a better understanding of the dominant pattern of foreign direct investment which demonstrates that it is the major developed market economies which are the main recipients of FDI. While there are clear incentives for firms to internationalize for this reason, the question that remains is how they will be able to compete effectively alongside national firms in these markets. If they start from a disadvantaged position, how will firms be able to overcome this?

The conventional answer to this question is that firms must have some source of competitive advantage which those in other countries do not have. The pioneering work on this issue was that of Stephen Hymer (1976) who argued that firms wishing to operate in foreign markets started at a disadvantage compared with domestic firms. This disadvantage stems from the greater expertise that domestic firms enjoy within the country in question: their familiarity with the language and business traditions; their expertise in the market; and their established links with key institutions such as government bodies. In order to undertake foreign direct investment, Hymer argued that firms must possess a 'firm-specific advantage' (also referred to as an ownership specific advantage) that would enable them to overcome the disadvantages of being foreign-owned.

This advantage could take a number of forms. It some cases it will stem from features of the domestic business system in which the firm originated. One example is where the financial system affords firms a stable source of finance, as has historically been the case in Swedish firms. Alternatively, the firm-specific advantage may be something that the firm has developed itself. The patents that pharmaceutical firms have over drugs they have developed are prime examples, as are the brand names possessed by soft-drink manufacturers and hotel chains. A further area in which firms may enjoy a firm-specific advantage is expertise in the management of people. Where this is the case, there are important implications for HRM. As Japanese MNCs expanded into Europe and North America in the 1980s and 1990s, for instance, they brought with them many practices developed in their home base. Many of these firms made concerted attempts to minimize waste and inventory through techniques such as 'just-in-time' production. The adjunct to the 'hard' aspects of Japanese-style production is a set of employment practices designed to minimize disruption and secure a degree of commitment to product quality. Thus, Japanese firms in the UK have exhibited a preference for a range of employee involvement practices and for either not recognizing a union at all or for dealing with a single union very much on their own terms (e.g. Oliver and Wilkinson 1992). A different example is in the fast-food sector. McDonald's has expanded internationally on the basis that it has developed a winning formula in the US that it seeks to replicate in other countries. This involves very tight control over the operation of its restaurants, highly standardized supplies and a concerted attempt to avoid unions wherever they operate (Royle 2000). Marginson (1994: 70) argues that where this is the motivation for firms to become multinational they are likely to be 'innovators' in labour practices; the transfer of the firm-specific advantage involves the adoption of practices that may be unusual in the host environment. In this context a key role for the HR function is to aid in the transfer of these innovations, an issue we consider in more depth in Chapter 7.

While the existence of firm-specific advantages helps to explain why foreign firms may be able to compete effectively in the 'backyard' of their competitors, it does not explain why they need to set up wholly owned subsidiaries in other countries. Given the complexities in co-ordinating production or service provision over great geographical distances and across a range of diverse business environments, why don't firms with a firm-specific advantage simply license or franchise to a different firm? As we saw in section one, many firms such as Nike and Benetton do just this, so why not all?

Many have argued that the answer lies in market failure. Many mainstream economists assume that markets will always operate efficiently and will spring up where there are economic agents who are interested in exchanging something. However, there are not well-developed markets in many of the factors which constitute a firm-specific advantage and, therefore, they cannot easily be traded. While a firm may be able to license a tangible asset like its brand name, it will be much more difficult for it to license an intangible asset. How can a firm accurately value something like expertise in work organization, for instance? If a firm's advantage lies in the trust relations it has developed with a key financier, how can this be traded or licensed? How can a firm guarantee through complex and contingent contracts that a brand name will be used in ways that do not rebound on it?

Where the advantage that a firm enjoys cannot be traded in the market there is an incentive for the firm to use it themselves in other business systems. This approach to why firms internalize is known as 'internalization' because the firm is deploying the assets it has within the legal boundaries of the firm. In other words, the hierarchy of the firm is used in preference to market exchange. Theoretically, the approach draws on the work of Williamson (1975) and others on transactions costs which we encountered earlier in the chapter, and has been developed by a number of writers (e.g. Buckley and Casson 1976; Rugman 1981; Dunning 1993). Where firms expand across borders in order to internalize an intangible asset, this requires the existence of structures which are capable of sharing knowledge and expertise across borders. There are a variety of structures which firms may use in order to facilitate such knowledge exchange, something that is discussed in more detail in Chapters 6 and 7. A number of MNCs have developed a cadre of managers and senior professional employees who roam across the organisation, taking with them knowledge of organizational innovations developed in one part of the group. The ways in which MNCs develop such a group is discussed in Chapters 9 and 10. A parallel development is for MNCs to instigate other structures which bring together key employees from different parts of the organization, such as international committees and meetings.

One problem with this focus on ownership-specific advantages is that it starts with a questionable assumption. The rationale for the condition that firms must possess an ownership-specific advantage if they are to become a multinational is that there are inherent disadvantages from operating internationally, such as linguistic and cultural differences between countries. Hence, the starting point is: why internationalize? Yet, there are also inherent *advantages*. The principal advantage stems from the geographical scope of a multinational's operations which accords it a powerful position in its dealings with nationally based institutions and associations. Thus, in negotiating tax breaks and aid packages with governments, MNCs may be able to extract concessions on the basis of their (perceived) 'footlooseness'. Similarly, in negotiating with trade unions, MNCs may seek to use the threat of relocation to gain acceptance of new working practices or changes to terms and conditions. Thus, for writers such as Dicken (2007), the correct question should be: why *not* internationalize? If there are inherent advantages from a high geographical scope, then it is pertinent to examine the extent to which MNCs have become widely spread internationally. To what extent have MNCs transcended their dependence on their home base? Should we see MNCs as being 'global' in nature, detached from their country of origin?

The arrival of the 'global' firm?

Over the last two decades it has become commonplace for senior managers of MNCs to describe their organizations as 'global' firms. For example, in 2009 a statement on Glaxosmithkline's website read:

> A number of critical forces are affecting the pharmaceutical industry. Rapid globalization of markets, the ease of global communications and the existence of an increasingly international and mobile pool of scientific and commercial talent mean that firms can serve more markets from fewer locations, while at the same time they have greater choice than ever before of location to consider when deciding where to locate new investments. (www.gsk.com)

Similarly, Ernst and Young claim that:

> We are the first major professional services organisation to bring a borderless approach to the emerging markets of CIS, India, the Middle East, Africa and the established markets of Europe. (www.ey.com)

Yet, such claims must be met with some scepticism. For example, Philip Condit, who became Boeing's chairman in February 1997, outlined his vision for the future of the company on taking up his position. Boeing, he said, would become less US-focused and instead would be transformed into a 'global enterprise' by 2016, its centenary year:

> I believe we are moving towards an era of global markets and global companies. I think it is advantageous that your workforce, your executive corps, reflect that. (Condit, quoted in the *Financial Times* 1997)

Yet, by 2009 only 22,000 out of the 160,000 of the employees of Boeing were working outside the US (www.boeing.com). While it may be global in some ways, such as sales, in others it seems to be rooted firmly in its original home base. What does academic research tell us about this issue?

In the late 1980s and early 1990s it became commonplace for managers and observers to talk about the 'globalization' of the firm. It was often asserted that many large MNCs were no longer dependent on their original home base; rather, they were positioned to serve a global market, they responded to the pressures and demands of the global economy, and they drew on knowledge and expertise from across the globe. Many MNCs, some argued, had become so internationalized that they had detached themselves from their home business system. The best known exponent of this line of argument was Ohmae (1990, 1995) in his writing concerning the 'borderless world'; he argued that the ability of the nation state to regulate and control economic activity has been dramatically reduced by globalization. At the core of this process, according to Ohmae, were 'global' corporations that were 'nationalityless' and able to shift to whichever part of the world promises the highest returns. Robert Reich wrote in a similar vein. In a famous article in the *Harvard Business Review* Reich addressed debates about national competitiveness by posing the question: 'Who is Us?'. Reich (1991) argued that a country's competitive position was not primarily determined by 'national' firms but rather by 'global' ones. The performance of the American economy, for instance, was shaped as much by foreign multinationals such as Thomson and Honda as by American firms like General Motors and IBM. In essence, Reich argued that nationality was no longer an important or meaningful concept in large MNCs. One interpretation of this apparent development is to see it as the logical consequence of the advantages that a firm accrues from becoming international. The more international the firm becomes, the more powerful it is in relation to domestically based actors such as governments and trade unions. Thus, there are strong incentives for firms to become increasingly spread across countries and to sever their ties with their original home base.

However, in the late 1990s other observers questioned the extent to which MNCs were global in nature. Reacting to some of the claims which were reviewed above, a counter-literature emerged. Many writers argued that, far from being detached from their home base, MNCs remained firmly rooted in, and influenced by, their country of origin. Ruigrok and van Tulder (1995), for instance, challenged the 'myth' of the global firm. Based on an examination of the largest 100 MNCs in the world, they concluded that 'not one of these can be dubbed truly global, footloose or borderless. The argument of the globalization of the firm is unfounded and untenable' (1995: 168). Legrain (2002) has argued that firms which are supposedly global or stateless are in fact firmly rooted in their home base. Doremus *et al.* (1998: 3) argued that MNCs 'are not converging toward global behavioral norms' but rather were deeply influenced by their country of origin. Perhaps the best known exponents of this view were Hirst and Thompson (1999: 95) who also referred to the myth of the global firm, arguing that the 'home oriented nature of multinational activity across all dimensions seems overwhelming'.

This counter-argument was made on a number of grounds. Principally, statistics concerning the geographical breakdown of the sales, assets and employment of MNCs demonstrated that most MNCs remained heavily concentrated in their home country and in the countries neighbouring it. The way in which MNCs were embedded in their home country showed up in a number of other ways: MNCs were owned largely by shareholders of the country of origin and raised finance predominantly at home; the key strategic functions in MNCs, such as the HQ and R&D facilities, were generally in the home country; and the senior managerial boards of MNCs were still dominated by home country nationals.

This alternative view throws doubt on the extent to which firms will automatically realise benefits by spreading their wings further and further afield. Indeed, it suggests that MNCs tend to retain strong linkages with their country of origin and, therefore, continue to be influenced by the business system in this country to a greater extent than any other system. Moreover, it also suggests that in making foreign investments multinationals favour locations which are near to their home country and only gradually reach out to countries further afield. Indeed, more recent evidence testifies to this regional dimension. Alan Rugman's conclusion of his analysis of the largest MNCs, for example, was that the vast majority are 'home region based', defined as having less than 50 per cent of their sales in the other two regions of the Triad. As he put it: 'globalization, as commonly understood, is a myth. Far from taking place in a single global market, business activity by most large multinationals takes place within any one of the world's three great trading blocks' (Rugman 2005: 6).

One explanation for this is that this is offered by the 'Uppsala' model. Developed by academics at the University of Uppsala, the basic idea behind the model is that the internationalization of the firm is a gradual process that arises from a series of incremental decisions rather than a few grand leaps forward. This is because firms lack the knowledge and resources about operating in other business systems due to the 'psychic distance' between countries, which is defined as the 'factors preventing or disturbing the flows of information between firms and markets' (Johansson and Wiedersheim-Paul 1975). As firms gradually acquire knowledge about other systems, they begin to enter new markets, initially through exporting via an independent representative, then through a sales subsidiary and finally through a full production facility. Crucially, psychic distance is highly correlated with geographical distance; while there are exceptions, generally speaking the business systems that are close to one another tend to have stronger commonalities in terms of the nature of the dominant institutions than those that are far apart. Thus, this provides an explanation for why MNCs tend to hold the majority of their foreign investments in countries that neighbour their original base.

This picture of gradual internationalization fits the evidence. The United Nations has for many years published data on the extent to which the largest 100 MNCs in the world are internationalized (see Table 5.1). Combining the ratios of foreign sales to total sales, foreign assets to total assets and foreign employment to total employment, a 'transnationality index' (TNI) is constructed in an attempt to measure the degree to which this group of firms are concentrated in their home country. During the last two decades the TNI has risen slowly but steadily, from 51 in 1990 to 62 in 2006 (UN 2008).

An overall assessment might be that MNCs are gradually increasing the extent to which they are spread across countries with this spread having a strong regional dimension. This raises a further question; given the diversity of business systems in which MNCs operate, how do they organize themselves across to manage units across these systems and what strategies do they pursue?

Key influences on strategy and structure in MNCs

> The world's largest companies are in flux. New pressures have transformed the global competitive game, forcing these companies to rethink their traditional worldwide strategic approaches. (Ghoshal and Bartlett 1998: 3)

So begins perhaps the best known book on 'strategy' in MNCs. Ghoshal and Bartlett identify three key forces on managers in international firms. First, by definition, multinationals operate in a variety of national 'cultures'; values, attitudes and tastes that people hold continue to differ across countries. This 'multiculturalism' that MNCs confront can be seen as a force for 'local differentiation', defined as the need to be responsive to the local environment. Second, in many industries, firms have come under great pressure to achieve economies of scale at the international level. Ghoshal and Bartlett argue that technological developments in the production of consumer goods such as radios, televisions and watches have meant that scale is a key factor in shaping competitive success. Many firms have responded through developing internationally integrated production processes. Thus, a second identifiable pressure on international strategy is the force of 'global integration'. Third, international firms are under pressure to respond to rapidly evolving markets, with products and technologies having shorter life cycles. One way of responding to this is through seeking to link their international operations and transfer expertise across them. Consequently, a further pressure is for 'world-wide innovation'.

These competing pressures on international strategy are evident in differing mixes from one sector to another and from one period to another. Bartlett and Ghoshal identify different organizational forms that are more or less suited to meeting these competing demands. Over the course of the twentieth century the nature of these pressures has

Table 5.1 The world's top 100 non-financial TNCs, ranked by foreign assets, 2006[a] (Millions of dollars and number of employees)

Ranking by: Foreign assets	TN1[b]	I[c]	Corporation	Home economy	Industry[d]	Assets Foreign	Assets Total	Sales Foreign	Sales Total	Employment Foreign	Employment Total	TN[b] (Per cent)	No. of affiliates Foreign	No. of affiliates Total	I[c]
1	71	54	General Electric	United States	Electrical & electronic equipment	442 278	697 239	74 285	163 391	164 000	319 000	53	785	1 117	70
2	14	68	British Petroleum Company Plc	United Kingdom	Petroleum expl./ref./distr.	170 326	217 601	215 879	270 602	80 300	97 100	80	337	529	64
3	87	93	Toyota Motor Corporation	Japan	Motor vehicles	164 627	273 853	78 529	205 918	113 967	299 394	45	169	419	40
4	34	79	Royal Dutch/Shell Group	United Kingdom, Netherlands	Petroleum expl./ref./distr.	161 122[o]	235 276	182 538[e]	318 845	90 000	108 000	70	518	926	56
5	40	35	Exxonmobil Corporation	United States	Petroleum expl./ref./distr.	154 993	219 015	252 680	365 467	51 723	82 100	68	278	346	80
6	78	64	Ford Motor Company	United States	Motor vehicles	131 062	278 554	78 968	160 123	155 000[f]	283 000	50	162	247	66
7	7	99	Vodafone Group Plc	United Kingdom	Telecommunications	126 190	144 366	32 641	39 021	53 138	63 394	85	30	130	23
8	26	51	Total	France	Petroleum expl./ref./distr.	120 645	138 579	146 672	192 952	57 239	95 070	74	429	598	72
9	96	36	Electricite De France	France	Electricity, gas and water	111 916	235 857	33 879	73 933	17 859	155 968	35	199	249	80
10	92	18	Wal-Mart Stores	United States	Retail	110 199	151 193	77 116	344 992	540 000	1 910 000	41	146	163	90
11	37	34	Telefonica SA	Spain	Telecommunications	101 891	143 530	41 093	66 367	167 881	224 939	69	165	205	80
12	77	88	E.On	Germany	Electricity, gas and water	94 304	167 565	32 154	85 007	46 598	80 612	51	279	590	47
13	86	82	Deutsche Telekom AG	Germany	Telecommunications	93 488	171 421	36 240	76 963	88 808	248 800	46	143	263	54
14	58	65	Volkswagen Group	Germany	Motor vehicles	91 823	179 906	95 761	131 571	155 935	324 875	57	178	272	65
15	73	57	France Telecom	France	Telecommunications	90 871	135 876	30 448	64 863	82 148	191 036	52	145	211	69
16	90	63	ConocoPhillips	United States	Petroleum expl./ref./distr.	89 528	164 781	55 781	183 650	17 889	38 400	43	118	179	66
17	56	89	Chevron Corporation	United States	Petroleum expl./ref./distr.	85 735	132 628	111 608	204 892	33 700	62 500	58	97	226	43
18	11	75	Honda Motor Co Ltd	Japan	Motor vehicles	76 264	101 190	77 605	95 333	148 544	167 231	82	141	243	58
19	36	62	Suez	France	Electricity, gas and water	75 151	96 714	42 002	55 563	76 943	139 814	69	586	884	66
20	45	48	Siemens AG	Germany	Electrical & electronic equipment	74 585	119 812	74 858	109 553	314 000	475 000	66	919	1 224	75
21	10	11	Hutchison Whampoa Limited	Hong Kong, China	Diversified	70 679	87 146	28 619	34 428	182 499	220 000	82	115	125	92
22	84	85	RWE Group	Germany	Electricity, gas and water	68 202	123 080	22 142	55 521	30 752	68 534	47	221	430	51
23	9	7	Nestlé SA	Switzerland	Food & beverages	66 677[e]	83 426	57 234[e]	78 528	257 434[h]	265 000	83	467	502	93
24	62	38	BMW AG	Germany	Motor vehicles	66 053	104 118	48 172	61 472	26 575	106 575	56	138	174	79
25	51	33	Procter & Gamble	United States	Diversified	64 487	138 014	44 530	76 476	101 220[h]	138 000	59	369	458	81
26	89	71	General Motors	United States	Motor vehicles	63 538	186 192	78 308	207 349	167 342	280 000	44	115	186	62
27	48	97	Nissan Motor Co Ltd	Japan	Motor vehicles	61 398	104 264	68 703	90 014	93 935	186 336	62	52	166	31
28	93	29	Deutsche Post AG	Germany	Transport and storage	60 938	286 709	44 807	75 957	137 251[e]	463 350	37	698	839	83
29	72	40	Eni Group	Italy	Petroleum expl./ref./distr.	58 113	116 307	62 429	108 023	36 691	73 572	53	157	199	79
30	50	28	Sanofi-aventis	France	Pharmaceuticals	55 342[o]	102 414	20 266[e]	35 595	71 325	100 289	61	179	215	83
31	98	70	DaimlerChrysler AG	Germany, United States	Motor vehicles	55 214	250 259	82 130	190 176	98 976	360 385	31	275	440	63
32	75	49	Pfizer Inc	United States	Pharmaceuticals	53 765	114 837	22 549	48 371	59 819	98 000	51	75	100	75
33	15	20	Roche Group	Switzerland	Pharmaceuticals	52 178	60 980	33 155	33 531	41 554[e]	74 372	80	184	206	89
34	44	72	Mitsui & Co Ltd	Japan	Wholesale trade	50 678	82 499	17 557	41 967	39 792[i]	41 761	66	273	444	61

(continued)

Table 5.1 The world's top 100 non-financial TNCs, ranked by foreign assets, 2006[a] (millions of dollars and number of employees) (continued)

Ranking by: Foreign assets	TNI[b]	II[c]	Corporation	Home economy	Industry[d]	Assets Foreign	Assets Total	Sales Foreign	Sales Total	Employment Foreign	Employment Total	TNI[b] (Per cent)	No. of affiliates Foreign	Total	II[c]
35	95	77	Mitsubishi Motors Corporation	Japan	Motor vehicles	48 328	96 559	37 270	176 410	19 0489	55 867	35	24	42	57
36	59	21	IBM	United States	Electrical & electronic equipment	47 392	103 234	55 507	91 424	231 248	355 766	57	330	373	88
37	2	15	Xstrata PLC	United Kingdom	Mining & quarrying	45 284	47 216	15 038	17 632	26 506°	28 198	92	109	121	90
38	49	39	Fiat Spa	Italy	Motor vehicles	44 715	76 785	46 394	65 026	96 261	172 012	62	398	502	79
39	31	10	Novartis	Switzerland	Pharmaceuticals	42 922	68 008	35 630	36 031	52 830°	100 735	71	294	318	92
40	52	47	Sony Corporation	Japan	Electrical & electronic equipment	40 925	98 498	52 045	71 331	103 900	163 000	59	256	340	75
41	29	26	Compagnie De Saint-Gobain SA	France	Non-metallic mineral products	39 729	54 887	37 224	52 184	151 974	206 940	72	828	984	84
42	60	41	BASF AG	Germany	Chemicals	38 705	59 648	37 194	66 002	47 951	95 247	57	384	493	78
43	66	84	Repsol YPF SA	Spain	Petroleum expl./ref./distr.	38 281	59 530	32 651	64 427	18 409	36 931	55	71	137	52
44	54	16	Hewlett-Packard	United States	Electrical & electronic equipment	37 664	81 981	59 414	91 658	101 915	156 000	59	235	262	90
45	83	2	Eads	Netherlands	Aircraft and parts	36 868	95 005	38 937	49 472	29 349	116 805	48	286	296	97
46	8	44	Philips Electronics	Netherlands	Electrical & electronic equipment	36 680	50 701	32 478	33 843	104 222	121 732	85	357	467	76
47	76	50	Renault SA	France	Motor vehicles	35 935	90 565	34 268	52 099	60 836	128 893	51	149	201	74
48	3	12	Linde AG	Germany	Industrial trucks, tractors, trailers and stackers	35 125	36 871	13 322	15 605	51 670	58 835	89	447	492	91
49	13	24	Lafarge SA	France	Non-metallic mineral products	34 793	39 265	18 047	21 213	57 995ʲ	82 734	81	347	399	87
50	19	61	Unilever	United Kingdom, Netherlands	Diversified	34 433°	48 824	45 078	49 733	135 000ᵉ	179 000	79	248	374	66
51	61	25	Altria Group Inc	United States	Tobacco	34 090	104 270	58 327	101 407	140 958ʰ	175 000	57	104	121	86
52	53	74	Veolia Environnement SA	France	Water supply	32 404	52 843	19 091	35 905	185 881	298 498	59	608	1 040	58
53	80	56	Johnson & Johnson	United States	Pharmaceuticals	32 130	70 556	23 549	53 324	71 756ⁿ	122 200	49	195	282	69
54	81	53	Endesa	Spain	Electric Utilities	31 389ᵏ	71 234	13 160ᵏ	25 819	14 092ᵏ	26 758	49	65	91	71
55	35	94	Anglo American	United Kingdom	Mining & quarrying	30 976	46 483	21 894°	33 072	123 000ᵉ	162 000	70	185	474	39
56	100	100	Petronas – Petroliam Nasional Bhd	Malaysia	Petroleum expl./ref./distr.	30 668	85 201	14 937	50 984	3 965	33 439	26	4	78	5
57	47	19	Mittal Steel Company NV	Netherlands	Metal and metal products	30 438ᵉ	112 166	46 985ⁱ	58 870	248 986	316 224	62	76	85	89
58	46	80	BHP Billiton Group	Australia	Mining & quarrying	28 817	58 168	35 187	39 498	18 964	33 861	65	104	187	56
59	79	86	Vivendi Universal	France	Diversified	28 533	56 694	9 625	25 146	21 451	34 694	50	71	142	50
60	64	91	Carrefour SA	France	Retail	27 955	62 601	51 047	97 731	315 781	456 295	55	158	386	41
61	17	31	Inbev SA	Netherlands	Consumer goods/brewers	27 688ʲ	34 566	12 122ⁱ	16 696	73 495ʲ	85 617	80	97	120	81
62	82	17	Samsung Electronics Co., Ltd.	Republic of Korea	Electrical & electronic equipment	27 011	87 111	71 590	91 856	29 472	85 813	48	78	87	90
63	28	96	BAE Systems Plc	United Kingdom	Transport equipment	26 195	35 624	20 171	25 327	51 839°	79 000	73	123	333	37
64	30	59	Christian Dior SA	France	Textiles	26 167	43 178	17 214	20 093	47 023	66 903	72	32	47	68
65	65	45	Bayer AG	Germany	Pharmaceuticals/chemicals	26 100	73 609	30 650	36 327	48 200°	106 000	55	273	359	76

		Company	Country	Industry										
66	24	Volvo AB	Sweden	Motor vehicles	25 822	37 647	33 210	35 081	55 360	83 190	77	279	341	82
67	6	Liberty Global Inc	United States	Telecommunications	25 479	25 569	6 349m	6 488	12 068h	20 500	85	128	132	97
68	5	WPP Group Plc	United Kingdom	Business services	25 061	28 849	9 295	10 870	69 202	77 686	87	932	1 434	65
69	27	SAB Miller	United Kingdom	Consumer goods/brewers	24 504e	28 736	14 247e	18 620	40 5559	66 949	74	146	161	91
70	39	Holcim AG	Switzerland	Non-metallic mineral products	24 419e	36 632	12 268d	19 117	66 777e	88 783	69	131	149	88
71	20	Cemex S.A.	Mexico	Non-metallic mineral products	24 411	29 749	14 595	18 114	39 505	54 635	78	493	519	95
72	97	Hitachi Ltd	Japan	Electrical & electronic equipment	23 905	89 653	27 840	88 117	122 196	349 996	31	382	796	48
73	91	Marubeni Corporation	Japan	Wholesale trade	23 788	40 969	8 876	31 461	12 188h	28 261o	43	202	354	57
74	21	Coca-Cola Company	United States	Beverages	23 787i	29 963	17 426	24 088	58 800	71 000	78	113	140	81
75	63	Metro AG	Germany	Retail	23 540	42 339	41 971	75 125	133 152	243 139	55	299	798	37
76	85	National Grid Transco	United Kingdom	Energy	23 526	55 730	7 908	15 998	8 761	18 776	46	48	203	24
77	4	Pernod Ricard SA	France	Beverages	23 307	25 645	7 039	8 083	14 808	17 684	87	317	350	91
78	38	TeliaSonera AB	Sweden	Telecommunications	23 152	29 047	7 439	12 342	18 970	28 528	69	128	161	80
79	16	CRH Plc	Ireland	Lumber and other building materials dealers	22 880	24 160	21 937	23 506	41 214o	79 560	80	514	583	88
80	12	Alcan Inc.	Canada	Metals and metal products	22 017	28 939	20 410	23 641	54 000	65 000	82	266	286	93
81	68	United Technologies Corporation	United States	Transport equipment	21 877	47 141	24 121	47 829	141 570	214 500	54	576	691	83
82	74	Dow Chemical Company	United States	Chemicals	20 651	45 581	30 952	49 124	20 290f	42 578	52	133	204	65
83	22	AES Corporation	United States	Electricity, gas and water	20 522	31 163	9 623	12 299	28 6939	32 000	78	161	207	78
84	69	Glaxosmithkline Plc	United Kingdom	Pharmaceuticals	20 1949	50 163	28 620e	42 732	56 937e	102 695	54	241	320	75
85	33	Diageo Plc	United Kingdom	Beverages	20 081	27 397	15 542	18 247	11 487	22 520	70	44	108	41
86	43	British American Tobacco Plc	United Kingdom	Tobacco	19 871e	34 896	11 125e	17 961	78 478e	97 431	66	220	284	77
87	70	Alcoa	United States	Metal and metal products	19 790	37 183	13 229	30 379	79 600	123 000	54	121	203	60
88	42	Bertelsmann	Germany	Retail	19 779	29 630	16 795	24 209	62 796	97 132	67	384	672	57
89	67	Thyssenkrupp AG	Germany	Metal and metal products	19 677	47 056	39 252	59 121	103 534	187 586	54	428	679	63
90	99	Hyundai Motor Company	Republic of Korea	Motor vehicles	19 581	76 064	30 596	68 468	5 0939	54 711	27	19	28	68
91	32	McDonald's Corporation	United States	Food & beverages	19 546	29 024	14 122	21 586	362 700	465 000	70	74	136	54
92	1	Barrick Gold Corp.	Canada	Gold mining	19 524	21 373	5 468	5 636	15 900	17 000	94	28	41	68
93	25	Nokia	Finland	Telecommunications	19 365	29 787	51 103	51 588	41 233	65 324	76	88	95	93
94	57	Thomson Corporation	Canada	Media	19 184	20 132	1 283	6 641	18 338h	32 000	57	141	150	94
95	55	Pinault-Printemps Redoute SA	France	Wholesale trade	19 144	29 487	12 422	22 495	41 894	78 453	58	246	355	69
96	88	Matsushita Electric Industrial Co., Ltd.	Japan	Electrical & electronic equipment	19 043	66 389	38 622	78 317	183 227	328 645	45	253	468	54
97	18	L'Air Liquids Groupe	France	Chemicals	18 895	21 461	10 813	13 736	26 199	36 900	79	249	348	72
98	23	Schlumberger Ltd	United States	Other services	18 688	22 832	13 959	19 230	54 054n	70 000	77	127	135	94
99	41	Singtel Ltd.	Singapore	Telecommunications	18 678	21 288	5 977	8 575	8 606	19 000	68	103	108	95
100	94	Statoil Asa	Norway	Petroleum expl./ref./distr.	18 603	50 394	16 553	66 294	11 448	24 576	36	62	147	42

(continued)

Table 5.1 The world's top 100 non-financial TNCs, ranked by foreign assets, 2006[a] (millions of dollars and number of employees) (continued)

Ranking by:			Corporation	Home economy	Industry[d]	Assets		Sales		Employment		TNI^b (Per cent)	No. of affiliates		
Foreign assets	$TN1^b$	I^c				Foreign	Total	Foreign	Total	Foreign	Total		Foreign	Total	I^c

Source: UNCTAD/Erasmus University database.

[a] All data are based on the companies' annual reports unless otherwise stated. Data on affiliates is based on Dun and Bradstreet's *Who owns Whom* database.

[b] TNI, the Transnationlity Index, is calculated as the average of the following three ratios: foreign assets to total assets, foreign sales to total sales and foreign employment to total employment.

[c] It the Internationalization Index is calculated as the number of foreign affiliates divided by the number of all affiliates. (Note: Affiliates counted in this table refer to only majority-owned affiliates.)

[d] Industry classification for companies follows the United States Standard Industrial Classification as used by the United States Securities and Exchange Commission (SEC).

[e] Data are for activities outside Europe.

[f] Data are for activities outside North America.

[g] Foreign employment data are calculated by applying the share of foreign employment in total employment of the previous year to total employment of 2006.

[h] Foreign employment data are calculated by applying the average of the shares of foreign employment in total employment of all companies in the same industry (omitting the extremes) to total employment.

[i] Data are for activities outside Asia.

[j] Data are for activities outside Western Europe.

[k] Data are for activities outside Spain and Portugal.

[l] Data are for activities outside Other Europe.

[m] Data are for activities outside Other Americas.

[n] Foreign employment data are calculated by applying the share of both foreign assets in total assets and foreign sales in total sales to total employment.

[o] Total employment data are calculated by applying the annual percentage increase of non-consolidated total emploment data to the consolidated total employment data from the previous year.

Note: The list covers non-financial TNCs only. In some companies, foreign investors may hold a minority share of more than 10 per cent.

evolved, and the authors identify periods in which particular organizational forms were in evidence. (The issue of terminology can be confusing here; some use the term multi-national or global firms in a generic sense while others attribute particular connota-tions to each. To avoid confusion, we use the terms in italics when there is a particular connotation.)

▶ The multinational form

The period from 1920 to 1950 is what Ghoshal and Bartlett call the 'multi-domestic' era. In these decades the basis on which competition took place differed significantly from one country to another; consumer tastes varied and protectionism by governments was rife, resulting in pressures for local differentiation being dominant. The strategy and associated structure best suited to these conditions is what Ghoshal and Bartlett term the *multinational* which they define as a collection of national companies which manage their local businesses with minimal direction from HQ (see Figure 5.1). This approach is very good at achieving national responsiveness and has much in common with Perlmutter's (1969) *polycentric* firm and Porter's (1986) *multi-domestic* approach.

What are the HR implications of this organisational form? A key implication is that there is likely to be very little influence on HR policy and practice in operating units from the corporate HQ; decision-making on issues to do with employment practice are highly decentralized in this type of firm. Accordingly, there is unlikely to be a signifi-cant number of expatriate managers as decisions will be left to local managers. A fur-ther implication is that there will be little requirement for knowledge and expertise to be diffused across borders as all parts of the production or service provision process are carried out in one location.

▶ The global form

The period from 1950 to 1980 was characterised by a number of developments: transport and communication costs began to fall in real terms; the minimum efficient scale fell making economies of scale more important; and trade became less regulated. During these decades American firms expanded their international operations, particularly into

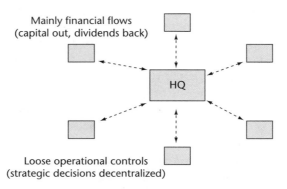

Figure 5.1 **The multinational firm: a decentralized federation**

Europe. One important motivation for this growth in foreign direct investment was to take advantage of the opportunity of realising economies of scale through the creation of 'mini-replicas' of home country operations. Thus foreign units are closely modelled on domestic ones. Ghoshal and Bartlett (1998) identify this as the *global* approach, arguing that it produces standardised products in a highly cost-efficient way and is therefore good at achieving efficiency through global integration. There are similarities here with Perlmutter's *ethnocentric* style in which home country values predominate and foreign subsidiaries are managed as a cultural extension of the parent (see Figure 5.2).

In terms of HR, the replication of the home country approach means that there is some implementation of home country practices in foreign subsidiaries, particularly in relation to work organization. Thus, there will be a distinctive parent company approach to HRM. One way in which this occurs is through the use of expatriates as 'enforcers' of HQ policy and, consequently, firms with the global strategy use a number of people on international assignments. One concern that some observers in host countries have expressed about this sort of multinational is that the replication of home country operations means foreign plants will tend towards being 'screwdriver' operations; that is, the high-tech operations such as research and development are retained in the country of origin and the subsidiaries are characterised by routine assembly work with a high proportion of jobs being low skill in nature.

▶ The international form

The 1950s to the 1980s was also characterized by a further pressure on MNCs, namely the importance of spreading innovations across the firm. Ghoshal and Bartlett describe the way in which many international organisations responded to this pressure: 'The strategy of a third group of companies is based primarily on transferring and adapting the parent company's knowledge or expertise to foreign markets' (1998: 17). These firms, termed *international,* are less centralised than the *global* firms since local management are able to vary the nature of the products or services to the national market, but are much more centralised than the *multinational* firms. This type of firm does not correspond directly to any of Perlmutter's types of multinational, but can be seen as a hybrid of the *polycentric* and *ethnocentric* firms.

The implementation of centrally developed innovations has implications for HR in foreign subsidiaries. Managers at local level are responsible for implementing such innovations and, more generally, for ensuring that the expertise and knowledge transferred from the centre is harnessed and deployed. Thus, while they are unlikely to be subject to the same degree of control that subsidiaries of *global* firms are subject to, there will certainly be requirements from the HQ with which they must comply. Relatedly, the role of managers on international assignments differs from those in *global* firms; they are less likely to be 'enforcers' of corporate policy, and more likely to be key points of contact between HQ and subsidiaries and facilitators of the transfer of expertise and knowledge from the centre (see Figure 5.3). Finally, concerns over the limited contribution of foreign-owned firms to the local economy are likely to be less acute in relation to *international* firms. Indeed, this group of firms may be seen as a mechanism through which new technologies and practices can be

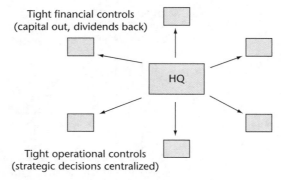

Figure 5.2 **The global firm: a centralized hub**

spread across borders, although some may harbour concerns that these innovations are developed abroad.

▶ The transnational firm

Over the last two decades or so Ghoshal and Bartlett argue that developments in technology and markets have meant that more and more industries are characterised by the simultaneous pressures to be locally responsive, achieve efficiency through global scale and to diffuse innovations across their sites. Thus, while each of the three types of firm identified above may be adept at responding to one of these pressures, none of them allows a firm to respond to all of them. The authors present a fourth type of firm, the *transnational,* as offering the 'solution' to these competing pressures. There is a clear prescriptive element in this respect; they see the *transnational* form as 'necessary for every company that operates in an international environment' (1998: 20).

The *transnational* involves the creation of an integrated network of sites, each of which possesses a distinct role. The plants within the network have differentiated roles in that their brief is to specialize in a particular part of the production or service provision process. As a result of this differentiation, the plants have some freedom to respond to local factors and so meet the pressure for local differentiation. The integration of international operations through the network also provides for scale efficiencies

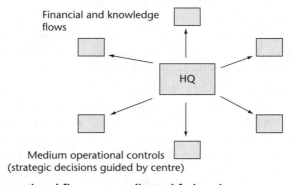

Figure 5.3 **The international firm: a co-ordinated federation**

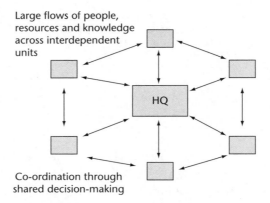

Large flows of people, resources and knowledge across interdependent units

HQ

Co-ordination through shared decision-making

Figure 5.4 **The transnational firm: an integrated network**

to be realised at the global level, thereby achieving a degree of global integration (see Figure 5.4). And the diffusion of knowledge and expertise within the interdependent network affords scope for world-wide learning. In this way, Ghoshal and Bartlett argue that the *transnational* can respond to all three of the key pressures on firms operating across borders. This organizational form has much in common with Perlmutter's *geocentric* firm, while the idea of an integrated network also features strongly in Hedlund's (1986) notion of the *heterarchical* firm.

The *transnational* has a number of important implications for HR. The practices in place at plant level will in part reflect innovations in other parts of the network, not just those in the home country as in *global* and *international* firms. Moreover, a key part of the facilitation of the network is a cadre of managers roaming from site to site, serving as the 'glue' holding the firm together and bringing about the exchange of knowledge and expertise. What distinguishes a *transnational* in this respect is that the international assignees will not only originate in the parent company. For those concerned about the role of a subsidiary in contributing to the development of a host country the *transnational* promises much, since each plant will be accorded a specialist role.

The idea of the *transnational* organizational form is a very important one for international HRM. Indeed, the concept of an integrated network is central to much recent writing in this field. Dowling *et al.* (1999) note that a number of authors have advocated the network form and claimed that a growing number of MNCs are moving towards it. The networked multinational, they argue, is characterized by five dimensions: 'delegation of decision making authority to appropriate units and levels; geographical dispersion of key functions across units in different countries; de-layering of organizational levels; de-bureaucratization of formal procedures; and differentiation of work, responsibility, and authority across the networked subsidiaries' (1999: 50). The idea of a network features strongly, if implicitly, in the 'integrative framework of strategic international human resource management' proposed by Schuler *et al.* (1993). They assert that MNCs 'are realising that every possible source of competitive advantage must be identified and utilized. And as they are searching, particularly firms pursuing total quality management, they are realizing that a systematic approach to developing human resource policies and practices may, in fact, give competitive advantage' (1993: 427). They go on, 'a major goal of MNEs is facilitating learning and the transfer of this learning across units' (1993: 427). Later in the article they argue that HR policies can assist in the integration of the business: 'In doing so they must be consistent with the needs of the business to achieve competitiveness, be flexible and facilitate the transfer of learning across units' (1993: 431). In empirical studies of MNCs, moreover, there is some support for the notion that some MNCs are characterized by interdependent networks involving flows of knowledge across the firm in many directions (e.g. Edwards and Tempel, forthcoming; Johnson and Medcof 2007; Noorderhaven and Harzing 2009; Persson 2006).

How useful is the concept of an integrated network in general and Bartlett and Ghoshal's *transnational* solution in particular? Are MNCs all finding it a 'necessary' element to operating internationally as the authors claim? And is it a key part of the 'solution' to managing across borders? We consider in turn the two main objections to this view, firstly that it sees strategy making as a deliberate, rational process, and secondly that it pays too little attention to the 'embeddedness' of strategy in its social context.

▶ The importance of organizational politics in MNCs

Many writers on strategy stress the importance of the micro-politics of organizations in the development of strategies. Firms are comprised of a range of groups each with their own goals and priorities. Moreover, each of these groups, to a greater or lesser extent, possesses some resource of value to others in the organization which they can use to advance their own agenda. In this way, strategies emerge as a result of bargaining and compromise between groups of organizational actors and, consequently, strategies tend to evolve slowly. Ghoshal and Bartlett's approach plays down the role of organizational politics; there is relatively little attention devoted to how different groups may have different aims and seek to advance them. Yet, much research into the internal workings of multinational companies and the development of 'strategies' in IHRM have revealed the importance of micro-political processes.

One obvious source of tension within MNCs is between managers at the corporate HQ and those in a subsidiary in a different country. The former group may seek to advance their own position by developing global policies, while the latter may strive to maximize their autonomy. As an example, Edwards *et al.* (1993) provide evidence that the French subsidiary of a British multinational was able to resist orders from the centre concerning the timing of a redundancy programme. In doing so, managers at the profitable French plant knew that the French market was important to the wider company and that corporate managers were dependent on them to serve this market. They knew that the HQ could not sack them and send expatriates to take over; few of the British senior managers spoke French and their understanding of the French legal and institutional context was poor. A related source of tension between groups of managers within MNCs is between expatriate and indigenous managers. The former may seek to establish themselves as key players in the operation to which they have been sent, while the latter may resent their presence. Broad's (1994) study of a Japanese MNC in Britain revealed the way in which British managers formed informal networks that

Japanese expatriates were excluded from. These networks served to share information from rumours and gossip in the plant and this information was kept from the Japanese, whose limitations in English meant they could not access the information directly.

While the managers of units within a multinational possess some sources of power, those at the HQ do so too, of course. The most obvious resource that the HQ controls is the funds for new investment. Research in the car industry has revealed the way in which corporate managers systematically compare the performance of their sites in different countries, and use these comparisons to exert pressure on actors at plant level to improve quality and costs. Commonly, these comparisons are tied to investment decisions so that, in effect, the plants compete against one another for the allocation of investment. In this way, the centre is able to exert growing influence over working practices at plant level (Mueller and Purcell 1992; Martinez and Weston 1994). Sisson *et al.* (2003) review evidence from a range of sources to show that such 'benchmarking' among MNCs is widespread, particularly within regions such as Europe.

Managers at the corporate HQ also have the ability to use the promotion of unit managers to senior positions within the company as a source of power. The pay and promotion prospects of unit managers can be tied in part to their willingness to be active participants in the network, both through inputting practices into it and through adopting practices that originated elsewhere. Once again, case study evidence has revealed the importance of this source of power in facilitating the multilateral diffusion of practices across borders; those managers promoted or given international assignments take with them knowledge of practices that have operated successfully in one part of the organization and spread this to other operations (Coller and Marginson 1998; Edwards 1998).

CASE STUDY

ABB – a test case of the transnational strategy

Perhaps the most widely cited example of a transnational company is ABB. This firm was formed through a merger between ASEA of Sweden and Brown Boveri of Switzerland and operates in a range of sectors, from industrial power to transport equipment. In the late 1980s and 1990s the firm engaged in a string of acquisitions across the world so that it has a significant presence in the Americas and Asia as well as Europe. The former CEO, Percy Barnevik, was renowned for supposedly creating a radically new approach to managing international operations. In his own words, ABB is simultaneously 'global and local, big and small, radically decentralised but with central control'.

Ghoshal and Bartlett themselves described ABB as a 'classic transnational organization' (1998: 259). A key element of this orientation, they argued, was the devolution of responsibility for operating performance to the managers of the 1,300 business units; accompanying this was the creation of a very small corporate HQ employing just 150 people. This was a key part of Barnevik's stated aim of putting 'individual initiative and personal responsibility...at the heart of the company's philosophy' (1997: 30–31). When there was a problem in one of the units, senior management of the company would 'reach down to the front lines', but their objective was to 'help rather than interfere' (1997: 189).

Coupled with devolution to operating units was an attempt to 'encourage global teamwork and cooperation between companies and countries' (1998: 265); the creation of the network which is central to the transnational form. Ghoshal and Bartlett ascribed the firm's success in doing so to two key aspects of the firm's approach. The first was creating 'stretch', defined as the setting of ambitious goals which are to be achieved through a set of common values. In ABB a 'policy bible' containing the firm's key principles was distributed across the organisation with the intention that this would appeal to individuals' own values and induce them to channel their creative capabilities for the good of the organisation. The second was to establish trust, which the authors argue is 'vital to the development and nurturing of the collaborative behaviour that drives effective revitalisation' (1998: 268–269). Apparently, an emphasis on employee involvement in decision-making, and a structure comprising numerous cross-national boards and teams, allowed a sense of 'organizational fairness and equity' to develop.

But is the process of managing international operations as straightforward as this? The interpretation that Ghoshal and Bartlett put on the workings of ABB has been challenged by Belanger *et al.* (1999). On the basis of a detailed case study of the firm across several countries, Belanger and his colleagues argue that Ghoshal and Bartlett too readily accepted top managers' views of how ABB operates and, consequently, downplayed the tensions and contradictions which are a key feature of organizational life in multinational companies.

In particular, the way in which 'learning' takes place was highly politicized, resting on competitive relations between plants which created pressure on local actors to adopt practices from other plants. Senior managers possessed a number of sources of power that enabled them to pressurise local management into adopting practices from other parts of the group. Perhaps most obvious among these was the management of the career patterns of managers in the company; those that were seen as obstructive to the working of the network faced the prospect of not progressing to more senior posts or, in some cases, being sacked. Further, business area management controlled capital investment decisions, and in some divisions also allocated orders from customers. Those plants which had been good 'corporate citizens' could be rewarded with new investment and orders, while those seen as problematic could be punished. These resources, Belanger *et al.* argue, enabled the centre to exert a growing influence over the plants.

Equally, however, local actors could draw on their embeddedness in local environments to shape the extent of corporate influence and the way it took place. One instance is the performance of the plants. A system known as the 'ABB Olympics' sought to assess and rank each plant in terms of a range of aspects of performance, such as costs, quality and throughput times. Those plants which performed well in these league tables were able to use this to increase their autonomy from business area and corporate management; the profits that their plant contributed to the group could be seen as a source of power. A further illustration of the political activity in which local actors can engage is the creation of an uneasy alliance of some local managers and the union in the Hull plant in Canada in response to the parent company's plans for restructuring.

The evidence presented by Belanger and his colleagues illustrates the important of political activity within MNCs. The establishment of an integrated network of plants collaborating with one another as envisaged by Ghoshal and Bartlett is likely to be a contested, rather than a straightforward, process. Indeed, the resources controlled by actors at plant level may be used to block the operation of a network as local actors seek to preserve their own autonomy. In sum, where a multinational seeks to integrate its operations into a network, the way this operates is likely to be governed more by power relations between different groups than by values and trust.

For further details on contrasting perspectives on ABB, see Belanger, J. *et al.* (1999); Belanger, J. *et al.*, (2003); Ghoshal, S. and Bartlett, C. (1998).

Question

What does the case of ABB tell us about the ease with which MNCs can establish collaborative networking between their sites?

The case of ABB together with wider research evidence, some of which was cited above, demonstrates the importance of micro-political processes in MNCs. This has implications for the 'integrated network' that appears to be favoured by many writers on international HRM. Such networks do not always operate in a harmonious, coherent way; rather they are political constellations of groups of organisational actors whose aims and priorities are often divergent. The extent to which organisational actors are able to achieve their aims when they diverge from those of other groups is determined in part by the resources they have at their disposal. As Kristensen and Zeitlin (2005) put it, the multinational is a 'battleground' in which subsidiaries represent and mobilize their own capabilities and national expertise. Hence, divergences of interest within a multinational are worked out through the exercising of power relations.

The implications of recognizing the contested nature of international networks are significant. In particular, some groups of actors or units within a multinational may be able to block the diffusion of practices; they may seek to resist pressure to adopt a practice which originated elsewhere and may also be reluctant to input information on new practices into the network for fear of it undermining their competitive position. This is not to deny that a multilateral sharing of information can and does occur through 'networking' within MNCs, but it is to emphasize that senior managers will often need to overcome resistance to this process and will use the resources at their disposal to bring this about. Edwards et al. (1999: 290) argue that in many MNCs diffusion occurs through networking between plants, with this being underpinned by HQ control over investment decisions and the prospects of plant managers. They used the term 'networking within hierarchy' to describe this process.

As we have implied, the way that micro-political processes within international networks of managers operate is shaped in part by the linkages between organisational actors and their environment. The sources of power that actors possess are in many cases a product of their environment, as demonstrated by the example of the French subsidiary of the British MNC described above. Thus, these actors are not detached, calculating individuals but rather are embedded in their environment, which we now explore in more depth.

▶ The 'embeddedness' of strategy

To some extent Ghoshal and Bartlett are sensitive to the notion that a firm's strategy is firmly embedded in its particular economic and social context in identifying a firm's 'administrative heritage', which they define as a company's 'existing organizational capabilities as shaped by various historical and structural factors' (1998: 39). This administrative heritage, which the authors argue makes firms to some extent 'captives of their past', stems from some factors internal to the organization, such as the role of the founders and leaders and the influence of the history of the firm. It also stems from the impact of national culture which gives a firm 'a way of doing things' and shapes the values and behaviour of senior management.

However, the institutionalist perspective demands a much fuller appreciation of the way a multinational's 'country of origin' is important in shaping the way it operates at the international level; as we have argued earlier in the book, there is much more to a national influence than simply 'culture'. The role of the family can be a crucial factor in creating variations between countries in the way firms operate. For instance, Whitley (1991) has described the importance of the family unit in Taiwan in creating a set of entrepreneurial small and medium sized firms, many of which are linked together through wider family networks. The role of the state, too, varies significantly from country to country. In relation to France, Whittington and Meyer (2000: 95) show how 'the state, elitist educational institutions, and the great financial and industrial enterprises have long been closely interlinked'. The nature of financial institutions also varies from country to country, with the bank-centred system of industrial finance in Germany in which investment banks hold significant stakes in firms and have close relationships with their managements contrasting with the market-centred system in the UK and USA where shareholdings are dispersed across a range of institutions and individuals and relationships between these and senior managers are distant. The notion of culture is clearly inadequate to capture these national differences as it neglects important institutional factors, leading many to prefer the term 'national business system'.

The distinctiveness of national business systems, despite current talk of globalisation, matters because most MNCs remain firmly rooted in their original country. As we have seen, most MNCs remain disproportionately focused on the home country across a number of dimensions. Even those MNCs that are highly internationalised in terms of sales are concentrated in their home country in others. In Ericsson, for example, the ownership structure at the end of 2008 meant that nearly half of the voting rights were controlled by six Swedish institutions (www.ericsson.com). This concentration of ownership and key activities in the home base means that the centre has a disproportionate influence on strategy formulation. Hence, international strategies continue to reflect a significant 'country of origin' effect.

For instance, a considerable body of evidence concerned with employment practice in the foreign subsidiaries of American MNCs indicates that they have been particularly hostile to trade unions and systems of collective representation, and have sought to implement HRM practices such as performance-related pay and employee involvement programmes (Almond and Ferner 2006). Japanese MNCs are also influenced by their domestic business system when they operate outside Japan, one aspect of which is the use of a high number of expatriates to oversee the adoption in their subsidiaries of some Japanese-style forms of work organization, such as team-based working and just-in-time production (Whitley *et al.* 2003). While there is less evidence for MNCs of other nationalities, the embeddedness of MNCs appears to create a detectable influence from the country of origin (see Ferner 1997b, for a review).

Crucially, MNCs may not be able to easily shed this effect; whether they like it or not, they may find that they cannot leave their 'national baggage', as Ferner and Quintanilla (1998) put it, at home. In this respect, Ghoshal and Bartlett (1998), in arguing that MNCs will move towards a transnational orientation over time, appear to overestimate the ease with which MNCs can shed their 'administrative heritage'.

CASE STUDY

AutoPower – shaking off its American origins?

The way in which MNCs are embedded in their country of origin, and the way that this continues to shape the way they operate, is clearly illustrated by the case of 'AutoPower'. This firm originated in the mid-west of the USA in the early part of the last century and rapidly became the major employer in a relatively small town. The founding family of the company took an active part in the management process, playing a key role in setting the style and values that characterized the organization. AutoPower is now a multinational employing approximately 30,000 people in 12 different countries.

The influence of the founding family has been significant. Management style in the firm's original location in the mid-west has been paternalistic: pay and conditions have tended to be favourable compared with other firms; job security has been high (until recently anyway); and employees have been provided with a range of fringe benefits. To some extent, this paternalism has been carried over into the firm's international operations, particularly those in Britain. The influence of the founding family can also be discerned in relation to its dealings with trade unions. Unlike many American firms that grew in the first half of the twentieth century, AutoPower did not experience bitter disputes with trade unions. The attitude of the founding family was to allow employees to decide whether to join a union and, if sufficient numbers did so, management would recognize and negotiate with them. This relatively relaxed, constructive approach to dealing with unions also shows up at the international level. A third area where the original owners were influential was in relation to 'diversity'. As long ago as the 1960s, senior managers were emphasizing the importance of having the composition of the workforce in all their locations reflect the ethnic composition of the community. Latterly, the firm has introduced a global policy stipulating that the benefits accruing to the wives and husbands of employees should also accrue to unmarried and same-sex partners.

As well as the style and values which were strongly influenced by the founding family, there have also been a number of global policies which have been devised in the company's HQ. One particular example is the system of teamworking. This was the product of a team of engineers and managers and involved the creation of teams of operators working flexibly within a cell. This model of organizing production was gradually diffused to all of the firm's operations internationally. All in all, it is clear that the nature of IHRM in AutoPower strongly reflects its American roots.

This 'ethnocentric' approach has been challenged by those in AutoPower's international operations. At a meeting of HR managers from across the company the presentation of a new corporate initiative for a global policy on the repatriation of employees who have been on international assignments provoked a mini-rebellion from HR managers outside the USA. Many complained that the development of the firm's international policies did not reflect the diversity of the company's operations, and that if it claimed to be a genuinely internationalized firm with international markets as its main growth area then its policies should reflect this.

This protest was acted upon by senior HR managers who appeared to recognize the legitimacy of the concerns. One response was to commission the HR managers from India and the UK to devise a 'template' outlining the way in which international HR policies would be devised in the future, allowing substantial input from HR people in the subsidiaries. Another indication that the firm was striving to be less US-focused was the appointment of a Chinese-American, who had been Head of HR in China, as Head of International HR. And perhaps most significantly, responsibility for the development of a new performance management system has been given to a British HR manager who is on an assignment in the corporate HQ and is leading an international team of eight, only two of whom are American. This is seen by many in the company as a marked departure from the way HR policies had been developed in the past, and a pointer to how they will be developed in the future.

However, the legacy of the firm's embeddedness in the USA has not proven so easy to shake off. Over the last few years the company has become more subject to pressures from outside financial institutions. A consequence has been that senior managers have begun to attach more importance to quarterly budgets and financial targets, since this is how they are assessed by the institutions. When a downturn hit the product market, the immediate response was to slash costs, an element of which was to greatly reduce the travel budget. This meant that convening meetings of the team members was impossible and the leader of the initiative has worked from the corporate HQ. Moreover, the interest in the experiment by senior HR people has waned as they have become focused on managing the redundancies which accompanied the downturn.

The upshot has been that the much celebrated shift towards subsidiary input into decision-making has had much less impact than had been envisaged. Some time after their creation the 'templates' guiding the development of international HR policies are not in evidence, and policies appear to be created and rolled out from the HQ in a way that they had previously. International networking in AutoPower proved to be quite difficult to realize.

For more details, see Edwards *et al.* (2007).

Question

Is it inevitable that MNCs will encounter difficulties in trying to make their approach less ethnocentric?

While the country of origin effect is an important influence on HRM in MNCs which it is not always easy to shed, neither is it set in stone. As multinationals mature and become more internationalised, the influence of the country of origin may diminish. Indeed, evidence from studies of German, French and Swedish MNCs indicates that many have adopted structures and practices traditionally associated with Anglo-Saxon MNCs, such as international product divisions with devolved responsibilities, share options and performance-related pay (e.g. Ferner and Quintanilla 1998; Mtar 2001; Hayden and Edwards 2001). These developments have eroded the influence of the country of origin, but they have not eradicated it; the MNCs in these studies still reflect their national origins in significant ways.

Conclusions

This chapter has considered how to define a multinational, contrasted various explanations for why firms internationalize and investigated the extent to which MNCs are global in orientation. It then examined how the changing nature of the external environment within which MNCs operate has had important implications for the internal organization of multinationals: differences persist in the nature of the national systems in which MNCs are located; globalization has presented opportunities for firms to realize more fully economies of scale at the international level; and rapidly evolving technologies and shorter product life cycles have created pressures on firms to engage in innovation and learning across their operations. As we have seen, much writing on strategic IHRM urges firms to create a flexible network in which units have differentiated roles, share expertise with one another and in which responsibility and authority is diffused. Indeed, there is some evidence that many firms are clearly seeking to instigate networks which have the capability of transferring knowledge and expertise across the firm.

However, in two important respects the popular vision of networks appears to be flawed. First, as is the case for all organizations, MNCs are political animals in which there are multiple interest groups each of which will seek to use the resources at their disposal to advance their own interests. This does not mean that networking will not occur but it does imply that senior management merely establishing the formal architecture of a network will not be sufficient on its own. Rather, the precise nature of networking will depend on the exercising of power. Second, networks transcend a range of distinctive business systems and are disproportionately influenced by the original home base of the multinational. In this way, even MNCs that are characterized by a highly internationalized network of operations continue to exhibit a 'country of origin' effect'.

Despite these qualifications, it is evident that an increasingly important element of the way that MNCs operate is with a common element across borders. Thus, in the next chapter we consider in more detail the rationale for such a global element and the ways in which they can achieve this in the HR function.

Review questions

1 What are the relative strengths and weaknesses of the narrow and broad definitions of MNCs?

2 Why do firms 'internalize' a competitive advantage and what are the implications of doing so for their role as employers?

3 Why do Bartlett and Ghoshal see the 'transnational' as the 'solution' to managing across borders?

4 What sources of power do managers in the operating units of MNCs commonly hold?

5 What are the sources of the 'country of origin' effect in MNCs?

Further reading

1 Dicken, P. (2007) *Global Shift: Mapping the Changing Contours of the World Economy*, London: Sage, Chapter 4.

The chapter contains a concise summary of many theories of internationalization and ways in which MNCs organize themselves.

2 Marginson, P. (1994) 'Multinational Britain: employment and work in an internationalised economy', *Human Resource Management Journal*, 4(4), 63–80.

The article explores the various motivations for firms to expand overseas and links each of these to the implications for their approach as employers. The analysis is located in a discussion of the British context.

3 Almond, P. and Ferner, A. (eds) (2006) *American Multinationals in Europe: Managing Employment Relations Across National Borders*, Oxford: Oxford University Press.

The book presents the results of a large study of American MNCs in a range of countries, providing both conceptual and empirical material.

4 Adenfelt, M. and Lagerstrom, K. (2006) 'Knowledge development and sharing in multinational corporations: the case of a centre of excellence and a transnational team', *International Business Review,* 15(4), 381–400.

This is an example of the range of studies that examine the ways in which MNCs exhibit a degree of networking across their operations in different countries.

References

Almond, P. and Ferner, A. (eds) (2006) *American Multinationals in Europe: Managing Employment Relations Across National Borders,* Oxford: Oxford University Press.

Belanger, J., Berggren, C., Bjorkman, T. and Kohler, C. (1999) *Being Local Worldwide: ABB and the Challenge of Global Management,* Ithaca: Cornell University Press.

Belanger, J., Giles, A. and Grenier, J. (2003) 'Patterns of corporate influence in the host country: a study of ABB in Canada', *International Journal of Human Resource Management,* 14(3), 469–85.

Bird, A., Taylor, S. and Beechler, S. (1998) 'A typology of international human resource management in Japanese multinational corporations: organizational implications', *Human Resource Management,* 37(2), 159–72.

Broad, G. (1994) 'The managerial limits to Japanisation: a case study', *Human Resource Management Journal,* 4(3), 52–69.

Buckley, P. and Casson, M. (1976) *The Future of the Multinational Enterprise,* London: Macmillan.

Coase, R. (1937) 'The nature of the firm', *Economica,* 4, 386–405.

Coller, X. and Marginson, P. (1998) 'Transnational management influence over changing employment practices: a case study', *Industrial Relations Journal,* 29(1), 4–17.

Corley, T. (1994) 'Britain's overseas investments in 1914 revisited', *Business History,* 36(1), 71–88.

Cowling, K. and Sugden, R. (1987) *Transnational Monopoly Capitalism,* Brighton: Wheatsheaf.

Dicken, P. (2007) *Global Shift: Mapping the Changing Contours of the World Economy,* London: Sage.

Doremus, P., Keller, W., Pauly, L. and Reich, S. (1998) *The Myth of the Global Corporation,* Princeton, NJ: Princeton University Press.

Dowling, P., Welch, D. and Schuler, R. (1999) *International Human Resource Management: Managing People in a Multinational Context,* Cincinnati: South Western.

Dunning, J. (1993) *Multinational Enterprises and the Global Economy,* Harlow: Addison-Wesley.

Edwards, P., Ferner, A. and Sisson, K. (1993) 'People and the Process of Management in the Multinational Company', *Warwick Papers in Industrial Relations,* No. 43, Coventry: IRRU.

Edwards, T. (1998) 'Multinationals and the process of reverse diffusion', *International Journal of Human Resource Management,* 9(4), 696–709.

Edwards, T., Almond, P., Clark, I., Colling, T. and Ferner, A. (2005) 'Reverse diffusion in US multinationals: barriers from the American business system', *Journal of Management Studies,* 42(6), 1261–86.

Edwards, T., Colling, T. and Ferner, A. (2007) 'The transfer of employment practices in multinational companies: towards an integrated conceptual approach', *Human Resource Management Journal,* 17(3), 201–17.

Edwards, T. and Ferner, A. (2002) 'The renewed "American challenge": a framework for understanding employment practice in US MNCs', *Industrial Relations Journal,* 33(2), 94–111.

Edwards, T., Rees, C. and Coller, X. (1999) 'Structure, politics and the diffusion of practices in multinational companies', *European Journal of Industrial Relations,* 5(3), 286–306.

Edwards, T. and Tempel, A. (forthcoming 2010) 'Reverse diffusion and national business systems: evidence from the British and German subsidiaries of American multinationals', *Journal of World Business,* 45(1).

Ferner, A. (1997a) 'Multinationals, "Relocation", and Employment in Europe', in Gual, J. (ed). *Job Creation: The Role of Labour Market Institutions,* London: Edward Elgar.

Ferner, A. (1997b) 'MNCs and the country of origin effect', *Human Resource Management Journal,* 7(1), 19–37.

Ferner, A. and Quintanilla, J. (1998) 'Multinationals, national business systems and HRM: the enduring influence of national identity or a process of "Anglo-Saxonisation"?', *International Journal of Human Resource Management,* 9(4), 710–31.

Financial Times (1997) 'Management: flight plan from Seattle: Philip Condit tells Michael Skapinker how he hopes to turn Boeing into a global company over 20 years', 12 March.

Frobel, F., Heinrichs, J. and Kreye, O. (1980) *The New International Division of Labour,* Cambridge: Cambridge University Press.

Gereffi, G., Humphrey, J. and Sturgeon, T. (2005) 'The governance of global value chains: an analytical framework', *Review of International Political Economy,* 12(1), 78–104.

Ghoshal, S. and Bartlett, C. (1997) *The Individualized Corporation: A Fundamentally New Approach to Management,* London: Heinemann.

Ghoshal, S. and Bartlett, C. (1998) *Managing Across Borders: The Transnational Solution,* London: Hutchinson.

Guardian (2002) 'New balls please', 24th June.

Hayden, A. and Edwards, T. (2001) 'The erosion of the country of origin effect: a case study of a Swedish multinational company', *Relations Industrielles,* 56(1), 116–40.

Hedlund, G. (1986) 'The hypermodern MNC', *Human Resource Management,* 25, Spring, 9–36.

Hirst, P. and Thompson, P. (1999) *Globalization in Question: The International Economy and the Possibilities of Governance,* (2nd edition), Cambridge: Polity Press.

Hymer, S. (1976) *The International Operations of National Firms: A Study of Foreign Direct Investment,* Cambridge, MA: MIT Press.

Johansson, J. and Wiedersheim-Paul, F. (1975) 'The internationalisation of the firm: four Swedish cases', *Journal of Management Studies,* 12, 305–22.

John, R., Ietto-Gillies, G., Cox, H. and Grimwade, N. (1997) *Global Business Strategy,* London: Thompson.

Johnson, W. and Medcof, J. (2007) 'Motivating proactive subsidiary innovation: agent-based theory and socialisation Models in Global R&D', *Journal of International Management,* 13, 472–87.

Jones, G. (2000) *Merchants to Multinationals: British Trading Companies in the Nineteenth and Twentieth Centuries,* Oxford: OUP.

Kristensen, P. and Zeitlin, J. (2005) *Local Players in global Games: The Strategic Constitution of a Multinational Company,* Oxford: Oxford University Press.

Lane, C. (1995) *Industry and Society in Europe: Stability and Change in Britain, Germany and France,* Aldershot: Edward Elgar.

Legrain, P. (2002) *Open World: The Truth about Globalisation,* London: Abacus.

Marginson, P. (1994) 'Multinational Britain: employment and work in an internationalised economy', *Human Resource Management Journal,* 4(4), 63–80.

Martinez, M. and Weston, S. (1994) 'New management practices in a multinational corporation: the restructuring of worker representation and rights', *Industrial Relations Journal,* 25(2), 110–21.

Mtar, M. (2001) 'French Multinationals' International Strategy', PhD thesis, University of Warwick.

Mueller, F. and Purcell, J. (1992) 'The Europeanisation of manufacturing and the decentralisation of bargaining: multinational management strategies in the European automobile industry', *International Journal of Human Resource Management,* 3(1), 15–34.

Noorderhaven, N. and Harzing, A. (2009) 'Knowledge sharing and social interaction within MNCs', *Journal of International Business Studies,* 40(5), 719–41.

Ohmae, K. (1990) *The Borderless World,* London: Collins.

Ohmae, K. (1995) (ed.) *The Evolving Global Economy: Making Sense of the New World Order,* Boston: Harvard Business Review Press.

Oliver, N. and Wilkinson, B. (1992) *The Japanization of British Industry: New Developments in the 1990s,* Oxford: Basil Blackwell.

Oman, C. (1994) *Globalisation and Regionalisation: the Challenge for Developing Countries,* Paris: OECD.

Perlmutter, H. (1969) 'The tortuous evolution of the multinational company', *Columbia Journal of World Business,* Jan.–Feb., 9–18.

Persson, M. (2006) 'The impact of operational structure, lateral integrative mechanisms and control mechanisms on intra-MNE knowledge transfer', *International Business Review,* 15(5), 547–69.

Porter, M. (1986) *Competition in Global Industries,* Boston: Harvard Business School Press.

Reich, R. (1991) 'Who is us?', *Harvard Business Review,* Jan.–Feb., 53–64.

Royle, T. (2000) *Working for McDonalds in Europe,* London: Routledge.

Rugman, A. (1981) *Inside the Multinationals,* London: Croom Helm.

Rugman, A. (2005) *The Regional Multinationals: MNEs and the 'Global' Strategic Management,* Cambridge: Cambridge University Press.

Ruigrok, W. and van Tulder, R. (1995) *The Logic of International Restructuring,* London: Routledge.

Schuler, R., Dowling, P. and De Cieri, H. (1993) 'An integrative framework of strategic human resource management', *Journal of Management,* 19(2), 419–59.

Sisson, K., Arrowsmith, J. and Marginson, P. (2003) 'All benchmarkers now? Benchmarking and the "Europeanisation" of industrial relations', *Industrial Relations Journal,* 34(1), 15–31.

UN (2008) *World Investment Report,* New York: United Nations.

Whitley, R. (1991) 'The social construction of business systems in East Asia', *Organization Studies,* 12(1), 1–28.

Whitley, R. (1999) *The Social Structuring of Business Systems,* Oxford: Oxford University Press.

Whitley, R., Morgan, G., Kelly, W. and Sharpe, D. (2003) 'The changing Japanese multinational: application, adaptation and learning in car manufacturing and financial services', *Journal of Management Studies,* 40(3), 643–72.

Whittington, R. and Meyer, M. (2000) *The European Corporation: Strategy, Structure and Social Science,* Oxford: Oxford University Press.

Williamson, O. (1975) *Markets and Hierarchies,* New York: Free Press.

Chapter 6

Global integration and international HRM

Adam Smale

Key aims

The aims of this chapter are to:

- outline the key drivers of global HRM integration in multinational corporations and present the arguments for why multinational corporations are likely to pursue more extensive integration (as opposed to differentiation) in the future;
- identify the range of mechanisms through which multinational corporations can facilitate the global integration of their HRM practices, and review how they are used;
- critically discuss when the global integration of HRM can be regarded as having been accomplished.

Introduction

In the previous chapters we have seen how the dilemma between globalization and differences embedded in national business systems lead to different strategic and structural responses by multinational corporations (MNCs). This chapter presents the arguments why MNC strategies and structures that support global integration, including the global integration of HRM practices, are becoming increasingly popular. In reference to the integration-differentiation dilemma, whilst this chapter presents the case for global HRM integration, Chapter 7 focuses on the arguments for differentiation by highlighting the limits of global integration, questioning the 'diffusability' of HRM practices into different national contexts, and taking into consideration the role of internal politics in MNCs and the way that they segment their production processes across borders.

The basic premise of this chapter is that the global integration of HRM in MNCs is becoming a more attractive proposition (Taylor 2006). The chapter will therefore firstly outline the key drivers behind this suggested move towards greater global integration (the 'why'), both in general and in relation to HRM specifically. Secondly, the chapter will look at the ways in which MNCs try to facilitate tighter global HRM integration (the 'how') by identifying the range of integration mechanisms they use, and how they are used. Lastly, the chapter engages in a critical discussion of when we can say that an MNC has actually accomplished global HRM integration.

The case for global HRM integration

Prior to embarking on a discussion about global integration in MNCs, it is first necessary to define what is meant by global integration, especially since it comprises two fairly abstract terms. In essence, global integration can be said to be about the achievement of at least one of three key objectives: (i) the *control* of foreign subsidiaries, (ii) the *transfer* of practices to those subsidiaries, and (iii) the appropriate *adaptation* of activities that requires both an understanding of parent practices and local conditions.

In terms of subsidiary control, the international management literature depicts integration as comprising both a formal, direct, control-based dimension and a more informal, indirect, co-ordination-based dimension. Accordingly, control has been defined as any process in which a person, group or organization determines or intentionally affects what another person, group or organization will do (Baliga and Jaeger 1984: 26), whereas co-ordination is referred to as a means through which the different parts of an organization (e.g. foreign subsidiaries) are integrated or linked together to accomplish a collective goal (Van de Ven *et al.* 1976). Global integration from a control perspective is thus both about control and co-ordination with these being used in combination to achieve consistency of international business activities across borders (Kim *et al.* 2003).

Since global integration requires activities in foreign subsidiaries to be centrally managed and/or made interdependent, those activities need to be transferred to the subsidiaries. The transfer of firm-specific practices (e.g. HRM) for the purposes of achieving consistency and alignment amongst foreign subsidiaries also addresses the need to integrate dispersed knowledge and practices, which is argued to be an important basis for competitive advantage in firms (Grant 1996).

Lastly, the third objective of making appropriate adaptations to activities makes the distinction that global integration does not imply total standardisation. In the same way that global strategy is argued not to mean doing everything the same way everywhere (e.g. Kanter and Dretler 1998), for global integration and the transfer of practices to be truly effective some degree of adaptation to account for national contextual differences is needed to move beyond simple imitation of those practices towards a deeper belief in their value (discussed later in this chapter). In reference to institutional theory, 'appropriate' adaptations to transferred practices do not denote a substantial shift away from global integration, but are intended to result in greater host legitimacy amongst regulatory, normative and cognitive institutions rendering the practice easier to comprehend and put into practice (Jensen and Szulanski 2004).

These three objectives of global integration, which could also be seen as 'lenses', are now used as a reference point for the issues covered in this chapter, starting with the discussion of those factors driving the global integration of HRM.

▶ Drivers of global integration

Before presenting arguments why the global integration of HRM is becoming more desirable, it is worth re-visiting the arguments why global integration in general is becoming more attractive for MNCs. To do this, the arguments are grouped into three categories of global integration 'drivers': (i) environmental drivers, (ii) strategic drivers, and (iii) structural drivers. You will note that these tie in with the discussion of strategy, structure and the international business environment in Chapter 5. There are strong interrelationships between these categories; some drivers of global integration are going to be related to drivers in the other categories. Nevertheless, the classification assists us in acknowledging the source of the driver, whether it's within or outside of the MNC's direct control, and provides us with a clearer picture of the direction these different, mutually reinforcing drivers of global integration might take over time.

Environmental drivers have already been discussed at length in Chapter 1 in connection with the forces of globalization. The novelty and limits of globalization notwithstanding, there are many features of globalization that are making global integration more feasible, more desirable and even more necessary. To name but a few – the diminishing significance of national borders, supranational integration, the dismantling of trade and investment barriers, the far-reaching deregulation of markets, the emergence of global customers, rapid developments in the capabilities and spread of new information- and web-based technologies, and the opening up of large developing economies such as the BRIC nations of Brazil, Russia, India and China – have contributed to the intensification of competition. One could argue they have also promoted the attractiveness of global integration to MNCs. Although some 84 of the world's largest 100 MNCs are headquartered in one of the Triad regions (North America, Europe and Japan), on average they have affiliates in 39 different foreign countries, and at 53 per cent they now employ more foreign nationals as a proportion of their total workforce (UN 2007). The growing levels of complexity that have arisen from operating in a large number of foreign locations comprising very different national business systems have increased the need for MNCs to foster some degree of control over foreign subsidiaries and to transfer common practices to them. However, this complexity also inhibits the MNCs' ability to do so. Put another way, the differences in how organizational practices are carried out in different parts of the MNC are both a prerequisite and a constraint for the transfer of practices. Whilst this chapter makes arguments for differences being a prerequisite, or a 'driver', Chapter 7 will present the case for them being constraints.

Environmental drivers of global integration put pressure on MNCs to take a course of action regarding their international strategy and structure. *Strategic drivers* capture the business advantages that are realizable by pursuing global integration. Evans *et al.* (2002: 105) list a number of such strategic drivers that they see as supporting the adoption of a globally integrated approach to managing the MNC. Achieving *economies of scale* can help a firm to lower its unit costs by centralising core value chain activities. This might take the form, for example, of creating a network of specialized operations which are then tightly controlled by a central hub. Establishing *value chain linkages* between, for example, R&D and manufacturing allows the firm to exploit its position as a leader in innovation and to be at the forefront of any technological and competitive changes. *Serving global customers* refers to the need for suppliers of products or services to become as globally integrated as their clients who determine things such as price, quality and delivery on an increasingly global basis. Global integration can also facilitate *global branding* insofar as it allows an MNC to promote a consistent brand image around the world and to benefit from an efficient application of marketing tools such as advertising and merchandising. *Leveraging capabilities* involves the transfer of valuable capabilities developed in a firm's competitive domestic market to its international operations. *World-class standardization,* on the other hand, refers to standardization and central control over complex core processes, which can help to ensure high quality and a competitive edge. The strategic driver of *competitive platforms* is based on the idea that if the HQ tightly controls subsidiaries it can allow them to respond quickly to shifts in the competitive landscape and also facilitates a more rapid global expansion of operations via the redeployment of resources. Lastly, *information advantages* refers to the advantages of being present in several different international locations when it comes to identifying and monitoring first-hand the prices of goods and services as well as the suppliers who provide them.

One could also add *business process outsourcing* to the list of strategic drivers, especially when it involves contracting out an activity to an offshore provider or to a shared service centre. The outsourcing industry has grown rapidly in recent years with most of the world's leading MNCs now outsourcing at least one of its core business processes (see Chapter 15). However, for outsourcing to an offshore service provider to work more effectively, the activity to be outsourced ideally needs to be carried out in the same way, or at least similar, in each location, otherwise the service provider would need to get up to speed on all the different ways that the activity is performed. In this sense, the global integration of a set of activities (e.g. HRM) is seen as a necessary step prior to reaping the benefits from their outsourcing.

Beyond the strategic drivers that confer certain competitive advantages to MNCs, there are characteristics of the MNC itself that lend themselves to global integration and thus the transfer of organizational practices. These are referred to here as *structural drivers*. Unlike strategic drivers, these characteristics can act as either facilitators or inhibitors of global integration. For instance, the first structural driver is the MNC's *country of origin,* and the corresponding 'country-of-origin effect' (discussed in Chapter 5) that this has on an MNC's tendencies, amongst other things, to transfer its HRM practices (see e.g. Ferner 1997). As mentioned, the evidence suggests that the way an MNC manages its international workforce, including the degree of global integration it seeks over its foreign subsidiaries, is disproportionately influenced by its roots in the domestic business system. More specifically, MNCs from countries that have been economically successful have an incentive to integrate those practices in their foreign subsidiaries that are seen as having contributed to this success. For instance, many US MNCs transferred 'Taylorist' forms of work organization and formalized payment systems to their European subsidiaries in the post-war period (e.g. Kogut 1991). More recent evidence reveals that several US MNCs transfer practices designed to increase the 'diversity' of their workforces, such as quotas on women in management positions and equal treatment for homosexual employees, in the belief that such diversity policies form a part of the firm's competitive advantage (Ferner *et al.* 2004). Similarly, in the 1980s many Japanese MNCs sought to integrate 'lean production' and its associated HRM practices, such as teamworking and employee involvement in maintaining quality standards, in their European and North American subsidiaries.

However, Pudelko and Harzing (2007) remind us that in the global integration-local differentiation dilemma, global integration does not necessarily involve the integration of practices found at MNC headquarters, but around a national management model perceived as representing global best practice. Indeed, in their study of HRM practices in the foreign subsidiaries of US, German and Japanese MNCs, they found that the '*dominance effect*' of the US model of HRM was more important than country-of-origin and localization effects in explaining the HRM practices found in the foreign subsidiaries. In support of the argument in this chapter that global HRM integration is becoming more desirable, Pudelko and Harzing conclude that there does appear to be convergence towards a worldwide best practices model of HRM.

A second structural driver of global integration is the nature of an MNC's *international management structures*. In particular, a structure that is based on national units, which Porter (1986) calls 'multi-domestic', limits the contact between actors in different countries, thereby constraining the scope for integration. In contrast, a structure that is based around international product divisions, which Porter terms 'global', deepens the linkages across borders within the firm. With respect to the HR function, Marginson *et al.* (1995) have shown that MNCs with a global structure are more likely to have regular meetings of HR managers across their sites, to have an international HR policy committee and to promote the mobility of staff through international assignments. All of these structures have the potential to act as mechanisms through which global integration occurs. Thus, while a multi-domestic structure limits the scope for global integration, a global structure promotes it. Many MNCs have moved towards adopting a matrix structure in which international divisions coexist with regional aspects to the structure, normally based around continents. This type of matrix deepens international management structures along two dimensions, providing significant scope for integration and the transfer of practices. The Benchmarking Survey of Global HRM (cited in Sparrow *et al.* 2004: 55) found that MNCs still operate with different international management structures, but over 67 per cent aimed to create an integrated organisation (referred to as 'geocentric') where there exists "*a balance between central coordinating processes and flexibility at the local level, with a strong global culture that fosters integration*". It would also appear in structural terms, therefore, that global integration has become an important goal for a majority of MNCs.

The third structural driver is a characteristic of foreign subsidiaries, namely their *mode of establishment*. In general, the constraints facing management at HQ in integrating foreign subsidiaries are greater when the subsidiaries have been acquired. This is because the firm inherits a pre-existing set of practices that may prove difficult to change, and also because the act of acquisition itself may create suspicion and resistance among employees in the acquired units. In foreign subsidiaries established as 'greenfield sites', on the other hand, HQ management has greater freedom to introduce their own practices. Accordingly, research suggests that MNCs that seek to implement practices that diverge from the 'norm' in a particular country grow mainly via greenfield investments. Indeed, we find more expatriates from HQ in greenfield sites (e.g. Harzing 1999) as well as HRM practices that more closely resemble those of the parent (Rosenzweig and Nohria 1994; Björkman and Lu 2001).

While the country of origin shapes the inclination of MNCs to achieve global integration and the firm's structure and method of growth affects the constraints that they face in so doing, the last structural driver is arguably even more important in shaping whether MNCs want to globally integrate and transfer organizational practices in the first place: the extent to which processes of production and service provision are integrated on an international basis, and where they are, how this occurs. This is referred to here as the *extent and nature of the integration of subsidiary operations*. Some MNCs are not integrated internationally in that their units in different countries operate independently of one another and perform quite different functions. This is the case in conglomerates which have sought to reduce risk through a high degree of diversification and in which senior management exercise financial control over their units but do not exercise operational control since technologies and patterns of work organization differ significantly (Edwards *et al*. 2009). You will notice from the explanations below that this last structural driver of scope and integration of subsidiary operations might also be classified as an 'industry effect' since certain structural configurations are more commonly found in specific industries (Ghoshal and Nohria 1993).

Where the international integration of subsidiary operations does take place it can take two primary forms, each of which has quite different implications for the extent of overall global integration. One of these is 'replicated production' in which units in different countries perform very similar operations. Examples of this are the large consultancy firms such as Accenture and IT service providers such as IBM, which are increasingly offering standardized services in different countries. In this case, the similarity in the nature of the operating units means that the HQ has a clear incentive to spread practices throughout its operations in order to apply lessons learned in one unit to other units in the MNC and to develop common policies to encourage the mobility of staff across their operations.

The other variant of integrated subsidiary operations is 'segmented production', which involves units in different countries performing distinct functions within a corporate production process. Gereffi (1999) uses the term 'global commodity chains' (GCCs) to describe the way in which segmented production can occur. Gereffi distinguishes between two types of GCC. First, 'producer-driven commodity chains' are 'those in which large, usually transnational, manufacturers play the central roles in coordinating production networks' (see Figure 6.1). These are characteristic of capital and technology intensive industries such as cars and computers. The way in which the Japanese motor firms have broken up the production of a car so that different parts of the process take place in different Asian countries is an example of this. Second, 'buyer-driven commodity chains' are 'those industries in which large retailers, designers and trading companies play the pivotal role in setting up decentralised production networks in a variety of exporting countries' (see Figure 6.2). This type of chain is found in labour-intensive consumer goods sectors such as clothing, household goods and consumer electronics. Firms like Nike and Gap, for example, have established this type of

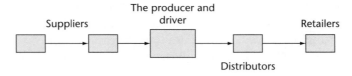

Figure 6.1 **Producer-driven chains**

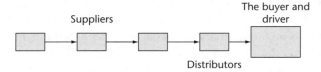

Figure 6.2 **Buyer-driven chains**

chain. In both these types of 'segmented production' chains the incentive to integrate practices is significant also, but different in nature from those associated with replicated production. Some coordination between these links in the chain is necessary, meaning that management has an incentive to ensure that there are cross-national teams of key staff, such as those in logistics and R&D, for example. However, since the functions performed in different countries are quite distinct from one another there is very little incentive to harmonize the firm's approach to managing most occupational groups (Edwards *et al.* 2009). Indeed, one of the limits to the standardization of HR policies across borders has been the acceleration in the distribution of MNCs' operational responsibilities to various third parties, leaving MNC structures to become more accurately described as 'differentiated networks' (Nohria and Ghoshal 1997). In many industries like automobile manufacturing and pharmaceuticals, MNCs in a relatively short period of time have gone from being 'doers' to 'integrators in a value net' (*Economist* 2007). We pick up on this idea of different forms of integration in the following chapter.

Having indentified a comprehensive list of environmental, strategic and structural drivers of global integration, it is worth noting that there is a weakness in this approach of implying that outcomes (i.e. global integration) follow unproblematically from these drivers. This is picked up in the next chapter and is based on arguments presented in Chapter 5 that there are various organizational actors involved in the integration (or 'diffusion') process, who will draw on their sources of power to further their own interests and thus encourage or obstruct integration efforts.

▶ Drivers of global HRM integration

The drivers discussed so far could apply to a wide range of MNC activities or business functions. The purpose of this section is to highlight additional drivers of global integration that are HRM specific, i.e. they encourage heightened levels of HQ control over subsidiary HRM practices. It is worth pointing out here that some argue that integration (and its associated drivers) really has its roots at the business function level (Kim *et al.* 2003). Thus, we equally need to look at how the HR function itself *contributes* to the process of globalization, and therefore global integration, in addition to how it might be affected by it. However, as Sparrow *et al.* (2004) suggest, the HR function at least currently is not one we could consider as being particularly globalised.

In their survey of HR professionals across 64 firms, Sparrow *et al.* (2004: 59–60) identified five 'organizational drivers' behind the globalisation, and functional re-alignment, of HRM. Touching on some drivers already mentioned elsewhere, they comprised the following: efficiency orientation (centralization and outsourcing of business processes);

the creation of core business processes; building rapid global presence (including the e-enablement of management); information exchange, organizational learning and partnership (including knowledge management), and the localization of decision-making.

A further driver of global HRM integration relates to the belief by top management that HRM is a key source of competitive advantage. Studies by, for example, Beechler and Yang (1994) and Bae *et al.* (1998) found that when an MNC's top management placed significant value on their HRM practices as part of their achieving superior performance, the integration of those HRM practices into their foreign subsidiaries was much more extensive than in the subsidiaries of MNCs which did not.

Another HRM-specific driver concerns perceptions of internal equity. The argument here is that if HRM policies and practices are carried out in much the same way in all MNC locations, subject to some minor local adjustments, then MNC employees will feel as though they are being treated equally and thus fairly (Rosenzweig and Nohria 1994). Of course, one can think of several cases where being treated the same is not likely to result in perceptions of fairness (e.g. individual, performance-related pay in a collectivist culture or conducting all managerial appraisals in English), but global HR policy frameworks are nevertheless argued to be more equitable than adhering to a multitude of different requests.

Cost minimization has also been cited as a reason for globally integrating certain aspects of HRM. Schmitt and Sadowski (2003) argue that there are economies of scale to be gained in HRM policy development and implementation if it takes place at HQ and transferred to foreign subsidiaries. Indeed, when compared to the greater costs associated with decentralization, MNCs in their study were shown to transfer various aspects of their parent HRM practices (e.g. variable compensation) to foreign subsidiaries. However, the relatively greater costs of centralising aspects of industrial relations (e.g. collective bargaining) led to stronger host-country effects and less transfer.

From an evolutionary perspective, the required organizational levels of integration now necessary to execute global strategies has led to calls for a strategic global HRM agenda (Kiessling and Harvey 2005). That is to say, the HR function is being pressured to become more globally integrated in order to support broader MNC strategies and follow suit with the activities of other business functions that have already become more globalized (e.g. manufacturing and logistics). Supporting this evolutionary view, Sparrow *et al.* (2004: 62) believe that the global HR function 'is both dependent upon and will be shaped by the globalising activity of two contiguous functions' – information systems, and marketing and corporate communications.

Taylor (2006), on the other hand, argues that global HRM integration is becoming more desirable due to a greater focus on the leverage of knowledge and organizational learning (or social capital) within the MNC's internal network, together with increasing pressures on MNCs to address the 'sustainability' agenda, which will require the international HR function to integrate economic, social and environmental criteria (the so-called 'triple bottom line') into subsidiary HRM practices (discussed in Chapter 12).

With regards to the impact of technology on global HRM, Sparrow *et al.* (2004: 83) conclude that 'the introduction of e-enabled HR, with the associated generic HR processes supported by IT systems that it entails, brings a significant change in the focus of the international HR function'. Indeed, the rise in popularity of 'integrating' technologies such as the SAP software platform, together with the 'push' of these technologies by IT and HR consultants, is reportedly transforming how HRM is delivered (Stone and Gueutal 2005). For some MNCs, such as Shell, the global integration of HRM, partly facilitated by integrative technology and the creation of one global HR system, has been a necessary step prior to the transfer of certain HR processes to shared service centres (see Chapter 15 for a discussion of HR outsourcing). Three 'business case' drivers of these globally integrated e-HRM systems are argued to include, firstly, the reduction of HR transaction costs and headcount, secondly, the substitution of physical capability by leveraging digital assets in the sense that HR information can be used flexibly on an infinite number of occasions at little or no marginal cost, and thirdly, the transformation of the HR 'business model' by e-enabling the HR function to provide strategic value to the business that it previously could not do, thus facilitating a movement away from transactional tasks to more strategic, business-driven roles (Stone and Guetal 2005; Reddington and Martin 2007).

In reference to the 'control' objective of global HRM integration, three 'control-based' benefits of globally integrated e-HRM systems are, firstly, bureaucratic control by establishing procedural standards about how the system is used and thus how core HRM processes should be carried out; secondly, output control by communicating goals and monitoring them through an array of sophisticated management reporting tools; and thirdly, control via centralisation by restricting access rights and introducing layers of electronic transaction authorization (Smale, 2008).

In summing up the arguments why the global integration of HRM is becoming more desirable to MNCs, Taylor (2006) comments that despite the number of potentially convincing motives, it is unclear from extant empirical research which drivers are most important for MNCs, and under which conditions. An equally, if not more important question is how MNCs should best go about achieving global HRM integration – a subject to which we now turn.

HRM integration mechanisms in multinational corporations

The question of how management at HQ can influence a unit's or individual's behaviour to make it consistent with the overall goals of the firm is not a new one. However, it has certainly taken on added significance in the context of geographically dispersed MNC operations where the dilemma of simultaneously achieving suitable levels of global integration and local responsiveness renders it much more complex. It is not surprising then that studies on the tools (or mechanisms) of integration have a long history. Indeed, a study by Martinez and Jarillo published in 1989, which summarized the empirical work conducted on this subject since 1953, reported on the findings of 85 studies.

The major trends to emerge from this research were that the number of integration mechanisms used by MNCs and their degree of subtlety were both shown to be on the increase (Martinez and Jarillo 1989). In addition to the bureaucratic and personal

mechanisms of control, MNCs have been actively using other forms of lateral or 'unobtrusive' (Coller 1996; Edwards 1998) types of integration mechanisms such as cultural
control (Baliga and Jaeger 1984) and normative integration (Ghoshal and Nohria 1989)
in order to harmonise cultural differences between foreign affiliates. Over time, we
have witnessed MNCs becoming more adept at deploying complementary mechanisms
that draw upon, for example, organizational context (Prahalad and Doz 1981), power
relations (Ferner and Edwards 1995), socialisation and networks (Harzing 1999), and
even emotional integration (Ghoshal and Gratton 2002).

In view of the extensive portfolio of integration tools that MNCs can now deploy,
several attempts have been made to categorise these tools using different criteria. In
turn, this has led to discussions about the relative merits of different types of integration mechanism. We concentrate here on classifications rooted in the control and co-
ordination literature, which has represented the theoretical foundation of most studies
conducted on global integration in MNCs.

▶ Types of global integration mechanisms

Much of the early research on integration mechanisms in firms approaches the issue from
a control perspective and the ways in which an organization can be managed so that it
achieves its objectives (Ouchi 1979). The control-based classifications of integration
mechanisms that have followed generally acknowledge there to be two fundamental targets of control – output or behaviour – and two different means of controlling them –
directly or indirectly. For instance, Harzing and Sorge (2003) present four major types of
corporate control mechanisms based on combinations of whether the mechanism is
direct/explicit or indirect/implicit, and personal/cultural or impersonal/bureaucratic/
Itechnocratic (see Table 6.1). Kim *et al.* (2003), on the other hand, present four 'global
integration modes' – centralization-, formalization-, information- and people-based
modes – which we will discuss in more detail in connection with the empirical evidence
on their usage in integrating HRM.

Centralization-based integration mechanisms (cf. Harzing and Sorge's centralization
and direct supervision) refer to where decision-making authority resides at MNC headquarters and are argued to be particularly effective in producing global scale, scope and
learning efficiencies. As a means to integrate HRM specifically, empirical studies have
shown HQ authority to be most frequently exercised in determining senior management pay, recruitment and development (Edwards *et al.* 1996) as well as in making

Table 6.1   **Classification of control mechanisms**

	Personal/Cultural (founded on social interaction)	**Impersonal/Bureaucratic/Technocratic (founded on instrumental artefacts)**
Direct/Explicit	Centralization, Direct supervision, Expatriate control	Standardization, Formalization
Indirect/Implicit	Socialization, Informal communica-tion, Management training	Output control, Planning

Source: Harzing and Sorge (2003)

decisions on financially sensitive HRM issues like headcount and salary expenditure (Martin and Beaumont 1999). In general, however, studies have found centralisation-based tools of HRM integration to be uncommon when compared to other more 'unobtrusive' tools (Edwards 1998). It has also been noted that the source of centralization in large MNCs can in fact lie at the regional, not global level (Ferner *et al.* 2004).

Formalization-based integration mechanisms (cf. Harzing and Sorge's standardization and formalization) refer to the codification and standardization of work procedures and policies on a global basis. Attempts by MNCs to devise global HRM policy frameworks have been shown to be commonplace (e.g. Tempel 2001). However, whilst some studies describe global HRM policies as a means of creating a common language across foreign subsidiaries (Hetrick 2002), others argue that formalization efforts are dependent on other less formal 'social' control mechanisms for their overall effectiveness (Ferner 2000).

Information-based mechanisms (cf. Harzing and Sorge's output control and planning) include those tools which facilitate the international flow of information whether it is via simple databases or via more complex electronic data interchanges. In essence, information-based integration is intended to be a means for HQ to communicate and regulate information that is central to strategic decision-making and thereby influencing the choices made by subsidiary managers. This mode of integration is likely to be most effective when the parent has to transmit information in large quantities, in a short period of time or when the information can be easily interpreted. As mentioned above, MNCs have been shown to use HR information systems to establish procedural standards about how HRM processes are carried out, to communicate HR goals and monitor them, and to introduce different levels of access rights and transaction authorisation (Smale 2008). Several other studies indicate that MNCs are rolling out e-HRM systems with similar integrative roles in mind (see e.g. Tansley *et al.* 2001; Ruël *et al.* 2004; Ruta 2005).

Lastly, *people*-based integration (cf. Harzing and Sorge's expatriate control and informal communication) involves person-to-person interaction facilitated through meetings, teams, committees, the use of integrators, and the transfer of people across units. People-based integration is considered most effective when involving tacit forms of knowledge that are best conveyed face-to-face. In terms of people-based integration of HRM, whilst some studies reveal the significance of expatriate presence in establishing subsidiary HRM practices that closely resemble the parent's (Rosenzweig and Nohria 1994; Björkman and Lu 2001), others describe the multifaceted roles that expatriates play in the transfer of HRM practices, including that of 'role model', 'boundary spanner', 'coach' (Hetrick 2002), and communicator of HRM-related knowledge (Gamble 2003). In addition to expatriation, HRM practices have traditionally been integrated through the global or regional networking activities of HR professionals who come together to share ideas and best practices (Harris *et al.* 2003). The integration of HRM in this group format is suggested to be on the increase in connection with the rise of informal networking and knowledge transfer 'spaces' such as HR Communities of Practice (Sparrow *et al.* 2004).

One type of integration mechanism that appears in Harzing and Sorge's (2003) classification but not in Kim *et al.*'s (2003) is that of socialization. Socialization, or corporate socialization, refers to the establishment of a strong corporate culture around a shared set of values, objectives and beliefs across MNC units (Nohria and Ghoshal 1994). The use of organizational culture by MNCs as a mechanism of control to change the work values of host-country employees has also been referred to as organizational acculturation (Selmer and de Leon 1996, 2002). This form of integration shares many similarities with the construction of a shared organizational identity whereby the MNC attempts to foster a shared sense of 'who we are' (e.g. Pratt and Foreman 2000). Although some are questioning the viability of this type of soft, informal mechanism of control (e.g. Welch and Welch 2006), recent case study evidence shows that many leading European, North American and Asian MNCs have to some extent attempted to integrate corporate culture or values into their HRM tools and processes (Stahl *et al.* forthcoming). In other words, MNCs are using HRM practices as a channel through which to strengthen and integrate corporate values throughout their foreign subsidiaries (e.g. by including the values in recruitment and appraisal criteria).

▶ Patterns of HRM integration mechanism usage

Whilst classifications like the above make us aware of the range of integration mechanisms at the MNC's disposal, they do not provide us with answers to the questions of (1) how they are used collectively (i.e. are they complementary or substitutes), (2) which ones are most important in the integration of HRM (e.g. compared to the integration of marketing or manufacturing), and (3) why MNCs are likely to place different emphasis on their usage. This section summarizes what the empirical research to date has to say on these issues.

Firstly, considering how integration mechanisms are used collectively, it is the general consensus that MNCs use multiple mechanisms in combination at different levels of intensity, otherwise referred to as a 'systems' approach (Kim *et al.* 2003). Also in the HRM literature we see MNCs using a diverse array of direct and indirect mechanisms in combination and at varying strengths (Edwards 1998; Tempel 2001; Smale 2008), suggesting that HRM integration mechanisms too are used as complements, not substitutes. In addition to this, we are told that there is intra-MNC variance in the usage and emphasis placed on certain mechanisms, indicating that the uniqueness of HQ–subsidiary relations requires HRM to be integrated in a number of different ways (Edwards *et al.* 1996). Patterns of mechanism usage are also found to differ between MNCs of the same nationality (Wolf 1997).

In terms of which mechanisms are more important in the integration of HRM, we have already pointed out above that centralisation-based methods are relatively uncommon and are generally reserved for a few select areas of HRM. We are also aware that information-based mechanisms in the shape of 'integrative' e-HRM technologies are on the rise. In addition, the role of expatriates as a people-based mechanism has been shown to be pivotal in facilitating the integration of HRM, in particular in their role of two-way communication regarding parent HRM practices and host subsidiary concerns (Hetrick 2002; Gamble 2003). Subsidiary HR managers also shape how integration mechanisms are used, determined by their level of HR competence, their relationships with subsidiary top management and corporate HR, and their networking activities with other local HR professionals working in other MNCs (Smale 2008). Answering the question about which mechanisms are more important, however, may also require us to distinguish between individual HRM practices. Based on the empirically supported assumption that some HRM practices are easier to integrate than others (see e.g. Lu and Björkman 1997; Myloni *et al.* 2004, 2007), we would expect to see a differential usage of integration mechanisms across individual HRM practices. For instance, Sparrow *et al.* (2004: 56-7) report the findings of a CIPD survey, which shows that the most centrally determined HRM practices include expatriate management, management development, and succession planning, whereas the most regionally/locally determined HRM practices include the recruitment of non-management personnel, training, and employment law.

The answer to the third question of why MNCs are likely to place different degrees of emphasis on their usage of different mechanisms is much less clear. Despite a wealth of research on control in MNCs, attempts to explain or predict patterns of mechanism usage remain largely inconclusive (see e.g. Harzing 1999; Hennart 2005; Björkman 2007). Although there is evidence of some country-of-origin effect (Harzing and Sorge 2003), we are not sure of the selection criteria MNCs use when assembling their configurations of integrating mechanisms. One potential reason for this lack of coherent findings is the arguably false assumption that management at HQ alone decide how integration will take place. In reality, integration is argued to be a highly contested and political process, characterized by the use of power resources by both the HQ and subsidiary management (Martin and Beaumont 1999; Ferner *et al.* 2005). For example, Ferner *et al.* (2004) suggest that subsidiary management's ability to leverage their role as 'interpreters' of the local context can act as a powerful means of resisting centralization- or formalization-based attempts at HRM integration. The 'political' nature of HRM integration (or 'diffusion') is discussed in more detail in the next chapter.

In summing up, MNCs can and do make use of a very wide range of global integration mechanisms, which they use in combination to differing extents. In this sense, HQ management's task is to try and find the most effective configuration of mechanisms in order to achieve the desired degree of consistency across foreign operations. We are still unsure precisely which criteria HQ management use when assembling these configurations, but evidence suggests that one size rarely fits all in terms of when to use certain mechanisms. Indeed, if the process of integration is as complex and political as suggested, then explaining patterns of HRM integration mechanism usage in MNCs is likely to remain elusive for some time to come.

Achieving global HRM integration

So far in this chapter we have discussed the key aims behind global HRM integration, the reasons why global HRM integration is becoming more desirable, and the different ways in which integration can be implemented. One important issue that remains, however, is how we identify the existence and extent of global HRM integration in MNCs.

Common to most studies of HRM in MNCs are attempts to explain variations in the extent to which HRM practices found in subsidiaries resemble those of the parent (denoting integration) as opposed to those of local firms (denoting differentiation) (see e.g. Rosenzweig and Nohria 1994; Björkman and Lu 2001). Indeed, the majority of the empirical literature is set against the associated global-local dilemma (for a detailed review see Edwards and Kuruvilla 2005). It has not been until recently that the weaknesses of assessing the degree of global HRM integration in this way have been highlighted. This section discusses these weaknesses under the headings of conceptual weaknesses and methodological weaknesses.

Turning to the *conceptual* weaknesses, reliance on the degree of resemblance to parent practices as an indicator of integration is problematic for a couple of reasons. The first is to do with the term 'resemblance'. Resemblance implies, and often entails in empirical work, an analysis of statements concerning whether the HRM practices that exist in the subsidiary are similar or dissimilar to those found in the parent. The conceptual bone of contention here is whether we (or HQ management) are satisfied that global integration has taken place when a similar HRM practice 'exists' in the subsidiary. Even if a practice exists, this tells us nothing about the extent to which subsidiary personnel value the practice or even use it. In the same way that Davenport and Prusak (1998) suggest that a successful transfer of knowledge involves its transmission, absorption and use, Kostova (1999) argues that the successful transfer of an organisational practice should be defined in terms of its institutionalisation, i.e. the extent to which recipient employees have both implemented *and* internalized the practice. According to Kostova, whereas 'implementing' refers to the adoption of formal rules, 'internalizing' means attaching symbolic meaning and value to the practice. This stricter conceptual definition of transfer is argued to be necessary given a subsidiary's scope to respond to the transfer in the form of different patterns of adoption ranging from 'active' to 'ceremonial' (Kostova and Roth 2002). Björkman and Lervik (2007) expand on this definition of transfer success to include the 'integration' of the practice in the recipient unit. In addition to implementation and internalization above, they define integration to mean the degree to which 'a transferred practice is connected and linked up with existing routines and practices' (2007: 322). This, they argue, sits more comfortably with the notion that HRM should not be viewed as a collection of individual practices, but is rather a system or configuration of practices that mutually reinforce each other and work in concert.

The second conceptual weakness concerns the term 'parent'. Although when talking about global integration and the mechanisms of integration it is common for us to refer to the parent as the source of HRM practices and the instigator of integration efforts, we could question whether global integration cannot originate from elsewhere. For instance, the study by Pudelko and Harzing (2007) reveals that some foreign MNC subsidiaries are just as likely, if not more, to integrate HRM practices from a 'global' best practices model (the dominance effect) rather than the parent's. Furthermore, an exclusive focus on parent resemblance is going to obscure the identification of global integration that may have taken place via 'reverse diffusion', i.e. the integration of subsidiary HRM practices into the parent and other foreign units (e.g. Edwards 1998). This is discussed further in Chapter 7. One final criticism of the 'parent' versus 'local' resemblance indicator, is the misleading assumption that it is always an either/or question, when in fact it is not. In a recent study of HRM practices found in MNC subsidiaries in China over a ten-year period from 1996–2006 (Björkman *et al.* 2008), the findings indicate that HRM practices in MNC units located in China had come to increasingly resemble both the practices found in local firms *as well as* the practices found at MNC headquarters. This can be interpreted as MNCs having been successful in integrating some of their parent HRM practices into their Chinese subsidiaries, whilst during the same time period those Chinese subsidiaries have modelled their HRM practices on other local firms, 'local' firms crucially including the Chinese subsidiaries of other MNCs. In this sense, pressures for the global integration (parent resemblance) and local differentiation (local resemblance) of HRM are not always in conflict.

In terms of *methodological* weaknesses one could argue that many of the existing studies on HRM in foreign subsidiaries have not asked the right people the right questions. For example, when asking subsidiary top managers to comment on the resemblance between subsidiary and parent HRM practices we are making the assumption that these respondents have in-depth knowledge of both. If those that are asked are expatriates, then we might expect this to be the case, although this is of course no guarantee, especially if they have no background or interest in HR. If those that are asked are host-country nationals, including those who have never visited HQ, then basing the measure of integration on their responses may prove to be misleading. Asking respondents to comment on the resemblance between subsidiary and 'local' HRM practices is more problematic still, since we often lack sufficient information on the kinds of 'local firms' the respondents are basing their comparisons (e.g. leading MNCs, state-owned enterprises, or small entrepreneurial firms).

In terms of asking the right people, many of the survey-based studies on HRM in MNCs have suffered from single-respondent (or 'common method') bias in the sense that findings are based on the sole responses of either corporate *or* subsidiary representatives. More specifically, the exclusive use of HR policy makers such as HR professionals and top management as key informants haven't allowed us to draw accurate distinctions between what is 'intended' by HQ versus what is actually 'implemented' lower down in foreign subsidiaries (Khilji and Wang 2006). Together with conceptual ambiguity regarding whether HRM practices are implemented, internalised or integrated, we may not know as much as we think about HRM practices in foreign subsidiaries and thus the extent of global HRM integration in MNCs.

Recent suggestions to address these conceptual and methodological weaknesses have included a focus on the perceptions of different HRM stakeholders. By studying differences in perceptions of HRM practices and differences in their perceived effectiveness (see e.g. Mitsuhashi *et al.* 2000; Farndale and Paauwe 2007), it is hoped that we can avoid the 'intended' versus 'implemented' dilemma and move towards a deeper understanding of what is 'espoused' versus 'experienced' (Wright and Nishii, 2007) that includes the reactions of subsidiary employees to the global integration of HRM.

CASE STUDY

Globally integrating diversity management at Transco

An underlying assumption in the field of international HRM is that unlike the practices attached to other business functions, HRM practices are among the most culturally and institutionally embedded in national contexts and are thus the most difficult to integrate globally, typically requiring high levels of local adaptation. This would especially seem to be the case for the HRM practice of diversity management, the global integration of which has been shown to be problematic even between the US and the UK (Ferner *et al.* 2005), which we are led to believe have broadly similar institutional arrangements.

In the mid-1990's Transco, a well-known European MNC operating in over 100 countries and employing more than 100,000 people, underwent significant organizational restructuring that saw the launch of its new 'Global Organization'. This represented a distinctive move away from its previous diversified strategy and multi-domestic orientation. This new 'global' approach included the streamlining of its core businesses, a matrix structure organizational design, and far-reaching efforts at process standardization. In terms of global HR strategy, this has translated into aims of greater standardization of HRM processes and the creation of a globally integrated HRM system.

Commencing in 1997, Transco introduced a global workforce diversity management (DM) drive as an extension of its global business principles and a reinforcement of its existing core values. The ten-year global integration plan sought to integrate diversity and inclusiveness into key business and HRM practices throughout their worldwide operations. In doing so, Transco aimed to attract and retain key global talent, allow for a clearer focus on diverse customers and markets, to increase productivity through improved employee engagement, and to strengthen its reputation within the global community.

Representing one of the smallest foreign units, Transco Finland was established nearly 100 years ago and employed over 1,700 people. Along with several other select European operations, Transco Finland was included in the first European wave of DM integration which began in early 2003. In terms of the Finnish national context for workforce diversity, Finland could be characterized as somewhat bipolar. On the one hand, the appreciation of individual differences such as ethnicity, cultural background and sexual orientation remained relatively underdeveloped, in part due to Finland's relative cultural, racial, religious and linguistic homogeneity in the past. On the other hand, Finland was also representative of a Nordic welfare state that emphasized an inclusive political ideology, which has served to promote with

good effect certain aspects of diversity. Perhaps the best example of this is gender equality where Finland earned third position in the most recent *Global Gender Gap Report* published by the World Economic Forum.

Since Transco's global DM policies and practices were largely based on the 'successful' US subsidiary's model, Transco's global DM integration was perhaps better described as involving first 'reverse diffusion' from the US subsidiary to Transco headquarters, and then 'forward diffusion' throughout the rest of the MNC. From the outset, the global integration of Transco's global DM practices to the rest of the MNC involved a significant investment in infrastructure and resources, reflected in the vast array of integration mechanisms used.

In terms of *people*-based mechanisms, diversity co-ordinators were deployed who had full working responsibility for the integration of DM into the Finnish subsidiary. In addition, 'diversity auditors' were dispatched to monitor DM integration progress and all local line managers were brought to the European headquarters for centrally delivered diversity training. Regarding *information*-based mechanisms, the internet was used to publish Transco's global values and commitment to managing diversity, and included its progress for the benefit of diverse stakeholder groups. The corporate intranet was extensively used in storing large volumes of diversity-related information, training material, organizational surveys and leadership self-assessment tools. *Formalization*-based mechanisms were the most extensively used, appearing to indicate that this was being treated as somewhat of an assurance process. Indeed, the local CEO had to sign an annual Diversity Assurance Letter, confirming how far the subsidiary has come in working towards agreed targets. Other formalization-based mechanisms included the integration of corporate diversity values (evidence of socialization) and global DM policy frameworks into regional diversity plans. Based on these plans, diversity and inclusiveness performance criteria were then formally integrated into unit- and individual-level balanced scorecards. Lastly, *centralization* was not used to a great a extent but did take the form of target setting and plans that were centrally determined by the corporate-level Diversity Council and Diversity 'Steering Group'. Whilst these bodies were strict about the standardization of Transco's DM values and global policy framework, they allowed room for local decision-making in how the values, policies and plans were to be implemented.

Subsidiary employee reactions to global DM integration were mixed. The polarized nature of the Finnish context for workforce diversity meant that whilst the integration of values and practices concerning gender equality was considered to be 'like cracking a nut with a sledgehammer', the integration (and open discussion) of diversity issues such as sexual orientation, religion and ethnicity were slow and, at times, painful processes. Since DM is arguably one of the most contextually embedded practices that an MNC can seek to transfer and integrate across borders, and since meaningful DM diversity interventions require changes in both individual and organizational attitudes and behaviours, we might have expected people-based tools of integration to be the most widely used. However, this form of global integration was not as common as the various forms of DM formalization. Whilst we might question the ability of formalization-based tools

to bring organizational and individual DM practices in line with the rest of the MNC, it was these tools that appeared to be the most effective in forcing Transco employees and managers to think about everyday diversity issues when self-initiative was not forthcoming.

On the whole, it seemed that whilst Transco Finland had been fairly successful in the routine 'implementation' of DM policies and practices and their 'integration' with other HRM practices, but it had made much less progress in their 'internalization' to the extent that subsidiary managers and employees all believed in their value and application.

For further details, see: Sippola and Smale (2007).

Question

Based on what we know about (a) the relative strengths and weaknesses of different integration mechanisms, and (b) the qualities of individual HRM practices that make them more or less susceptible to global integration, how appropriate were the mechanisms used by TRANSCO to integrate diversity management into the Finnish subsidiary? How would you have done it differently?

Conclusions

This chapter has presented the key arguments for the global integration of HRM (the 'why'), outlined the ways in which MNCs can and try to facilitate global HRM integration (the 'how'), and critically discussed how we can identify the existence and extent of global HRM integration in MNC subsidiaries.

All this has pointed to several interesting questions. Firstly, whilst we are led to believe that the forces of globalization are turning MNCs' attention towards the integration side of the integration–differentiation dilemma (Ghoshal and Gratton 2002), it is unclear how far this will extend to the most contextually embedded set of business practices – HRM. Taylor (2006) foresees that existing drivers and 'emerging' motivations connected to sustainability and organizational learning will further promote the attractiveness of global HRM integration, but there is not much large-scale empirical research on whether MNCs are following this path.

Studies on HRM in MNC subsidiaries have traditionally focused on 'structural' explanations that include a range of home-country, host-country, MNC, and subsidiary factors. An often neglected factor is the mechanisms through which HRM practices are integrated throughout the MNC. This chapter has highlighted that we know much more about the types of mechanisms used compared to the questions of how they are used and why. Perhaps more importantly, we have a poor understanding about the impact of integration mechanism usage on HRM integration, organizational and individual outcomes.

Some mechanisms of integration have been in use for decades, whilst others have only recently gained in popularity. Two of these that are likely to shape HRM integration in the future are e-HRM and its associated 'integrative' technologies (see Strohmeier 2007 for a good review of the research), and the use of corporate values (i.e. socialization). Sitting at opposite ends of the spectrum in terms of their directness of approach, integrative HRM systems (e.g. SAP or PeopleSoft) will be an interesting test of the limits of global HRM integration, whereas the fostering of cultural integration via the use values-based HRM practices might provoke some interesting responses from subsidiary personnel.

As in any field of study there is always scope for more improvement, whether it is in the form of greater accuracy in what we are measuring or a more nuanced perspective from which to try and understand something. In studies of global HRM integration, this chapter has highlighted a need for stricter definitions of 'global integration' that include the notions of 'internalization' and 'integration', as well as for methodological considerations into what we ask to whom. To assist in making this happen, future research needs to make use of more sophisticated modelling techniques (Wright and Nishii 2007), 'richer' qualitative case-study methods (Martin and Beaumont 1999), and more cross-cultural researcher collaboration (Edwards and Kuruvilla 2005). It is possible that when subjected to this level of scrutiny we find that the global integration of HRM and the associated transfer of HRM practices is not quite so straight forward as presented here, as we discover in Chapter 7.

Review questions

1 (a) What are the key drivers of global HRM integration? (b) Which drivers do you think are currently the most influential and which drivers do you think will be the most influential in the future, and why?

2 What tools (or mechanisms) of global integration can MNCs use to achieve tighter HRM integration amongst their foreign subsidiaries, and what kinds of factors might determine when and how they are used?

3 What conceptual and methodological issues need to be taken into account when assessing the extent of HRM integration (or transfer) in foreign MNC subsidiaries?

Further reading

1 Evans, P., Pucik, V. and Barsoux, J. (2002) *The Global Challenge: Frameworks for International Human Resource Management,* Boston: McGraw-Hill, Chapter 3: 'Exploiting Global Integration', 101–51.

Comprehensive review of global integration drivers, global integration mechanisms and how to implement globally integrated strategies. Also includes interesting cases and several references to further reading.

2 Taylor, S. (2006) 'Emerging Motivations for Global HRM Integration', in Ferner, A. Quintanilla, J. and Sánchez-Runde, C. (eds) *Multinationals, Institutions and the Construction of Transnational Practices,* Basingstoke: Palgrave Macmillan, 109–30.

Good discussion of forces driving the global integration of HRM specifically, including a look forward at possible future drivers.

3 Kim, K., Park, J.-H. and Prescott, J.E. (2003) 'The global integration of business functions: a study of multinational businesses in integrated global industries', *Journal of International Business Studies,* 34(4), 327–44.

Provides a useful classification of four global integration 'modes' (centralization-, formalization-, information- and people-based) based on an in-depth review of the control and co-ordination literature. The study investigates the use and effectiveness of these modes in integrating different business functions.

4 Björkman, I. and Lervik, J.E. (2007) 'Transferring HR practices within multinational corporations', *Human Resource Management Journal,* 17(4), 320–35.

Argues convincingly for a more in-depth understanding of HRM transfer outcomes (i.e. implementation, integration, internalization), and expands upon existing explanations of HRM practice transfers to foreign MNC subsidiaries.

References

Bae, J., Chen, S. and Lawler, J. (1998) 'Variations in human resource management in Asian countries: MNC home-country and host-country effects', *International Journal of Human Resource Management,* 9(4), 653–70.

Baliga, B.R. and Jaeger, A.M. (1984) 'Multinational corporations: control systems and delegation issues', *Journal of International Business Studies,* 15(2), 25–40.

Beechler, S. and Yang, J.Z. (1994) 'The transfer of Japanese-style management to American subsidiaries: contingencies, constraints, and competencies', *Journal of International Business Studies,* 25(3), 467–91.

Björkman, A. (2007) 'Towards Explaining the Use of Control Mechanisms in Foreign Subsidiaries of MNCs', Unpublished doctoral dissertation, Swedish School of Economics and Business Administration, No. 168., Helsinki, Finland.

Björkman, I. and Lervik, J.E. (2007) 'Transferring HR practices within multinational corporations', *Human Resource Management Journal,* 17(4), 320–35.

Björkman, I. and Lu, Y. (2001) 'Institutionalization and bargaining power explanations of HRM practices in international joint ventures – the case of Chinese–Western joint ventures', *Organization Studies,* 22(3), 491–512.

Björkman, I., Smale, A., Sumelius, J., Suutari, V. and Lu, Y. (2008) 'Changes in institutional context and MNC operations in China: subsidiary HRM practices in 1996 versus 2006', *International Business Review,* 17(2), 146–58.

Coller, X. (1996) 'Managing flexibility in the food industry: A cross-national comparative case study in European multinational companies', *European Journal of Industrial Relations,* 2(2), pp. 153-72.

Davenport, T.H. and Prusak, L. (1998) *Working Knowledge,* Boston, MA: Harvard Business School Press.

Economist (2007) 'Revving up: How globalisation and information technology are spurring faster innovation' Special Report on Innovation, pg.3.

Edwards, P., Ferner, A. and Sisson, K. (1996) 'The conditions for international human resource management: two case studies', *International Journal of Human Resource Management,* 7(1), 20–40.

Edwards, T. (1998) 'Multinationals, labour management and the process of reverse diffusion: A case study', *International Journal of Human Resource Management,* 9(4), 696–709.

Edwards, T. and Kuruvilla, S. (2005) 'International HRM: national business systems, organizational politics and the international division of labour in MNCs', *International Journal of Human Resource Management,* 16(1), 1–21.

Edwards, T., Margihsen, P., Edwards, P., Ferner, A. and Tregaskis, O. (2009) 'A Transnational Logic in the Management of Labour in Multinational Companies? Understanding Variation by Nationality and International Integration', Paper presented at the SASE Conference, Paris, 14–16 July.

Evans, P., Pucik, V. and Barsoux, J. (2002) *The Global Challenge: Frameworks for International Human Resource Management,* Boston: McGraw-Hill.

Farndale, E. and Paauwe, J. (2007) 'Uncovering competitive and institutional drivers of HRM practices in multinational corporations', *Human Resource Management Journal,* 17(4), 355–75.

Ferner, A. (2000) 'The underpinnings of 'bureaucratic' control systems: HRM in European multinationals', *Journal of Management Studies,* 37(4), 521–39.

Ferner, A. (1997) 'Country of origin effects and HRM in multinational companies', *Human Resource Management Journal,* 7(1), 19–37.

Ferner, A. and Edwards, P. (1995) 'Power and the diffusion of organizational change within multinational enterprises', *European Journal of Industrial Relations,* 1(2), 229–57.

Ferner, A., Almond, P., Clark, I., Colling, T., Edwards, T., Holden, L. and Muller-Camen, M. (2004) 'The dynamics of central control and subsidiary autonomy in the management of human resources: case-study evidence from US MNCs in the UK', *Organization Studies,* 25(3), 363–91.

Ferner, A., Almond, P. and Colling, T. (2005) 'Institutional theory and the cross-national transfer of employment policy: the case of 'workforce diversity' in US multinationals', *Journal of International Business Studies,* 36(3), 304–21.

Gamble, J. (2003) 'Transferring human resource practices from the United Kingdom to China: the limits and potential for convergence', *International Journal of Human Resource Management,* 14(3), 369–87.

Gereffi, G. (1999) 'International Trade and Industrial Upgrading in the Apparel Commodity Chain', *Journal of International Economics,* 48, 37–70.

Ghoshal, S. and Gratton, L. (2002) 'Integrating the enterprise', *Sloan Management Review,* 44(1), 31–38.

Ghoshal, S. and Nohria, N. (1989) 'Internal differentiation within multinational corporations', *Strategic Management Journal,* 10(4), pp. 323–37.

Ghoshal, S. and Nohria, N. (1993) 'Horses for courses: organizational forms for multinational corporations, *Sloan Management Review,* 34(2), 23–35.

Grant, R.M. (1996) 'Prospering in dynamically-competitive environments: organizational capability as knowledge integration', *Organization Science,* 7(4), 375–87.

Harris, H., Brewster, C. and Sparrow, P. (2003) *International Human Resource Management,* London, UK: CIPD.

Harzing, A.-W. (1999) *Managing the Multinationals: An International Study of Control Mechanisms,* Cheltenham: Edward Elgar.

Harzing, A.-W. and Sorge, A. (2003) 'The relative impact of country of origin and universal contingencies on internationalization strategies and corporate control in multinational enterprises: worldwide and European perspectives', *Organization Studies,* 24(2), 187–214.

Hennart, J.F. (2005) 'Control in Multinational Firms: the Role of Price and Hierarchy', in Ghoshal, S. and Westney, D.E. (eds) *Organization Theory and the Multinational Corporation* (2nd edition), Basingstoke: Palgrave MacMillan, 149–71.

Hetrick, S. (2002) 'Transferring HR ideas and practices: globalization and convergence in Poland', *Human Resource Development International,* 5(3), 333–51.

Jensen, R. and Szulanski, G. (2004) 'Stickiness and the adaptation of organizational practices in cross-border knowledge transfers', *Journal of International Business Studies,* 35(6), 508–23.

Kanter, R.M. and Dretler, T.D. (1998) '"Global strategy" and its impact on local operations: Lessons from Gillette Singapore', *Academy of Management Executive,* 12(4), pp. 60-8.

Khilji, S.E. and Wang, X. (2006) ''Intended' and 'implemented' HRM: the missing linchpin in strategic human resource management research', *International Journal of Human Resource Management,* 17(7), 1171–89.

Kiessling, T. and Harvey, M. (2005) 'Strategic global human resource management research in the twenty-first century: an endorsement of the mixed-method research methodology', *International Journal of Human Resource Management,* 16(1), 22–45.

Kim, K., Park, J.-H. and Prescott, J.E. (2003) 'The global integration of business functions: a study of multinational businesses in integrated global industries', *Journal of International Business Studies,* 34(4), 327–44.

Kogut, B. (1991) 'Country Capabilities and the Permeability of Borders', *Strategic Management Journal,* 12(1), 33–47.

Kostova, T. (1999) 'Transnational transfer of strategic organisational practices: a contextual perspective', *Academy of Management Review,* 24(2), 308–24.

Kostova, T. and Roth, K. (2002) 'Adoption of an organizational practice by subsidiaries of multinational corporations: institutional and relational effects', *Academy of Management Journal,* 45(1), 215–33.

Lu, K. and Björkman, I. (1997) 'HRM practices in China-West joint ventures: MNC standardization versus localization', *International Journal of Human Resource Management,* 8(5), pp. 614–28.

Marginson, P., Armstrong, P., Edwards, P. and Purcell, J. (1995) 'Managing labour in the global corporation: a survey-based analysis of multinationals operating in the UK', *International Journal of Human Resource Management,* 6(3), 702–19

Martin, G. and Beaumont, P. (1999) 'Co-ordination and control of human resource management in multinational firms: the case of CASHCO', *International Journal of Human Resource Management,* 10(1), 21–42.

Martinez, J.I. and Jarillo, J.C. (1989) 'The evolution of research on coordination mechanisms in multinational corporations', *Journal of International Business Studies,* 20(3), 489–514.

Mitsuhashi, H., Park, H.J., Wright, P. and Chua, R. (2000) 'Line and HR executives' perceptions of HR effectiveness in firms in the People's Republic of China', *International Journal of Human Resource Management,* 11(2), 197–216.

Myloni, B., Harzing, A.-W.K. and Mirza, H. (2004) 'Host country specific factors and the transfer of human resource management practices in multinational companies', *International Journal of Manpower,* 25(6), 518–34.

Myloni, B., Harzing, A.-W.K. and Mirza, H. (2007) 'The effect of corporate-level organisational factors on the transfer of human resource management practices: European and US MNCs and their Greek subsidiaries', *International Journal of Human Resource Management,* 18(12), 2057–74.

Nohria, N. and Ghoshal, S. (1994) 'Differentiated fit and shared values: alternatives for managing headquarters–subsidiary relations', *Strategic Management Journal,* 15(6), 491–502.

Nohria, N. and Ghoshal, S. (1997) *The Differentiated Network: Organizing Multinational Corporations for Value Creation, San Francisco,* CA: Jossey-Bass.

Ouchi, W.G. (1979) 'A conceptual framework for the design of organizational control mechanisms,' Management Science, 25(9), 833–48.

Porter, M. (1986) *Competition in Global Industries,* Boston: Harvard Business School Press.

Prahalad, C.K. and Doz, Y.L. (1981) 'An approach to strategic control in MNCs', *Sloan Management Review,* 22(4), pp. 5–13.

Pratt, M.G. and Foreman, P.O. (2000) 'Classifying managerial responses to multiple organizational identities', *Academy of Management Review,* 25(1), 18–42.

Pudelko, M. and Harzing, A.-W.K. (2007) 'Country-of-origin, localization, or dominance effect? An empirical investigation of HRM practices in foreign subsidiaries', *Human Resource Management,* 46(4), 535–59.

Reddington, M. and Martin, G. (2007) 'Theorizing the links between e-HR and strategic HRM: A framework, case illustration and some reflections', *Proceedings of the First European Academic Workshop on Electronic Human Resource Management,*??

Reddington, M., Martin, G. and Bondarouk, T. (2008) 'Manager perceptions of e-HR outcomes: A framework, case illustrations and some reflections', *proceedings of the 2nd European Academic Workshop on Electronic Human Resource Management,* Aix-en-Provence, France.

Rosenzweig, P. and Nohria, N. (1994) 'Influences on human resource management practices in multinational corporations', *Journal of International Business Studies,* 25(2), 229–51.

Ruël, H.R., Bondarouk, T. and Looise, J.K. (2004) 'E-HRM: innovation or irritation. An explorative empirical study in five large companies on web-based HRM', *Management Revue,* 15(3), 364–80.

Ruta, C.D. (2005) 'The application of change management theory to HR portal implementation in subsidiaries of multinational corporations', *Human Resource Management,* 44(1), 35–53.

Schmitt, M. and Sadowski, D. (2003) 'A cost-minimization approach to the international transfer of HRM/IR practices: Anglo-Saxon multinationals in the Federal Republic of Germany', *International Journal of Human Resource Management,* 14(3), 409–30.

Selmer, J. and de Leon, C.T. (1996) 'Parent cultural control through organizational acculturation: Local managers learning new work values in foreign subsidiaries', *Journal of Organizational Behavior,* 17, 557–72.

Selmer, J. and de Leon, C.T. (2002) 'Parent cultural control of foreign subsidiaries through organizational acculturation: A longitudinal study', *International Journal of Human Resource Management,* 13(8), 1147–65.

Sippola, A. and Smale, A. (2007) 'The global integration of diversity management: A longitudinal case study', *International Journal of Human Resource Management,* 18(11), 1895–916.

Smale, A. (2008) 'Foreign subsidiary perspectives on the mechanisms of global HRM integration', *Human Resource Management Journal,* 18(2), 135–53.

Sparrow, P., Brewster, C. and Harris, H. (2004) *Globalizing Human Resource Management,* London: Routledge.

Stahl, G., Björkman, I., Farndale, E., Morris, S., Paauwe, J., Stiles, P., Trevor, J. and Wright, P. (2008 forthcoming) 'Global talent management: How leading companies build and sustain their talent pipeline', *California Management Review.*

Stone, D. and Gueutal, H. (2005) *The Brave New World of eHR: Human Resources Management in the Digital Age,* San Francisco, CA: Jossey-Bass.

Strohmeier, S. (2007) 'Research in e-HRM: Review and implications', *Human Resource Management Review,* 17(1), 19–37.

Tansley, C., Newell, S. and Williams, H. (2001) 'Effecting HRM-style practices through an integrated human resource information system', *Personnel Review,* 30(3), 351–70.

Taylor, S. (2006) 'Emerging Motivations for Global HRM Integration', in Ferner, A., Quintanilla, J. and Sánchez-Runde, C. (eds) *Multinationals, Institutions and the Construction of Transnational Practices,* Basingstoke: Palgrave Macmillan, 109–30.

Tempel, A. (2001) *The Cross-National Transfer of Human Resource Management Practices in German and British Multinational Companies,* Munich: Hampp.

Van de Ven, A.H., Delbecq, A.L. and Koenig Jr., R. (1976) 'Determinants of coordination modes within organizations', *American Sociological Review,* 41(2), 322–38.

Welch, D.E. and Welch, L.S. (2006) 'Commitment for hire? The viability of corporate culture as a MNC control mechanism', *International Business Review,* 15(1), 14–28.

Wolf, J. (1997) 'From "starworks" to networks and heterarchies? Theoretical rationale and empirical evidence of HRM organization in large multinational corporations', *Management International Review,* 37(1), 145–69.

United Nations (2007) *World Investment Report: Transnational Corporations, Extractive Industries and Development,* UNCTAD: New York and Geneva.

Wright, P.M. and Nishii, L. H. (2007) 'Strategic HRM and Organizational Behavior: Integrating Multiple Levels of Analysis', *CAHRS Working Paper,* #07-03, Ithaca, NY: Cornell University, School of Industrial and Labor Relations, Center for Advanced Human Resource Studies (http://digitalcommons.ilr.cornell.edu/cahrswp/468).

Chapter 7

The diffusion of HR practices in MNCs

Tony Edwards, Chris Rees and Miao Zhang

Key aims

The aims of this chapter are to:

- examine the features of the host environment that inhibit diffusion, or require that practices be altered to fit local conditions;
- consider the possible directions in which practices flow across a multinational;
- investigate the organizational characteristics of MNCs that promote or hinder diffusion, particularly the nature of integration;
- examine the processes of diffusion, focusing on the relationships between actors at different levels of the organization.

Introduction

A central theme so far in this book has been the opportunities and challenges that differences between national business systems pose for MNCs. For instance, in Chapter 5 we saw how these differences have led to a number of organizational forms being adopted by MNCs, none of which provide a completely satisfactory structure with which to deal with the various pressures that they face. One key element of many of these organizational forms, particularly the much-vaunted 'transnational' structure, is the emphasis placed on the diffusion of practices across a firm's international operations. Similarly, in the previous chapter we examined the motivations for global integration and how this may be achieved; in doing so, we noted that there are clear implications of greater integration for the transfer of HR practices.

In this chapter we consider four specific aspects of the diffusion of practices. First, are some employment practices more readily diffused than others? And in what ways are practices amended to fit a new environment? Second, from which national business systems are practices likely to emerge? And, relatedly, which units are likely to be the recipients of diffusion? Third, are some MNCs more likely to transfer practices across their operations than others? What are the characteristics of integration in particular that predispose MNCs towards engaging in the transfer of practices? Fourth, through what mechanisms and channels are practices transferred? How do various organizational groups persuade and cajole others into accepting the transfer of practices?

In addressing these questions, we view differences in national business systems as at the same time enabling and constraining the transfer of practices. These differences are a prerequisite for transfer since without the diversity of practices that result from distinct national systems there would be little incentive to look to diffuse practices across sites in different countries. There is a parallel here with Gray's (2002) argument that globalization is brought about by variations in national forms of organizing economic activity; if it was not for these variations, Gray argues, there would be little incentive for economic activity to cross borders. Differences between national systems also constrain the scope for diffusion, however, since they act as a force for MNCs to adapt to local conditions. In this way, 'varieties of capitalism' simultaneously create and close off scope for diffusion. Moreover, diffusion within MNCs can be one force for change in national business systems themselves since the introduction of new practices can be subsequently diffused throughout a host economy. These themes run throughout the chapter.

The 'diffusibility' of employment practices

Throughout this book we emphasize the 'embeddedness' of employment practices in particular national contexts. That is, practices originate and become established in a given legal, institutional, political and cultural context. To some extent, they are dependent on this context and cannot operate in a different environment. The extent of this dependence varies from one area of HRM to another; in other words, the 'diffusability' of some practices is higher than that of others.

The ease with which a practice can be diffused across a multinational is shaped partly by its dependence on 'supportive and distinctive extra-firm structures' (Hayden and Edwards 2001). These extra-firm structures can underpin the operation of a practice that would not function in their absence, and include such things as legal obligations on firms, institutions in the labour market, and the values, expectations and assumptions that characterise employment relations in a particular country. All employment practices, of course, are to some extent dependent on these legal, institutional and cultural 'props'. The ease with which a practice can operate outside its original home environment – in other words, the extent to which a practice is 'diffusable' – is determined in part by its dependence on these props.

One area of HR in which these props are central is training. Some aspects of a firm's approach to training are dependent on supportive institutions, an example of which is the 'dual' system of training in Germany. The role of the colleges, training bodies, employers associations and trade unions in administering, monitoring and certifying the system provides crucial support for firm-level practices; without these supports, firms are unlikely to find it feasible to operate such practices. Consistent with this, Dickmann's (1999, 2003) studies of German multinationals showed that they have been constrained in their attempts to introduce German-style vocational training into their UK subsidiaries because the British economy lacks the 'broader business institutions necessary to underpin particular practices' (Edwards and Ferner 2004). Of course, some training practices, particularly those that are employer-led, are more diffusable in that they are less dependent on a set of supportive institutions.

The distinctive characteristics of the national business systems in which MNCs operate can also limit the diffusion of practices in a further way. Managers at the HQ of a multinational may seek to operate a practice in a number of countries but might be prevented from doing so by the legal, institutional or cultural 'constraints' of the country to which the practice is directed. Organizational actors in the recipient unit may try to resist its introduction and may use their legal powers, rights provided by institutions, or appeals to the importance of local 'custom and practice' in order to thwart the HQ's plans (Almond and Ferner 2006). In this sense, some practices may not be 'diffusable' because of the constraints posed by the nature of the host business system.

One area where such constraints are notable is in relation to practices designed to secure greater numerical flexibility, which may have to be adapted to fit the prevailing labour market traditions in each country. For instance, the tendency to use part-time workers is dependent on there being a pool of workers willing to accept such jobs. Other forms of numerical flexibility, such as annualized hours, temporary contracts and changes in shift patterns, have to be negotiated with employee representatives and a multinational's ability to transfer them across its sites is clearly influenced by the attitudes and strength of organized labour in the countries in which it operates. However, these constraints clearly do not close off scope for diffusion altogether, particularly to those countries which are relatively deregulated and where unions are weak, and some evidence points towards MNCs being able to use their power to lever change in shift patterns (Martinez and Weston 1994).

In many instances, therefore, these constraints are partial rather than absolute: that is, managers at the HQ may be able to diffuse a practice, but it may need to be altered so that it can be implemented in the new business system. As Edwards and Ferner (2004) put it, a 'practice may not operate in the same fashion in the recipient as in the donor unit but, rather, may undergo *transmutation* as actors in the recipient seek to adapt it to pre-existing models of behaviour, assumptions and power relations'. Thus, the formal substance of a practice may be diffused but the operation of this practice may differ between countries.

One illustration of this process is the adoption by many US-based automotive firms of Japanese forms of work organisation over the last decade or so. Maccoby (1997) argues that in implementing these practices, American companies have tended to attach less emphasis on the devolution of responsibility to teams of operators which characterises the nature of teams in Japan, and instead have retained the distinctive supervisory relationships characteristic of their US-based operations. In a similar vein, Broad (1994) has shown how the British managers in a UK transplant of a Japanese multinational resisted moves by the parent firm to shift responsibility for quality to teams of operators, preferring to retain the right to take decisions in this area themselves. Broad (1994: 58) argued that this reflects the 'traditional obsession of British managers with prerogative and secrecy'. A further example is Edwards and Zhang's (2008) study of an American multinational, which showed how practices in the field of performance management were diffused to the Chinese operations but were adapted by local actors in ways that the parent company were not aware of. In all three cases, practices were diffused, but took on a different form in the new environment.

Differences between national business systems, therefore, limit the diffusability of employment practices. This is partly because practices are dependent on the 'props' present in the system in which they originate, and partly because their introduction to other countries is subject to the 'constraints' posed by the recipient systems. We have also seen how practices can be modified, or 'transmuted', to fit the new environment. However, it is the differences between national business systems that also create the potential for cross-border diffusion in the first instance, as MNCs seek to gain a competitive advantage through transferring practices perceived as delivering improved performance across their operations. Are the practices that they seek to diffuse drawn from a wide range of countries, or are some countries likely to be the main 'suppliers' of such practices?

The hierarchy of economies and the diffusion of practices

In Chapter 5, we reviewed the evidence concerned with the influence of a multinational's original home base, arguing that there is a detectable 'country of origin effect'. That is, the ways that MNCs manage their international workforces are disproportionately influenced by their roots in the domestic business system. However, we also noted that this effect is not set in stone but rather evolves over time; in other words, it provides a strong influence on the decisions of actors in key positions, but leaves open the scope to draw on elements of other business systems in which the multinational operates. The way in which they seek to do so is shaped in part by the relative strength of these various national economies. A strongly performing economy is likely to attract attention from actors in senior positions in firms in other countries, creating a dynamic of emulation at the international level. This idea has been developed by Smith and Meiksins (1995) who argue that the international economy contains a hierarchy of national economies. Those countries whose economies have performed strongly are at or near the top of this hierarchy, and this 'dominant' position creates interest amongst actors in other countries in emulating the practices associated with these 'dominant' economies. A part of this interest can be in HRM, such as methods of work organization, systems of pay and appraisal, or practices in relation to employee development.

One example of these 'dominance effects' is the role of the American economy in the post-war period. The USA emerged from the Second World War with its military and political position enhanced, and its economy relatively unscathed. Thus American firms were in a strong position to grow in international markets, and did so partly through exporting and partly through engaging in foreign direct investment. The consistent growth in the American economy and the strength of many big American firms during the 1950s and 1960s led many to refer to the 'Pax Americana'. During this time, elements of the American business system were diffused – albeit often in amended form – to other countries. Hence, US MNCs were active in diffusing practices such as 'Fordist' forms of work organization, approaches to negotiating such as productivity bargaining, and formalized and standardized procedures in many areas of HRM (see Edwards and Ferner 2002 for a review). During this time, therefore, the USA served as a key source from which practices could be diffused.

During the 1980s, however, the performance of the US economy began to falter, and the perception that the American economy was dominant began to evaporate. Indeed, a whole raft of books, articles and reports were concerned with 'American economic decline'. The Japanese economy at this time was enjoying a sustained boom and large

Japanese firms came to dominate many sectors. In automotive, for instance, firms such as Nissan, Honda and Toyota set up production sites in Europe and North America and increased their market share in these areas at the expense of indigenous firms. In electronics and financial services, similarly, Japanese firms grew in international markets. The strength of the Japanese economy led to great interest in 'lean production' – a set of practices including worker involvement in teams or groups which had responsibility for product quality and were designed to minimize waste and throughput time. The way in which these practices were implemented in the foreign subsidiaries of Japanese MNCs, and their adoption by western firms, became the subject of much attention (e.g. Oliver and Wilkinson 1992). Similarly, the German economy had recovered from postwar devastation to a status of one of the world's leading economies. German firms made great strides into international markets, particularly in sectors such as chemicals and engineering. Their success was widely ascribed to the operation of 'diversified quality production', a strategy of serving niche markets with high quality, customized products involving highly skilled workers (Streeck 1992). Towards the end of the twentieth century and in the first few years of the twenty-first the situation has changed once again, with the new conventional wisdom perceiving the Japanese and German economies to be 'sclerotic' and unable to deal with the challenges of globalization while the American economy regained its hegemony, owing in part to its flexibility and apparent dynamism.

The idea of the 'dominance' of particular economies shaping the direction in which practices flow across borders has much intuitive appeal. However, in its simplest form, the dominance effects argument is open to two main criticisms. The first is that it rests on an assumption that rates of economic growth differ markedly between the major developed countries and that these differences reflect divergences in forms of economic organisation. In fact, differences in rates of economic growth are not as great as is often assumed. For instance, while the 1970s and 1980s was seen as a period of economic decline by many in the US, the growth rate of the American economy was actually higher than that in Germany, Sweden and the UK. Only compared with the Japanese economy was there a marked difference and even this was less significant than is often supposed. Similarly, while the popular perception in recent years of 'coordinated market economies' (CMEs) such as Germany and Japan has been that they are saddled with rigidities that harm economic performance, their growth rates in the last two economic cycles have not been too far behind the 'Anglo-Saxon' economies of the US and UK, while Sweden, another CME, has outperformed these countries (see Table 7.1).

Moreover, even where there are significant differences in economic performance between countries, only a part of this can be explained by divergences in forms of economic organisation. Some of the explanation lies in the process of 'convergence and catch-up'. Economists such as Krugman (1994) argue that the rapid growth of the German and Japanese economies in the post-war period was due to the process of recovery following the decimation of their industrial bases during the war. Similarly, the remarkable growth rates in the 'Asian Tiger' economies up until 1997 was due, according to Krugman, to one-off gains from using existing resources more intensively. Many academics, notably Abramovitz (1994), have criticized Krugman for overstating his case, arguing that the 'social capability' of a national economy – defined as the ability to take

Table 7.1   **Real GDP growth, 1961–2008 (average annual percentage change)**

	1961–73	*1974–84*	*1985–98*	*1999–2008*
US	4.0	2.2	2.9	2.6
UK	3.1	1.3	2.4	2.6
Germany	4.3	1.8	2.2	1.5
Sweden	4.2	1.8	1.5	2.8
Japan	9.7	3.3	2.6	1.4

Source: Hall and Soskice, 2001: 20; updated from US government statistics (www.ers.usda.gov)

advantage of technological opportunities – is an important determinant of its perfor-mance. Nonetheless, even Abramovitz accepts that differences between economic growth rates across nations can only be partially explained by this social capability.

The second criticism is that the notion of dominance risks reifying a national econo-my. That is, the incentive to emulate elements of a particular national business system creates a danger of implying that a country is characterized by a homogeneous set of structures and practices that operate across firms, and that companies in other countries can identify and seek to emulate these. This is, of course, not the case. We saw in Chapters 3 and 4 how national business systems contain important intra-national varia-tions. In the USA, for instance, managerial style in HRM differs markedly across the economy: between those developed in the 'sun-belt' states such as Texas and those in the 'rust-belt' cities such as Detroit; between 'welfare capitalist' and 'New Deal unionist' firms; between 'high-tech' firms embedded in areas such as the Research Triangle in North Carolina and the 'low-road' firms that compete on the basis of cost-minimization. Thus, two sets of managers in, say, the UK which both seek to emulate 'American' prac-tice may have in mind quite different things.

These two points question the usefulness of the dominance effects approach. However, despite these criticisms, it retains some utility. We see dominance effects as a way of categorizing commonly held views by managers – as a management ideology, in other words. Viewed in this light, the notion of dominance captures the interest that exists amongst organizational actors, particularly senior managers, in emulating prac-tices which originate in other countries. One particularly useful aspect to the concept is in helping to distinguish different forms of diffusion. In MNCs from 'dominant' or 'hegemonic' countries this effect is likely to reinforce the country of origin effect, giving rise to 'forward' diffusion in which practices are diffused from home to host countries. Thus, as we have seen, during the 1980s and 1990s much attention centred on the way in which Japanese MNCs exported some practices characteristic of the Japanese business system, notably 'lean production' and its associated employment practices, and the sub-sequent adoption by local firms of such practices (e.g. Elger and Smith 2005; Whitley *et al.* 2003).

However, in MNCs which are not from 'dominant' or 'hegemonic' countries diffu-sion can occur in the opposite direction; this has been termed 'reverse diffusion' and involves practices originating in foreign subsidiaries and subsequently being adopted in the domestic operations. This is particularly likely in MNCs in which key actors perceive their country of origin to exhibit weaknesses and other countries in which the firm has subsidiaries to have 'solutions' to these weaknesses. Where this is the case, these actors can use their foreign subsidiaries in 'dominant' systems, such as the USA. Alternatively, in other countries that have been open to the influence of these dominant systems through high levels of foreign direct investment, such as the UK, to learn about new practices.

The shift in the conventional wisdom during the 1980s and 1990s towards a view that the deregulated, market-based Anglo-Saxon economies have provided a stronger platform for growth than the institutionalized economies of continental Europe and Japan is associated with a growing body of evidence that demonstrates that many continental European firms adopted structures and practices characteristic of the USA and UK. For instance, many German MNCs used their British subsidiaries as sources of new practices, moving towards adopting performance-related bonuses for managers, identifying and developing 'high potentials' as a way of creating a cadre of 'international' managers, issuing an explicit set of values often referring to the importance of 'shareholder value', and implementing 'business re-engineering' programmes (Ferner and Quintanilla 1998; Ferner and Varul 2000; Tempel 2001). Similar moves towards the adoption of 'Anglo-Saxon' practices appeared to be evident in French MNCs (Mtar 2001; Thory 2008) and in a case study of a Swedish multinational (Hayden and Edwards 2001). At the time of writing, it is too soon to say whether the impact of the financial crisis of 2007–8 and the subsequent global recession triggers a new shift in the conventional wisdom. It will be interesting to observe over the next decade how key actors in MNCs view the merits or otherwise of different national systems.

At a more fundamental level, the notion of dominance effects can be used to analyse the way that MNCs from developing nations operate. There is some evidence of Chinese MNCs looking to their subsidiaries in the UK for new practices that they absorb and transfer back to China as part of a process of catching up with the practices of the developed market economies (Zhang and Edwards 2007 and see the case study that follows).

CASE STUDY

CFS – adaptation, absorption or retention

CFS is a state-owned financial enterprise with over 1,000 domestic branches and 500 foreign subsidiaries and branches. There are two subsidiaries operating in the UK, one of which, Old-CB, has a long history in the country, while the other, New-CB, has only two years of operating experience in Britain.

Old-CB was established in the 1940s. Until the1980s, it was a representative agent of the government and carried out financial services for Chinese exporting and importing businesses. It was strongly controlled by the government and had little link with the UK market. As a result, most staff in this branch were Chinese expatriates and very few were recruited locally. Most management practices were modelled on practices in China rather than those in the UK. For example, the staff in this subsidiary were employed with the 'job for life' status that was enjoyed by most professional employees in China. Moreover, the salary rose in line with age and tenure rather than performance, and there was only a modest gap in salary between top managers and the most junior staff.

The parent company, CFS, began to lose its monopoly position in China during the 1980s as the government gradually opened up the domestic market. Simultaneously, the firm began to expand internationally. As the oldest overseas branch, Old-CB was accorded a key role in extending the company's business into international markets from the early 1990s, losing its 'agent' status and becoming more autonomous. Its main task became to learn how to do business in a competitive environment, and a key part of this involved greater use of local managers and the adoption of local management practices in some areas. One such area is in the pay structure, with pay being linked to individual performance and the gap in pay between the highest and lowest earners rising significantly. Crucially, this subsidiary took on the role of training managers from the home country and other subsidiaries, setting up a training centre to run courses on a range of aspects of doing business in market environments. So far, the subsidiary has trained more than a thousand Chinese managers, including most top-level managers and heads of departments.

In relation to the important issue of training, therefore, the subsidiary has taken on a 'vanguard' status within the wider company, and it is evident that practices in this area are being 'reverse diffused'. However, the subsidiary does not have complete autonomy, and is still strongly controlled by the parent firm. Many top managers and over half the staff are Chinese or with a Chinese background, and a Chinese management style is still evident. British management practices have been applied mainly in the areas which are strongly shaped by the demands of the local labour market and regulations, such as the recruitment process and pay for non-managerial staff, but a Chinese influence was detectable on other types of HR practice. For example, the

importance of harmony in work relations are still stressed, and the selection and pay packages of senior managerial positions remain controlled by the parent company.

New-CB's establishment was a key part of the global strategy of the parent company. At the beginning of its establishment, this subsidiary was intended to become the headquarters in Europe, in charge of the business of all other related subsidiaries and branches. According to the description of one of founders of this subsidiary, the UK was perceived as advanced in HR terms, making it an ideal base for this plant. CFS invested significantly in the subsidiary in the hope that it would serve as the basis for learning for the wider firm, and whether it made a profit or not was seen as secondary to its key task of absorbing local management practices.

In the first two years of its existence, this subsidiary used a strategy of 'localisation' in HRM. That is, most top managers and all middle managers were British and HRM policies and practice were based on those of local companies. For example, recruitment, remuneration and appraisal systems were all modelled on those in place in similar organisations in the UK. Moreover, practices operating in this subsidiary were subsequently diffused to the HQ and to other sites. One example is that of an appraisal system that had been implemented in the site after senior staff learned about it in operation in a similar local UK company. Knowledge of this practice was passed to the HQ and given the status of 'best practice', with other subsidiaries expected to implement it. Thus, this subsidiary also has a 'vanguard' role in transferring practices within the company.

From these two cases, it is clear that this Chinese multinational attempted to use a strategy of 'localization' to absorb UK management practice. However, the extent to which this process of 'reverse diffusion' occurred was constrained by various factors. For example, following the Asian financial crisis in 1997 the subsidiaries business was severely impacted and the parent company changed its previous plans, reducing the size and security of New-CB, and the HQ moved to establish greater control over staff remuneration, reducing the autonomy it previously enjoyed. Currently, this subsidiary is focusing on its own survival and cost reduction programme, rather than serving as a site for others to learn from. In this respect, the case study has much in common with that of AutoPower, considered in Chapter 5 as well as this one, in which attempts to establish a network of HR managers working collaboratively across borders was derailed by adverse trading conditions.

For more details, see Zhang and Edwards, 2007.

Question

Why might the internationalization process of Chinese companies, such as CFS, differ from those of other nationalities?

The evidence on the diffusion of practices, whether forward or reverse, raises again the issue of how practices operate differently in the recipient unit. We saw above how the transfer of Japanese-style practices lead to changes in the way they operated as they were assimilated into a different institutional context and were interpreted differently by organizational actors at plant level. Similarly, the evidence concerning the reverse diffusion of Anglo-Saxon practices in German MNCs demonstrated that they were 'being assimilated in such a way as to change their significance' (Ferner and Varul 2000: 137). For example, the Anglo-Saxon emphasis on 'shareholder value' takes on a quite different meaning where shareholders are 'insiders' such as investment banks and families that have had close ties to the firm for a long period. Consequently, the authors argue that 'international "borrowings" from different business systems do not necessarily prefigure homogenisation and convergence among national models' (2000: 137).

Thus, the hierarchy of economies creates a dynamic that shapes the direction and form of cross-national diffusion within MNCs, and this has the potential to lead to significant changes in the nature of HRM in subsidiary units. Given this, it is pertinent to ask whether all MNCs will engage in cross-national diffusion, or whether it is likely to be found in certain types of MNCs. Do the characteristics of MNCs, such as the way they are integrated, affect the incidence of diffusion?

Corporate characteristics promoting and hindering diffusion

The literature on the diffusion of practices within MNCs has produced some mixed, even contradictory findings. For instance, some studies have shown broad similarities between the employment practices of foreign and local firms in a given national economy, while others have revealed marked differences which are attributed to diffusion from the centre of MNCs. One illustration of this is in Ireland where the work of Turner and his colleagues (2001), suggesting that foreign-owned firms have adapted their approach to fit in with the Irish system of industrial relations, contrasts sharply with other research (Geary and Roche 2001) claiming that the employment practices in foreign firms differ significantly from those in Irish firms. How can we make sense of such contrasting findings? One approach is to recognise that not all MNCs will look to diffuse practices across borders but that some key organizational features make it more or less likely to happen. We adopt this approach, focusing on the nature of integration that we came across in the previous chapter and expanding on this.

Examining the extent and nature of integration provides grounds for understanding why some MNCs have little incentive to transfer practices across borders. One motivation for a firm to expand into other countries is to seek to achieve *financial economies* from autonomous sets of operating units. Hill and Hoskisson (1987) argue that an explanation for why firms derive financial economic benefits from diversifying into unrelated areas with little in the way of linkages between operating units or divisions can be found in the 'markets and hierarchies' paradigm developed by Williamson (1975) and others. From this perspective, the limitations of information flows in capital markets mean that the hierarchy of the firm may be a relatively efficient mechanism for managing business units that have little in common with one another. As Hill and Hoskisson put it (1987: 332–333), 'firms pursuing a strategy of unrelated diversification can achieve a more nearly optimal allocation of resources, and "police" the divisions more effectively than the external capital market could if each division were an independent enterprise'. Thus, the attraction of growing internationally in this way is that the multinational firm acts as an 'internal capital market' (Marginson 1992). MNCs pursuing financial economies operate as a series of 'stand-alone' sites that have responsibility for a particular product or service and have no operational linkages with other parts of the multinational. Consequently, they have considerable autonomy on employment practices; the HQ role is confined to pressurizing the managers of business units to produce good financial returns but it lacks either the inclination or the mechanisms to exert central influence on functions such as HR, leaving operating units to their own devices. Thus, in this type of MNC, which we might term *non-integrated*, there is little incentive to transfer practices across borders.

The purest form of non-integration appears to be relatively rare, and many high profile diversified conglomerates, such as Hanson Trust, have been broken up into more focused businesses. Accompanying this it seems has been a growth of integrated MNCs which look to realize synergies across borders. Yet, as we saw in the last chapter integration can take different forms, notably *segmentation* or *replication,* with each having rather different implications for the transfer of practices. Segmentation involves each operating unit performing a distinct part of the production or service provision process in a vertically integrated chain. In this scenario, each site supplies components or services to others, receives components or services from others, or both. The advantages of achieving vertical integration internationally arise in part from the opportunities it presents to concentrate distinct operating functions in the national context with the most conducive conditions (Berger 2005), thereby exploiting locational specialization. As noted in the previous chapter, a stream of research analysing 'global value chains' has analysed the segmentation of production between and within firms across borders (e.g. Gereffi *et al.* 2005; Levy 2008) while a growing body of research has charted the way in which subsidiaries of MNCs have taken on distinct roles within interdependent network structures (e.g. Bouquet and Birkinshaw 2008).

The implications for the transfer of HR practices of this form of integration vary from one area of HR to another. The distinct role for the sites means that they differ from each other in the occupational mix of staff, while the tasks that employees are required to perform and the technologies they operate also differ. Therefore, there is relatively little incentive to apply common forms of work organization, for example,

across these quite different operating units. Indeed, it is this argument that has sometimes been used to argue that MNCs tend to make a virtue out of differentiating their
approach to each country (e.g. Kahancova and van der Meer 2006; Wilkinson *et al.*
2001). In other areas of HR, however, segmented production generates strong incentives to develop international policies. First, where there are vertical linkages between
sites, there is an incentive for the HQ to ensure that flows of components and services
between the operating units occur smoothly and they might seek to do this by developing the mobility of key groups of staff across their international operations. Moreover,
MNCs that are segmented have been those that are often criticized for exploiting vulnerable workforces. One response has been to establish minimum employment standards that apply across sites through a CSR code.

The option of pursuing segmentation is only open to those firms that can separate
the stages in a production process and place them in different locations. As we saw in
the previous chapter, this is clearly feasible in sectors such as clothing and electronics
and is increasingly used in parts of the service sector, such as finance where face-to-face
customer contact has been replaced to a large extent by international call centres
(Dicken 2007). However, the option of segmenting operations across borders is not so
easy in other sectors, particularly those in which MNCs face a requirement to have a
local presence if they are to serve the national market. In some sectors there is an
immediacy between firm and consumer that results in strong pressures towards establishing facilities in each national market the firm wishes to serve, as in fast-food and
newspaper printing (Bair and Ramsay 2003), and high transport costs make a local presence attractive in sectors such as the production of 'white goods' (Nichols and Cam
2005). In these sectors, functions cannot easily be concentrated in one location and
many MNCs respond by replicating their functions across countries.

Replication involves the creation of similar operating units performing essentially
the same roles as their counterparts in other countries, with sites employing a similar
profile of workers who perform comparable tasks and use the same technologies. MNCs
may adopt this approach because of the economies to be derived both from developing
'tangible interrelationships' through jointly developing new technologies and shared
inputs and from encouraging the instigation of 'intangible interrelationships' through
the diffusion of expertise across borders (Hill and Hoskisson 1987; Marginson 1992). As
Hill and Hoskisson argue, the realization of these benefits requires 'a corporate system
for identifying such opportunities' (1987: 334). It is evident that in replicated MNCs
the context of the employment relationship is similar across sites, suggesting that there
is considerable scope for an international dimension to HR in general and the transfer
of practices in particular.

An important source of synergies in this scenario is the adoption of international
management structures that facilitate the development of a standardized approach
across sites; realizing the benefits to be gained from both tangible and intangible interrelationships requires a corporate system for identifying what form these may take (Hill
and Hoskisson 1987; Taylor *et al.* 1996). Such structures create a locus of authority on
strategic issues that have knock-on effects on the HR function. More specifically, a
company way concerning a single model of production or service provision of the sort
we might expect in standardized MNCs has implications for global HR policies and the

transfer of practices across sites. This global dimension to HR is feasible and attractive because the sites not only share many features with their counterparts in other countries in terms of their occupational mix and the basic technologies employed but also because the standardized nature of the product means that the work process is very similar across sites. Thus MNCs that adopt a replicated approach have strong incentives to develop key staff for international assignments since such mobility is a primary mechanism through which interrelationships between sites are realized, and to operate common patterns of work organization, which can mesh with a standard product.

This approach to identifying the factors that promote or hinder the transfer of practices has been 'structural' in that it has focused on key organizational characteristics and highlighted the way in which the cross-border transfer of practices is more likely to occur in some MNCs than in others. In particular, while many MNCs are moving towards network forms of organization, these take many different forms. Hence, this approach is potentially more productive than those which group all MNCs together and compare them with local firms. However, one weakness in the approach is that it risks implying that outcomes, in this case the diffusion of practices, follow unproblematically from environmental and organizational factors. As argued in previous chapters, we should not assume that actors in the HQ can exert control over their international operations; rather, the authority of the HQ is commonly contested and challenged. Thus the structural approach should be complemented with attention to the way in which organisational actors at a variety of levels exercise choices, which may either encourage or obstruct diffusion. This 'political approach' highlights the ways in which organizational actors can draw on their sources of power in order to further their own interest, and is revealing about the processes through which diffusion takes place.

The process of diffusion

Management at the HQ of a multinational may see clear benefits in transferring practices across their international operations. In order to facilitate the transfer of knowledge and expertise across its sites, the HQ may establish a range of formal mechanisms that bring together actors from different parts of the multinational. These formal mechanisms can take the form of regular meetings and conferences of managers whose coverage is wide ranging, or working parties and task forces with more particular remits.

However, as we saw in Chapter 5, transferring expertise through the formal architecture of a network may not be straightforward since management at subsidiary level may seek to maximize their independence and look to block diffusion as a part of this, and use the sources of power they possess in their dealings with HQ. It may be imperative, for example, that the firm has an operating plant in the market it wishes to serve; this is a requirement in many service industries, of course. Generally, a local operating presence will require expertise concerning the local environment and market and the dependence of the HQ on local managers is a source of power for the latter group. Furthermore, within a foreign subsidiary of an MNC, 'domestic' managers may be able to lessen the influence of expatriates through their greater familiarity with the language and culture of the host country, as was illuminated by Broad's (1994) study of a

Japanese transplant in Wales. The ability of managers at unit level to form alliances with other local stakeholders can also be a source of power for this group in dealing with higher-level managers (Almond and Ferner 2006; Kristensen and Zeitlin 2005). Belanger *et al.* (2003) found that managers in one of the Canadian sites of ABB formed an uneasy alliance with the union in order to shape the sites response to the corporate restructuring programme.

Of course, managers at HQ level also possess sources of power which can be used to overcome resistance at local level and ensure that plants engage in diffusion. One of these is the formal authority that comes from their position in the managerial hierarchy, which can lead to formal directives or edicts on practices to be adopted at plant level. There are numerous examples of this in the literature; perhaps most famously, IBM's 'Blue Book' was used to stipulate policy in a number of areas of HR such as single status and employee representation. More generally, most MNCs have formal policies and guidelines on issues such as the deployment of staff on international assignments. However, there are significant constraints on the extent to which MNCs issue formal policies and guidelines on employment practice. Coller (1996) argues that this is because such 'direct control' involves the costs of, firstly, restricting the ability of plant managers to respond flexibly to the local environment and, secondly, de-motivating them through constraining their involvement in policy making. In a similar vein, Ferner (2000: 521) argues that 'formal "bureaucratic" controls depend for their effective operation on informal systems and the power relations they embody'.

Indeed, the literature suggests that many MNCs seek to rely on a range of more informal ways of influencing employment practices at plant level. These include forms of personal control such as developing the mobility of key staff across the company. Employees on international assignments fulfil a range of roles, but one of these is to take with them experience and knowledge of organizational practices. In some cases international assignees are given a specific brief to oversee the implementation of a particular practice or system. Bureaucratic forms of control can also be underpinned by 'social' control, such as attempts by senior managers to forge a distinctive 'corporate culture' which shapes the operation of the mechanisms identified above. One aspect of this is moves by the corporate HQ to ensure that there are common 'rules of the game' across the firm, such as shared understandings over the importance of sticking to formal budgetary targets (Ferner 2000).

This more 'unobtrusive' forms of control, as Coller (1996) terms it, has much in common with the 'transnational' strategy and structure outlined by Ghoshal and Bartlett (1998). This involved the creation of a network of actors from different countries, with each node of the network performing a distinct function and sharing expertise with other parts of the network. As we argued in Chapter 5, however, this vision of a network underplays the potential resistance to diffusion across the firm and the role of the centre in breaking down this resistance. Accordingly, the formal mechanisms that are established in order to facilitate transfer may also be complemented by the HQ threatening formal sanctions for those actors at unit level not engaging in transfer. The generation of internal competition between plants for new investment and new orders is a key way in which this can take place. This internal competition creates pressure on managers and worker representatives at plant level to adopt practices favoured by the

HQ. The HQs of such firms can also reduce their dependence on any one plant through sourcing the same product or component from more than one location, reducing the uniqueness of any one plant. In this way the HQ can reduce the degree to which it is dependent on a particular plant and use internal competition for investment and orders in order to pressurize actors at plant level into adopting practices that operate successfully elsewhere within the group.

In many cases, these kinds of 'coercive comparisons' are not possible, however. A principal reason for this is that the market in one country cannot be served from another location. As noted above, this is the case in many service industries, such as retail and catering, which require a physical presence in the market. Where coercive comparisons are not feasible, managers at the HQ may seek to use an alternative sanction, namely control over managerial careers. There is some evidence that the pay and promotion prospects of plant managers are influenced in part by their willingness to engage in the sharing of best practice across sites (see case study). Thus, the HQ ensures that a network of managers moving around the organisation take with them knowledge of practices which have operated successfully in one part of the organisation and disseminate this information to other plants.

CASE STUDY

Engineering Products – networking... but with the centre in charge

How does diffusion across a multinational occur? In particular, in what circumstances will subsidiary managers be inclined to both share innovations they have developed with other plants and adopt practices pioneered by others? As we have seen, many writers on international HRM argue that the diffusion of practices can and should occur through the operation of a network of plants across countries. The workings of such a network in facilitating diffusion were the subject of a recent case study of a British multinational in the engineering sector that we call 'Engineering Products'. The firm is nearly 100 years old and has had international operations for several decades. In recent years it has reduced the number of product lines it offers and now operates three primary divisions, the largest of which, automotive components, was the area studied. This division is a first-supplier to the large car assemblers, and is both highly integrated in the sense that it produces standardized products and highly internationalized in that it is spread across a number of countries. Indeed, only 15 per cent of the division's employees are based in the UK.

The division has a number of structures capable of transferring expertise and knowledge across borders, many of which the HR function has played a key role in creating. One key aspect of this is the management of overseas assignments. At any one time the division has around 60 people from various functions on long-term assignments of over a year in countries which are not their own. Spending time on an international assignment has become a key criterion in deciding whom to promote to senior positions within the firm. In addition to these long-term assignments, there are a number of other individuals on short-term visits of a few weeks or months, some of whom travel to learn about a practice operating elsewhere and others of whom travel to 'spread the word' about something developed in their unit. The division also has a number of mechanisms designed to bring together specialists from different functions: the 'Manufacturing Councils' facilitate exchange of information between manufacturing managers and engineers; the 'International College of Engineering' runs training courses on practices and technologies favoured by the HQ; while the HR function convenes regular meetings (at least twice a year) to discuss developments in HR practice and the scope to harmonise these across countries.

There was little evidence that the centre had used these mechanisms to exercise 'direct' control: there are few formal guidelines on HR practice across their international assignments and respondents at both plant and HQ level were keen to emphasize that the degree of central intervention in decision making was limited. However, there was compelling evidence that the mechanisms identified above were used by those at the centre of the division to exercise unobtrusive control in order to bring about the flow of practices across the firm's plants. There were a number of instances of this diffusion. First, the American operations have been pioneering a set of 'key competencies' that engineers across the firm should possess. Managers in the US were given the task of devising a training programme that would deliver these competencies, to be implemented by the International College of Engineering. Second, the French plant had developed a form of organizing the factory floor which involved dividing it into a series of small production units each with their own support services. The aim was to develop a stronger focus among the workforce on serving an 'internal customer', the next unit in the production process. This practice was diffused through the chief executive of the French plant being accorded the status of 'internal consultant', roaming from one subsidiary to another advising plant managers on the implementation of this system. Third, a form of cellular assembly had been developed in the Spanish plant involving the reorganization of the

assembly line into a series of U-shaped cells. Within these cells workers are required to perform a range of tasks and responsibility for quality and output levels is shared among team members. A team of Spanish engineers who had developed this practice were sent on a string of short-term assignments to the other plants, while the Spanish plant built and installed the U-shaped cells.

What tactics was the centre able to use to ensure that the sites engaged in the cross-national transfer of practices? A two-pronged approach was evident. The primary way in which the HQ created an imperative on actors at plant level to adopt practices favoured by the centre was to exercise 'coercive comparisons'. In recent years, the firm's customers had moved away from their own plants commissioning components from suppliers in their own country, towards the HQ placing orders with the HQs of a select band of suppliers who are themselves multinationals. In effect, this strengthened the hand of senior managers in their dealings with the plants since they were able to allocate production to those sites that produce the best quality products at the lowest cost. This source of power created an imperative on plants whose performance was poor to adopt practices favoured by the centre. One respondent at the divisional HQ described the way in which this pressure had led to the 'greater co-ordination of manufacturing processes to make sure that the world's best practices are shared and adopted across the organization'. He went on to state that if, in a hypothetical case, one of the subsidiaries refused to accept that a practice favoured by the HQ should be implemented the centre would initially try to 'persuade them and then instruct them and eventually fire the chief executive'.

However, while this pressure may be effective in ensuring that plants adopt practices diffused from elsewhere, it might make actors at plant level reluctant to share innovations with those in other plants for fear of undermining their own competitive position. Thus the second element of central influence was to give individuals at plant level an incentive to provide practices for the rest of the group by making it clear that doing so would enhance their own prospects for pay rises and promotion. Instances of this are the French and Spanish managers who had identified the improvements in work organization; not only were they given short-term international assignments as a 'reward' but it was also evident that this would count in their favour if they were to apply for positions outside their own plant.

For more details, see Edwards (1998).

Question

Why do you think that the HQ relied primarily on competition between sites and control over managerial careers as opposed to more direct forms of control?

It appears that in many MNCs diffusion occurs through networking between plants, underpinned by the HQ retaining control over investment decisions and the prospects of plant managers. This is the process that has been referred to as 'networking within hierarchy' (Edwards *et al.* 1999).

Conclusions

The chapter has considered several issues relating to the transfer of practices across borders: the extent to which practices can be transferred and operate in a new environment; the key patterns in terms of the direction of transfer; the type of MNCs most likely to engage in diffusion; and the processes through which diffusion takes place. In dealing with these questions, we have integrated into the analysis the role of both nationally distinct business systems and the internal politics of multinationals. Indeed, the inter-dependence between these two sets of factors has been, and will continue to be, a theme of the book; groups of actors within MNCs derive some of their power and influence from their familiarity with their local or national context, while the actions of large MNCs have the potential to shape the evolution of national systems. This approach is even more to the fore in our analysis of cross-border mergers and acquisitions in the next chapter.

Review questions

1 Why are some HR practices more diffusible than others?

2 What are the limitations to the concept of 'dominance' effects in shaping the transfer of practices across borders?

3 What are the different ways in which production or service provision can be integrated in MNCs and what are the implications for the transfer of practices?

4 Do you think that MNCs will look to engage in transfer of practices to an ever increasing extent in the future?

Further reading

1 Edwards, T., Rees, C. and Coller, X. (1999) 'Structure, politics and the diffusion of practices in multinational companies', *European Journal of Industrial Relations*, 5(3), 286–306.

The article discusses 'structural' and 'political' approaches to the diffusion of employment practices across borders within MNCs and argues that the two approaches can be integrated.

2 Ferner, A. (2000) 'The underpinning of bureaucratic control systems: HRM in European multinationals', *Journal of Management Studies*, 37(4), 521–39.

The paper tackles the nature of formalized, 'bureaucratic' forms of control in MNCs and argues that their efficacy is dependent on the informal workings of firms.

3 Edwards, T. and Zhang, M. (2008) 'Multinationals and national systems of employment relations: innovators or adapters', *Advances in International Management*, vol. 21, 33–58.

The paper is based on a case study of an American multinational in China and explores the ways in which practices are transferred across borders but also adapted to the national context.

4 Wilkinson, B., Gamble, J., Humphrey, J., Morris, J. and Anthony, D. (2001) 'The new international division of labour in Asian electronics: work organization and human resources in Japan and Malaysia', *Journal of Management Studies*, 38(5), 675–95.

The way in which Japanese MNCs 'segment' their international operations so that the various parts to the production process take place in different countries is elaborated upon. The authors argue that this segmentation (though they do not use that term) is a key driver of the nature of HR practices in place at each site.

References

Abramovitz, M. (1994) 'The Origins of the Postwar Catch-up and Convergence Boom', in Fagerberg, J., Verspagen, B. and von Tunzelmann, N. (eds) *The Dynamics of Technology, Trade and Growth*, London: Edward Elgar.

Almond, P. and Ferner, A. (eds) (2006) *American Multinationals in Europe: Managing Employment Relations Across National Borders*, Oxford: Oxford University Press.

Bair, J. and Ramsay, H. (2003) 'MNCs and Global Commodity Chains: Implications for Labor Strategies', in Cooke, W. (ed.) *Multinational Companies and Global Human Resource Strategies*, Westport: Quorum.

Belanger, J., Giles, A. and Grenier, J. (2003) 'Patterns of corporate influence in the host country: a study of ABB in Canada', *International Journal of Human Resource Management*, 14(3), 469–85.

Berger, S. (2005) *How We Compete: What Companies Around the World are Doing to Make It in Today's Global Economy*, New York: Doubleday.

Bouquet, C. and Birkinshaw, J. (2008) 'Weight versus voice: how foreign subsidiaries gain attention from corporate headquarters', *Academy of Management Journal*, 51(3), 577–601.

Broad, G. (1994) 'The managerial limits to Japanisation: a case study', *Human Resource Management Journal*, 4(3), 52–69.

Coller, X. (1996) 'Managing flexibility in the food industry: a cross-national comparative case study of European multinational companies', *European Journal of Industrial Relations*, 2(2), 153–72.

Dicken, P. (2007) *Global Shift: Reshaping the Global Economic Map in the 21st Century*, London: Sage.

Dickmann, M. (1999) 'Balancing Global, Parent and Local Influences: International Human Resource Management of German Multinational Companies', Unpublished PhD thesis, London: Birkbeck College.

Dickmann, M. (2003) 'Implementing German HRM abroad: desired, feasible, successful?', *International Journal of Human Resource Management,* 14(2), 265–83.

Edwards, T. (1998) 'Multinationals, labour management and the process of diffusion', *International Journal of Human Resource Management,* 9(4), 696–709.

Edwards, T. and Ferner, A. (2002) 'The renewed "American Challenge": a framework for understanding employment practice in US MNCs', *Industrial Relations Journal,* 33(2), 94–111.

Edwards, T. and Ferner, A. (2004) 'Multinationals, national business systems and reverse diffusion', *Management International Review,* 24(1), 51–81.

Edwards, T., Rees, C. and Coller, X. (1999) Structure, politics and the diffusion of practices in multinational companies', *European Journal of Industrial Relations,* 5(3), 286–306.

Edwards, T. and Zhang, M. (2008) 'Multinationals and national systems of employment relations: innovators or adapters', *Advances in International Management,* vol. 21, 33–58.

Elger, T. and Smith, C. (2005) *Assembling Work: Remaking Factory Regimes in Japanese Multinationals in Britain,* Oxford: Oxford University Press.

Ferner, A. (2000) 'The underpinning of bureaucratic control Systems: HRM in European multinationals', *Journal of Management Studies,* 37(4), 521–39.

Ferner, A. and Quintanilla, J. (1998) 'Multinationals, national business systems and HRM: the enduring influence of national identity or a process of "Anglo-Saxonisation"?', *International Journal of Human Resource Management,* 9(4), 710–31.

Ferner, A. and Varul, M. (2000) '"Vanguard" subsidiaries and the diffusion of new practices: a case study of German multinationals', *British Journal of Industrial Relations,* 38(1), 115–40.

Geary, J. and Roche, W. (2001) 'Multinationals and human resource practices in Ireland: a rejection of the "new conformance thesis"', *International Journal of Human Resource Management,* 12(1), 109–27.

Gereffi, G., Humphrey, J. and Sturgeon, T. (2005) 'The governance of global value chains: an analytical framework', *Review of International Political Economy,* 12(1), 78–104.

Ghoshal, S. and Bartlett, C. (1998) *Managing Across Borders: The Transnational Solution,* London: Hutchinson.

Gray, J. (2002) *False Dawn: The Delusions of Global Capitalism,* (2nd edition), London: Granta.

Hayden, A. and Edwards, T. (2001) 'The erosion of the country of origin effect: a case study of a Swedish multinational company', *Relations Industrielles/Industrial Relations,* 56(1), 116–40.

Hill, C. and Hoskisson, R. (1987) 'Strategy and structure in the multiproduct firm', *Academy of Management Review,* 12(2), 331–41.

Kahancova, M and van der Meer, M. (2006) 'Coordination, employment flexibility, and industrial relations in Western European multinationals: evidence from Poland', *International Journal of Human Resource Management,* 17(8), 1379–95.

Kristensen, P. and Zeitlin, J. (2005) *Local Players in Global Games,* Oxford: Oxford University press.

Krugman, P. (1994) 'The myth of Asia's miracle', *Foreign Affairs,* Nov.–Dec., 62–78.

Levy, D. (2008) 'Political contestation in global production networks', *Academy of Management Review,* 33(4), 943–63.

Maccoby, M. (1997) 'Is there a best way to build a car?', *Harvard Business Review,* Nov.–Dec., 75(6), 161–7.

Marginson, P. (1992) 'European integration and transnational management–union relations in the multinational enterprise', *British Journal of Industrial Relations,* 30(4), 529–45.

Martinez, M. and Weston, S. (1994) 'New management practices in a multinational corporation: the restructuring of worker representation and rights', *Industrial Relations Journal,* 25(2), 110–21.

Mtar, M. (2001) 'French Multinationals' International Strategy', PhD thesis, University of Warwick, Coventry.

Nichols, T. and Cam, S. (2005) *Labour in a Global World: Case Studies from the White Goods Industry in Africa, South America, East Asia and Europe,* Basingstoke: Palgrave Macmillan.

Oliver, N. and Wilkinson, B. (1992) *The Japanization of British Industry: New Developments in the 1990s,* Oxford: Basil Blackwell.

Porter, M. (1986) *Competition in Global Industries,* Boston: Harvard Business School Press.

Smith, C. and Meiksins, P. (1995) 'System, society and dominance effects in cross-national organisational analysis', *Work, Employment and Society,* 9(2), 241–67.

Streeck, W. (1992) *Social Institutions and Economic Performance: Studies of Industrial Relations in Advanced European Capitalist Countries,* London: Sage.

Taylor, S., Beechler, S. and Napier, N. (1996) 'Toward an integrative model of strategic international human resource management', *Academy of Management Review,* 21(4), 959–85.

Tempel, A. (2001) *The Cross-National Transfer of Human Resource Management Practices in German and British Multinational Companies,* Mering: Hampp.

Thory, K. (2008) 'The internationalisation of HRM through reverse transfer: two case studies of French multinationals in Scotland', *Human Resource Management Journal,* 18(1), 54–71.

Turner, T., D'Art, D. and Gunnigle, P. (2001) 'Multinationals and human resource practices in Ireland: a rejection of the "new conformance thesis": a reply', *International Journal of Human Resource Management',* 12(1), 128–33.

Whitley, R., Morgan, G., Kelly, W. and Sharpe, D. (2003) 'The changing Japanese multinational: application, adaptation and learning in car manufacturing and financial services', *Journal of Management Studies,* 40(3), 643–72.

Wilkinson, B., Gamble, J., Humphrey, J., Morris, J. and Anthony, D. (2001) 'The new international division of labour in Asian electronics: work organization and human resources in Japan and Malaysia', *Journal of Management Studies,* 38(5), 675–95.

Williamson, O. (1975) *Markets and Hierarchies: Analysis and Anti-trust Implications,* New York: Free Press.

Zhang, M. and Edwards, C. (2007) 'Diffusing "best practice" in Chinese multinationals: the motivation, facilitation and limitations', *International Journal of Human Resource Management,* 18(12), 2147–65.

Chapter 8

HR in cross-border mergers and acquisitions

Tony Edwards and Chris Rees

Key aims

The aims of this chapter are to:

- examine the pressures on firms to integrate HR policies in the two parties to the merger, focusing on the role of the nationality of the parent firm in shaping this process;
- consider the features of host countries which influence the nature of restructuring in the post-merger period;
- highlight the 'political' dimension to cross-border M&As, including the role of a range of groups within a firm who will seek to influence the character of the new firm;
- establish the challenges that firms face in learning from acquired operations.

Introduction

Cross-border mergers and acquisitions (M&As) are of particular concern to those interested in IHRM. The process of merging two firms, whether they be from different countries or not, raises a number of HR issues: the details of the merger and its likely implications for employees must be communicated; management must decide on the extent to which they will seek to integrate pay and benefit policies; and the employment consequences of the restructuring that follows most mergers must be confronted. The impact of a merger or acquisition, particularly the nature of restructuring, depends in large part on the rationale for it and the context in which it takes place. For example, a merger based on adverse trading conditions, over-capacity and the desire to cut costs is much more likely to lead to large-scale redundancies than one based on an expansion into new markets (Aguilera and Dencker 2004). The impact of cross-border M&As are also likely to be strongly shaped by national effects. These national effects show up in two ways; firstly in terms of the orientation of the parent or larger firm in the merger, something we have termed the 'country of origin' effect in earlier chapters; and secondly the way that HR issues are handled differently at national level, or 'host country effects'. We consider both aspects of these national effects in this chapter.

The 1990s witnessed a boom in cross-border M&As, with their value increasing from $150 billion in 1990 to more than $1,000 billion in 2007 (UN 2009). Rather than being

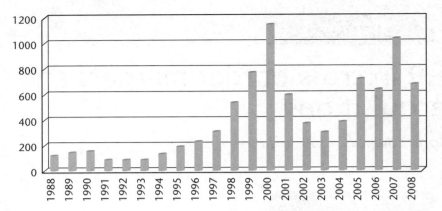

Figure 8.1 The growth in cross-border mergers and acquisitions ($ billions)
Source: UN (2009)

a steady rise, the value of cross-border M&As has been highly cyclical with sharp rises in the late 1990s of very nearly 50 per cent per annum, a subsequent fall in the first few years of the millennium, sharp rises again between 2004 and 2007, before a subsequent fall in 2008 (see Figure 8.1). This latter period was one in which there were a string of very large deals, including the famous – or notorious perhaps, given subsequent events – acquisition of ABN-AMRO by a consortium led by the Royal Bank of Scotland (RBS). In the year 2007 alone, there were 96 cross-border mergers which were valued at more than $3 billion (UN, 2008). Thus, cross-border M&As have been one of the principal ways in which firms have reorganized themselves internationally.

Cross-border M&As can transform companies in terms of their scale, structure and geographical orientation. A prime example is RBS, mentioned above, which acquired either partial stakes in, or full ownership of, banks in a number of countries in the 10 years or so prior to the 'credit crunch' of 2007–8. The aggressive expansion, particularly the purchases of companies near the peak of the stock market boom in 2007, was one factor in the company's huge debts, leading to the UK government taking a majority stake to keep the company afloat. RBS is not an isolated case in terms of the problems it encountered following overseas acquisitions. Many sources of evidence testify to the poor financial performance that is experienced by firms that have engaged in a series of cross-border M&As (Habelian *et al.* 2009). By 2002, it was evident that one-third of the cross-border M&As that had been reached in the second half of the 1990s were beginning to unravel, as firms sold off divisions and sites they had previously acquired (BBC News 2002). Moreover, a report by KPMG into cross-border M&As in Europe found that the majority of deals had failed to improve financial performance. The report argued that 'the process of entering into M&A transactions is often less than perfect, with key elements left too late and post-completion integration tackled haphazardly' (KPMG 1999: 23). The greater likelihood of cultural differences between parties to a cross-border merger when compared with domestic mergers may bring more acute challenges that help explain this disappointing performance. However, differences between the parties may also bring greater potential for learning. Stahl *et al.* (2004: 90–92) argue that this may explain why, while cross-border M&As are associated with poor performance, they actually compare favourably with domestic M&As.

The importance of cross-border M&As as drivers of corporate restructuring demands a close inspection of the processes involved. Throughout we make use of our own empirical research into cross-border M&As to illustrate the points (Rees and Edwards 2003; Edwards *et al.* 2008). This has taken the form of a series of case studies looking at the handling of HR issues in the British arm of firms formed through a cross-border merger. For reasons of confidentiality, the companies are often referred to with pseudonyms.

The national orientation of the parent in cross-border M&As

One of the key issues facing a firm that has been created through a cross-border merger is the extent and process of integration between the two firms. One pressure to integrate comes from the incentive to present a uniform face to global clients. In some service industries, such as management consultancy, and in some manufacturing industries, such as automotive components, firms are selling principally to other MNCs requesting a service or product which has few differences across countries. This necessitates the firm standardizing many aspects of its own operations, including HR issues such as work organisation, training and service delivery. In other cases, cross-border M&As are justified to shareholders on the basis that they will allow significant cost-cutting to take place. This requires the merged firm to remove duplicate functions and shed excess capacity, another force towards integration. A further reason why merged firms will look to integrate their HR policies across borders is that it will promote the mobility of staff across the company. Standard pay scales and benefits policies, at least for managerial and professional workers, is one way of facilitating such mobility.

However, in Chapter 3 we noted a number of significant differences in the framework of employment relations across countries. The distinctiveness of 'national business systems' shows up in a number of respects. One aspect of this is in relation to managerial backgrounds. In France and Germany it is common for senior managers to have technical backgrounds, whereas in Britain and the USA finance and accounting backgrounds dominate. This has implications for the sort of control mechanisms adopted at firm level. Historically, many large French and German firms have favoured a 'functional' corporate structure in which senior managers are involved in a range of technical and operational matters in the various units. In contrast, most British and American firms have strongly favoured a 'multi-divisional' structure in which the HQ merely exercises financial controls over divisions which operate with devolved responsibilities (Mayer and Whittington 2002). A further difference between countries concerns the use by firms of 'internal labour markets' in which recruitment is to junior positions with more senior positions being largely filled from internal promotions: while this has been a common practice in Japan, in other countries, such as the UK, there is much greater recourse to the external labour market and, consequently, much greater inter-firm mobility of labour. The laws and institutions that afford employees the right to be consulted about, and influence, decisions which affect their job security, pay prospects and the nature of their day-to-day work also differ markedly from country to country, with one contrast being between the highly regulated and codified system of employee representation in Germany and the more deregulated American system. One illustration of how national differences are evident in a firm formed through a cross-border merger is provided by Vaara and Tienari (2003) in their study of the Scandinavian financial services group Nordea. The authors cite the views of managers within the organization and show how 'national stereotypes' were constructed and endured. While these did not represent an 'absolute truth' concerning how people behaved, they did help those within the organization to make sense of why others behaved as they did. Thus, 'according to these "strong" stereotypes, Swedes were frequently seen as consensus-driven, Finns as action-oriented, Danes as negotiating merchants and Norwegians as people who go straight to the point in decision-making' (2003: 62).

These national differences are central to understanding the competing pressures on firms as they acquire or merge with those in other countries. The differences create pressure for national 'differentiation' of HR policies, for a company's approach to be responsive to the peculiarities of national systems. This is developed in the next sub-section. National differences are also significant, however, for the way they shape the extent and nature of integration. As we saw in Chapters 5, 6 and 7, most international firms are embedded in their original country in a range of ways: finance is raised and ownership is concentrated predominantly at home; senior managerial positions are filled largely by nationals of the home country; the government in the country of origin often has close ties with, and influence over, large MNCs; and so on. This embeddedness gives rise to a 'country of origin effect' in the way they manage their workforces. Thus we might expect this effect to inform the way that the dominant firm in a cross-border merger seeks to integrate its acquisition into the wider firm.

Indeed, the available evidence suggests that MNCs are significantly influenced by their original nationality in this respect. One illustration is a study by Faulkner *et al.* (2002) which examined acquisitions of British firms by foreign MNCs. Over the period of 1985 to 1994, the researchers examined through a postal survey the nature of post-acquisition change in 201 cases, with the parent firms being American, Japanese, French and German. While they found that there were some changes that appeared to occur whatever the nationality of the parent firm – most firms had sought to establish a clear link between pay and performance, for example – their findings also revealed significant differences by nationality in the handling of HR issues in the post-acquisition period, particularly in relation to recruitment, development and termination practice. One of the clearest findings was the preference among American firms for formal and regular appraisals, with these being used to ensure good performance; consistently substandard performance could easily lead to 'separations' under such systems. More generally, American firms exhibited a centralised, forceful and hands-on approach to integration, including an emphasis on trying to shape the culture of the acquired unit. Japanese firms also exhibited some distinctive ways of integrating acquired firms: they were less likely to rotate managers between different tasks; they favoured seniority as an important criterion for promotion; and they took a slower, more considered approach to change than the Americans. French acquirers also appeared to introduce some nationally specific practices in the post-acquisition period, such as emphasising formal qualifications as criteria for promotion. The authors also argued that there was a 'glass ceiling' for promotion for non-French managers. German acquirers tended to emphasis technical expertise in recruiting, but generally they adopted a highly decentralized approach to decision making on HR issues and, relatedly, attached less emphasis on using HRM in an integrative way.

Where the acquiring firm is clearly bigger than the acquired unit, this 'country of origin effect' seems to show through clearly. However, what happens where the two parties to a merger are of a comparable size? In such cases the orientation of the merged firm is less clear-cut. This is a significant issue because in the last decade or so a number of cross-border mergers have involved broadly similar sized firms, creating what has been termed 'bi-national' firms. Bi-nationals are so-called because the merger results in them having strong roots in two rather than one business system. This shows up in a number of ways. In terms of the ownership of merged firms, the overwhelming focus on one financial system that is characteristic of most MNCs is strongly eroded. The roots that bi-national firms have in two systems also show up in the cosmopolitan nature of the management board. It is common for a board in a firm formed through an agreed merger to be comprised of proportionate numbers of managers from each party to the merger. For example, with the creation of Astra-Zeneca, the top four managerial positions were divided up between two Britons and two Swedes. The international expansion of formerly state-owned companies has reduced a further source of national influence from the parent, namely that of the state. France Telecom, for example, has undertaken a string of acquisitions overseas, funded by raising finance on the financial markets in France and elsewhere, thereby reducing its ties with the French state. More generally, the wave of cross-border M&As in the late 1990s was one force towards the increased international spread of MNCs, something that is picked up in the growth of the UN 'Transnationality Index' (see Chapter 5).

In the case of bi-nationals which are created through cross-border M&As, is it possible to predict how the management of people will be handled? In particular, are there likely to be discernable national effects. Three possibilities exist. First, two national management styles may continue to be evident some time after the merger with full integration between the two parties to the merger being weak. If quite different styles do exist, there may be tensions between the two. Second, an integrated style may emerge following the merger which is a hybrid of the two styles. Third, an integrated style may also emerge based on one of the styles characteristic of one of the two firms. The case study of HealthCo shows how all three of these possible scenarios can be evident in a bi-national firm.

CASE STUDY

HealthCo

The pharmaceuticals and health care sector witnessed a number of mergers in the late 1990s. One of these brought together a British company with one which was predominantly American, forming a new group that has very strong bases in the UK and in the USA, as well as a notable presence in a number of others. The firm is officially registered as a British company, but has a split stock market listing in the UK and America, an HQ that is split across the two countries, and has a mix of nationalities on the company's management board – Americans and Britons comprise almost equal numbers, while other nationalities are represented too. The firm is therefore an excellent one in which to investigate the way in which a company formed through a cross-border merger has a detectable country of origin effect. Is it possible to detect particular national influences over the management style of HealthCo or is this a cosmopolitan, globally influenced firm? If the former, does the British or American influence show up more strongly?

The evidence from nearly 40 interviews in HealthCo suggests that it has been strongly influenced by the American system, something that shows up in a number of respects. First, the firm has a number of global HR policies on issues such as performance-related pay. The influence of the centre was much more marked in the predominantly American party to the merger than in its British counterpart, which was described as being like an 'absentee parent' by a number of Americans. A relatively centralized approach to decision making on HR issues is a characteristic feature of American MNCs more generally (see Ferner *et al.* 2004). Second, in the manufacturing side of the business all of the sites were required to introduce a process known as 'Lean Sigma', which is a way of identifying waste and potential economies in the organization of production. An American firm of consultants led the introduction of this. Third, since the merger the firm has introduced a new policy on the length of time that 'contingent', or temporary, workers can be employed continuously. Responding to a legal ruling in the US, the firm imposed an 18-month maximum time limit on the use of such workers in America and Britain, even though the law in the UK is different. Fourth, in relation to 'diversity' the American operations are clearly perceived as being more advanced than those in other countries and have served as the model on which practices in other countries have been developed, such as 'diverse marketing teams'.

In short, the merger has created a firm with no clear-cut national 'centre of gravity', but one that is shifting towards America. The interviews demonstrate that this shift appears to be partly explained by the attractions of the US to senior managers, such as the widespread perception of it as a fast-moving, dynamic system and one that is 'more advanced' in some areas such as diversity. One manager summed up this influence: 'All our competitors, or the majority of our competitors, are in the States. So you know 70 per cent of our competition is in the United States so role models of how people behave in our industry almost seem very influenced by the US.'

However, the influence of the HQ, which we have argued is distinctively American, is of course mediated by the dominant features of the various host country systems that the firm operates within. For example, the pace at which restructuring has taken place has been swifter with less consultation in the UK than in Germany, partly reflecting the legal requirements for negotiation with employee representatives. The central influence was also constrained by country level managers who were reluctant to give up their autonomy, something that was particularly marked in countries with operations belonging to the British party to the merger.

Source: Edwards *et al.* (2006).

Question

To what extent can the concept of 'dominance' effects help explain the direction the company took following the merger?

The case study of HealthCo has demonstrated not only the influence of the business systems of the main parties to a cross-border merger but also the influence of host country systems in shaping the effects of a merger. It is to this that we now turn.

Restructuring at national level and the legacy of distinctive national systems

The regulation of M&As has some common aspects across countries. This is particularly so within the EU where there is a common legal framework setting out a minimum set of employee rights during M&As. This framework stems from the EU Acquired Rights

Directive (77/187/EEC), which was revised in 1998 (98/50/EC), concerning the safe-guarding of employees' rights in the event of a transfer of ownership of companies. In essence, the acquiring firm must respect most of the obligations that the acquired firm had towards its employees. In particular, the Directive states that:

- terms and conditions existing in a collective agreement must be observed until such an agreement expires or is replaced with a new one;

- a transfer of ownership does not of itself constitute a justifiable reason for dismissals (though that does not mean that none will occur – they can take place for 'eco-nomic, technical or organizational reasons');

- the status of employee representatives should be preserved following a merger or acquisition;

- these representatives are entitled to be consulted as to the likely or planned eco-nomic and social implications of the transfer, with this consultation occurring 'in good time' before the transfer is carried out.

The Directive has been implemented into national law in all EU member states, with only limited variation at national level, and is a requirement for new 'accession' coun-tries. Thus, where M&As bring together firms from different EU countries, there is to some extent a common legal framework governing the process.

Despite this EU-wide framework, there are marked differences in the extent of regu-lation across EU countries since some have additional provisions concerning employee participation in M&As (see EIRO 2001). In the Netherlands, for example, there are a number of institutional means through which employees' rights are protected, notably through the 'Merger Code' and the Works Council legislation. These require that man-agement in the companies involved in a merger inform both sets of works council rep-resentatives and also inform union representatives. Management must provide the works council with information concerning the likely impact of the merger, provide a justification of its decision, and show that it has taken account of workers' interests. Crucially, works councils have the right to seek external expert assistance and can chal-lenge management's proposals; if they do so, then the proposals must be postponed for a month, during which time the works council can go to a Labour Court to challenge the decision. If this court feels that management have not done enough to safeguard employees' interests it can prevent management's plans being implemented. In addi-tion, a merged firm wishing to make redundancies must get the approval of a 'District Employment Services Authority', and the firm's Supervisory Board must approve any major changes involved in post-merger restructuring. Even after the current revisions to the 'Merger Code', which have marginally weakened the position of unions and works councils in the target company and made hostile takeovers slightly easier, it is clear that Dutch workers enjoy considerable legal and institutional protection during M&As.

In Spain, there are also national level provisions safeguarding employees' rights, though these are not as strong as those in the Netherlands. Spanish firms are obliged to consult with both works councillors and trade unionists. In particular, the 'Workers' Statute' gives employee representatives the right to be consulted on the same basis as shareholders; since shareholders must be informed in writing at least one month before a general shareholders meeting at which the merger proposals are to be discussed, so workers must be informed at the same time. Moreover, where a merger or acquisition involves 'any incidence that affects the volume of employment' worker representatives must be given at least 15 days to issue a report containing their views, and this must be received and considered by management before a merger is consummated, though they are not obliged to implement its proposals. However, while worker representatives do not have the power to block or even delay job losses involved in a merger, where collective redundancies of roughly 10 per cent of the workforce are not agreed by worker representatives and management, the plans must go for approval to a 'labour authority' at either local, regional or national level, whichever is most appropriate.

In the UK, by contrast, the ability of employees to influence the merger process is weaker and the framework protecting employees' rights is more minimalist. The European Directives were transposed into UK law through the Transfer of Undertakings (Protection of Employment) Regulations (1981), known as TUPE. This Act, which has been subsequently amended to comply with the new European directive, gives employees the basic rights of consultation that exist across the EU. In addition, legislation on collective redundancies also gives employees the right to be consulted 90 days before any such redundancies are made. However, beyond these provisions any influence that employees possess stems from their bargaining power in relation to their employer, either in an organized way through the influence of unions or through their possession of skills which mean they are of value to their employer. In essence, therefore, managers have a freer hand in the UK to make changes following a merger than they do in most European countries.

Differences in the regulation of M&As within the EU are even greater when compared with other countries, such as those in North America and Asia. Variations in legal frameworks are only one element, of course, of wider differences in systems of employment relations. These differences encourage the decentralisation of decision-making on HR issues in firms formed through a cross-border merger. In other words, 'host country effects' significantly shape the handling of HR issues.

The importance of these national level institutions and regulations shows up in a recent study of Franco-German mergers. Corteel and Le Blanc (2001) argued that 'social issues' – by which they mean pay, working time, holidays, pensions and so on – are governed by a national logic, and that these are 'lastingly rooted at national level'. Thus in the companies they examined, the differences between the French and German operations in terms of pay, benefits and working time arrangements that existed prior to the merger continued to exist following the merger. Managers had not sought to integrate practices in this area, principally because they recognised the importance of national level regulations and the strength of the 'social partners' in the two countries.

Our own current research confirms this picture. Interviews with HR managers in the British arm of 12 firms which have been involved in a cross-border merger or acquisition (of which HealthCo is one) highlighted how remuneration is strongly conditioned by national level factors. Pay and benefits are clearly one of the areas where differences in practices become immediately apparent following a merger. The MNCs have a strong incentive to integrate these policies, particularly where they want employees to be geographically mobile. However, a key constraint on managers is that integration will only be readily agreed by employees if it takes the form of 'upward harmonization'. Thus, host country effects lead to the creation of a 'patchwork quilt' of various sets of pay and conditions across borders (Rees and Edwards 2003).

The difficulties in integrating remuneration policies across sites in different countries also exist, albeit to a lesser degree, between sites within countries. The TUPE regulations in the UK, and the role of unions in securing collective agreements in many organizations, mean that levels of pay and benefits continue to differ across sites that formerly belonged to different firms. An IT services company in our research, which had taken on groups of workers gradually from a range of other firms through the subcontracting of their IT functions, now has 27 sets of terms and conditions in its British operations. In a French industrial firm, managers were quite clear that while they would like pay levels to be similar across their operations in France, there is little prospect of employee representatives agreeing to this. Thus, the 'patchwork quilt' exists within as well as between countries.

The way in which cost savings are made is also something which is strongly shaped by host country effects. As we indicated above, many cross-border mergers are motivated by a desire to reduce costs through removing duplicate functions and concentrating activities in particular locations. However, the ease with which plants can be closed and employees made redundant differs across countries. Corteel and Le Blanc (2001) present a fascinating case which demonstrates this, namely the merger between the German-owned Quante and the French firm Pouyet. Following this merger, the IG Metall union in Germany and the unions in France were successful in preventing any cutbacks leading to compulsory lay-offs in France or Germany. However, the firm did close a plant in the UK, where workers did not have the same legal protection. For Corteel and Le Blanc 'it is reasonable to argue that...a logic aiming at preserving national employment levels to the detriment of employees located on other territories prevailed'.

The implication of Corteel and Le Blanc's argument is that a range of groups are able to shape the restructuring process which follows a cross-border merger. It is not simply the product of systematic planning by senior management, nor is restructuring simply the result of a rational trade-off between the advantages of integrating policies across borders on the one hand versus differentiating policies to national level on the other. Rather, it is a highly political process in which a variety of groups look to defend or advance their own interests and use whatever sources of power they control to do so. We now consider this political dimension in more detail.

The political dimension to cross-border M&As

Much of the writing on M&As in general and cross-border M&As in particular stresses the importance of managers following plans, guidelines and checklists if they are to make a merger a success. For instance, Schuler *et al.* (2003) provide a series of guidelines for HR practitioners to follow, such as 'state-of-the-art HR policies and practices should be used' (2003: 70). Similarly, Stahl *et al.* (2004) identify a number of HR issues that have to be confronted in a cross-border merger, such as assessing culture in the due diligence phase' and 'undertaking a human capital audit'. While such guidelines may to some extent be useful to practitioners, in this section we emphasize the internal disputes that arise within MNCs concerning the nature of integration and restructuring in the post-merger period.

Mergers and acquisitions, whether domestic or cross-border, are a time when organisational structures and styles are 'unfrozen' and new ones are created. As Meyer and Lieb-Doczy (2003: 479) put it, 'managers ought to be aware of the evolutionary processes within the firm' following a cross-border M&A. During this process, there are many individuals and groups within the organisations concerned who will look to defend or advance their own interests. A merger is a time when a lot is 'up for grabs': the structure of the merged firm must be determined; key positions need to be filled; the units that are to close or suffer the deepest cuts have to be identified; and so on. While the forces of competition and the demands of the financial markets mean that there are external demands that pressurise companies into prioritizing certain outcomes, the process of reaching the eventual course of action is a highly political one. A range of organizational actors possess some scope to influence the overall direction of the firm and, hence, this direction is not solely the product of a rational process of planning by senior managers responding to external pressures; it is also the product of a series of internal negotiations and compromises.

This perspective on organizations generally is well developed in the academic literature on strategy making and organizational change. What is sometimes referred to as the 'processual approach' to strategy (Whittington 2001) emphasizes the range of sources of power within organizations that exist, with these not solely residing with those actors at high points in the formal hierarchy. Thus, writers such as Mintzberg are sceptical about the mainstream view that strategy making is a rational and objective process. Instead, they see strategies as emerging from a series of negotiations, compromises and 'bodges'. As a consequence, the outcomes of strategy can include goals other than just the maximisation of profits for the organization as a whole and can reflect such considerations as the desire of a powerful group to safeguard the future of a unit in which they work. This political perspective helps us understand organizations of any sort, but seems essential to incorporate into an analysis of cross-border M&As. This is partly because mergers are times when a range of issues need to be resolved, as argued above, but also because cross-border M&As involve new operations in different business systems and the divergence of interests within such operations is likely to create fertile ground for political activity.

This perspective is also evident in the literature on MNCs, which are seen by some as 'loosely coupled political systems' (Forsgren 1990). The detailed case study work of Bélanger et al. (1999) into ABB is testament to the resources controlled by those in operating units of a large multinational. As we saw in Chapter 6, on occasions these resources can be used to obstruct policies issued by the corporate centre. These political processes should be seen as central to the way that the firms as a whole react to developments and challenges from the context in which they operate. As Edwards et al. (1993: 3) put it: 'political processes are not separate from structural forces, but represent the working out of responses to them'.

Our own case study work highlights a number of ways in which the process of merging firms across borders is highly political. Where international mergers bring together firms of roughly equal sizes, perhaps the most obvious example is the composition of the senior managerial positions. If a merger is billed as a 'merger of equals' it is important symbolically for the top management team to be comprised of equal numbers from both firms. For example, in the UK arm of the large French industrial firm referred to above, the issue of proportionate 'balance' in choosing people for senior positions was seen as crucial. This was influenced by the French parent company, where balance between the three companies that had merged was highlighted explicitly by the CEO as central to its success. In a different company, one manager argued that this process of dividing up the positions according to the proportionate size of the companies could mean that the most able and best qualified people were not always selected – or as he put it, 'you can end up with a complete dingbat in a senior position'. Despite this, even this manager saw achieving balance as necessary for the merger process to be seen as fair by employees of both 'legacy' companies. In other words, achieving balance may mean that the firm does not appoint the best person for the job, but this is often deemed a price worth paying in order to create an impression of fairness.

The way in which senior managerial posts are distributed was identified by Vaara and Tienari (2003) in their discussion of the creation of Nordea. Because of the sensitivity of the mergers being seen as one party being dominant, both to those in the organisations and to those outside, particularly the national governments, it was seen as essential that they were portrayed as 'mergers of equals'. For this impression to be created it was agreed that there should be 'an even distribution of positions in board and executive management' (2003: 95). While this was largely seen as legitimate in the immediate post-merger period, it soon became evident that maintaining this balance was creating tensions with other priorities that the firm had developed, such as stressing the importance of competencies in selecting managers for key positions and increasing the proportion of women in senior levels of management.

The political dimension to cross-border mergers also shows up in the struggle for influence by organizational actors from different functions. Of great relevance here is the role of those in the HR function; a perennial concern for HR practitioners in the UK and in many other countries is their relatively low status within organizations, leading to the danger from their perspective of being marginalized during major organizational changes such as international M&As. In one of the IT companies in our study the HR Director indicated that the function had not been involved in key strategic decisions during an acquisition, such as the choice of partner and the speed with which it would be integrated, nor had they even had much influence over many of the HR issues thrown up by the acquisition, such as the consultation process and recruitment to key positions within the acquired unit. However, in other cases it was evident that HR practitioners have used the merger or acquisition as an opportunity to raise the profile of HR within the organization. One example was the persistent efforts by an 'HR Partner' at an American financial services group to convince other managers, particularly those with an accountancy background, of the benefits of involving her in the setting up of joint ventures in various European countries. These efforts took the form of stressing the impact on the bottom-line of mishandling HR issues, such as the legal penalties of contravening the Acquired Rights Directive and supplementary national regulations.

A further question that is an aspect of many cross-border M&As, and is highly political, is that of where the main brunt of cost cutting is to be felt. Based on their study of Franco-German mergers, Corteel and Le Blanc (2001) argue that a company's overall work load is governed by a 'national fair balance rule'. This rule means that orders from customers are distributed among the firm's sites not only according to the costs and performance of these sites, but also according to what is seen as just. In other words, these decisions are governed partly by 'rationality', but also by 'fairness'. The impetus for this often stemmed from informal deals that were struck during the merger negotiations; these were not binding following the merger, but breaching them would risk creating serious grievances in the units which came off worse. As one of their respondents put it: 'If we were willing to work, politically, we had to distribute the load in a fair way'. However, their data also point to the limits of the 'national fair balance rule', particularly the way it is limited to certain territories. As discussed in the previous subsection, the British plant of the firm formed through the merger of Quante and Pouyet was closed, partly in order to preserve employment levels at the French and German operations. Moreover, the authors also stress that the rule can become strained over time, leading to its renegotiation.

Overall, this line of analysis indicates that it is the diffusion of control of resources across a range of groups within a merged organisation that results in the process being so highly political. One of the resources that is controlled by staff at unit level within MNCs is knowledge of, and expertise in, local institutions and regulations. This knowledge and expertise can be used to advance or protect their own interests. The Corus case study considered below illustrates the interdependence between local institutions and regulations on the one hand, and the influence of different groups within merged firms on the other.

CASE STUDY

Corus

The merger of British Steel with Hoogovens in June 1999, forming the Anglo-Dutch group known as Corus, provides an interesting example of what can happen when firms from two quite different business systems join together. One key difference between the two countries concerns the nature of employee relations; as we have seen, the Dutch system affords employees more scope than their British counterparts to influence the restructuring that follows a merger. This has had significant implications for relations between different units of the firm in general, and for the form that cost cutting has taken in particular.

The merger took place in the context of over-capacity in the sector. Other mergers between steel firms have occurred, notably that between Usinor of France, Arbed of Luxembourg and Aceralia of Spain, with a prime motive being the opportunity to realise cost savings through removing duplicate functions. At the time of the Corus merger, managers promised shareholders that savings of £194 million a year would result. It was evident that this would mean large-scale redundancies.

By early 2001, with the market for steel turning markedly down, it was apparent that Corus would be suffering very large financial losses. In February of that year management announced that 6,000 employees in the British operations would be losing their jobs. The union representing most of the

British workforce, the Iron and Steel Trade Confederation (ISTC), pressurized the company to amend its plans, advancing counter-proposals which included buying a plant from the company and short-time working to tide the company over until the market picked up. However, the legal framework in the UK meant that these proposals would have to find support from managers if they were to have any impact, and the company was adamant that they should press on with their original plans. Meanwhile, in the Netherlands redundancies were also taking place. Only six months after the merger, there had been a 'wildcat' (unofficial) strike at the huge and profitable Ijmuden plant following the announcement that the steel manufacturing department would be shut with the loss of 590 jobs. In 2001 it was announced that 1,100 further jobs would be cut as the company's losses became apparent.

During the first two years or so of the post-merger period it appeared that employee representatives were liasing more closely across the two countries. When the axe fell on 6,000 British workers in early 2001 the Dutch Trade Union Federation (Federatie Nederlandse Vakbeweging, FNV) wrote to the ISTC, pledging support for their campaign of opposition to the cuts. Moreover, the Dutch union hinted that it might support a boycott at the Ijmuden plant of any work that was to be transferred from the UK to the Netherlands.

Even after the large scale cuts of 2001 the company's troubles continued. The share price at the end of 2002 stood at less than half of its value at the time of the merger. This added to the pressure on senior managers, and in response the company signalled a move away from its 'multi-metal' strategy by proposing to sell its aluminium business to Pechiney of France. This met strong resistance from employee representatives, and also revealed tensions between the different parts of the business across the two countries. According to press reports, many in the Dutch part of the firm had come to resent the merger, seeing it as a takeover of a profitable Dutch business by an ailing British one. In late 2002, it became evident that the Dutch supervisory board, which is made up of a mixture of managers and employee representatives, was threatening to use

its power to veto the proposed sale of the aluminium business. Members of the board were concerned that the proceeds from the sale of this part of the business, which stemmed mainly from Hoogovens, were to be used to pay off group debt rather than re-invested in the Dutch part of the business. The implication was that further cuts would have to occur in the UK if the supervisory board was to approve the sale. Indeed, the chair of the board Leo Berndsen is reported to have said that if senior managers 'don't tackle structurally the problems in the UK, Hoogovens will become Corus's cash cow'. The supervisory board did indeed use its power to bock the sale, throwing the company's future into doubt for a while. Management's response was to seek further rationalizations in the British part of the business, involving yet more redundancies. Between 2004 and 2007 the company's fortunes turned upwards, mainly off the back of steep rises in the steel price, and its share price rose steeply. The booming steel sector more generally led to fresh merger interest and in 2007 the company was taken over by Tata, an Indian conglomerate. This acquisition was quickly followed by the recession of 2008 onwards, leading to fresh bouts of cost-cutting.

The case of Corus in general, and the dispute over the sale of the aluminium business in particular, demonstrate the way in which actors at local level within MNCs can draw on their embeddedness in the local institutional framework and use it as a source of power within the company. As we have already seen in this chapter, the ability of British workers to shape management's plans during and after a merger is much more limited than that of their Dutch counterparts. The significance of the role of the Dutch supervisory board in particular, and the institutions and regulations in the Netherlands more generally, is evident not only in the way that they have limited the restructuring in the Netherlands itself, but also in the knock-on effects on restructuring in other countries.

Question

Why will the concerns of employee representatives be different in other types of cross-border mergers?

Cross-border M&As and organizational learning

This section addresses a key question about cross-border M&As, namely to what extent do organizations engaged in international M&As learn from their experiences? In particular, it investigates the extent to which expertise and practices in the operations that are acquired are transferred to the parent company. Growing by acquisition automatically increases the diversity of expertise and practice in the wider firm; no two firms will have identical practices, nor will the body of expertise be the same. Thus in contrast to firms that do not grow at all, firms growing through M&As receive fresh input in terms of technologies and practices. Moreover, in comparison with firms that grow through 'greenfield' investments, there is also more of an external input into companies growing through M&As as they inherit a set of pre-established practices and a body of expertise giving them great potential to engage in knowledge transfer from their acquired operations (Edwards 2000). This is especially so for international M&As and making use of this diversity is a key aspect of the integration process (Bjorkman *et al.* 2007; Stahl and Voigt 2008). Schuler *et al.* (2003: 114) argued that 'capturing and consolidating the learning and knowledge that has been generated throughout the IM&A process is perhaps the most important activity' during the full integration stage. Despite this, there is rather little empirical evidence on this phenomenon in practice (Habelian *et al.* 2009). Some studies look at how international acquisitions provide firms with the knowledge to operate in the market in which they have made the acquisition (e.g. Zou and Ghauri 2008), but there are few that look at ways in which knowledge and expertise is spread to the rest of the firm. In one study Bresman *et al.* (1999: 439) concluded that while 'the immediate post-acquisition period is characterised by imposed one-way transfers of knowledge from the acquirer to the acquired,... over time this gives way to high quality reciprocal knowledge transfer'. However, they were not writing about HR specifically and we need to know more about the extent and nature of transfer from the acquired operations back into the rest of the multinational. In doing so, we draw on a recent study of this issue (Edwards *et al.* 2008).

Edwards *et al.*'s (2008) survey analysis showed that while some firms do indeed absorb new knowledge and practices from acquired units, on average firms growing through international M&As are not more likely to learn from their foreign units than those that have not grown in this way. They then used the case studies to explore this issue further, with variation evident in the extent to which the transfer of knowledge was a key aim of management in the post-merger period. In three of the firms there was no evidence that the acquired units had instigated a process of corporate-wide learning. This was the case in AmeriBank, US Industrial, and New Finance. In one of the others, Euro Cure, the acquisition was motivated by 'an acquisition of knowledge...an acquisition of their potential and their future' but this had not fed through. At the time of their research, however, this had not fed through into concrete instances of transfer from the acquired operations.

In two of the other case studies it was possible to identify practices and expertise that had been absorbed into the parent company. One of these was InterServ, which was bought partly for its management style. According to the respondents in the acquired company, the acquiring firm was deliberately purchasing another whose ethos and approach differed markedly from its own yet which it very much admired, describing the acquired firm as 'fast moving' and 'vibrant'. This had opened the door for those in the UK operations that had been acquired to push a number of their ideas and practices to the parent firm, enabling them to raise their own profile within the much larger company of which they had become a part. There were three examples of new company-wide initiatives that had been developed by those in the UK, including a share plan, an employee survey and a new talent management system. The other case study firm in which the acquired units had exerted influence on the rest of the firm was Global Drug. Acquisitions in this sector in recent years have been characterized by big pharmaceuticals firms purchasing much smaller biotechs, which often lack the financial backing and expertise necessary for long-term success. Since most biotechs do not have the resources or experience to take a drug beyond research and development, through several phases of clinical trials and on to end-stage marketing and sales, they are an attractive source of knowledge to large pharmaceuticals firms looking to enhance their pipeline or to fill a gap in a particular drug category. The acquisition in question in Global Drug was of a very small bio-technology company in the US that had very particular expertise in a specific technology that was of great interest to the acquiring firm. Clearly, what were being absorbed in this case were not innovative HR practices, but the absorption of the technical expertise had clear HR consequences. As one manager put it, 'We did appreciate that it would take time to get to the point of saying we have acquired the technology transfer'.

How should the patterns in the data be viewed? Clearly, expertise is absorbed into the wider firms in some cases, but this is clearly far from a straightforward process. Edwards *et al.*'s (2008) research highlighted six factors that lead some acquiring firms to engage in transfer across the firm while others did not.

▶ The motivations for the acquisition and the assumptions held about the nature of the acquired units

One factor that shapes the extent to which acquiring firms learn from acquisitions is the assumptions that they have about the quality of the companies that they buy. In some cases the senior managers driving the acquisition may be motivated by a desire to tap into expertise in the company that they are purchasing but in other cases the acquired firm is perceived in a less positive light, particularly when the national system in which it is located is viewed negatively. Thus the acquiring firm is unlikely to learn from its new operations, an example of which was AmeriBank's acquisition of a Polish bank. This acquisition was motivated by a desire to establish a significant presence in a new market but it was clear that they were not expecting to be able to learn from the firm that they acquired. As one respondent put it, 'What they had didn't really matter that much'. The acquired firm was viewed by the parent as having some 'irrelevant' processes, such as the manual counting of money, and some 'outdated' benefits, such as meal tickets and holiday homes. More generally, HR was seen as a low-status function that needed to be 'professionalized'. This approach to acquisitions in which the acquired firm is seen as having little to offer is likely to be common in those cases where a well-established company from a developed economy is acquiring a much smaller firm in a transition economy. Thus, AmeriBank's approach was certainly not illogical; those in the Polish bank had local market knowledge and contacts with key intermediaries, but were unlikely to be able to teach the parent much about how to manage its international operations. This approach of assuming that the acquired firm may have little to offer is also likely to be found in cases where a failing company is acquired; in a scenario where the parent has rescued a firm on the brink of collapse, it is unlikely to then search for distinctive practices or expertise in the acquired operations. In other contexts, however, the assumption that the parent firm has little to learn may be less justified and may represent a missed opportunity to learn. As we will see, this was evident in some of the other case study companies.

▶ A centralized model in the acquiring firm

A second factor, and one which is related to the first, is the extent to which the parent firm has a centralised approach to managing its international workforce. An example of this is US Industrial and its acquisition of a much smaller British firm, a move that was part of the parent firm's emphasis on growth into new business areas. However, despite this being the motivation for the acquisition, *US Industrial* largely imposed its structure and culture on to the organisation it acquired. With an ethnocentric mindset, the firm's HR policy and practice emanated from Head Office with strategic decisions being made centrally. A part of this approach was to make cost savings through rationalizing the acquired units and installing 'change leaders' from US Industrial. There were signs that the ethnocentric perspective in US Industrial had led to the firms not appreciating other ways of doing things and, therefore, losing opportunities to learn from their new subsidiary. A joke in the organization concerning its approach to acquisitions was that the company's actual name stood for a phrase equivalent to 'You Must Comply', representing the heavy-handed approach to managing post-merger integration. Overall, then, while centralization can deliver many benefits to the organisation, such as global consistency on a business model that may have worked well in the home country, the case indicated that where the predominant model in an acquiring firm is centralization, such an approach can lead to a blinkered perspective which in turn can impede learning from the new organization.

▶ The lack of a strategic approach to acquisitions

A third factor, and one that is also related to the issue of how effectively an acquirer is able to see the diversity of practice and expertise that it has bought, concerns the extent to which it adopts a deliberate strategy of integrating any such practice or expertise. In some of the firms, as we have seen, the acquisitions were motivated by a desire to take advantage of what the acquired operations possessed with a view to utilising this in other parts of the firm. However, in one of the other companies, New Finance, there was no such strategic approach. This company had expanded quickly through a range of acquisitions paid for largely in shares, the value of which had risen sharply as the stock market at that time looked very favourably on firms that used the internet as the main vehicle for accessing customers. It acquired financial service providers in a number of countries with the inflated valuation of the parent company meaning that it was possible for senior managers to buy up companies without having to build a convincing case to analysts concerning the scope for rationalizations. In describing its approach to acquisitions outside the US, one respondent indicated that the company 'took almost a shotgun type approach, no real clue of what they were doing'. Thus, New Finance lacked a coherent plan to its growth that meant it never achieved the equilibrium needed to put in place the mechanisms to enable learning. With so many acquisitions in a short space of time, it was unable to stop and reflect on the potential learning opportunities in its latest purchase because it was already in the process of the next one. Thus, once in possession of the new entity, there were no plans in place to learn from acquired operations. This case study illustrates a key challenge to be overcome if international acquisitions are to result in learning, namely the need for a deliberate approach to learning involving the establishment and maintenance of channels through which knowledge can be transferred.

▶ Central resistance to the acquired units taking the lead in policy development

A fourth factor concerns the openness to learning from acquired units on the part of those at the centre of the company. In the case of InterServ, the message of valuing the British firm's dynamism and innovative approach was not matched by the attitudes of many in the HR function at the firm's HQ. The respondents in the UK described the parent firm as having an 'old fashioned HR team' that relied on a rather 'bureaucratic' approach and which had not 'even been involved in the acquisition'. This apparently had caused some resentment, particularly when the senior corporate management at the HQ were heaping praise on the approach of the acquired firm. This had led to some heated exchanges involving an HR person at the HQ saying to a British counterpart 'if you are so good why weren't you the acquirer?' Those in the central HR function were seen as keen on a form of integration that involved their pre-existing model being the basis for how the company should operate. As one respondent put it, 'what they would dearly like to do from a management perspective is for us to adopt their approach lock, stock and barrel'. In this context, the UK operations leading on some new policy developments had caused some tensions within the HQ, with the HR Director apparently being irritated that senior managers were looking outside the country of origin in allocating the role of leading new initiatives. Accordingly, there was an acceptance on the part of those in the British operations that to be effective in transferring expertise they had to tread carefully, not going in 'with all guns blazing'. Thus, if the organization is to utilize the expertise and practices of its acquired units then there must be a commitment from those at the centre of the company to welcoming input from these operations and sensitivity on the part of those in the acquired firm concerning how their messages will be received.

▶ The 'situated' nature of some knowledge and expertise

A further challenge to be confronted in utilizing knowledge and practices across business units in firms that have grown through acquisition is that some of this will have been developed in a distinctive context and might not easily be transferred to a different setting. This is particularly likely to be the case in international M&As due to the cultural and institutional differences across borders. The situated nature of expertise shows through strongly in the case of Euro Cure. The deal in question was motivated by 'an acquisition of knowledge...an acquisition in their potential and their future'. Yet, to a high degree the knowledge was 'situated' in that it could not easily be transferred across locations. A crucial factor in this respect was that researchers with particular expertise could not easily move to a different branch of research: 'when you get into the deep science, people can't move from one field to a completely different scientific arm'. Thus, the firm realized that there were some synergies between the two firms that could be realized but there was little attempt to embark on a challenging process of 'taking two entities and blending them into one'. The HR implications of this were that the acquiring firm adopted a largely decentralized approach to managing its acquired operations. As one put it, 'we are saying to them just keep doing what you were doing'. This limits the opportunities for 'cross-fertilization' in areas that are common to both, such as the support functions, as where the remits of the two entities are so different and there exists little overlap, this limits the scope for knowledge to be transferred across the merged organization.

▶ Adopting an incremental approach to accessing expertise in acquired units

The case of Euro Cure also illustrated a further challenge in learning from international acquisitions. In considering the firm's approach to post-acquisition integration, it was acknowledged that there was a danger in getting the knowledge and expertise out of the acquired unit in an over-zealous manner, resulting in missing the opportunity altogether and rendering the acquisition futile. As one respondent put it, 'Our CEO said what is not going to happen is that everybody has jumped on this new toy, ripped it apart and we have gone and bust the damn thing'. This tension can be overcome to some extent, which shows through very clearly in the case of Global Drug. This company had been through a number of acquisitions and had a clear plan for how they fit into the company's structure, in which HR seemed to be very well placed to influence the approach to acquisitions, including who was acquired. As we saw above, the key challenge in the acquisition of the small bio-tech company in the US was to absorb the expertise they had in such a way that was sensitive to how the parent company would be perceived. In this case it was evident that the technology being acquired was completely different to the technology that they had been using previously and to some degree this in itself was a barrier to learning. It was described as 'not going there and adding a few pieces to your existing knowledge, it is going back to the beginning and learning a different way of doing the same job'. The technology was seen as 'taking some learning' and to try and gradually absorb it the parent company sent small 'scouting parties' which were characterized as 'Trojan horses'. This had to be handled delicately as senior HR people were anxious to avoid a perception forming in the acquired unit that the new parent was acting in a heavy-handed way in stripping away the acquired firm's distinctive capabilities. In order to reassure the acquired employees of this, certain exceptions to corporate policies were permitted, some of which, such as the free cafeteria that had taken on iconic status, were symbolic of a continuing degree of independence. This was described as 'making sure that they felt that the micro-climate of their culture...would be retained' and by giving assurances such as 'we are acquiring you but we are not absorbing you'. Thus, the specificity of the knowledge and the way it has been situated in a particular and distinctive company presented a challenge to the acquiring company. The respondents argued that with such specialist knowledge it was hard to know when the transfer was complete and the desired knowledge had been acquired: 'We did appreciate that it would take time to get to the point of saying we have now acquired the technology transfer. There is no document that will assure that. It is a state of mind'. Thus where gathering knowledge or expertise is central to the purpose of the acquisition or merger, an incremental approach to extracting this from the acquired unit is important.

Conclusions

The material in this chapter has both theoretical and practical implications. Theoretically, we have argued that the extent and form of integration between firms engaged in a cross-border merger will be shaped by the national business system of the dominant firm, but will also be constrained by the peculiar features of the various national systems in which the merged firm operates. We have also argued, however, that the integration process, and the restructuring and learning that are key parts of this integration in most mergers, is also highly political. In particular, we have attempted to show that the structural aspects of national systems on the one hand and the political processes within merged organizations on the other are interdependent. As we hope is now clear from this and earlier chapters, this approach is not only relevant to the issue of cross-border M&As, but is also integral to the way we understand the operation of multinationals more generally.

In practical terms, the preceding analysis of cross-border M&As has far-reaching implications. One of the central findings in much research on international mergers, as we have seen, has been their high failure rate. The severe problems at RBS and Corus are examples of the problems experienced by firms that have engaged in a string of acquisitions. In light of the above material concerning both the quite different regulatory contexts in which mergers and acquisitions take place across countries, and the highly politicised nature of the post-merger period, it is perhaps not surprising that such problems and difficulties are so widespread. An appreciation of the nature of these likely challenges on the part of both 'deal-makers', and those such as HR practitioners who are involved in the subsequent integration, is essential if cross-border mergers are to achieve the aims of those who initiate them.

Review questions

1 Why are cross-border mergers and acquisitions more complex than domestic ones?
2 In what ways do national effects condition the post-merger restructuring process?
3 In what ways is the process of restructuring 'political'?
4 What are the key obstacles to be overcome if a firm wants to learn from an acquisition it makes in another country?
5 If you were asked to highlight the key issues to an HR manager who is about to go through her first cross-border merger, what would you tell her?

Further reading

1 Rees, C. and Edwards, T. (2003) *The HR Implications of International Mergers and Acquisitions*, CIPD Research Report, London: CIPD.

2 Edwards, T., Budjanovcanin, A. and Woollard, S. (2008) *International M&As: How can HR Play a Strategic Role?* CIPD Research Report, London: CIPD.

The reports summarize two research projects carried out for the Chartered Institute of Personnel and Development in the UK, providing details on a series of case studies of a variety of mergers, acquisitions and joint ventures.

3 Faulkner, D., Pitkethly, R. and Child, J. (2002) 'International mergers and acquisitions in the UK 1985–94: a comparison of national HRM practices', *International Journal of Human Resource Management*, 13(1), 106–22.

The article reports the findings of a study of foreign acquisitions of UK firms, studying the impact of these acquisitions on HR practices.

4 Stahl, G., Pucik, V., Evans, P. and Medenhall, M. (2004) 'Human Resource Management in Cross-Border Mergers and Acquisitions', in Harzing, A. and van Ruysseveldt, J. (eds) *International Human Resource Management*, London: Sage.

The chapter provides an interesting discussion of how cross-border M&As present opportunities for firms to learn from the diversity of their operations and then some detail on the key HR issues that firms encounter in the post-merger period.

5 Vaara, E. and Tienari, J. (2003) 'The "Balance of Power" Principle: Nationality, Politics and the Distribution of Organizational Positions', in Soderberg, A. and Vaara, E. (eds) *Merging Across Borders: People, Cultures and Politics*, Copenhagen: Copenhagen Business School Press.

A very interesting discussion of the way in which senior managerial positions were distributed in the creation of the Scandinavian financial services group Nordea.

References

Aguilera, R. and Dencker, J. (2004) 'The role of human resource management in cross-border mergers and acquisitions', *International Journal of Human Resource Management*, 15(8), 1355–70.

BBC News (2002) 'Most international mergers fail', www.bbc.co.uk/business/.

Belanger, J., Berggren, C., Bjorkman, T. and Kohler, C. (1999) *Being Local Worldwide: ABB and the Challenge of Global Management*, Ithaca: Cornell University Press.

Bjorkman, I., Stahl, G. and Vaara, E. (2007) 'Cultural differences and capability transfer in cross-border acquisitions: the mediating roles of capability complementarity, absorptive capacity, and social integration', *Journal of International Business Studies*, 38, 658–72.

Bresman, H., Birkenshaw, J. and Nobel, R. (1999) 'Knowledge transfer in international acquisitions', *Journal of International Business Studies*, 30(3), 439–62.

Corteel, D. and Le Blanc, G. (2001) 'The Importance of the National Issue in Cross-Border Mergers', Paper presented to a Conference entitled 'Cross Border Mergers and Employee Participation in Europe, Ecole des Mines, Paris, 9 March.

Edwards, T. (2000) 'Multinationals, international integration and employment practice in domestic plants', *Industrial Relations Journal*, 31(2), 115–29.

Edwards, P., Ferner, A. and Sisson, K. (1993) 'People and the Process of Management in the Multinational Company: A Review and Some Illustrations', *Warwick Papers in Industrial Relations*, No. 43, Coventry: IRRU.

Edwards, T., Budjanovcanin, A. and Woollard, S. (2008) *International Mergers and Acquisitions: How Can HR Play a Strategic Role?*, CIPD Research Report, London: CIPD.

Edwards, T., Coller, X., Ortiz, L., Rees, C. and Wortmann, M. (2006) 'How important are national industrial relations systems in restructuring in multinational companies? Evidence from a cross-border merger in the pharmaceuticals sector', *European Journal of Industrial Relations*, 12(1), 69–88.

EIRO (2001) *Industrial Relations Aspects of Mergers and Takeovers*, www.eiro.eurofound.ie/2001/02/study/TN0102401s.html.

Faulkner, D., Pitkethly, R. and Child, J. (2002) 'International mergers and acquisitions in the UK 1985–94: a comparison of national HRM practices', *International Journal of Human Resource Management*, 13(1), 106–22.

Ferner, A., Almond, P., Clark, I., Colling, T., Edwards, T., Holden, L. and Muller, M. (2004) 'The transmission and adaptation of "American" traits in US multinationals abroad: case study evidence from the UK', *Organization Studies*, 25(3), 363–91.

Forsgren, M. (1990) 'Managing the International Multi-Centre Firm', *European Management Journal*, 8(2), 261–7.

Habelian, J., Devers, C., McNamara, G., Carpenter, M. and Davison, R. (2009) 'Taking stock of what we know about mergers and acquisitions: a review and research agenda', *Journal of Management*, 35(3), 469–502.

KPMG (1999) *Unlocking Shareholder Value*, London: KPMG.

Mayer, M. and Whittington, R. (2002) 'For Boundedness in the Study of Comparative and International Business: The Case of the Diversified Multidivisional Corporation', in Geppert, M., Matten, D. and Williams, K. (eds) *Challenges for European Management in a Global Context*, Basingstoke: Palgrave Macmillan.

Meyer, K. And Lieb-Doczy, E. (2003) 'Post-Acquisition Restructuring as Evolutionary Process', *Journal of Management Studies*, 40(2), 459–82.

Rees, C. and Edwards, T. (2003) *The HR Role of International Mergers and Acquisitions*, CIPD Research Report, London: CIPD, 1–35.

Schuler, R., Jackson, S. and Luo, Y. (2003) *Managing Human Resources in Cross-Border Alliances*, London: Routledge.

Stahl, G. and Voight, A. (2008) 'Do cultural differences matter in mergers and acquisitions? A tentative model and examination, *Organization Science*, 19(1), Jan.–Feb., 160–76.

Stahl, G., Pucik, V., Evans, P. and Medenhall, M. (2004) 'Human Resource Management in Cross-Border Mergers and Acquisitions', in Harzing, A. and van Ruysseveldt, J. (eds) *International Human Resource Management*, London: Sage.

United Nations (2008) *World Investment Report*, New York: United Nations.

United Nations (2009) *World Investment Report,* New York: United Nations.

Vaara, E., Risberg, A., Soderberg, A. and Tienari, J. (2003) 'Nation Talk: The Construction of National Stereotypes in a Merging Multinational', in Soderberg, A. and Vaara, E. (eds) *Merging Across Borders: People, Cultures and Politics,* Copenhagen: Copenhagen Business School Press.

Vaara, E. and Tienari, J. (2003) 'The "Balance of Power" Principle: Nationality, Politics and the Distribution of Organizational Positions', in Soderberg, A. and Vaara, E. (eds) *Merging Across Borders: People, Cultures and Politics,* Copenhagen: Copenhagen Business School Press.

Whittington, R. (2001) *What is Strategy? And Does it Matter?* London: Thomson.

Zou, H. and Ghauri, P. (2008) 'Learning through international acquisitions: the process of knowledge acquisition in China', *Management International Review,* 48(2), 207–26.

Part 2

THE MANAGEMENT OF INTERNATIONAL HRM

Chapter 9

International management development

Jean Woodall

Key aims

The aims of this chapter are to:

- outline the changing scope of international management development and international manager roles;
- explore more fully the significance of learning theory for international management development;
- outline specific international management development interventions that are commonly used;
- reflect on future developments.

Introduction

Since the first edition of this book, much continues to be written about the selection and preparation of managers for international roles in global organizations, and much of the literature continues to be of a rather descriptive and prescriptive nature. In general, the focus on identifying high-potential employees for expatriate assignments and devising executive development programmes for them, persists, and, as argued in the first edition of this book, this can lead to a very narrow perspective on international management development (IMD). So it is important to take a broader view that incorporates a number of other factors.

The first of these factors is the organizational context within which the international manager operates. Multinational companies (MNCs) can have quite diverse structures – they are not simply headquartered in a 'home' country with foreign operations run by expatriates. The scale of the operations controlled by MNCs and their global reach have given 'host' and 'third' country nationals a more significant role in the management process. Also, the rapid changes in company fortunes as a consequence of globalization mean that the international manager can face a potentially shorter, more uncertain career as operations are switched between countries. In addition, the growth of partnering, outsourcing, and off-shoring, involves more technical and professional specialists in international management work, many of whom are employed on short-term contracts. This has serious implications for the range of roles required of international managers (as outlined in the next section), and in turn starts to raise issues about the nature of the IMD provided. Should it be confined purely to executive development for a select group of high-potential expatriates? Or is this something that should be extended to include other managers at all levels, in different roles and at different stages of their careers? Finally, what does this mean for host country and even third country nationals who hitherto might not have been included within IMD activity?

Another factor concerns the scope of activities that are included in IMD. It involves more than simple training and development and also comprises succession planning and performance management, and even extends into personal and family welfare. In particular, it is important to situate IMD within the context of management learning. Unfortunately, much of the debate on IMD continues to take place in isolation from the insights on learning that have emerged over recent years (Briscoe and Schuler 2004; Sparrow *et al.* 2004; Tayeb 2004; Caligiuri *et al.* 2005; Parkinson and Morley, 2006). These insights can be summarized as follows:

- the importance of responding to individual learning styles (Kolb 1983);
- the growing significance of informal and incidental learning that takes place through everyday work activities as opposed to formal off-the-job training sessions (Marsick and Watkins 1990); there is also evidence that work experiences of a negative as well as a positive kind can be very important for individual learning and career development (McCauley *et al.* 1994);
- linked to this, the growing awareness of the ways in which formal work-related activities can be harnessed as learning tools;
- the growing interest in organizational and team learning as well as individual learning;
- a growing awareness that the wider organizational culture and the specific learning culture of the organization can encourage or inhibit individual, team and organizational learning;
- the potential contribution of information and communications technology (ICT) to individual, team and organizational learning as well as knowledge transfer; in particular, this underpins the enthusiasm for knowledge management (KM) and corporate universities.

The changing scope of international management development

Until the 1990s, the international manager was typically a senior-level corporate employee who was mid-to-late career, male and Caucasian, and who had a 'trailing spouse'. Usually 'he' was embarking on an international assignment of at least two years, which was often presented as a reward towards the end of a long career with the organization. The pre-departure development would be confined to a 'briefing' from existing expatriates returning or visiting the home country, occasionally supplemented by the opportunity to make a short visit to the overseas site. Formal international development programmes that included a wider range of pre-departure support were rare. Indeed, the administration of international human resource management (IHRM) was usually separate from corporate management development activities and mainly preoccupied with arranging international salary packages and dealing with relocation issues such as visas, work permits and housing. This model was developed largely by US multinationals, although it was also widely adopted in the UK.

However, by the mid-1980s it was becoming clear that this 'neo-colonial' model was exhibiting serious flaws (Scullion 1993). First, the rate of expatriate turnover was much higher than in comparable management groups, with hidden indirect costs to the business as well as the expense of replacement and development. This in turn led to shortages in the supply of international executives, thereby severely constraining the potential for overseas business development. The expatriate with 'trailing spouse' (usually female, although males are increasingly facing this predicament – see Selmer and Leung 2003) was being replaced by dual career couples who exhibited a greater reluctance to embark on an international assignment unless it offered career development for both partners. This was also related to changing patterns of female employment and family life, so that expatriates with school-age children were reluctant to disturb the children's education or to send them home to boarding school. Furthermore, traditional stereotypes and host country social conventions reinforced women's continued under representation among the ranks of international managers (Harris 2004). Finally, there was growing evidence that the process of repatriation was not a satisfactory experience for most managers, who on their return often experienced culture shock, lost career opportunities and even unemployment.

These trends were still evident at the start of the twenty-first century. Forster (2000) argued that the idea of the 'international manager' as originally conceived is now a myth. It is rather a 'loose description of someone who is potentially or currently abroad on a one-off international assignment' (2000: 126). Short-term travel assignments are increasingly used by European, Japanese and US MNCs and involve people drawn from a wide range of business functions – human resource managers, corporate lawyers, engineers, computer programmers and hardware designers, and finance, marketing and sales personnel. Forster's study of 500 expatriates in 36 UK companies showed that a substantial number of respondents experienced psychological difficulties in adjusting to a foreign culture, and even more so at the stage of repatriation. He saw this as contributing to a declining interest in continuing an international career, and concluded that the form of international assignments would need to change from a long-term stay overseas to more frequent short-term cross-border job swaps, short assignments or participation in multicultural virtual project teams. This would require managers with international competencies, who were able and willing to undertake such short assignments. It would mean that the frequency of traditional expatriate postings with male employees and trailing female spouses would become less common in the future (Forster 2000). Thus, if international managers are required to carry out a greater variety of roles, it is important to consider what has led to this.

The growth of global business has been mainly fuelled by an expansion of merger and acquisitions, alliances and joint ventures, rather than just organic growth on the part of MNCs (Evans, Pucik and Barsoux 2002, and see Chapter 8). The accompanying developments within the internal labour markets of international businesses has meant that the 'job-for-life' culture of many organizations has ended, and this in turn has contributed to a reduction in the supply of potential expatriate managers. There are three aspects to this. Mergers and acquisitions often resulted in a breach of psychological contracts and trust among management teams, so that expatriate managers were often reluctant to stay with the new organisation (Stahl *et al.* 2004). The downsizing of the 1980s and 1990s affected many older senior and middle managers – many of whom provided the core group from which the international management cadre was drawn. Multinational corporation succession plans for developing a cadre of potential international managers were therefore disrupted. Secondly, the global reach of organizations and the entry into emergent markets, often in areas of the world facing political unrest and problems of security, proved unattractive to the traditional expatriate with their 'trailing spouse' and family. In addition, the growth of alliances and joint ventures required greater input from technical and professional specialists from finance, marketing, sales, IT and logistics – a group that hitherto had not been at the centre of international management development activity. Finally, the growth in the use of contract staff and the tendency to outsource whole areas of activity such as IT, facilities and even professional areas (such as HR and marketing), meant that organisations were often being represented in international activity by individuals who were not directly employed by them. International management is now conducted by an ever more diverse group of individuals, carrying out an even wider variety of roles, and who may engage in a greater variety of international assignments (Harris *et al.* 2003; Mayerhofer *et al.* 2004).

At the same time, these new developments have created an ever greater hunger for a steady supply of international managerial talent. It is no accident that the McKinsey consultancy declared 'the war for talent' in the late 1990s (Chambers *et al.* 1998, cited in Scullion and Collings 2006b), as shortages of international managers became an increasing problem for international businesses. The contradictions of globalization are being played out within the sphere of human resource policy and strategy. On the one hand, central HR functions are called upon to play an even greater role in relation to expatriates in terms of search, career development, management development and support for dual career households. On the other hand, a growing proportion of individuals involved in international management roles are outside the scope of central HR policies for international management. In some cases this is because responsibility has been devolved to HR managers in subsidiaries so that they can recruit and develop local managers – host country nationals. In other cases project managers within alliances and joint ventures take responsibility for recruiting and developing their international project teams who meet virtually as well as in real time, but often facing serious problems of implementation (Schuler *et al.* 2004).

So the popular conception of the role of the international manager as a mid-career expatriate who relocates overseas in order to assume a senior management position in a subsidiary of the parent company needs to be dispelled. Managers now need to fill different roles at various stages of corporate international development (Hendry 1994; Woodall and Winstanley 1998). This variety of management roles has implications not only for the type of development required, but also for the skills to be developed.

However, before looking at these skills and the interventions used to develop them, it is important to reflect more fully on management learning.

Learning theory and international management development

At the start of this chapter we mentioned the relative neglect of research evidence on learning by specialists in IMD. It is ironic that many MNCs have been introducing many innovative human resource development (HRD) practices, but that these have been confined to their domestic operations. Their international management development policies remained immune to such innovation. This was certainly the case until the early 1990s, but has since changed. Particularly in the USA, the growing interest in developing international managers has led many MNCs to draw upon wider theoretical insights into learning gained from the academic world (Maznevski and DiStefano 2000; Black and Gregersen 2000; Caligiuri *et al.* 2005; Parkinson and Morley 2006). The framework underpinning IMD initiatives now draws heavily upon a number of key principles. Among these are: that adults learn most effectively when the learning is embedded in meaningful experiences; that behavioural skills are improved through observation and practice and with feedback from others; that learning also requires the ability to search for and identify new patterns of thinking so that individual cognitive frameworks are able to accommodate new assumptions; that most learning is informal and incidental, rather than planned and formal; and that challenging experiences, often quite negative in nature, can be powerful learning tools. We shall now examine each of these in turn, and indicate their significance for the development of international managers, highlighting potential IMD interventions that will be dealt with more fully in a later section of this chapter.

▶ The effectiveness of learning embedded in meaningful experiences

The four-stage model of learning outlined by David Kolb (1983) has been an extremely influential tool for employee development in the USA and the UK over the last 20 years. The four stages of the learning cycle: experiencing, reflecting, conceptualizing and experimenting, have been used to demonstrate that effective learning involves multiple interactions with experience and passing through all four stages. However, at the same time, Kolb's research revealed that individual learners display learning style preferences that corresponded to each stage of the learning cycle: the activist, reflector, theorist and pragmatist learning styles. The implications of this are twofold. First, effective learning requires some correspondence between experience and learning style: the 'activist' who is forced to listen to a long lecture or to read a detailed company handbook will not learn well, but might respond very well to a practical assignment (the reverse would be true for the 'theorist'). Second, the individual learning style preference can be an obstacle to learning from certain types of learning experience. Again, the 'activist' will avoid reflecting on their activities and drawing conclusions from this, leading to potential mistakes. Thus, it is important to assist individuals to become aware of their individual learning styles and to identify ways of ensuring that their learning is effective.

Another set of learning theories that recognize the importance of meaningful experience to learning are to be found in 'humanistic' adult learning theory, and in particular the work of Knowles (1989) and Rogers (1969). Both are much more focused on the emotional and personal development aspects of learning than Kolb. Rogers argues that in an ever-changing environment, teachers and trainers must become 'facilitators' of learning, setting a climate of trust, eliciting individual and group aims, providing access to resources, accepting and sharing emotional as well as intellectual contributions and, above all, accepting their own limitations as teachers. Similarly, Knowles, in his principles of adult learning – self-styled as 'andragogy' – stresses the importance of a leaner-centred, experience-based approach that takes into account the wider life experiences and personal motivations of learners.

Therefore, experiential learning theory tells us that international management development programmes should offer a variety of learning opportunities delivered at an appropriate time to enable the manager to draw the most out of their experience, and to build upon it. This means that the design of such programmes should start to go beyond pre-departure awareness training, and build in real-life experiences with opportunities to stand back, reflect, draw conclusions and try out alternative courses of action and behaviours. It explains why cross-cultural awareness training is more usually done after arrival at the overseas destination, rather than pre-departure, and why a number of international leadership development programmes now take place over a number of years, not only prior to departure but also during the overseas assignment. Work-related projects, mentoring schemes and international seminars become important tools for ensuring that programme participants can draw upon all stages of the learning cycle.

▶ Developing behavioural skills in an interactive context

A further principle of learning is the recognition that it is as much a social as an individual experience. The Kolb model is focused on the individual, but the work of Bandura (1977) has shown the importance of the process of learning through observation and imitation. Feedback from others can provide a 'reality check' for the potential perceptual distortions to which we all can succumb. In addition, the identification of positive and negative role models provides another cognitive 'prod' to encourage the adoption of positive, and avoidance of negative, behaviours. Above all, a supportive social environment with strong social cohesion is important to enable the learner to feel that they can take reasonable risks in their behaviour with others.

This has been recognized in the design of international leadership programmes. While a great deal of attention has been devoted to the *identification* of international leadership competencies (see below), it is quite clear that their development requires an appropriate environment for practice. So, a group-based international leadership development programme will provide the opportunity for acquiring the essential skills of learning, managing relationships (including communication, motivation, decision-making, conflict management) and managing uncertainty. This will be done in an environment where the development of strong social cohesion and trust will enable participants to explore and experiment without creating the potential for intention to be misinterpreted. Action learning set methodologies are particularly good at assisting international managers achieve the mastery of these skills before they acquire the leadership responsibility (Maznevski and DiStefano 2000; Marquardt 2004). Often, however, the acquisition and development of these skills will be the 'spin-off' from working with colleagues on a shared task or problem.

For this reason, it is increasingly common for such international leadership programmes to include an element of action learning. Action learning was popularized by Revans (1982) in the 1960s as a method that is learner-led rather than trainer-led, and yet is able to provide a great deal of structure to the learning process with minimal direction. Revans believed that the most effective managerial learning takes place within the context of real-life problems that are of a non-routine nature and that present a challenge to the manager concerned. Action learning aims to create a collective learning experience through the creation of learning sets of five or six people that meet to discuss, and question each other about, the challenging, work-related problems to which they have each been assigned. They negotiate the use of their meeting time, and are usually assisted by a facilitator who will point them in the direction of an appropriate source of expertise and will assist with group learning, when requested. The key point is that managers are motivated to take responsibility for their own learning and to focus on action rather than just analysis. While supportive, the learning set culture is not 'soft'. There is emphasis on 'learning by doing' and working together to reframe problems. There is only limited tolerance of failure. Such learning sets can be built in towards the latter part of an international leadership development programme, and can be a useful tool in consortium programmes of several organizations (Marquardt 2004). They are also an important means of support for the international manager once they are alone back in their post.

▶ Learning as the ability to reframe cognitive maps

The quality of an inquisitive and challenging mindset is often found in the lists of international management development competencies. However, while it is easy to identify this ability, it is much more difficult to know how it can be developed. Thus it is not surprising that many companies with long histories of extensive international activity, such as BP, Standard Chartered Bank, and IBM, pay a great deal of attention to global leadership attributes when hiring or promoting people. The ability to reframe mental maps in a rapid and dramatic manner is essential if international managers are to become aware that what is considered to be 'best practice' in one country is not necessarily the same in all countries. Thus, international managers need to be able to do more than solve problems – they also need to be able to reframe them.

Argyris's work (1990, 1994) has drawn attention to the limitations of a narrow definition of management learning tied to problem solving, as this leads managers to overfocus on identifying and correcting errors in their external environment, rather than to question and confront the way in which the problem is defined. Similarly, managers may not be able to learn from a successful experience as it often leads to the complacent assumption that the same behaviour will result in the same outcomes in all circumstances, and may well encourage overconfidence in their individual ability. Drawing heavily on theories of group dynamics and personal change, Argyris describes how even highly intelligent professionals and managers will explicitly espouse theories – private assumptions – that they think they use every day, but which in fact they do not. Furthermore, managers and professionals are usually unaware of the assumptions that they do use to design and manage their actions. In this situation, the difference between 'espoused theory' and 'theory in use' means that unwittingly they screen out certain information. Consequently, their attempt to manage and control their environment results in the adoption of 'defensive routines' as they display 'skilled incompetence' in their efforts to avoid surprise, embarrassment or threats. The outcome is 'single-loop learning', in which the response to a problem does not involve any change in assumptions, norms and values. To avoid skilled incompetence, managers have to learn new skills, and especially to question and confront their assumptions, and to explore and take calculated risks. This will enable 'double-loop learning' to occur. Yet, Argyris observed that managers and professionals can be among the most resistant to double-loop learning because of their strong task-focus and desire to avoid failure.

Thus, the need to provide an environment to encourage double-loop learning is essential for successful international management development programmes. Such programmes now usually incorporate this in a workshop format or in one-to-one coaching. It involves three stages (Black and Gregersen 2000), starting with *unfreezing* activities that will shake up the old mental map. Remapping involves presenting the participants with a noticeable contrast of interpretation or behaviour. This is the principle behind the use of cultural assimilators in cross-cultural awareness training (see below). The second stage takes this further through placing the international manager in a situation where they are forced to confront these contrasts. This will be most effective where it involves a real work assignment or project. The third stage involves presenting them with a conceptual framework that indicates the variables that change between countries and cultures. The key is ensuring that managers are provided with frequent opportunities, either in a group or with an executive coach, to develop their double-loop learning skills.

▶ Taking advantage of informal and incidental learning and making use of developmental challenges

There is thus a paradox presented by the above principles. Effective learning needs to be embedded in meaningful experiences, but managers often engage in defensive routines that only result in single-loop learning. Furthermore, individuals may not be aware that they are learning. Marsick and Watkins (1990) noted that much learning is 'incidental' as well as 'informal'. While informal learning can be planned or intentional, incidental learning is usually the by-product of some other activity, such as carrying out a task or interactions with other people. As such it is neither planned nor intentional, but rather is tacit, taken–for–granted and implicit in everyday management assumptions and actions. There is much evidence that adults are more likely to learn from non-routine rather than from routine experiences (Marsick and Watkins 1990;

McCall *et al.* 1988; Gold *et al.* 2007). This obviously raises the question of how international managers can best take advantage of the opportunities for incidental learning. In
the first place, the nature of their work means that formal learning opportunities are
difficult to access, but opportunities for informal and incidental learning abound. This
has two implications for IMD. First, the manager has to be exposed to new experiences,
but at the same time usually needs help to recognize these as learning opportunities.

Furthermore, the nature of the learning opportunities may not always be positive.
Research undertaken to identify the developmental components of managerial jobs
(McCauley *et al.* 1994) highlighted that several developmental challenges are highly
negative in nature – such as having to manage a business turnaround, cutbacks, or a
troublesome boss or colleague. International managers are probably more likely to
encounter such negative experiences. The challenge then becomes how to learn from
them. However, what is clear is that individual managers require support to encourage
them to reflect, either privately, in a group or with an executive coach. Again, research
(Wood-Daudelin 1996) has shown that those managers who had a personal coach or
were part of a group were much better able to recall and analyse their learning from a
highly developmental experience. This perhaps accounts for the very rapid increase in
the use of executive coaching for international managers.

The implications for IMD are that managers need to be sensitized to the opportunities for incidental learning and to be open to the fact that this might well occur by
means of negative as well as positive experiences. However, if such learning is to occur
then individual managers will need support to encourage them to reflect. This is why
many MNCs now use action learning sets, individual mentors and executive coaches as
ways of enabling this.

International management development initiatives

Given the tremendous diversity of international manager roles, the reluctance of many
managers to embark on a long-term expatriate career and the above-mentioned insights
from theories of managerial learning, there have been a number of new initiatives in
IMD programmes since the early 1990s. These include:

- the identification of international leadership competencies as a basis for developing
  managers for international assignments;
- cross-cultural awareness training;
- multicultural team building and development;
- IMD for women.

Each of these will now be considered in turn.

▶ Identifying and developing international leadership competencies

Most models of leadership have been generated in the USA, and there is general agreement that they have been helpful in assisting US managers to lead in a domestic context
where the focus is on the use of hierarchical structures and institutional position.

However, the rise of globalization has shown how culture impacts on norms and values, and therefore European, Asian and Latin American leadership models are often very different from US approaches (Morrison 2000). The dangers of establishing an 'ethnocentric' leadership model have been recognized for some time (Adler and Bartholomew 1992; Black and Porter 1991), and Yeung and Ready (1995) found significant differences in the national emphasis on key leadership capabilities. So while Australians believe that global managers need to lead change, Korean and Japanese leaders disagree. Similarly, French employees value leaders who would be skilful in managing internal and external networks, but this was far less important for US, German, Australian, Italian, Korean and UK managers. Also, the current US vogue for transformational (Bass and Avolio 1994) and distributive (Gronn 2002) leadership models does not translate easily to many parts of the world, especially Asia where authoritative, decisive and forceful action is prized. Nonetheless, this has been ignored by some specialists in IMD who are preoccupied with the search for generic competencies (Briscoe and Schuler 2004; Scullion and Collings 2006a). They argue that those who possess the ability to deal with ambiguity and uncertainty, who are analytical, risk-taking, action-oriented, multidimensional figures, and who are not aggressively defensive, but are in touch with their own emotions and sensitive to the needs of others are more likely to succeed as international managers than those who do not possess these attributes.

Yet, a review of the research literature on global leadership (Morrison 2000) shows that evidence supporting the need for such qualities is inconclusive and very ambiguous

Table 9.1 **Competencies of the global executive**

Open-minded and flexible in thought and tactics	The person is able to live and work in a variety of settings with different types of people and is willing and able to listen to other people, approaches and ideas.
Cultural interest and sensitivity	The person respects other cultures, people,a nd points of view: is not arrogant or judgemental; is curious about other people and how they live and work; is interested in differences; enjoys social competency; gets along well with others; is empathetic.
Able to deal with complexity	The person considers many variables in solving a problem; is comfortable with ambiguity and patient in evolving issues; can make decisions in the face of uncertainty; can see patterns and connections; and is willing to take risks.
Resilient, resourceful, optimistic and energetic	The person responds to a challenge; is not discouraged by adversity; is self-reliant and creative; sees the positive side of things; has a high level of physical and emotional energy; is able to deal with stress.
Honesty and integrity	Authentic, consistent, the person engenders trust.
Stable personal life	The person has developed and maintains stress-resistant personal arrangements, usually family, that supports a commitment to work.
Value-added technical or business skills	The person has technical, managerial or other expertise sufficient to provide his or her credibility.

Source: Briscoe and Schuler (2004: 277)

in focus, covering such topics as competencies, cultural differences, the impact of nationality on managerial values and the impact of culture on management style. In addition, the scientific rigour is variable and ranges from descriptive to analytical studies and from convenience samples to large-scale, multi-country surveys. Thus, it is not surprising that many international businesses, such as PricewaterhouseCoopers, resort to developing their own company-specific models (Hoeksema and de Jong 2001). However, sometimes the manner in which these competencies are derived is not particularly rigorous, relying on an unvalidated 'wish list' generated by senior executives (Connor 2000; Alldredge and Nilan 2000), but the involvement of a large number of managers from across the organisation is essential in order to build commitment to such competence schemes. Table 9.1 provides a typical list of such global competencies.

Scullion and Collings (2006b) take this further, by making a contrast between what they see as a 'global mindset' and a 'domestic mindset, as outlined in Table 9.2.

However, it is interesting to reflect on whether this might be a false polarity. Is the 'traditional domestic mindset' *really* espoused by organizations these days? Are the 'global mindset' qualities acceptable in all cultures? Can these qualities be developed, or are some of them immutable aspects of an individual's personality? Are some individuals more susceptible to development than others? How is it possible to develop such qualities? These questions can only be answered by looking more closely at how individuals learn, and as we have seen above, they can learn in different ways in different circumstances. While there is considerable controversy over the nature of global leadership competencies, there does appear to be more consensus over developing managers to use them. Global organizations concerned to expand capacity are aware of the acute shortage of new general managers and are concerned to identify people earlier in their careers. Thus, corporate leadership development programmes providing training and workshops at intervals over a period of two years or more are now common (Neary and O'Grady 2000; Connor 2000). A typical programme structure is outlined in Example 9.1 on page 174.

This structure is very common among leading global companies, including British Airways, and IBM. Usually the content of the programme will cover a number of themes such as global strategy, leadership style and behaviour, culture and organizational capabilities, and in some programmes there is further emphasis on cross-cultural

Table 9.2 Global mindset compared to traditional 'domestic' mindset

Traditional domestic mindset	Global mindset	Personal characteristics
Functional expertise	Broad and multiple perspectives	Knowledge
Prioritization	Duality – balance between contradictions	Conceptual ability
Structure	Process	Flexibility
Individual responsibility	Teamwork and diversity	Sensitivity
Predictability	Change as opportunity	Judgement
Trained against surprises	Open to what is new	Learning

Source: Scullion and Collings (2006b)

training or multicultural team building (see below). However, as already outlined in the previous section on learning, the major aims of such programmes are to encourage participants to reframe their cognitive maps and to provide opportunities for guided reflection upon experience and for exposure to peers from other cultures. It is also very common in the USA for programmes to be developed in collaboration with university business schools and to be hosted in a variety of locations. However, Townsend and Cairns (2003) argue that the development of globally capable managers requires experiential development that goes beyond competency. This is necessary to move beyond simple skill and knowledge acquisition to the development of understanding and self-efficacy.

The problem is that such leadership development programmes are costly, as are expatriate assignments. They are thus only available to a small proportion of organizational personnel and, as we have seen, the number of employees involved in international business activities is increasing. While short-term travel assignments are increasingly used by European, Japanese and US multinational firms, there is little strategic use of these experiences for development purposes. Too often the managers are 'cocooned' and isolated from the host country experience, staying in an international hotel and having little opportunity to socialize with host country nationals. Oddou *et al.* (2000) provide many examples of how the experience could be enhanced for such managers.

EXAMPLE 9.1

A typical global leadership development programme

- **Annual appraisal** in all operating units used as the basis for identifying 'hi-pos' (high potential younger managers).

- Names forwarded to a **global database**.

- **Assessment centres,** often held bi-annually.

- **First workshop,** using diagnostic instruments (e.g. Myers-Briggs Type Indicator, 360-degree feedback, self-assessment) and one-to-one executive coaching to create an individual personal development plan with action points.

- Use of **other interactive learning techniques,** such as case studies, break-out group assignments, team-building interactions, and project work, to encourage networking.

- Following the first workshop, **action learning projects** of either an individual or group nature are assigned to be worked on between the first and second workshops, and meetings with the **executive coach** continue, possibly supplemented by the assignment of a **mentor from senior management**.

- **Second workshop,** at which the outcomes of the action learning projects are presented, often to senior management.

- Continued meetings with **executive coach and senior management mentor,** and **periodic international management seminars** at later stages.

▶ Cross-cultural awareness training

The growth in expatriation by the 1990s was accompanied by an alarming increase in the number of curtailed assignments. In the USA this was estimated to have reached up to 50 per cent (Eschbach *et al.* 2001). While there are many reasons for international assignment failure (see above), culture shock was viewed as a major contributory factor. Culture shock has been described as:

> an adjustment reaction syndrome caused by cumulative, multiple, and interactive stress in the intellectual, behavioural, emotional and physiological levels of a person recently relocated to an unfamiliar culture, and is characterized by a variety of symptoms of psychological shock. (Befus 1988)

The experience of culture shock usually follows an initial 'honeymoon' on arrival, and results from a frustration with the host culture as it becomes apparent to the manager that past behaviours are inappropriate but what is desirable is not apparent. This is where cross-cultural awareness training plays a major role. There is evidence that integrated cross-cultural training that begins prior to departure, is designed for trainees in a specific context and continues intermittently during the foreign posting is the most effective means of doing this (Eschbach *et al.* 2001).

Research in the 1990s indicated that in both the USA and Europe, between half and two-thirds of companies are providing cross-cultural training for their international managers (Bennett *et al.* 2000) but more recent research (Parkinson and Morley 2006) suggests that the actual amount of such training is rather limited, and with relatively little thought given to underpinning theory and objectives (Graf 2004). Companies such as Monsanto, General Electric and Motorola place a great deal of emphasis on such cross-cultural training. There are many techniques that can be used. It involves more than the provision of factual information on the host country, and should move into the psychological and emotional domains to develop an awareness of the cultural differences. A 'cultural general assimilator' (Brislin 1998) is a frequently used technique. This is an instrument based on over 100 critical incidents that capture the experiences, feelings and thoughts that all who embark on an overseas experience in a different culture might encounter. The incidents are grouped into eight categories: host customs, interaction with hosts, settling in, tourist experiences, the workplace, the family, schooling and returning home. The use of the cultural general assimilator is usually more effective after exposure to the culture, and the critical incidents present an opportunity for discussion and exchange of views. They can then be used as the basis for a number of interactive exercises, including role play.

In general, cross-cultural training tends to be seen mainly as a tool for assisting international managers to adjust to the host culture, and ignores the need to develop mutually respectful and trustful relations with members of the host culture both within and outside the company. However, it is also a major means for helping managers develop so that they can perform effectively. The failure of international assignments is not only to be measured in the costs of early repatriation. Delays in start-up of an international project, low productivity, disrupted relations with local nationals, damage to the company image and lost opportunities can all be averted by cross-cultural training.

EXAMPLE 9.2

A model cross-cultural training programme

Content

- General and country-specific cultural awareness.
- Area studies, history, geography, politics, economics.
- Frameworks for understanding and valuing cultural differences.
- Planning for a successful international assignment.
- Intercultural business skills for working effectively in the local environment.
- Understanding cultural variations for those with regional responsibilities.
- Business and social customs in the host country.
- International transition and stress management.
- Practical approaches to culture-shock management and lifestyle adjustment.
- Information on daily living issues.
- Special issues: partners and families abroad.
- Repatriation as a pre-departure issue.

Training delivery methodologies

- Led by a multicultural team of facilitators, including both host nationals and international managers who have recently returned.
- Learner-centred, taking account of individual learning styles.
- Methods to enhance cultural self-awareness (e.g. culture general assimilator, culture inventories).
- Interactive methods, such as case studies, critical incidents, simulations, video, role play and guided discussion.
- Mentors (both recently returned international managers and host nationals).
- Access to an executive coach after arrival.

delivered both prior to, and subsequent to, departure. It is generally argued that pre-departure training should occur between three and five weeks before leaving, and should be followed up between eight and twelve weeks after arrival. The content and delivery methods for a typical cross-cultural training programme are outlined in Example 9.2.

Cross-cultural training is not only needed for those who depart on international assignments, but is also needed for home-based employees who are in face-to-face or 'virtual' contact with other nationals. More specialized training in subjects such as cross-border communication and teamwork, cross-cultural negotiations and region-specific business briefings may also be needed.

❯ Multicultural teamworking

Becoming sensitive to other cultures is an important quality for international managers, but for many they need to be able to take this one step further as they become members of international management teams. International businesses increasingly rely on multi-cultural teamworking as more and more organizations get involved in joint ventures and partnering arrangements. Companies that make extensive use of international teams include Unilever, HSBC, Shell, IBM, Deutsche Bank and SAP. The types of team can vary enormously in terms of their duration, composition and location. They can be home or overseas based, as well as 'virtual' and transnational (Snell *et al*. 1998). This means that managers need to be able to understand and cope with the processes of communication and decision making in different settings. Problems can arise in multicultural teams around the different ways in which decisions are taken, tasks are allocated and work co-ordinated. Also attitudes to time (especially deadlines and punctuality), the ways in which meetings are conducted, how poor performance is evaluated, how conflict is resolved and how negotiation takes place are other key issues.

Such teamworking requires an understanding of cross-cultural differences in organizational behaviour – especially communication, motivation and decision making (Adler 1997; Smith 1992). Thus while the standard techniques of development are required, the processes for arriving at common understanding and 'norms' are likely to require slower and more explicit discussion of processes. The problem is that in many international organisations, team development tends to be delivered in an *ad hoc* manner, and the constraints of business deadlines often allow little time for it to take place. Furthermore, the growing sophistication of ICT and a reluctance to contemplate travel and relocation mean that international organizations are expecting their international teams to function very soon after start-up. However, the desirable team member qualities, such as adaptability, ability to communicate, commitment to membership, openness to others and understanding of the wider business context, cannot be developed remotely. They require an initial period of intensive contact and regular follow-up meetings.

In most cases such teams require a leader, and care is required in selecting and developing the leader, especially when the team operates as a part-time parallel organization to the rest of the core business. Such team leaders require sophisticated group management skills and the capacity to act as a role model. They must also have the ability to manage the team's external environment – cultivating relations with the management sponsors of the team and with different parts of the parent organization. Very often there will be multiple leaders in virtual teams.

❯ International management development for women

It has been estimated that women make up between 2 per cent and 15 per cent of international managers (Harris 2004), and in both the UK and the USA the proportion of expatriates who are women has remained constant at around 2 per cent to 3 per cent (Scullion 1993; Adler *et al*. 2000). There has been a tendency to assume that societal norms, domestic arrangements and women's preferences are the main obstacle. However, Adler (1984) has debunked these and other commonly held myths about women's lack of interest in international management, and Harris (2004) indicates the critical influence of home country organizational policies on women's prospects in international management. In particular, the interplay of formal company policies and informal processes can have an effect upon women's perceptions of the opportunities available. While the majority of UK and US companies have espoused equal opportunity policies, this certainly does not translate into a growing proportion of women in international management. This is ironic in the light of the research on international management competencies (Barham and Devine 1991), which shows that women tend to be more sensitive to cultural differences and are therefore more able to work effectively with managers from other countries. However, the barriers to their participation are not necessarily within the control of women managers themselves. The major obstacles often lie in the unacknowledged assumptions and prejudices held by senior managers and within the policies for career and succession planning. These can be difficult to overcome.

This chapter now concludes with a case study that illustrates the challenges for international management development within the complex business environment of a single MNC operating in two different countries in the Far East.

CASE STUDY

Inter-InsuranceCo

The start of the twenty-first century has seen considerable concentration and global expansion in financial services. Inter-InsuranceCo is one such company. Headquartered in the UK, it now sells insurance, pensions and savings products throughout the world. Expansion in Asia began in 2002 as India and China, in particular, were perceived to be the main growth markets, and direct competitors to Inter-InsuranceCo were already operating there. So India and China were markets that were imperative to enter, but also where the returns on investment could not be expected to be large for some time to come.

Inter-InsuranceCo Joint Venture in India	*Inter-InsuranceCo Joint Venture in China*
In 2002 Inter-InsuranceCo set up a joint venture, in which it had a 26 per cent equity stake, with a local Indian insurance company. The business now sells insurance, pensions and savings products through a workforce of over 10,000 and over 100 branches across India. There are plans to continue expansion and build a 50,000 strong workforce. However, the regional HR manager for Asia (who is originally from Hong Kong, but with extensive international experience) has noticed some strange practices in the new operation: 1 Resistance to matrix management on the part of many middle and junior managers, who will only accept direction from their line manager. Employees are uncomfortable with being empowered, and many managers see this as a threat to their authority. This adversely affects many cross-business projects.	This joint venture operates across 12 cities within China, and is based on a 50 per cent ownership by Inter-InsuranceCo and the Chinese partner is a state owned enterprise. There are no British managers in the JV, and out of the 1,000 employees, most are Chinese nationals with around 10 managers brought in from Taiwan and Singapore. A new chief executive has been brought in from Singapore who does not have previous experience of working in a JV or China. In particular, there are five senior managers who were transferred into the JV from the state owned enterprise, and who have little experience of business. The regional HR manager for Asia (who is originally from Hong Kong, but with extensive international experience) has observed the following practices: 1 The persistence of strong hierarchical management and authoritative decision-making. Matrix management is not easily understood.

2 Teamworking is therefore problematic, although capability is not at all an issue, as employees are highly qualified. The problem is getting people to work in ways that are unfamiliar, and to a large extent, counter-cultural.

3 The notion that effective management requires growing and developing subordinates is perceived as very threatening by many managers.

4 Non-observance of a number of global HR practices. Examples include many staff making claims for additional payment in lieu of taking annual leave, and tolerance of a high level of sickness absence, because employees expect to be able to take a number of sick days. The introduction of 360 degree feedback has been particularly contentious.

5 Resentment of standard vetting of employees for police records, which is perceived by the parent company as essential to satisfying standards of integrity and trust in client dealings. The perception of employees is that this is a breach of trust.

6 Expectations that family members of employees will be automatically be included in organizational events such as seminars and workshops, and even entitled to preferential treatment when apply for job vacancies.

The regional HR manager has decided to recommend bringing in a senior manager from the UK Head Office to replace the local managing director. However, Head Office are suggesting that it might be better to bring someone familiar with global processes who will work alongside the current managing director, and who will also assist with implementing some international management development activities...

2 Resistance to teamworking as most people prefer working in silos and do not want to share and communicate.

3 Resistance to western methods of performance management from most staff who are accustomed to the old ways that operated within the state owned enterprise. Managing by means of objective-setting, and review of achievement against key performance indicators has proven difficult to get accepted. Furthermore, there is a distaste for providing and receiving subjective feedback on individual performance.

4 There is a degree of bewilderment about the significance of the corporate statement in respect of values, ethics and integrity. Support for openness, adaptability, and respect for others is not easily achieved.

5 The regional HR manager is wondering whether it might be better to approach the Chinese partner about replacing some of the local line managers with experienced international managers from the UK. However, he knows that the Head Office is reluctant to do this, because it goes against the original terms agreed for the joint venture. So, he is now looking for alternative suggestions...

Question

What suggestions would you make for a management development strategy for both these joint ventures?

Future developments

While the previous discussion has focused on the main interventions in the field of IMD, there are some potential new developments on the horizon. One review (Brewster *et al.* 2001) of the implications of globalization for HRM has shown that the fastest increase in internationalization has been among small and medium-sized enterprises. To date, there has been little research on IMD for this sector. Furthermore, increasing competition is forcing many global organizations to cut back and often outsource IMD activities. In some cases independent consultancies have emerged specializing in particular aspects of IMD, such as cross-cultural awareness training or executive coaching. However, several leading international management schools such as London Business School, INSEAD, IMD and several 'Ivy League' US business schools have expanded their international manager programmes and also work closely with the corporate sector to deliver customized executive development. Furthermore, developments in ICT and the growing interest in KM across the corporate sector have brought a new perspective to IMD, in which sophisticated software and 'corporate universities' play a major role (Prince and Stewart 2002). The potential for accelerating communication is enormous, but can only be realized if organizations adopt a strategic approach. This involves a precise analysis of the company's international involvement and the ways in which it is likely to develop, before considering what is required of international managers. The current policies and practices for developing international managers need to be open to critical scrutiny before alternative methods are proposed, and the wider implications for corporate careers for women and host country nationals as well as for white male expatriates need to be addressed.

Review questions

1 How have the roles of international managers changed in the last two decades or so?

2 What aspects of learning theory are useful tools for thinking about IMD?

3 What would you regard as the key competencies that international managers should have? To what extent will these vary according to the context?

4 Do you think that technological developments, particularly in relation to international communication, will mean that firms will need to rely on international managers more or less in the future?

Further reading

1 Chartered Institute of Personnel and Development website: http://www.cipd.co.uk/subjects/intlhr/manageia.htm

The Chartered Institute of Personnel and Development (CIPD) in the UK provides a range of practical sources of information on the subject of international development. A flavour of these, together with some further references and links, can be found at the above web address.

2 Forster, N. (2000) 'The myth of the "international manager"?', *International Journal of Human Resource Management,* 11(1), 126–42.

This article challenges a number of myths that are associated with managers who operate at the international level.

3 Harris, H. (2004) 'Women's role in international management', in Harzing, A.W. and van Ruysseveldt, J. (eds) *International Human Resource Management,* London: Sage.

This chapter provides an excellent overview of the research into women and international management.

4 Morrison, A. (2000) 'Developing a global leadership model', *Human Resource Management,* 39(2 & 3), 117–31.

This article reviews the evidence concerned with the factors that affect the nature and success of global leadership.

References

Adler, N. (1984) 'Women do not want international careers and other myths about international management', *Organizational Dynamics,* 13(2), 66–79.

Adler, N. (1997) *International Dimensions of Organisational Behaviour* (3rd edition), Cincinnati: South Western Press.

Adler, N. and Bartholomew, S. (1992) 'Managing globally competent people', *Academy of Management Executive,* 6(3), 52–65.

Adler, N., Brody, L.W. and Osland, J.S. (2000) 'The Women's Global Leadership Forum: enhancing one company's global leadership capability', *Human Resource Management,* 39(2 & 3), 208–25.

Alldredge, M.E. and Nilan, K.J. (2000) '3M's leadership competency model: an internally developed solution', *Human Resource Management,* 39(2 & 3), 133–45.

Argyris, C. (1990) *Overcoming Organizational Defenses: Facilitating Organizational Learning,* Boston: Allyn and Bacon.

Argyris, C. (1994) *On Organizational Learning,* Oxford: Blackwell.

Bandura, A. (1977) *Social Learning Theory,* Englewood Cliffs, NJ: Prentice Hall.

Barham, K. and Devine, M. (1991) *The Quest for the International Manager: A Survey of Global Human Resource Strategies,* London: Economist Intelligence Unit.

Bass, B.M., and Avolio, B.J. (1994) *Improving Organizational Effectiveness through Transformational Leadership,* Thousand Oaks, CA: Sage.

Befus, C.P. (1988) 'A multilevel treatment approach for culture shock experienced by sojourners', *International Journal of Inter-Cultural Relations,* 12, 381–400.

Bennett, R., Aston, A. and Colquhoun, T. (2000) 'Cross-cultural training: a critical step in ensuring the success of international assignments', *Human Resource Management,* 39(2 & 3), 239–50.

Black, S. and Gregersen, H. (2000) 'High impact training: forging leaders for the global frontier', *Human Resource Management,* 39(2 & 3), 173–84.

Black, J. and Porter, L. (1991) 'Managerial behavior and job performance: a successful manager in Los Angeles may not succeed in Hong Kong', *Journal of International Business Studies,* 22, 291–317.

Brewster, C., Harris, H. and Sparrow, P. (2001) *Globalisation and HR,* London: Chartered Institute of Personnel and Development (CIPD).

Briscoe, D. and Schuler, R. (2004) *International Human Resource Management,* London: Routledge.

Brislin, R.W. (1998) 'A Culture-General Assimilator: Preparation for Various Types of Sojourns', in J.B. Keys and R.M. Fulmer (eds) *Executive Development and Organizational Learning for Global Business,* Binghampton, NY: International Business Press.

Caligiuri, P., Lazarova, M, and Tarique, I. (2005) 'Training, Learning and Development in Multinational Organisations,' in H. Scullion and M. Linehan (eds) *International Human Resource Management: A Critical Text,* Basingstoke: Palgrave Macmillan.

Chambers, E.G., Foulon, M., Hanfield-Jones, H. and Michaels, E. (1998) 'The war for talent', *McKinsey Quarterly.*

Connor J. (2000) 'Developing the global leaders of tomorrow', *Human Resource Management,* 39(2 & 3), 147–57.

Eschbach, D.M., Parker, G.E. and Stoeberl, P.A. (2001) 'American repatriate employees' retrospective assessments of the effects of cross-cultural training on their adaptation to international assignments', *International Journal of Human Resource Management,* 12(2), 270–87.

Evans, P., Puciv, V., and Baroux, J.L. (2002) *The Global Challenge: Frameworks for International Human Resources Management,* MA: McGraw Hill.

Forster, N. (2000) 'The myth of the "international manager"?', *International Journal of Human Resource Management,* 11(1), 126–42.

Gold, J., Thorpe, R., Sadler-Smith, E. nd Woodall, J. (2007) 'Continuing profesisonal development in the legal profession – a practice-based perspective,' *Management Learning,* 38(2), 1–16.

Graf, A. (2004) 'Assessing intercultural training designs,' *Journal of European Industrial Training,* 28(2–4), 199–214.

Gronn, P. (2002) 'Distributed leadership as a unit of analysis,' *The Leadership Quarterly,* Vol. 13, 423–51.

Harris, Brewster, C. and Sparrow, P.R. (2003) *International Human Resource Management,* London: Chartered Institute of Personnel and Development.

Harris, H. (2004) 'Women's Role in International Management', in Harzing, A. W. and van Ruysseveldt, J. (eds) *International Human Resource Management,* London: Sage.

Harzing, A. and van Ruysseveldt, J. (2004) (eds.) *International Human Resource Management,* London: Sage.

Hendry, C. (1994) *Human Resource Strategies for International Growth,* London: Routledge.

Hoeksema, L. and de Jong, G. (2001) 'International co-ordination and management development: an application at PricewaterhouseCoopers', *Journal of Management Development,* 20(2), 145–58.

Knowles, M. (1989) *The Adult Learner: A Neglected Species,* Houston: Gulf Publishing.

Kolb, D. (1983) *Experiential Learning: Experience as the Source of Learning and Development,* Englewood Cliffs, NJ: Prentice Hall.

Marquardt, M. J., (2004) *Optimizing the Power of Action Learning: Solving Problems and Building Leaders in Real Time,* Washington, DC: Davies Black.

Marsick, V. and Watkins, K. (1990) *Informal and Incidental Learning in the Workplace,* London: Routledge.

Mayerhofer, H., Hartmann, L.C. Michelitsch-Riedl, G. and Kollinger, I. (2004) 'Flexpatriate assignments: a neglected issue in global staffing', *International Journal of human Resource Management,* 15(8), 1371–89.

Maznevski, M. and DiStefano, J. (2000) 'Global leaders are team players: developing global leaders through membership on global teams', *Human Resource Management,* 39(2 & 3), 195–208.

McCall, W., Jr., Lombardo, M. and Morrison, A. (1988) *The Lessons of Experience: How Successful Executives Develop on the Job,* Lexington, MA: Lexington Books.

McCauley, C., Ruderman, M., Ohlott, P. and Morrow, J. (1994) 'Assessing the developmental components of managerial jobs', *Journal of Applied Psychology,* 79, 544–60.

Morrison, A. (2000) 'Developing a global leadership model', *Human Resource Management,* 39(2 & 3), 117–31.

Neary, D. and O'Grady, D. (2000) 'The role of training in developing global leaders: a case study at TRW Inc', *Human Resource Management,* 39(2 & 3), 185–93.

Oddou, G., Mendenhall, M. and Bonner Ritchie, J. (2000) 'Leveraging travel as a tool for global leadership development', *Human Resource Management,* 39(2 & 3), 159–72.

Parkinson, E. and Morley, M.J. (2006) 'Cross-Cultural Training', in H. Scullion and D.G. Collings (eds) *Global Staffing,* London: Routledge.

Prince, C. and Stewart, J. (2002) 'Corporate universities – an analytical framework', *Journal of Management Development,* 21(4), 794–811.

Revans, R. (1982) *The Origins and Growth of Action Learning,* Bromley: Chartwell Bratt.

Rogers, C. (1969) *Freedom to Learn,* Columbus, OH: Charles E. Merrill.

Schuler, R.S., Jackson, S.E., and Yeo, Y. (2004) *Managing Human Resources in Cross-Border Alliances,* London: Routledge.

Scullion, H. (1993) 'Creating International Managers: Recruitment and Development Issues', in Kirkbride, P. (ed.) *Human Resource Management in Europe: Perspectives for the 1990s,* London: Routledge.

Scullion. H. and Collings, D.G. (2006) 'Alternative forms of international assignments', in Scullion, H. and Collings, D.G. (eds) *Global Staffing,* London: Routledge.

Scullion, H. and Collings, D.G. (2006b) 'International Talent Management', in Scullion, H. and D.G. Collings (eds) *Global Staffing,* London: Routledge.

Selmer, J. and Leung, A.S.M. (2003) 'Provision and adequacy of support to male expatriate spouses', *Personnel Review,* 32(1), 9–21.

Smith, I. (1992) 'Organizational behaviour and national cultures', *British Journal of Management,* 3, 39–51.

Snell, S., Snow, C., Davison, S. and Hambrick, D. (1998) 'Designing and supporting transnational teams: the human resource agenda', *Human Resource Management,* 37(2), 147–58.

Sparrow, P. (1999) 'International Recruitment, Selection, and Assessment', in Joynt, P. and Marlin, R. (eds) *The Global HR Manager: Creating the Seamless Organisation,* London: Chartered Institute of Personnel and Development (CIPD).

Sparrow, P., Brewster, C. and Harris, H. (2004) *Globalizing Human Resource Management,* London: Routledge.

Stahl, G.K., Pucik, V., Evans, P. and Mendenhall, M.E. (2004) 'Human Resource Management in Cross-Border Mergers and Acquisitions,' in A.W.K. Harris, H.

Tayeb, M. (2004) *International Human Resource Management: A Multinational Company Perspective,* Oxford: Oxford University Press.

Townsend, P. and Cairns, L. (2003) 'Developing the global manager using a capability framework', *Management Learning,* 34(3), 313–27.

Wood-Daudelin, M. (1996) 'Learning from experience through reflection', *Organizational Dynamics,* 24(3), 36–49.

Woodall, J. and Winstanley, D. (1998) *Management Development: Strategy and Practice,* Oxford: Blackwell.

Yeung, A. and Ready, D. (1995) 'Developing leadership capabilities of global corporations: a comparative study in eight nations', *Human Resource Management,* 34(4), 529–47.

Chapter 10

Recruitment and selection of international managers

Fiona Moore

Key aims

The aims of this chapter are to:

- outline the factors that influence the recruitment and selection of international managers;
- consider how the recruitment and selection of international managers differs from that of more locally based managers;
- examine issues of gender, ethnicity, cross-cultural variation and economic development in the recruitment and selection of international managers;
- consider how processes of globalization have affected the traditional patterns of recruitment and selection for international managers.

Introduction

Recruitment is a significant issue in international human resource management, for the simple reason that a failed expatriate assignment can be a serious waste of money and time for both the manager and MNC in question. Unfortunately, however, many companies still tend to use an informal and/or generic recruitment and selection programme when selecting their international staff, and ignore the impact which the tension between local embeddedness and the drive to global integration has on the question of who to recruit and how. This chapter builds upon the issues raised in the previous chapter to consider what is involved in the successful hiring of expatriate managers in theory and in practice, and to discuss ways of setting up recruitment and selection programmes which enable firms to find the right people for the job, before examining broader issues of diversity in international recruitment and selection and the impact of the changing needs of businesses under globalisation upon the process of choosing successful international managers.

In international management, it has been said that 'managers who are unwilling or incapable of generating global learning practices significantly reduce the effectiveness of an organisation' (Berrell *et al.* 2002: 92). In other words, selecting the wrong person for an expatriate assignment can give the organisation a bad image, or cause friction with host-country employees, or reduce profits, or give a new business venture a bad start. Many writers on the subject of expatriates also agree that 'expatriate failure', i.e. a case where an expatriate is unable to complete his/her assignment successfully, has a huge financial cost for the company: Forster (2000: 128–9) estimates that, in a 1995 survey (thus far the most recent of its kind), the cost of moving a single American expatriate to the UK for two years, including selecting, training and monitoring the assignee, was at least £250,000 (about $500,000). This figure does not include the cost of housing and other material benefits. The cost of sending a third-country national (see below), an increasingly common practice, is little better, and may in some cases be even higher. As Berrell *et al.* (2002) note that the first step of developing a successful management and development programme is to recruit and hire the right people for the job, we shall consider how these practices can be used to bring about the most successful result for the assignment.

One of the key problems with many expatriate recruitment and selection programmes is that they tend to focus on standard, traditional hiring practices, with some cosmetic alterations. However, many researchers are coming to realise that, given the differences between companies and the contested nature of globalization, this approach is detrimental to good performance. Bartlett and Ghoshal (1997) point out that, at each managerial level, managers may play similar roles and have similar responsibilities, but have a different size and scope of activities. This holds true for international management as well, if not more so: although they may all broadly be 'managers,' they have different situations and different responsibilities in different locations, and cannot be treated as a single category. Furthermore, as Berrell *et al.* note, 'there is…a shortage of managerial talent capable of operating internationally…the globally friendly senior manager is a scarce and, therefore, an expensive commodity' (2002: 92). International human resource managers are thus best advised to abandon 'generic' hiring practices in favour of more specialized ones.

In this chapter, we shall first consider the issues surrounding the development of a recruitment programme, then those regarding the selection of international managers, and the difference between theory and practice in both instances. We shall then look at two case studies of the recruitment and selection of Japanese international managers, with a view to comparing and contrasting the two situations. We shall finally develop themes referenced elsewhere in this book to consider issues of diversity in recruitment, recruitment and selection issues as they relate to the developing world, and to address the question of how the traditional concept of the 'international manager' has changed through the increasing use of rapid global transportation and new communications technologies, before drawing some general conclusions about recruitment and selection in the era of globalization. We shall now define some general concepts in recruitment and selection before going on to address issues within this field in greater detail.

Key concepts and definitions

Recruitment can be defined, broadly speaking, as the practice of deciding what the company needs in a candidate and instigating procedures to attract the most appropriate candidate for the job. In recruitment, the human resource manager will need to identify the key traits of the required individual (through working out a *job description* and *person specification*) and, through advertising and/or approaching individuals who might be suitable, finding a person with these traits. Recruitment thus involves identifying the needs of the company regarding the position to be filled, and attracting suitable candidates for the job.

Selection, by contrast, involves choosing the right candidate for the position from the ones who have been recruited. It involves testing and evaluating the skills and attributes of these individuals to determine which are the best ones for the job at hand. Selection should be, according to ACAS guidelines, 'effective, efficient and fair' – effective in picking the right person, efficient in doing it with minimal fuss and expense, and fair in that it should preclude discrimination (Beardwell *et al.* 2004). This holds true as much when selecting international managers as when selecting those who will be working closer to home.

Finally, a word on how we will define the *international manager* for the purposes of this chapter. The term is, broadly speaking, used of a manager who is sent on an international assignment; the stereotypical image most people have of such a manager is of a fairly young elite individual who takes an international assignment for about three years before returning home. Increasingly, however, writers are coming to use the term 'international manager' to mean someone with a more or less completely global orientation, who specializes in international assignments: Leonard (2002) furthermore identifies what she calls 'transpatriates', individuals who operate globally rather than in specific local cultures. Forster (2000) argues that both the stereotypical expatriate and the transpatriate are the exception (only about 8 per cent of any given company at any point in time), and that the concept of 'expatriation' includes more variety, including permanent migrants, short-term assignments, cross-border job swaps, and multicultural project teams. He further notes that that many international recruitment and selection programmes make a basic *a priori* assumption that managers fit the above stereotypes, and treat them accordingly, regardless of whether they fit the model or not, to the detriment of both individual and firm. More recent research has suggested that not only is Forster's analysis correct, but that increasingly, more expatriates are following these less traditional paths (Collings *et al.* 2007; Cullen 2007). This means that human resource managers need to adopt more flexible mindsets in terms of recruiting and selecting such individuals.

In this chapter, therefore, we will define an international manager in broad terms as a manager on an assignment which requires working and/or living for a time outside of their home country, recognizing that this definition includes a good deal of variation. We shall now examine the issues involved in recruiting such individuals for an international assignment.

Criteria for recruitment

As noted above, international recruitment involves defining what the assignment entails and what sort of person is needed for it, and then considering how to attract that person. This process has, however, been given little attention, to the point where

Dowling and Welch (2004) identify four myths which have grown up surrounding the recruitment of international managers, which shape managers' expectations:

1 There is a universal approach to management.
2 People can acquire multicultural behaviours without outside help.
3 There are common characteristics shared by all successful international managers.
4 There are no impediments to mobility.

In practice, however, both managers and assignments can vary widely in terms of what they need and the characteristics required. To this, we can also add a fifth myth:

5 The differences between national cultures and legal regimes are ultimately superficial and have little to no impact on expatriate assignments.

We shall here outline the factors affecting the criteria for recruitment, considering the role of the company, the needs of the person, the nature of the assignment, legal issues and the amount and type of training and development required.

▶ The company

As we saw in Chapters 5 and 6, companies have different needs and strategies in the international sphere, and different relationships to the global and the local. When recruiting international managers, these strategies are arguably the first thing which should be taken into account, with particular regard to what sort of expatriate would best fit with the company's strategy.

Bartlett and Ghoshal (2002) note that companies tend to take different forms when operating across national borders, depending on the degree to which the company aims for global integration versus embeddedness in various national contexts. These differences have an impact on the type of person needed for expatriate assignments in each case. A more centralized MNC, for instance, would, generally speaking, want expatriates with a strong head-office focus, who are able to transfer knowledge to, and maintain control of, subsidiaries and branches (see also Chapter 7). A more decentralized company would favour managers who are flexible, entrepreneurial and capable of making crucial decisions on their own. More globally oriented companies might want a manager who can integrate and serve as a 'bridge' between different markets. There is also the question of what the company expects the subsidiary or branch to achieve over the course of the assignment, which has a bearing on the skills required of the expatriate.

The selection of expatriates is also affected by more nebulous factors. The company's culture, for instance, may favour a more flexible outlook or a more regimented one (certain international hotel chains, for instance, refuse to allow any deviation from a certain set of standard management procedures); a company may also favour promoting talent within the company or hiring people with the relevant skills from elsewhere (also called 'growing their own' versus 'poaching'). A company's international image is also significant: certain German banks, for instance, want to be seen as 'German' wherever they are, and so favour the placing of particularly German-focused people in key international management positions, while certain German manufacturing corporations wish to cultivate a more international image, and consequently favour the hiring of third-country nationals or Germans with considerable international experience. 'Soft' qualitative factors might thus affect the question of who to hire for an international assignment.

Money is also an issue. Before deciding on who to recruit, the company must consider how much they want to spend on the assignment, how much they are willing to invest in the training and development of the manager, and whether they would be willing to provide financial or other incentives to successful candidates. The question of how much to spend on the manager's family is also an issue (see below). These criteria affect, for instance, whether one hires a manager with the relevant technical skills but few intercultural abilities with the aim of training them in the latter area, or a manager with both sets of skills (who might demand a higher price). It also might raise issues of equal opportunities, which will be discussed in greater detail below. When recruiting international managers, therefore, the strategy, culture and financial position of the company must first be taken into account.

▶ The nature of the assignment

Next, the nature and length of the assignment must be considered. An expatriate assignment lasting only a few months, for instance, requires less preparation and less of a disruption to the lifestyle of a manager than one lasting for three years. Similarly, an assignment involving travel to a variety of countries requires a different sort of preparation to one involving moving to one other country. The circumstances of the assignment might also be significant, as one would need different skills and capabilities for each of the following common reasons for expatriation:

- teaching a new process;
- helping a branch through a matrix integration;
- setting up a new branch or representative office;
- assisting with a joint venture;
- facilitating knowledge transfer between a subsidiary and its head office.

When recruiting candidates, therefore, HR managers must consider the following questions: *What are the needs of head office from the expatriate? What sort of role does the expatriate need to play in the assignment? How long will he or she be required to play it?* Once these questions have been answered honestly, a clearer picture of the type of candidate required may emerge.

Furthermore, it is not only the needs of the head office which have to be taken into account under these circumstances. Whether or not the subsidiary's needs are being considered affects how the expatriate will be treated by their new colleagues, how well they are able to carry out their duties and, ultimately, the success of the assignment. This can be seen in a study of performance management by Li and Karakowski (2001). They conducted a laboratory study of Asian-American and European-American subjects, in which individuals were shown videotapes of a group of students making a decision on an investment project, and then were required to evaluate the behaviour of particular individuals in the videotape. The results demonstrated that their standards of performance appraisal differed significantly: what one group considered appropriate behaviour for a manager, the other considered inappropriate, with, for instance, European subjects approving of behaviour which Asian subjects considered aggressive. Consequently, a person who is hired according to his/her compatibility with head office behavioural norms and practices might find their actions a severe liability in other national contexts. Berrell *et al.*, furthermore, note that involving the management of the subsidiary in the recruitment and selection of the international staff to be assigned there encourages trust between both parties (2002: 93). The nature of the assignment and the needs and wishes of the subsidiary thus must be considered when recruiting managers for international assignments.

The location of the assignment must also be taken into consideration. Expatriates moving from a more to a less developed country may find it particularly difficult to adjust to their new location. Furthermore, if they are being paid according to Head Office rates, they may incur resentment from local managers (Bhanughopan and Fish 2007; Dowling and Welch 2004: Chapter 6). Even between countries at a similar level of economic development, cultural differences may be difficult for expatriates to overcome. The economic and social differences between an international manager's country of origin and of assignment must also be taken into account.

▶ The person

It is equally crucial to consider the nature and motivations of the sort of person who the company requires for the international assignment. Managers do not always take international positions for the same reasons, but may do so from a combination of motivating factors, including:

- career advancement;
- financial incentives;
- interest in the area;
- interest in travel.

More nebulous criteria can also play a role. Behrend *et al.* (2009), for instance, note that companies which emphasised their pro-environmental credentials had greater success in recruitment than those which did not. It is worth considering these when advertising the position, as these may provide ideas as to how to attract the right person; for instance, one might investigate what sort of compensation package would be most attractive to the desirable candidate, or whether prior knowledge of the country would prove beneficial.

Furthermore, it is worth considering whether or not the expatriate's interests are in fact aligned with those of the company. While Harzing's (2001a; 2001b) studies of expatriates reveal that many are sent over as a more or less formal means by which head office can maintain control over the branches, a more qualitative study has revealed that expatriates tend to view the building of an international career as more important, and may become disillusioned and leave the company when this career fails to materialise (Moore 2006). Furthermore, it is possible for companies to make false assumptions about an individual's characteristics: Selmer (2002) notes that American companies frequently send Chinese-American managers on assignment to China, only to find that their beliefs that the managers' ancestry will give them a familiarity with the culture are severely mistaken. Finally, people who are interested in the assignment only for financial or career-related reasons may not actually be interested in the assignment. It thus may be worth considering whether the company and the candidate's aims and goals are aligned or in conflict.

The personal qualities of the candidate should also be taken into account. Crucial to many assignments is the ability of an individual to adapt to particular circumstances. This is an essential skill for international management, which may be even more important than previous knowledge of the country/region to which the expatriate is to be sent. This also affects the nature and amount of guidance from head office which will be required. The problem is that adaptability, being a psychological attribute, may be difficult to measure. It may also stem from character traits which are not highly valued in business. As Gregersen *et al.* (1996) note, often adaptability is the result of qualitative skills like empathy, ability to compromise and to get along with other people, as opposed to skills like competitiveness, aggression and so on, rather than of practical, quantitative skills. Consequently, the managers with the right abilities may be ignored or passed over because the recruiters do not consider their personality appropriate for a key management position.

It is also debatable whether prior experience of working in the country of assignment is an asset or a liability. On the plus side, prior experience can save the company money, as it would mean that linguistic and intercultural training may not be required; Selmer (2004) notes that many European MNCs currently establishing a presence in China are deliberately selecting managers who speak one or more Chinese languages, as these can be expensive and time-consuming for Westerners to learn. On the negative side, however, there is always the possibility of the manager becoming biased towards the subsidiary's culture rather than maintaining a degree of impartiality, or, when the assignment is over, deciding that s/he wants to stay in the country.

Finally, it is worth considering the personal skills of candidates. As noted above, expatriates tend to show a certain demographic similarity, which is surprising when one considers the variety of assignments currently being conducted. This suggests that there is a hidden problem, in that companies are simply hiring people who express an interest in the assignment rather than actively recruiting the best ones for the job in question. As noted below, in the section on gender and ethnicity, there are also reasons why a qualified manager might not put themselves forward for the assignment. Companies thus may need to engage in more imaginative recruitment practices, to attract candidates who might not otherwise apply for the job.

▶ Legal issues

When outlining the recruitment criteria, managers should consider what the hiring regulations are in the home country and the host country, especially whether there exist regulations forbidding companies from hiring non-local staff unless they can prove that they are essential. It is also worth considering how long a person can legally work in the country of assignment, and whether it has any legal impediments to the immigration of certain groups (see the section on gender and ethnicity, below). The hiring of third-country nationals and the potential development of "transpatriates" raises particular issues in legal terms, especially when taking into account how the company can provide such individuals with social security, a pension and other essential benefits (Polak 2002). However, legal issues are subject to change over time. Since the 1950s, EU countries have moved towards making it easier for EU nationals to travel and work in the different member states. By contrast, since 11 September 2001, American visa requirements for foreign expatriates have become much more stringent.

As no two international assignments are the same, it is therefore advisable for managers not to attempt to come up with a universal formula for expatriate managers when developing criteria for recruitment, but to consider the individual circumstances of the assignment, the ideal characteristics of the manager required, and the degree to which the organisation is willing to compromise. We shall now consider issues involved in the selection of the appropriate candidate.

Selection

As with recruitment, how the selection of candidates for international positions is done varies from company to company, and situation to situation. We shall here consider some of the more common methods of selecting candidates, and their advantages and disadvantages, as well as some of the issues which they raise.

▶ Informal methods

Traditionally, despite the abundance of literature on the subject, little consideration has gone into the specific requirements of an international assignment in practice, and instead candidates have been selected informally, based on personal contacts. Harris and Brewster (1999) call this the 'coffee-machine' system of selection, in which the selection of the candidate is down to a manager saying to a colleague as they both take a coffee break, 'we need someone to take over the Beijing assignment' and the colleague responding, 'well, Perkins has been to China, he might do it'. To play devil's advocate for a moment, it has been mentioned above that what often makes or breaks an international assignment is not the formal qualifications of the assignees but their ability to get by in a particular situation. Under those circumstances, a colleague's feelings about the candidate's suitability might be as reliable a guide as anything else.

Unfortunately, however, one has little way of knowing whether any given manager's judgement in this area is particularly sound. Perkins' manager might be putting forward a suitable candidate, but he might equally be trying to do a friend a favour, or rid himself of a troublemaker or ambitious subordinate. It is also not a particularly fair method of selection, in that better candidates might be passed over simply because they don't happen to know the manager getting the coffee at that particular time. Similar objections exist to the common practice of using seniority as the main consideration (Berrell *et al.* 2002), as seniority does not necessarily mean capability, particularly in the international arena. Selection on the basis of connections or seniority thus has a number of problems, and is strongly discouraged as a means of selecting an international manager.

▶ Formal methods

Formal methods, while more reliable, are not entirely problem-free. Selection on the basis of past experience, for instance, is often deemed a reliable guide to future performance. However, simply because a manager performs well in the home context, or in a particular host country environment, it does not follow that they will do well wherever they are assigned. Indeed, as countries and people change over time, it does not even necessarily mean they will do well in the country of their first assignment! As Bartlett and Ghoshal note:

> One problem is that profiles that have been generated often include an inventory of personality traits, individual beliefs, acquired skills and other personal attributes and behaviours assembled…with little logical linkage to bind them. Furthermore, these profiles are often developed based on surveys of current managers or analysis of the most successful individual performers in the existing context. (1997: 104)

The use of such criteria, firstly, fits the prior needs of the corporation, not the current ones (as well as failing to take the motivations of the managers themselves into account); secondly, it does not consider individual variation; and, finally, it encourages people to formulate a kind of 'ideal type' manager which actually bears little relation to the realities of individual managers.

There is also the case of selection by skill. As noted in earlier chapters, it is unfortunately common among MNCs to treat international experience or global awareness as a kind of 'bolt-on'; if you need a manager for a car factory, for instance, you select a good engineer and give him some intercultural training. The problem is that some skills and experiences cannot be formally taught. While doing research at German MNCs, for instance, I encountered several cases of German expatriates who were competent at their jobs, but whose lack of ability to communicate, on an emotional level, with the staff of the British office to which they were assigned resulted in mutual alienation (Moore, forthcoming). While one might discover hidden intercultural capabilities in some international assignees, it is best to treat these as pre-existing skills and abilities rather than as something which can be developed in any suitable person. Formal selection methods thus may be as problematic as informal ones; while they may be used as criteria for making the initial selection, other methods will be needed subsequently to determine the best candidate.

▶ Tests and examinations

In theory, at least, formal tests and assessments are more objective than the selection methods we have considered above, in that they are less based on advantageous friendships or on formal criteria which may or may not be good indicators of future performance (Hum 2006). As expatriate assignments become more common, and consequently more consideration goes into the selection of candidates, more emphasis is being placed on using formal tests, examinations and so forth.

Some of the means of selection are fairly familiar, such as:

Interviews. When interviewing a candidate for an international assignment, it is worth having a variety of people from different parts of the organisation consider the candidate – even, perhaps, have them assessed by people both from head office and the office to which they are being assigned. In this way, a balanced assessment of the candidate's skills can be found.

References/résumés. These can provide a useful indication of a candidate's skills and background, but it is worth bearing in mind that success in one international assignment might not necessarily mean success in another. Also, some assignments require a global orientation rather than previous experience.

In addition, more specialized means of selection may be used:

Selection tests. These are often used for non-international assignments; however, in the case of selecting an expatriate, they may also include tests for linguistic ability, intercultural ability, psychological fitness for expatriation, and other, assignment-specific, criteria (Hum 2006).

Assessment centres. These, again, are normally used for the selection of a candidate for non-international positions. However, they can be useful in assessing abilities such as flexibility, quick thinking, coping with multi-ethnic teams and handling difficult situations. In the future, we may increasingly see assessment centres geared towards international assignments (Hum 2006). However, as Berrell *et al*. note, the key problem with selection is that 'it is exceedingly difficult to simulate cultural influences' (2002: 92), meaning that it is doubtful that an assessment centre may prove to be a better guide than any other to the expatriate's potential fitness for the assignment.

Specific monitoring of disadvantaged groups. This is a legal requirement in some cases, and should be practiced even when it is not, for reasons discussed below. The purpose is to ensure that the selection is effective, efficient and fair for all candidates.

Whatever criteria are used initially to select candidates, they should thus be followed up with tests and assessments. It is worth bearing in mind, however, that tests can also show bias, as can examiners, when selecting candidates.

▶ Third-country nationals

As some more globally integrated companies are now beginning to recruit cross-nationally rather than simply to look for an applicant at the head office, more complex and specific criteria for selection are needed. Such expatriates are known as third-country nationals, as opposed to being from the home or host country of the MNC. The advantages of selecting such individuals are that one can hire the best person for the job, regardless of their head office connections or their place of origin; they are also widely believed to be more impartial than head office employees sent to branches (or vice versa), and, given that there are three rather than two cultures involved, to find it easier to cultivate a global mentality. However, they are also harder to recruit, and it can be harder to control for cultural differences in the selection process, and to arrange for training, compensation and so forth. It is also worth questioning whether it is really easier to develop a global mentality in this way than any other. It is thus very much down to the individual assignment and company whether to select third-country nationals or not.

▶ Selecting for specific abilities and competencies

Finally, MNCs will want to select candidates with specific abilities and competencies which might prove useful in the assignment. The fact that many MNCs starting operations in China select expatriates on the basis of their ability to speak Chinese languages, and/or an assumed familiarity with the culture based on family background (Selmer 2002), can be a mixed blessing. On the one hand, it saves the cost of training, but on the other hand it might mean that a better performer in other areas is passed over. Although Berrell *et al.* (2002) say that companies engaged in international joint ventures benefit actively from recruiting people who have lived for extended periods in the other culture, so that they can facilitate knowledge transfer, it might be less useful in other areas in which knowledge transfer is less of an issue than particular technical skills or the ability to be a negotiator. Overall, managers need to have 'effective cross-cultural communication, a capacity to be non-judgemental, empathy, flexibility and a high tolerance for ambiguity' (Berrell *et al.* 2002: 92), but quite what these entail in the particular circumstances of the assignment is more ambiguous.

Entrepreneurial skills are often cited as advantageous in international managers, as they may find themselves developing a new venture effectively on their own, or steering an established branch on a particular course. However, the importance of these skills depends on how isolated the branch is, how much of a controlling role the expatriate has been given, and the company's overall strategy *vis-à-vis* its branches.

In sum, then, selection, like recruitment, is very much dependent on the particular context of the assignment: the needs of the company, the skills of the candidates, and the role the manager will play in the organization. It is advisable to use both traditional and non-traditional selection methods to find the right individual for the position.

CASE STUDY

Hamada versus Sakai

Japanese expatriates are a particularly interesting group to consider in this context because the economic circumstances, expectations of expatriates and attitude to globalization of Japanese MNCs has changed dramatically over the past 30 years. By comparing and contrasting two studies of Japanese expatriates conducted ten years apart, Hamada's *Under the Silk Banner* (1992) and Sakai's *Japanese Bankers in the City of London* (2000), we can see how the needs, circumstances and attitudes of the expatriates and their companies change over time in response to outside events, impacting on the recruitment and selection of international managers.

Hamada's study was based on interviews with Japanese expatriate managers in the mid-1980s. At this time the emphasis in Japan was strongly on the idea of managers as 'company men', who would remain loyal to the company, making it the focus of their personal lives as well as their business activities (see Rohlen 1974) and of centralized companies focused on a Japanese head office. Japan was also internationalizing rapidly after a period in which business was largely domestic. Consequently, companies tended to prefer a model of expatriation based on a group of Japanese expatriate top managers and senior managers controlling the branch, with local junior managers and staff handling day-to-day issues.

At the same time, the Japanese managers were concerned about the personal impact of the internationalization process. Hamada's interviewees were reluctant to go overseas and concerned about losing their social networks within the company: under the traditional Japanese corporate system, senior employees look after and encourage the careers of their juniors, who in turn support their seniors, but staff posted overseas find themselves struggling to maintain their position within this network. Women were virtually non-existent within this cadre: Lam (1992), writing at the same time as Hamada, noted that women were usually passed over for expatriate positions on the grounds that they would be expected to leave the company once they married. The wives and children of expatriates often stayed in Japan; given that Japanese men were expected to form their social lives around the company, this is not too surprising, but the perceived difficulty of making an overseas move was also a factor.

In terms of recruitment and selection, then, the companies had a strong stake in ensuring that the people sent over are loyal and focused on Japan and the head office. There is the additional problem, however, that the international assignment might incur feelings of disloyalty in managers cut off from their networks and families. Furthermore, the fact that overseas postings were not regarded as avenues for career advancement meant that

they had difficulty attracting the best staff for such positions. Japanese companies in the 1980s were thus forced to rely on employee loyalty to maintain successful expatriate assignments.

By the time of Sakai's study, however, much had changed. During the 1990s, Japan had undergone a severe financial crisis, which had a similarly drastic effect on traditional Japanese company structure. In addition, the intervening years had seen the development of a cohort of what Goodman (1993) calls 'international youth': Japanese children raised wholly or partly abroad, who are consequently more internationally focused. Japan had thus become more flexible and globalized as a result of its experiences.

Consequently, among Sakai's interviewees, we see more interest in an international career among Japanese managers; as the system collapsed and reformed itself, managers felt less bound by the old social hierarchies and traditions of company loyalty, and sought non-traditional employment patterns, including going abroad. They also displayed more flexible approaches to international management: a notable portion of Sakai's interviewees were either Japanese already settled in England who were recruited to Japanese banks, or expatriates who settled and became locals. Although women still faced discrimination, the loss of the 'career for life' among male employees had put them on a more equal footing with the men. With the 'international youth' becoming more and more of a prestigious group, families were becoming less concerned about going abroad. In view of these changes, also, the head offices were more inclined to allow their subsidiaries greater control over their own affairs, resulting in a relaxing of the Japan-centric international management practices noted by Hamada.

Furthermore, Sakai's study clearly shows that the Japanese companies' relationship to home and host countries changes over time. In the 1960s, she notes, banks focused for the most part on domestic concerns and providing financial support for Japanese companies overseas; in the 1970s they become more focused on the international, due to financial and political pressures from Japan to expand into other economies. Following the collapse of the Japanese 'bubble economy' in the 1990s, the banks again changed their practices, hiring more foreign employees (and, apparently, allowing them greater status within the organization); layoffs and redundancies became more common. Many of her interviewees felt that the Japanese national business culture was changing to become more like that of the USA or Britain: no lifetime employment, a focus on generalists rather than specialists, and less of a sense of belonging to the company. With these changes, patterns of recruitment and selection also changed, from wanting staff who are focused on the head office, loyal to the company and technically skilled, to more flexible patterns focusing increasingly on intercultural skills and linguistic abilities.

The two studies of Japanese expatriates thus demonstrate that the needs and strategies of both companies and expatriates change over time and under different circumstances; the requirements of the company, and the concerns of the expatriate, were quite different in Hamada's and Sakai's studies. Finally, the main lesson that we can learn is that recruitment and selection patterns for international managers can, and should, vary depending on the circumstances of the individual assignment.

For more details, see Hamada (1992), Sakai (2000), Goodman (1993), Lam (1992) and Rohlen (1974).

Question

What impact do you think the changes in expatriation in Japanese companies identified by comparing Hamada's and Sakai's studies have had on (a) what the manager expects from the company? and (b) the company's criteria for recruiting a suitable candidate?

Diversity issues in international recruitment and selection

Although women can have advantages over men in certain expatriate assignments, even, sometimes, in countries where female managers are not the norm, women have a harder time winning expatriate assignments, partly because of the common belief in Western business contexts that they 'will not be taken seriously' in less egalitarian countries, and partly because they traditionally take on more of the family's childcare responsibilities. This is a problem for many companies, both because of increasing equal opportunities legislation in many countries, and because MNCs are increasingly concerned to hire the best candidate for the job. We shall here consider some of the issues involving diversity in international recruitment and selection, focusing on those relating to gender and ethnicity, although of course many other traits may form a basis for discrimination, such as age (Riach 2009), sexual orientation (Colgan et al. 2009), religion (Bell 2007) or class (McLeod et al. 2009).

▶ The problem

As noted in Chapter 9, international management has long remained the preserve of white male employees – or, as Davison and Punnet (1995: 418) put it, the preserve of male employees of the 'elite race' (Chinese males in Chinese firms, white German males in German firms, and so forth). This is despite the fact that demographics in the home countries of these firms have been changing. In North America, for instance, equal-opportunity initiatives have meant a rise in the numbers of women and ethnic minorities in management, which is not reflected in the same firms' international management practices. Also, Davison and Punnett (1995) note that, though most if not all firms recognise that they can benefit from diversity, and that firms which avoid systematic discrimination are more effective internationally, they still maintain discriminatory hiring practices. Despite advances in equal opportunity practices, then, women and ethnic minorities are still discriminated against in international management.

These practices may, furthermore, actually be *preventing* women and ethnic minorities from obtaining international posts. Davison and Punnet (1995) argue that many companies try to take a 'gender and race blind' approach to hiring, but, rather than being therefore able to pick the best candidate for the job, they frequently damage the assignment. In the first place, to try and ignore gender and race is to deny the real fact that discrimination exists; Linehan and Walsh (1999) note that of their sample of female international managers, none had been asked or suggested by their colleagues for the assignment, but all had deliberately put their names forward. Secondly, this approach ignores the advantages which gender and race may bring to the assignment, particularly as these are situations in which intangible assets may count, and in which an innovative approach may be necessary. To be 'colour blind' is thus not to grant everyone an equal chance, but to ignore workplace realities.

This is all the more significant because discrimination in recruitment is often the result of unconscious biases rather than any systematic process. Thomas (1990) notes that the overwhelming number of white male managers in American corporations is because the senior management of such corporations also tend to be white men, who are more favourably disposed towards people who resemble themselves, and with whom they can empathise (this is supported by Davison and Punnet's (1995) study, which suggested that female and black candidates were more favourably viewed by female and black assessors than by white and/or male assessors). Subconsciously, managers may decide that a female candidate would be 'unambitious', or that a black manager would 'have trouble fitting in'. Women are also often seen as being more likely to have 'split loyalties', as they attempt to balance their role within the company with their role within their families. Alternatively, they may not consider them at all, as they do not fit their stereotype of what an international manager looks like.

In addition, Linehan and Walsh also suggest that male senior managers may subconsciously feel threatened by an ambitious woman (1999: 523). Furthermore, they note that studies of uncertainty suggest that people under those conditions are more inclined to fall back on stereotypes than otherwise, which would further preclude the hiring of candidates from groups traditionally stereotyped as unambitious or unreliable (this can also potentially be a barrier against the hiring of individuals with physical or mental disabilities, neither of which in themselves preclude an aptitude for international management). The strongest barrier to the selection of women and minorities as international managers would thus seem to be subconscious prejudice.

Finally, different countries have different regulations and traditions regarding discrimination, equal opportunities and positive discrimination. When engaging in the selection of international managers, it is thus advisable to be aware of the regulations in the home and the host country regarding the hiring of disadvantaged groups, and to take these into account. One should also consider the International Labour Organization's regulations concerning race and gender, in particular the ILO Convention Concerning Discrimination in Respect of Employment and Occupation (Convention 111). In many places there can be significant benefits to being seen to be an equal-opportunities employer.

▶ Hiring women and ethnic minorities: the pros and cons

Another reason to recruit women and ethnic minorities as international managers, aside from the legal argument, is that they may have advantages which white male managers do not have. Adler and Izraeli (1994) cite the case of an American female manager who did very well in Japan, despite the fact that the Japanese indigenous business culture is strongly male-biased, because an American woman was seen as a novelty or curiosity, and so her contacts were better able to remember her than more conventional male expatriates. It may also be the case that, in a male-dominated business culture, businessmen may not see a female manager as a potential rival, and thus may be more open with her than with male managers. Taylor *et al.* (2004) also cite the case of a black American female interviewee, who said that, due to her experience of discrimination in her home country, she was less upset than her white male colleagues when she faced discrimination in Japan. Linehan and Walsh (1999) note that, as managers come to realise that relational skills and inter-cultural competencies may be worth more than technical skills as success factors in the international business arena, the stereotype of women as better relators and facilitators than technicians may come to work to the advantage of female managers. There are thus a number of inherent advantages to recruiting women and ethnic minorities as international managers.

There are, however, also disadvantages. Discrimination can be a source of stress, particularly when a woman or minority manager moves from a more egalitarian business culture to a more segregated one. American women in Germany, for instance, found what they saw as the 'casual sexism' of their German colleagues offensive (British women, however, did not, indicating that what are seen as acceptable forms and levels of discrimination vary from culture to culture) (Taylor *et al.* 2004). This can also lead to situations of cross-cultural misunderstanding, in which a local manager may cause offence to an international manager without realizing it, or vice versa, due to differences in attitude to gender and ethnicity. Furthermore, in some cases, discrimination goes beyond simple bias and stereotyping; in some countries, for instance, women may not be allowed to travel without a male escort, and in apartheid-era South Africa, a black manager would have been barred from dealing with white colleagues. The legal recognition of gay and lesbian spouses, also, varies strongly from country to country, and, in countries with a federal system such as the USA, may also vary from state to state. It is also possible that a male trailing spouse will face more problems than a female one, due to the lack of an extant support group, and of finding himself in a non-traditional social role (that of stay-at-home spouse and/or parent) at the same time as he moves to a foreign setting. When selecting women and minorities as international managers, one must bear in mind both the particular advantages and disadvantages that they face; one should not, however, let the disadvantages blind one to the potential benefits of such a choice.

▶ Family

For managers of both genders, the happiness of a spouse and children can have a strong impact on the morale and adaptability of an expatriate. Even in the most traditional expatriate situation, the attitudes of the family can be crucial to its success or failure; in a now classic study, Steinmetz (1965) focuses on the role of wives in the traditional male-centred expatriate assignment, demonstrating that the wife's happiness had a measurable impact on that of the expatriate himself. It is, therefore, in the interests of the MNC to ensure that the expatriate's family is also adequately provided for.

Furthermore, as dual-career couples increasingly become the norm, situations may arise in which one spouse may be forced to choose between their partner's expatriate assignment and their own career. As Forster notes, 'It is often relocating partners who have the most to lose from a move abroad – particularly if this means they have to give up work or…put their careers on hold' (2000: 131). Despite the fact that some companies are now trying out compensation policies for spouses, including hiring an executive search consultant to find a new job for the spouse in the area to which the manager is being assigned, Forster's research indicates that the bulk of trailing spouses simply give up employment altogether for the duration of the assignment (see Table 10.1).

Forster also notes that, increasingly, many people who might otherwise be suitable candidates for an international assignment are refusing the offer or failing to put their names forward because they do not want their partner to be forced to choose between the assignment and their own job. When hiring international managers of whatever gender, then, the situation and welfare of the family should be a key consideration.

Whereas in the past, most of the literature has assumed expatriates to be white and/or elite males with families, and while managers have consequently focused their selection processes upon this group, it should not be assumed that such individuals are therefore the best candidates for an international assignment. HR managers must thus be particularly careful in the case of international assignments to ensure that the recruitment and selection process is egalitarian, and takes into account the particular strengths and weaknesses of women and minorities in this situation, as well as considering the impact of the move on the expatriate's family.

▶ The developing world

Finally, the nature of present-day geopolitics means that assignments where a manager goes from a more-developed to a less-developed country, or indeed vice versa, are not only becoming more common, but are increasingly seen as more desirable on the part

Table 10.1 **Career patterns of partners of expatriates**

Before the move		After the move	
Part-time	32%	Part-time	9%
Full-time	34%	Full-time	11%
Not employed	34%	Not employed	80%

(*Source:* Forster 2000: 131)

of ambitious expatriates and MNCs keen to pursue interests in potentially lucrative markets such as China and India (Shen and Edwards 2004; Cullen 2007). It is worth noting that such assignments can incur issues not normally considered in the traditional international assignment. As noted earlier, issues of relative power can incur problematic relations between the international manager and his/her local contacts; there may also be a greater danger of resorting to damaging stereotypes, and/or misunderstanding the nature of the local culture and the social qualities necessary for the assignment (Li and Karakowski 2001), meaning that care must be taken to select a manager with particularly good skills in the areas of communication and sensitivity, as well as, in some cases, an understanding of local norms and values. It is also worth noting that the definition of 'development' is a particularly flexible one: while many people still consider such complex and sophisticated economies as China and South Korea as 'developing', parts of the 'developed' USA (for instance, the former automobile-manufacturing centres of Michigan) are socially and economically underdeveloped (Mickelthwait and Wooldridge 2000: Chapter 13). Such issues must increasingly be taken into account when selecting international managers.

The changing international manager

In our final section, we shall briefly consider whether the case of international recruitment and selection supports or contradicts the theory that 'international managers' are emerging as a distinct group in the business world, what the implications are for recruitment and selection in either case, and the potential implications for how we think about globalization.

It has been suggested in the past that the increasing recognition of international management as a distinct case within recruitment and selection is furthering the emergence of the 'international manager' as a distinct class (Gregersen *et al.* 2004; Selmer 2004). By selecting less for practical or technical skills, and more for such things as 'intercultural ability' and 'global awareness', it is possible that MNCs are in fact developing a cadre of people who specialise in international management, and who ultimately will become a group who go from assignment to assignment, like diplomats (Forster 2000). If this is in fact the case, then the possibility of the development of such a group should form a key part of any MNC's international recruitment and selection programme. Recruitment and selection should also focus less on the particular *national* context of the assignment, and more on the international development of the manager.

On the other hand, there is considerable evidence to support Forster's rejection of the development of such a managerial class, in an article tellingly entitled 'The Myth of the "International Manager"?'. As noted in the previous chapter, Forster (2000) argues, in line with the more general arguments of Hirst *et al.* (2009), that managers are not, and can never be, 'rootless'; everyone has to come from somewhere and go to somewhere else, and few people are psychologically capable of moving from region to region at regular intervals. The most successful international managers, he notes, are not the ones who keep on moving, but the ones who like their assignment so much they opt to stay in the country. This has been confirmed by, among others, Harzing and Christensen (2004), who argue that the complexity of the modern international assignment means that concepts such as 'expatriate failure' as traditionally understood no longer apply. Furthermore, it has been suggested by such researchers as Bartlett and Ghoshal (2002) and Tomlinson (1999) that globalization is as much a state of mind as anything else; a manager can remain locally rooted, and yet be global or international by virtue of their orientations, values, beliefs and use of communications and transportation technology, suggesting that if a globalized managerial elite is emerging, it will not be defined in terms of people's international assignments, but more in terms of their attitudes and activities (Collings *et al.* 2007). There thus appears to be support for Forster's position.

If this is the case, HR managers must be more flexible in terms of international recruitment and selection, thinking less in terms of developing the individual over the long-term, and more in terms of the particular position to be filled, and the specific requirements and competencies needed for it (Collings *et al.* 2007). While this need not preclude companies from developing general guidelines and policies for international management, they must also recognise that this term covers a wide and diverse field.

While it is possible that international managers may be developing into a distinct group, then, the situation, as always in globalization, is probably more complex, involving processes which encourage both convergence and divergence. The flexibility and variety of international assignments means that the important thing for human resource managers is to focus on the specific circumstances of the assignment in question, and the particular pressures involved.

Conclusions

In sum, the one certain thing in international recruitment would seem to be the *lack* of certainty. While one can identify certain general skills and abilities which can be useful under particular circumstances, the nature of globalization and the political manoeuvring which the implementation of IHRM policy involves means that it is impossible to identify hard-and-fast criteria for all expatriates, or for that matter all expatriate assignments. Each situation must therefore be taken on its own merits; the strategy of the company, the MNC's relationship with home and host country cultures (see, for instance, Rao 2009), the tension between global and local interests within the MNC and the agendas of the candidate and their family need to be taken into account; and the recruitment and selection programme designed accordingly. As Bartlett and Ghoshal put it, 'instead of forcing the individual to conform to the company's policies and practices, the overall objective is to capture and leverage the knowledge and expertise that each organisational member brings to the company' (1997: 114).

Key points to remember in international recruitment and selection are:

● Be flexible; remember that things change rapidly in the global sphere and that a variety of different political and cultural pressures are involved.

- Consider carefully the nature of the assignment, the cultures of the home and host country, the company's needs, the expatriate's needs and the subsidiary's needs before developing a recruitment programme.

- Don't be gender/race blind, but remember the problem of subconscious prejudice – ask yourself what you really need, and be wary of discrimination.

- If there are problems, or even expatriate failure, the key thing is to *learn* from the experience. If you do, this can offset the short-term cost by producing long-term improvement.

- Don't be afraid of taking risks – it can prove beneficial in the long run!

Recruitment and selection in the international sphere are thus very much context-dependent, and it is consequently very difficult to predict who will do well. However, with care and consideration, it may be possible to strongly reduce the risk of failure and produce successful international managers.

Review questions

1 In expatriate selection, how important are cultural factors as opposed to past knowledge and experience? Discuss the pros and cons of hiring an expatriate based on each criterion.

2 Develop an advertisement to recruit an international manager for one of the corporations described in any of the books in the References section, below. Be sure to take all possible considerations into account.

3 You are a HR manager at a large multinational firm. You are asked to help select a candidate for an international assignment to a country where local women face a considerable amount of discrimination. The two candidates have equal qualifications; one is a man with no intercultural experience at all, the other is a woman with considerable past experience in the country in question. Which would you choose and why?

4 'International assignments are so complex and diverse that there is no point in developing specialised programmes for the recruitment and selection of international managers.' Argue for or against this statement, with reference to Forster (2000) and Harzing and Christensen (2004).

Further reading

1 Bartlett, C.A. and Ghoshal, S. (1997) 'The myth of the generic manager: new personal competencies for new management roles', *California Management Review,* 40(1), 92–116.

While not specifically dealing with recruitment and selection, this article challenges the received 'one-size-fits-all' approach to international management and argues for a more customized approach.

2 Dowling, P.J., Festing, M. and Engle, A.D. (2008) *International Human Resource Management: Managing People in a Multinational Context* (5th edition), London: Thompson, Chapter 5.

A comprehensive, if brief and slightly managerialist, overview of the issues involved in international recruitment and selection.

3 Linehan, M. and Walsh, J.S. (1999) 'Recruiting and developing female managers for international assignments', *Journal of Management Development,* 18(6), 521–30.

Good consideration of the issues involved in the recruitment and selection of women in international management.

4 Shen, J. and Edwards, V. (2004) 'Recruitment and selection in Chinese MNEs', *International Journal of Human Resource Management,* 15(4), 814–35.

A good overview of international recruitment and selection generally, with particular reference to issues relating specifically to expatriates and MNCs from developing countries.

References

Adler, N. and Izraeli, D. (1994) *Competitive Frontiers: Women Managers in a Global Economy,* Oxford: Blackwell.

Bartlett, C. A. and Ghoshal, S. (1997) 'The myth of the generic manager: new personal competencies for new management roles', *California Management Review,* 40(1), 92–116.

Bartlett, C. A. and Ghoshal, S. (2002) *Managing Across Borders: the Transnational Solution* (3rd edition), London: Random House.

Beardwell, I., Holden, L. and Claydon, T. (2004) *Human Resource Management: A Contemporary Approach,* London: Prentice Hall.

Behrend, T., Baker, B. and Thompson, L. (2009) 'Effects of pro-environmental recruiting messages: the role of organizational reputation', *Journal of Business and Psychology,* 24(3), 341–50.

Bell, M. (2007) 'Accommodating religious diversity at work', *British Journal of Administrative Management,* 57, 6–16.

Berrell, M., Gloet, M. and Wright, P. (2002) 'Organisational learning in international joint ventures: implications for management development', *The Journal of Management Development,* 21(2), 83–100.

Bhanugopan, R and Fish, A. (2007) 'Replacing expatriates with local managers: an exploratory investigation into obstacles to localization in a developing country', *Human Resource Development International,* 10(4), 365–81.

Collings, D. G., Scullion, H. and Morley, M.J. (2007) 'Changing patterns of global staffing in the multinational enterprise: challenges to the conventional expatriate assignment and emerging alternatives', *Journal of World Business,* 42(2), 198–213.

Colgan, F. *et al.* (2009) 'Equality and diversity in the public services: moving forward on lesbian, gay and bisexual equality?', *Human Resource Management Journal,* 19(3), 280–301.

Cullen, L.T. (2007) 'The new expatriates', *Time,* 11 May.

Davison, E. D. and Punnett, B. J. (1995) 'International assignments: is there a role for gender and race in decisions?', *International Journal of Human Resource Management,* 6(2), 412–41.

Dowling, P. and Welch, D. (2004) *International Human Resource Management: Managing People in a Multinational Context,* London: Thompson.

Forster, N. (2000) 'The myth of the "international manager"?', *International Journal of Human Resource Management,* 11(1), 126–42.

Goodman, R. (1993) *Japan's 'International Youth': The Emergence of a New Class of Schoolchildren,* Oxford: Clarendon Press.

Gregersen, H. B., Hite, J. M. and Black, J. S. (1996) 'Expatriate performance appraisal in US multinational firms'. *Journal of International Business Studies,* 27(4), 711–39.

Gregersen, H. B., Harrison, D. A., Black, J. S. and Ferzandi, L. A. (2004) 'You Can Take it With You: Individual Differences and Expatriate Effectiveness', in Boyacigiller, N. and Kiyak, T. (eds.)

Proceedings of the 46th Annual Meeting of the Academy of International Business, East Lansing, MI: Academy of International Business, 185.

Hamada, T. (1992) 'Under the silk banner: 'The Japanese Company and Its Overseas Managers', in Sugiyama Lebra, T. (ed.) *Japanese Social Organization,* Honolulu: University of Hawaii Press, 135–64.

Harris, H. and Brewster, C. (1999) 'The coffee-machine system: how international selection really works', *International Journal of Human Resource Management,* 10(3), 488–500.

Harzing, A.-W. (2001a) 'An analysis of the functions of international transfer of managers in MNCs', *Employee Relations,* 23(6), 581–98.

Harzing, A.-W. (2001b) 'Of bears, bumblebees and spiders: the role of expatriates in controlling foreign subsidiaries', *Journal of World Business,* 36(4), 336–79.

Harzing, A.-W. and Christensen, C. (2004) 'Expatriate failure: time to abandon the concept?', *Career Development International,* 9(7), 616–26.

Harzing, A.-W. and van Ruysseveldt, J. (eds) (2004) *International Human Resource Management.* London: Sage.

Hirst, P. Q., Thompson, G. and Bromley, S. (2009) *Globalization in Question: The International Economy and the Possibilities of Governance* (3rd edition), Cambridge: Polity Press.

Hum, B. J. (2006) 'The selection of international business managers: part 1', *Industrial and Commercial Training,* 38(6/7), 279–86.

Lam, A. (1992) *Women and Japanese Management: Discrimination and Reform.* London: Routledge.

Leonard, O. (2002) 'Away winners', *Financial Management,* March, 42.

Li, J. and Karakowski, L. (2001) 'Do we see eye-to-eye? Implications of cultural differences for cross-cultural management research and practice', *Journal of Psychology,* 135(5), 501–17.

Linehan, M. and Walsh, J. S. (1999) 'Recruiting and developing female managers for international assignments', *Journal of Management Development* 18(6), 521–30.

McLeod, C., O'Donohoe, S. and Townley, B. (2009) 'The elephant in the room? Class and creative careers in British advertising agencies', *Human Relations* 62(7), 1011–39.

Micklethwait, J. and Wooldridge, A. (2000) *A Future Perfect: The Challenge and Hidden Promise of Globalisation,* London: William Heinemann.

Moore, F. (2006) 'Strategy, power and negotiation: social control and expatriate managers in a German multinational corporation', *International Journal of Human Resource Management,* 17(3), 399–413.

Oberg, K. (1960) 'Culture shock: adjustments to new cultural environments', *Practical Anthropology,* 7, 177–82.

Polak, R. (2002) 'Retirement programs for cross-border transfers', *Compensation and Benefits Management* 18(3), 24–8.

Rao, P. (2009) 'The role of national culture on Mexican staffing practices', *Employee Relations,* 31(3), 295–311.

Riach, K. (2009) 'Managing "difference": understanding age diversity in practice', *Human Resource Management Journal,* 19(3), 319–35.

Rohlen, T. P. (1974) *For Harmony and Strength: Japanese White-Collar Organization in Anthropological Perspective.* Berkeley: University of California Press.

Sakai, J. (2000) *Japanese Bankers in the City of London: Language, Culture and Identity in the Japanese Diaspora.* London: Routledge.

Selmer, J. (2002) 'The Chinese connection? Adjustment of Western vs. overseas Chinese expatriate managers in China', *Journal of Business Research,* 55, 41–50.

Selmer, J. (2004) 'Do You Speak Chinese? Language Proficiency and Adjustment of Business Expatriates In China', in Boyacigiller, N. and Kiyak, T. (eds) *Proceedings of the 46th Annual Meeting of the Academy of International Business,* East Lansing, MI: Academy of International Business, 104.

Shen, J. and Edwards, V. (2004) 'Recruitment and selection in Chinese MNEs', *International Journal of Human Resource Management,* 15(4), 814–35.

Steinmetz, Lawrence L. (1965) 'Selecting managers for international operations: the wife's role', *Management of Personnel Quarterly,* 4(1), 26–30.

Taylor, S., Napier, N. K. and Blair, A. (2004) 'Women Expatriates Working in Germany: Factors of Success', in Boyacigiller, N. and Kiyak, T. (eds) *Proceedings of the 46th Annual Meeting of the Academy of International Business,* East Lansing, MI: Academy of International Business, 186.

Thomas, R. R. (1990) 'From affirmative action to affirming diversity', *Harvard Business Review,* March–April, 107–17.

Tomlinson, John (1999) *Globalization and Culture,* Cambridge: Polity Press.

Chapter 11

International and comparative pay and reward

Guy Vernon

Key aims

The aims of this chapter are to:

- outline the commonalities and differences in the approaches to reward typical in different national environments;
- consider the roles of culture and of institutions in driving this cross-national variation;
- outline the approaches to reward strategy common in MNCs;
- characterize the 'strategic space' available for the international management of reward;
- consider how this might best be used in pursuit of improved performance.

Introduction

As is often observed, with many tangible resources easy to obtain, the management of people appears increasingly central to the achievement of competitive advantage. Pay, or extrinsic reward, is of obvious centrality in the employment relationship: to the recruitment, retention and motivation of employees. Moreover, it often seems symbolic of management style. Within multinational companies (MNCs), reward constitutes an area of HRM policy in which an overall direction, harmonization or even standardization appears very much less subject to processes of local implementation than other areas. The administrative nature of pay arrangements, and the relative simplicity of administering pay across national borders, appears to lend itself better than many other aspects of HRM to deliberate multinational strategy. Strategic international reward appears to offer an opportunity for HRM, and for HR functions, to be more active in the multinational arena. Yet, international HR functions must steer a careful course between Scylla and Charybdis in their approach to reward. On the one side lurk dangers of an unthinking universalism in the approach to pay and pay systems, most of all a universalism that is ethnocentric, involving the extension of practices from the country of origin to all countries of operation. On the other side the danger is of an unthinking conformity with existing or typical practice in the various countries of operation. In this context, a strategic approach to pay, deliberately steering a course between these dangers, appears to have much potential.

Despite the focus on expatriate, international, or at best senior subsidiary managers in much of the classic literature on international reward, and even now in much management discussion, there is a much bigger agenda; the reward of non-managerial employees, who comprise the majority of the workforce and in most cases the vast bulk of the pay bill. Even if there has been little change in the general stance of MNC managements since the late 1980s – when Wood and Peccei (1990) for example found a lack of interest among the managers of UK MNCs in the cross-national standardization of pay structures – this does not eliminate the space for such strategic contemplation. An international reward strategy extending beyond the treatment of expatriates does not require a commitment to such standardization.

Discussion of pay systems is complicated by the prevalence of a variety of terminologies, variously employed across, and even within, national boundaries. Essentially, though, we may distinguish between three bases of pay, or elements of pay packages. First, and predominantly for most employees, is a rate for the job, or pay for the post. Second, competence-based pay, assessed by qualifications or relevant experience, or a seniority element, based upon age or tenure, which is often seen as related. Finally, and subject of the most intense discussion, there is variable pay or pay for performance. Each of these is considered in the discussion here.

This chapter overviews the issues arising in the international management of reward, giving careful attention to the available evidence. It begins by outlining the international and comparative situation with regard to reward. It then moves to consider the activity of MNCs in this arena. Building upon this, the chapter then considers the 'strategic space' for the international management of reward, contemplating the constraints implied by national cultures and institutions but also the nature of the contestation and politics over reward within the management hierarchy itself. Of course, a key issue is how this space might best be used in the promotion of performance; thus, evidence on 'best practice' is the subject of the following section. Finally, some conclusions are advanced about the lessons which may be drawn from the evidence we now have on what does and doesn't deliver, and on the role that HR functions may play in the shaping of strategy in this area.

International trends in reward: uncertainty and ambiguity

Kessler (2007) stresses the value of a clear, detailed description of roles and a transparent and thorough means of linking these roles to pay. This emphasis on job classification and job evaluation, resulting in a clear pay hierarchy based upon the job or post held, was traditionally regarded as critical in generating a sense of equity or fairness in organizations. Employees may still be more comfortable, even with very great variations in earnings, if some sense of procedural justice based on such systems prevails. Whilst there is little international data on organizations' usage of job evaluation, it is certain that pay arrangements still often hinge on such systems in larger and multinational organizations. Yet, job classification and job evaluation are now often slighted in discussions of reward strategy as rigid or outdated. There seems a general tendency for managers internationally to have become increasing sceptical about the value of such systems – indeed sometimes it seems that any support for them is seen as a mark of a lack of concern for organizational performance.

Almost all management discussion of pay focuses on pay beyond post. Pay for person (almost always alongside the rate for the job or post) has a long history in continental Europe, and perhaps particularly the Nordic countries, but is now the subject of increased attention internationally. Recent years have seen the growth in some countries of discussion of skills or competence based pay in particular. Lack of data makes it difficult to judge whether this has carried over into a general international shift in practice, and indeed precludes consideration of comparative variation later in the chapter.

With regard to pay-for-performance (PfP), certain countries have seen marked increases in organizations' usage of certain forms of PfP, with for example the usage of individualized performance related pay (PRP) spreading rapidly across UK workplaces in the period 1998–2004 (Kersley *et al.* 2006) – and likely thereafter. This however is exceptional. Whilst the historical and international data provided by the Cranet survey (discussed further later) shows a clear and almost universal tendency for organizations to offer more information to employees about finance and strategy, this has not been allied to a general international growth of financial participation or indeed any other form of PfP. This is remarkable given the continued attention to, or perhaps often better obsession with, PfP amongst both managers and reward specialists.

Cross-national variation in reward and its basis

Whilst there is very little indication of any general international trends in the practice, as opposed to the discussion, of reward, cross-national comparative variation in current practice is clear. Whatever the direction of movement of organizations might be, multi-faceted globalization has not brought international homogeneity in pay practices. Even in the new millennium, organizations clearly face variations across their countries of operation in the reward structures and pay arrangements that are common. This section details the extent of these differences.

▶ Job classification, job evaluation and pay hierarchies

Job evaluation systems score jobs or posts on the basis of characteristics such as knowledge, responsibility, communication or working conditions and then link these job scores to pay grades. Clearly, job evaluation can have a more meaningful role where there are more pay grades, but as van Sliedregt *et al.* (2001) show in the Dutch context the existence of a large number of fine-grained grades can lead to inconsistency in job evaluation. This is a particular danger if there are, as is often the case, a relatively small number of broad job classes. In practice then, job evaluation may often not be as objective or clear cut as is sometimes believed. Still, the potential contribution of job evaluation in legitimating pay structures may be such that this should lead not to an abandonment or neglect of the system but rather to a more intense effort to operate it effectively.

Pay structures in the US and Germany – intriguing contrasts

Grund (2005) offers a fascinating analysis of the pay structure in a multinational with manufacturing operations in the US and Germany at the turn of the millennium. The plants feature near identical technology and similar production processes. Both US and German plants exhibit convex pay profiles, with the absolute pay gap between levels or grades generally increasing through the jobs hierarchy. Interestingly, he also finds that in principle and in practice pay for the higher blue collar grades exceeds that for the lower clerical grades in Germany, in contrast to the US where there is a continuous pay hierarchy from the lowest blue collar to the highest white collar. This is consistent with the general expectations of Marsden (1999), who suggests that the existence for blue collar workers of occupational labour markets based on certifiable (often apprenticeship) skills raises their overall status within German organizations. Perhaps as the flip side to this though, Grund (2005) finds that promotions through grades are much rarer in the German case, and that German blue collar workers face a glass ceiling which all but prevents a transition into white collar roles or management.

Overall pay inequality across the employees, managerial and non-managerial, of the plants is much greater in the US than in the German case. The pay inequality across the grades is similar in the two cases, but pay inequality at any particular grade is much lower in the German case. In practice, the German firm features a traditional bureaucratic narrow-grading whilst the US firm features broad-banding, to an extraordinary extent with regard even to some non-managerial

grades, for which the pay range sees maximum pay at well over 200 per cent of minimum pay. In consequence, some 84 per cent of the overall pay inequality in the German operations is attributable to grade compared to only 60 per cent in the US case. The difference in the significance of grade for pay is not attributable to comparative variation in age, tenure, or even education in the US versus the German operations. Rather, it is due to institutional features, and in particular the implications of German works council's co-dermination for pay systems and influence of German industry level agreements on base pay. The relatively weighty joint regulation of pay arrangements in the German case has foreclosed the possibility of the differential pay increases based on (apparently ad hoc and subjective) merit assessments which have marked the US operations. However, both age and tenure are a significant influence on pay in both national operations, with pay increasing with each at least until late career. Interestingly, despite the freedom of plant management from joint regulation in the US case, age and tenure matter rather more in the US case than in the German. This is consistent with Marsden's (1999) notion that the US is (still) broadly characterized by firm internal labour markets seeking to reward organization specific skills with seniority based pay, in contrast to Germany's occupational labour markets rewarding of certified skill.

Question

Is there anything surprising in the US–Germany contrast here?

◗ Overall pay inequality

The overall extent of pay inequality within workforces reveals much of the incentives that employees have to demonstrate individual achievement or climb organizational hierarchies, whether by exerting effort in their current role, acquiring qualifications or certifying competences, impressing their line managers, or moving from one organization

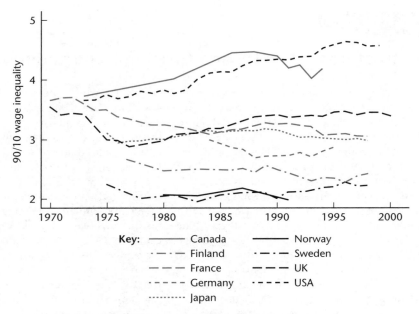

Figure 11.1 Time series plot of 90/10 wage inequality
Source: based on data from OECD (2001)

to another (e.g. Brown *et al.* 2003). Until recently, comparative data were readily available on the distribution of gross earnings across national workforces: the extent of earnings inequality (e.g. OECD 2001). Figure 11.1 shows for a number of OECD (Organization for Economic Co-operation and Development) nations a gauge of the spread of the overall earnings distribution of full-time employees: the ratio of earnings towards the top of the earnings distribution to the earnings of those towards the bottom. More specifically, it shows the ratio of the earnings of those at the 90th percentile of the earnings distribution (in the relatively comfortable position that only 10 per cent of employees earn more than them) to the earnings of those at the tenth percentile (in the relatively uncomfortable position that only 10 per cent earn less than them). Very roughly, this data reflects the ratio of the pay of a middle manager in a large organization to the pay of a cleaner in the various countries.

A good deal of similarity might be expected in these ratios across nations, particularly perhaps within the advanced industrialized world. We might also assume convergence in these ratios, perhaps particularly in the 1990s in the wake of the fall of state socialism, the explosion of multinational activity and indeed the resurgence of the USA as an economic power. The evidence, though, is rather at odds with such views. At the turn of the millennium, those towards the top of the earnings distribution in the USA earned four-and-a-half times as much as those towards the bottom. In the Nordic countries the ratio was barely two-and-a-quarter: half as great. The UK lies between these extremes, though it is becoming increasingly separated from the continental European situation. Generally, the enormous differences between nations show no signs of narrowing.

▶ Pay for performance

So much for cross-national variation in the earnings distribution. What of systems of pay for performance (PfP) more specifically? PfP may take the form of bonuses or special payments related to individual, team, departmental or organizational performance. This performance itself may be assessed in a multiplicity of ways: 'hard' objective or 'soft' subjective. The most comprehensive data available on comparative usage of PfP comes from Cranet (see e.g. Brewster *et al.* 2007), an international survey of more than 7,000 organizations in almost 40 countries in Europe and beyond, although some other more detailed information is available for particular countries.

Cranet shows that amongst the more established European Union countries organizational usage of individualized PRP for front-line employees is most common in Switzerland, Italy, Greece, Germany Austria and Finland, where upwards of 20 per cent of organizations use PRP for manual employees and typically upwards of 30 per cent use them for clerical employees. Such PRP is much less used in the UK and indeed the USA (upwards of 10 per cent for manual and 20 per cent for clerical), whilst the lowest levels of usage are found in Sweden (5–10 per cent for each) (Brewster *et al.* 2007: Figures 15 and 16). This pattern of usage, with the relatively unregulated Anglo-Saxon nations featuring towards the bottom of the ranking, clearly belies any simple notion that organizational deployment of PRP is associated with the weakness of unions or labour law.

Comparisons between Finland and the UK are worthy of further attention as there is detailed evidence here from large-scale national surveys about the application of PRP across these nations' employees, rather than merely on organizational usage. Across the economy as a whole (including the public sector), the available data suggest that a quarter of all UK employees are subject to individual PRP. Yet, some 23 per cent of Finnish manual employees and some 40 per cent of lower-level clerical employees are subject to merit pay *specifically*. The proportions are still higher for upper clerical employees/managers. While merit pay is the predominant form of individual PRP in Finland, other forms are of course present, such that one may say with much confidence that a minimum of a third of Finnish employees have some form of individual PRP (Emans *et al.* 2003: Tables 1, 12 and 15). There is thus little doubt that the prevalence of individual PRP is greater in Finland than in the UK. This is a remarkable finding given the strength of unions and collective bargaining in Finland versus that in the UK.

The cross-national comparative pattern of usage of team or department based pay returned by Cranet features many of the same countries at the extremes as with PRP, although Finland features still more strongly in this regard than for individualized PRP, and Sweden ranks towards the top here – with upwards of 20 per cent of organizations using such systems for their employees – rather than right at the bottom. Usage in these Nordic countries is an indication that team or department based PfP is not only consistent with, but perhaps encouraged by, powerful unions. The UK and the USA are for group based PfP, as with individualized PRP, placed towards the bottom of the rankings, with usage rates of around 10 per cent (Brewster *et al.* 2007). Limited social regulation of work appears no more supportive of the usage of group based than individualized PfP.

Turning to financial participation, generally speaking organizational usage of profit-sharing for front-line employees is more widespread than their usage of employee share ownership programmes (ESOPs). France is outstanding in that more than 70 per cent of organizations deploy profit sharing amongst manual employees. This is precisely what we would expect given French law mandating profit sharing in all but the smallest private sector organizations (Brewster *et al.* 2007). Finland ranks second, with 38 per cent of organizations rewarding manuals in this way, demonstrating that powerful unions are quite consistent with profit-sharing. Germany, Austria, Switzerland and the Netherlands lie at around 20 per cent uptake. The UK and the USA feature in the next bunch, with around 10 per cent of organizations using profit sharing for manuals, whilst such systems are still rarer in Italy (Brewster *et al.* 2007: Figure 19). Employee share ownership programmes are used comparatively extensively in Denmark, particularly for manual employees, showing that powerful unions are consistent with PfP in this sense too. ESOPs are though most extensive of all in France – perhaps as the mandated sharing of profits is sometimes distributed to employees in the form of shares. The UK also figures prominently, as we might expect given the Thatcherite 'popular capitalism' enthusiasm for employee share ownership (Brewster *et al.* 2007).

Poutsma *et al.*'s (2006) work on larger listed private sector organizations in four European countries shows that some sort of broad based financial participation, extending beyond executives and senior management to at least half of all employees, features in a majority of cases, with the proportion ranging from 50–70 per cent depending on country. Interestingly, broad based profit sharing schemes – including at least 50 per cent of all employees – are more common in larger organizations, although employee share ownership is less (*sic*) common in larger organizations. Internationally, it seems that to an important extent profit-sharing is the form of scheme chosen in the very largest listed companies whilst employee share ownership is the form chosen in those rather smaller – even though it is sometimes the case that profit shares are distributed in the form of companies' equity.

The discussion so far concerns only the prevalence of PfP, not its significance in the typical financial reward package. Typically, PfP accounts for less than 5 per cent of non-managerial employees' packages. Perhaps more importantly, anecdotal evidence suggests that in practice there is an extremely tight bunching of the actual payouts from pay for performance. The payout to individuals from PRP tends to vary little across teams or departments in practice, and the payout to teams or departments varies little within each organization in practice. Generally speaking then, while pay for performance now quite commonly forms an element of the pay of employees across Europe, it tends to be a very limited element and, moreover, an element that is, in practice, very insensitive to variations in the performance on which it ostensibly depends (see Brewster *et al.* 2007). Certainly, though, pay for performance not only applies to most senior managers and executives but also constitutes a sizeable proportion of their pay. Most commonly by far this takes the form of pay based on organizational performance. In Belgium, despite its almost total irrelevance to most employees, it represents more than 40 per cent of base salary for executives (Emans *et al.* 2003). Although systematic data are difficult to come by, it appears that, quite generally across Europe and North America at least, pay for performance is of much importance in the pay of the most senior managers. Even here, though, there must be doubts about the extent to which this pay for performance is actually linked to performance since bunching in actual payments appears common.

What do MNCs do with reward?

The very independence of an MNC from a particular country of operation affords an opportunity to move beyond the common presumptions of a particular nation, presumptions that may be particularly strong with regard to pay. Moreover, MNC status offers opportunities for the imposition of strategy. Where operations are more integrated, strategic action by the headquarters (HQ) or corporate region may be buttressed by implicit or explicit threats that particular facilities or subsidiaries will not be favoured with investment. Regardless of integration, some threat of sale may be employed by the HQ or region for leverage. Moreover, if the subsidiary is developed, perhaps on a greenfield site, rather than acquired, the opportunities for a 'clean sheet' appear to beckon. There seems little doubt that within any particular MNC approaches to reward generally involve greater homogeneity in their treatment of management, and most of all international cadres of management, across their countries of operation. Moreover, the total value of managers' compensation packages, however calculated, is becoming increasingly detached from that of non-managerial employees. Where MNCs are Anglo-Saxon in origin, this is very often a matter of the diffusion of compensation systems from home to foreign operations (e.g. Björkman and Furu 2000). Where they are not, it is a matter of the general dominance of such Anglo-Saxon approaches to the compensation of management, an influence attributable at least in part to the general perception of the success and centrality of the USA regarding productivity, competitiveness and profitability/shareholder value.

There is also evidence of some convergence of practice across MNCs, regardless of their countries of origin or of sector. The compensation of senior managers, and most particularly of the international cadre that multinationals are particularly keen to promote (Wigham 2003), is subject to increasing homogeneity across the corporations of the advanced industrialized world. Individual PRP is of much significance for middle managers, and pay systems linked to subsidiary or corporate performance or specifically to share prices are of significance for the pay of senior managers. This is true even in the companies of the traditional exemplars of organized capitalism, such as Germany or even, although less so, Sweden. This should, however, not be taken as indicating complete homogeneity, except perhaps as an intended strategy among some senior HR specialists. The country of origin of corporations, among other influences, continues to matter to an extent.

Björkman and Furu's (2000) interesting study concerns the payment systems applied to the top managers of 110 foreign-owned subsidiaries in Finland, focusing in particular on the significance of pay for performance as a proportion of fixed income. They show that on average pay for performance constitutes somewhere between 11 per cent and 25 per cent of the fixed income of such managers, but that there is marked variation, with some managers facing almost no pay for performance while others face pay for performance of more than 50 per cent of their base fixed salary. They show that pay for performance constitutes a greater proportion of base salary where the Finnish operations are sales subsidiaries, a lower proportion where they are production or research and development (R&D) subsidiaries. They also show that in subsidiaries that are treated as centres of excellence, managers tend to be more subject to pay for performance. Moreover, US ownership tends to imply a greater use of pay for performance. This careful study shows that variation in the pay systems applied to subsidiary managers remains. Moreover, it is not only that there is variation according to the role of the subsidiary in the activities of the multinational. The nationality of the multinational remains of relevance to the pay system applied.

With regard to the lower-level, or less high-flying, employees of MNCs, there are certainly examples of MNCs that have determinedly pursued the introduction of uniform systems across their national operations. In part, MNCs have sought to do this by operating outside the systems of pay determination that predominate in their countries of operation. Muller (1998) notes that several Anglo-Saxon multinationals operating in Germany have opted out of employers' associations, so remaining outside of the industrial bargaining that remains the general rule and is of particular relevance in some industries.

Perhaps unsurprisingly, fast-food retailers, and perhaps most of all McDonald's, have sought similarity in compensation practice across their outlets, regardless of national location. In the case of McDonald's, this is a matter of exporting an approach to compensation from the domestic, US, operations. Most particularly, this involves avoidance of, and resistance to, meaningful collective bargaining over pay, and a focus on containing wage costs. In the case of Germany, it is also a matter of an ongoing struggle to prevent the formation of works councils that would have the right to co-determine pay systems (Royle 2000, 2004).

Nonetheless, as Royle (2000) shows, the real pay levels of McDonald's counter staff, adjusted for the purchasing power of currencies, shows marked variation within Europe, with, for example, real pay typically more than 50 per cent higher in the Nordic nations than in the UK. Even McDonald's has not been able to escape entirely the realities of the political economies or national business systems in which it operates. Even aside from the necessity of legal compliance on some matters, McDonald's must both attract staff and offer them a reward package that they consider legitimate in some sense. This necessitates adjustment to the societal norms and generally prevailing pay practices that institutions have served to shape.

More generally, US MNCs have sought to export specific pay practices to foreign operations. One of the US financial services multinationals studied by Bloom *et al.* (2003) has determinedly sought to export the equity based incentives that it employs at home to its foreign operations. In the cases of some of its countries of operation, this has been extremely difficult as the ownership of shares by employees is illegal, but the company has circumvented this problem by structuring reward around a formula that reflects equity values. Bloom *et al.* (2003) also discuss a US high-tech MNC that has sought to standardize compensation across its national operations, though apparently in this case not only exporting practice from the US, but also seeking to draw on prevailing practice in all national locations to forge a globally integrated reward system.

In sum, there is considerable evidence of MNCs, and in particular US-based MNCs, seeking to export or, perhaps in a more integrative way, standardize pay systems. This is of potential general import given not only the growing importance of MNCs but also, via aggressive acquisition strategies, the increasing predominance of US MNCs in particular. There is, however, rather less evidence that even the standardization efforts of US-based MNCs typically result in a commonality of practice on the ground. Indeed, where there has been detailed attention to pay practice as this situation develops, most strikingly in the case of McDonald's, what is apparent is not the homogeneity of compensation but rather, whatever the strategic intention of the corporation, its sensitivity to the prevailing practices of the nations in question. As Edwards and Ferner (2000) note, practices undergo transformation or 'transmutation' when transferred (see also Chapter 7). This transmutation can be substantial. MNCs seeking standardization do not generally secure all that they hope; indeed, the result of a determined standardization may often be rather unexpected.

Determined efforts by MNCs to impose universal approaches or practices are indeed notable precisely because they are at odds with a general tendency for MNCs to show at least some sensitivity to the conditions prevailing in their nations of operation, or to quickly develop such sensitivity when obstructed. At the level of non-managerial employees this is perhaps most often a result of unconscious drift rather than a strategic intent to adapt, with national subsidiaries, which have often been acquired relatively recently and are only to a limited degree integrated or even understood by the corporation, allowed to continue much as before in terms of pay practice. Before its acquisition by Ford, Volvo was famed for its repertoire of approaches to employment relations, HRM and compensation practices (e.g. Berggren 1994). Volvo's sensitivity to local conditions, and preparedness to let subsidiary managements decide on pay systems was very likely exceptional. However, prevailing pay practice at the Swiss-Swedish ABB, once an exemplar of the business literature, is revealing. Despite the famed internationalization of the company, and indeed its status as an integrated, global company in the Bartlett and Ghoshal (1998) sense, Belanger *et al.* (1999) show that HRM generally, and pay systems specifically, differed on the ground.

Moreover, it is not only European companies that abstain from the pursuit of standardization. Bloom *et al.* (2003) record that a 'global high-tech' company that they studied went to such lengths to allow local variation that there were different pay systems even across its five Californian operations. Shire (1994) found that General Motors introduced quite different pay systems in its German and Austrian operations when seeking a shift to teamworking from the early 1990s. The works council in Germany was concerned to preserve the relatively egalitarian wage structure. With German management feeling no particular attachment to the principle of individual incentives within teams, the matter was not pursued. In Austria, where the sectoral agreement was rather less exacting and where the works councils were rather less interested, something much closer to corporate management's original intention was achieved. Moreover, despite a prevailing view in the literature that Japanese companies, like US ones, tend to export domestic practices, Bloom *et al.* (2003) found that a highly internationalized Japanese MNC sought to be a 'good citizen' right across its extensive operations by complying with prevailing local practice.

The 'strategic space' for international reward strategy

All this, however, concerns what currently prevails rather than what might be forged by MNCs with an international reward strategy – in terms for example of the pay-for-performance which is so often the focus for discussion. Evidence on the existing approaches of multinationals is not at all the same thing as a picture of what is possible. In line with the arguments introduced in Chapters 2–4, we have seen in this chapter that the national context of operation of an organization, in terms of the culture and expectations of employees, and in terms of the social regulation of work by labour law and by unions and employers' associations, may be viewed as defining the limits or boundaries of the space within which the organization may operate. These external features thus describe the confines of what we might term a 'strategic space' within which approaches to reward (and other aspects of people management) are shaped. These confines are various, and variously exacting, depending on the country concerned.

However, with regard to the approach to the pay of higher-level employees, the expatriates, senior managers and general managers of national subsidiaries on which the literature most focuses, the constraints posed by the external environment are generally very limited. This is reflected in the relative homogeneity of pay arrangements for such employees. For these employees a balance must be struck between conflicting objectives of organizational uniformity and local conditions in a manner that takes account of the reference groups to which these staff compare themselves. Consideration must be given to the total remuneration package and to purchasing power and taxation for the recruitment, retention, motivation and mobility of international staff. In all this, the key constraint is what is acceptable and motivating to the individuals concerned. However, the varying accounting and tax treatments of payments of stock and the actual legality of pay in the form of stock or specifically options across nations does represent an additional consideration, perhaps particularly since the emergence of corporate governance failings in, for example, Enron (Bloom *et al.* 2003; Dunn 2004).

For less high-flying employees, national contexts are of more consequence. One facet is national culture. Schuler and Rogovsky (1998) explore the link between national culture and indicators of national prevalence of PfP across a dozen nations from across and beyond the advanced industrialized world. They depend on the influential cultural classification of Geert Hofstede, derived from his extensive survey of global IBM employees in the early 1970s (see Chapter 3 for a discussion and critique). Schuler and Rogovsky (1998) find that nations that are characterized by greater uncertainty avoidance, such as the Latin nations, tend to feature pay systems in which seniority and some notion of skill weigh heavily. There is, moreover, less focus on specifically individual performance related pay in such nations. Conversely, nations with lower uncertainty avoidance, notably the 'Anglo-Saxon' nations, tend to focus less on seniority or skill, and more on specifically individual PRP. They present a similar pattern of findings for the focus on employee share ownership or options. Schuler and Rogovsky (1998) also find that nations characterized by greater individualism, most strikingly the Anglo-Saxon nations, tend to have a greater focus on pay for performance generally, and still more strongly a focus on individual pay for performance. Nations with less individualism, most prominently Spanish or Portuguese-speaking countries, tend to focus less on pay for performance. The findings for the focus on share ownership or options are similar.

Schuler and Rogovsky (1998) also show that nations characterized by greater 'masculinity', in the sense of a focus on assertiveness regarding the acquisition of wealth in contrast to a focus on personal relationships, tend to have more focus on individual bonuses, which applies to most categories of employees. Thus, more 'masculine' nations, principally the Anglo-Saxon ones but also Germany and to a remarkable extent Japan, generally tend to feature individual PRP among professional and technical staff, clerical staff and manual employees. The contrast here is with the general situation in the less masculine Scandinavian nations, and indeed the Netherlands, which tend to have a lesser focus on such payments for these non-managerial employees. Interestingly, though, there was no relationship between the focus on individual bonuses for managers specifically and nations' masculinity. Thus, there are substantial indications here of some link between Hofstede's uncertainty avoidance, individualism and masculinity dimensions and pay systems. In contrast, Schuler and Rogovsky find that only the focus on employee share ownership or options is related to the fourth of Hofstede's dimensions: power distance. Nations with the greatest tolerance of status differentials, generally the Latin, tend to feature less of such a focus, while those with the lowest power distance, the Anglo-Saxon and Scandinavian, tend to feature more.

It should, however, be stressed that this general overview highlights the extent to which culture can explain something of the cross-national comparative pattern of reward, rather than the (great) extent to which national culture and reward practices are independent. To a significant extent, nations consist of clusters of sub-cultures (Brewster *et al.* 2007) – Bloom *et al.* (2003) stress variability *within* nations in the expectations of employees. Moreover, it may not only be that national culture is multi-dimensional in the manner that Hofstede allows, but also that it is contradictory, allowing various quite diverse alternatives. It is quite clear that national culture does not dictate the pay systems in operation.

MNCs face some rather harder constraints in the form of the social regulation of pay, whether by governments or by unions and employers' associations. MNCs inevitably encounter some substantive regulation by national governments that immediately affects the pay arrangements possible in a particular location. Statutory pay minima exist, sometimes varying with the age of employees or their status as trainees, in most OECD nations and a third of the nations of the established advanced industrialized world (OECD 1998). Self-evidently, such minima only affect the pay of the very worst paid, representing a constraint on MNCs, which tend to pay rather better than domestic companies, only at the margin. In general, the observance of substantive statutory regulation of pay arrangements presents little in the way of constraints to MNCs.

Within the advanced industrialized world at least, collective bargaining and the statutory representation of employees is an issue of much greater significance for an international approach to pay arrangements than is substantive statutory regulation. For companies of Anglo-Saxon origin operating in northern Europe in particular, this joint regulation of pay can seem difficult to grasp, perplexing, even forbidding. Enterprises covered by collective bargaining are thus immediately subject to procedural regulation with regard to the development of pay systems, procedural regulation that will result in at least some substantive (joint) regulation of pay arrangements. What are the implications of this for MNCs?

It is very clear that national systems of collective bargaining influence the extent of pay inequality. The bulk of the cross-national variation in overall inequality documented earlier is the result of marked variation at the bottom of the distribution; in the extent to which the relatively low paid are short of the average earner. There is a remarkably strong relationship between the (national) density of union membership and the compression of bottom-end earnings inequality in particular (Rueda and Pontusson 2000; Pontusson *et al.* 2002; Rueda 2003; Vernon 2010). Even *within* the oft-distinguished groups of social market economies (principally northern Europe) and liberal market economies (Anglo-Saxon nations), density bears a strong relationship with earnings inequality. In the light of recent work on the significance of union density (Vernon 2006), this is best regarded as expressive of the impact of the weight of collective bargaining at multiple levels in constraining company and workplace level reward structures (Vernon 2010).

Yet, as Sisson (1987) notes, multi-employer agreements, whether confederal or industrial/sectoral, do not typically dictate pay practices. Rather, they lay down pay minima of various forms, often defining a hierarchy of minimum rates linked to job classifications. Multi-employer agreements tend not to restrict PfP specifically, though their specification of minimum pay rates generally implies that any such component must be made in addition to pay levels which some employers may already find quite exacting (see Vernon *et al.* 2007). There is then often subsequent negotiation, whether formal, with unions, or informal, with works councils ostensibly independent of unions, at the level of the establishment or (national) enterprise.

Whilst attitudes to PfP can vary dramatically between local union organizations and works councils, even within a single industry in one country, there is little evidence that the strength of such employee representation is generally an impediment to the introduction of PfP (Vernon *et al.* 2007). Whilst it is impossible to do justice to the range of views present across union leaderships, and most of all across local union organizations or works councils, there are a number of concerns which are commonly found in such circles (Vernon *et al.* 2007). Typically, unions prefer competence based pay to PfP, but generally concede some place for the latter if the basis of bonuses is transparent and objective, if the performance related component of total compensation is contained in the 5–10 per cent region, and if its implementation and functioning is subject to joint regulation. Typically, unions have preferred PfP based on group or company performance than on individualized performance, seeing both threats to solidarism and the potential for victimization in PRP. Thus, for example, the comparatively very powerful Swedish unions have not generally resisted the individualization of pay, but have been much more comfortable with this individualization occurring on the basis of variable competence development – with the whole workplace process framed by multi-employer agreements.

However, it is remarkable that where unions have a strong company or workplace presence which is one element in a larger infrastructure of joint regulation of pay, they are now sometimes more willing to consider PfP much more sympathetically – even if this takes the form of individualized PRP. As Nergaard *et al.* (2009) discuss, local representatives acting in such circumstances feel more secure, buttressed by the wider institutional context, and can also more readily view PfP as a complement to, rather than substitute for, basic increases, as to a substantial extent these are decided elsewhere. This is perhaps particularly true given a formal articulation of negotiations at different bargaining levels (see Stokke 2008). One might also note that national union organizations or confederations cannot freely indulge in posturing on PfP if their member unions have workplace presence, and are much more likely to be sensitive to the costs of their policy statements if leaderships are well articulated with local organizations (Vernon *et al.* 2007).

Regarding financial participation, whilst attitudes do vary across unions, generally they are quite accepting. Even where they are not only powerful but used to negotiating around pay they are often prepared to regard such schemes as a bonus in a number of senses, and as something on which they do not need to negotiate. The presence of local unions or works councils generally nurtures broad based profit sharing, and is weakly encouraging of more extensive participation in it, although does impede employee share schemes and employee take up of them (Poutsma *et al.* 2006).

Thus, much more flexibility exists within joint regulation within even those nations that are subject to its denser forms than is commonly thought. Nonetheless, a number of companies in Germany have recently demonstrated the possibility of operating beyond the coverage of industrial-level collectively bargained agreements. Withdrawing from employers' associations, some employers of all sizes negotiate company-level agreements independent of the prevailing sectoral agreement (Hassel 1999), a possibility allowed by the very limited legal extension of collective agreements in Germany (Traxler *et al.* 2001: 185). Since 1989 an industry association specifically for fast food has existed in Germany, established essentially by McDonald's after almost two decades of adverse publicity (Royle 2004). Yet collective bargaining is extremely unstable in the sector, with companies sometimes participating in industrial negotiations, sometimes concluding company agreements and sometimes, it seems, not having an agreement at all. Moreover, as noted earlier, McDonald's has determinedly sought to avoid the representation of its German employees in works councils (Royle 2000, 2004).

Whatever the difficulties which result, it is clear that even in the most organized capitalism, individual employers can thus sometimes opt to shape pay without the immediate procedural confines of joint regulation. This appears at first glance to substantially loosen the confines of their 'strategic space' with regard to reward. Much of this is illusory, however. Inescapably, employers in a particular nation must face the political economy in which they are located. This consists not merely of the institutions of collective bargaining, which they may in some cases be able to circumvent, but the substantial national environment that these institutions have in part shaped. The broader environment, consisting of national culture generally but more specifically including the pattern of employment, the earnings structure and the prevailing systems of pay, inevitably impact all employers. Thus, regardless of their participation in collective bargaining or indeed their efforts to avoid the statutory representation of employees in works councils, employers must recruit, retain and motivate staff; they cannot operate in a vacuum.

While there are thus certainly definite constraints, the complexity and ambiguity of the external environment offer much room for management manoeuvre. Yet, inside the strategic space which external confines define, intra-organizational influences, and in particular management activity, is at play. Given that we might expect particularly varied management cultures and ideologies within MNCs, and perhaps even some form of relatively autonomous, transnational, culture, we might expect MNCs to exhibit approaches to reward which are rather more considered and innovative – and less drawn by Scylla or Charybdis. However, MNC status confers not only opportunities but also constraints for the HR practitioner, some of which may be insurmountable. As we have seen, there is much evidence that the country of origin of multinationals tends to be related to the nature of their approach to pay. Of course, the extent to which this is expressive of a set of constraints to which HR must submit is far from clear. Certainly, though, as we have seen, different companies from the same country of origin, and indeed involved in similar industries or even activities, do pursue different approaches, something that we might take as indicative of a true space for contemplation and a strategic approach to reward.

The space enjoyed by HR in contemplating reward strategy is shaped by the standing of HR within the corporation, and indeed the importance attached by senior managers generally to consideration of matters of reward specifically. MNCs that are centralized offer certain opportunities for the strategic use of reward across national boundaries. However, subsidiary managements may resist the suggestion that their pay arrangements should be shaped by HQ. Then, of course, the competencies and attitudes of general, line and HR managers may present varying possibilities in terms of individual negotiations or indeed appraisals, and these may be difficult to surmount. The strategic space to reward is ultimately and importantly filled by organizational politics which can be at least as confining as the external pressures of the social regulation of work and the expectations of employees (see Chapter 2). Yet, the internal environment of the MNC does not dictate the approach to reward any more than does the external context. How should HR and reward managers seek to act in the strategic space available? Strategic approaches to HR should, of course, give cognisance to the performance implications of various practices. It is to the evidence available on pay arrangements and performance that we now turn.

Best practice in international reward

Despite the enormously varied practice of organizations, particularly internationally, might there be some best practice in reward? Most importantly, does there exist some best practice which is evidence based – rather than based in social norms about what is acceptable or mere presumptions about what works? Expectancy theory suggests that individuals are motivated to perform better for their organizations where they feel that their efforts will lead to better performance, that this better performance will be recognized and rewarded and that the rewards offered are valued by the individuals concerned. The popularity of individualized incentives amongst employees and amongst managers contemplating the pay systems they deploy can be read as expressive of the common sense nature of this theory (see e.g. Kessler 2007). Yet, is this an evidence based best practice, or a supposed best practice *in spite of the evidence*?

The evidence that individualized incentives deliver better business performance is remarkably limited. Cases that they do rest remarkably heavily on Lazear's (2000) study. This shows that the mid-1990s introduction of a piece rate pay system (though preserving some minimum hourly guarantee) at 'Safelite', an autoglass installer in the US, was associated with a 44 per cent increase in the number of units installed per person per day. It does not appear that this enormous increase can be attributed to a shift in the (physical or machine-embodied) technologies employed, but was the result of a shift in the approach to people management under a new management team. Lazear interprets his detailed findings as expressing in equal measure a simple incentivization of continuing employees and of turnover in the workforce, involving almost exclusively the recruitment of new employees particularly individually productive rather than the departure of those particularly unproductive on this basis. Yet, the study leaves much unclear, in part as the extent of change in people management beyond the realm of pay systems is obscure, leaving the suspicion that the productivity boon could have been generated by other initiatives. Then, the appropriateness of this very narrow performance measure, and so the significance of this performance achievement, even in this particular case, remains rather debatable. Moreover, the potential of such an approach in other work contexts is of course unexamined. This work context may well be rather peculiar in terms of the technical and social possibilities of simplifying and individualizing work tasks, implying that the dangers of individualized incentives undermining teamwork and organizational commitment are less threatening in this case.

Newman and Nollen's (1996) study is of note here. Their statistical analysis of a single US MNC examined the relationship, across 176 work units based in 18 (mostly advanced industrialized) nations, between financial performance and the fit of management practices with the national cultures of the host nations. Amongst the foci of the authors is what they term 'merit based reward', an encompassing concept relating not only to practice with regard to merit pay but to the possibilities of promotion, particularly on the basis of individual performance. Their careful work shows (1996: Table 5) strong results regarding the congruence between management practices and host cultures and financial performance. In more masculine national cultures, emphasising activity and achievement, merit based rewards are generally associated with superior performance. In more feminine cultures, emphasising contemplation and inter-personal relationships, merit based rewards are generally associated with inferior performance. Although this is a study of a single MNC, these findings at least suggest that we should not assume that what works in one country will work in another.

A fascinating recent study of over 300 US hospitals provides some evidence on the importance of both the levels and distribution of pay for organizational performance (Brown *et al.* 2003). Both higher pay levels and a more compressed pay structure are associated with better operational outcomes, whilst the best financial performance may be delivered either by combining higher pay levels with greater pay inequality, or alternatively lower pay levels with a more compressed structure. Given the widespread belief amongst managers that greater pay dispersion is performance promoting, these are interesting findings, particularly as the detail suggests that an organization operating around the market median pay level – by definition, the typical organization – performs better if its pay structure is more compressed.

These sector and country specific findings find some echo in an international study by Rogers and Vernon (2003). This examines the relationship between the pay structure and the growth in labour productivity growth (here value added at constant purchasing power parity) across the manufacturing sectors of nine advanced industrialised nations through 1970–95. The results suggest that whilst greater inequality is productively motivating at the top end of the earnings distribution, lower inequality is productively motivating at the bottom. It may be, as Rogers and Vernon (2003) suggest, that whilst the incentives provided by a stretched pay structure may motivate those whose pay levels are already relatively high, marked earnings inequality at the bottom end of the earnings distribution degrades and demotivates lower grade employees, provides little incentive for managers to offer them training or reflect on the organization of their work, and leads to a profound and dysfunctional stratification within the organizational hierarchy.

What then of the performance impact of financial participation? This might be thought to meet fewer cultural barriers than does individual incentivization, is not stratifying if schemes are made generally available across the workforce, and is typically more favourably regarded by unions as long as it is also seen as additional to existing payments. Kuvaas (2003) notes that financial participation such as profit-sharing and employee share ownership offers a form of pay-for-performance which does not endanger intrinsic motivation or effective teamwork, and which holds out the promise of greater employee loyalty, better morale, and an improved sense of attachment, belonging and organizational identification. Kruse (1993) famously argued that profit-sharing could act via employee attitudes and motivation to improve financial performance, and presented some evidence on the link to the bottom line.

A substantial body of further work has deepened our understanding. Coyle-Shapiro et al.'s (2002) longitudinal findings on the implications of profit-sharing for attitudes and behaviours in a British organization, suggest that the (affective) organizational commitment of employees is promoted by their perceptions of the appropriateness and legitimacy of the profit sharing scheme implemented. Kuvaas' (2003) longitudinal study, in the very different context of a Norwegian organization, features remarkably similar findings. This is a long way from demonstrating the relevance of any particular form of financial participation to employee commitment, let alone organizational performance, however.

Some international evidence is available on the link between financial participation and organizational performance. Kalmi et al.'s (2005) study of larger listed organizations in four European countries offers some evidence based upon managers' perceptions of the outcomes of financial participation where schemes are in place. It is the non-findings which are striking. Whilst almost 90 per cent of managers regard improved productivity as a relevant aim for financial participation in principle, there is no relationship between managers' perception of the impact of financial participation on productivity and the extent of employee coverage of either profit-sharing or equity schemes, even controlling for a number of other plausible influences on management perceptions of such impacts. D'Art and Turner (2004) deploy Cranet data to analyse the relationship between profit-sharing for front-line staff and organizational performance for almost 3,000 organizations across 10 European countries. They show, controlling for a number of other established influences on performance (e.g. size, market conditions, country of operation), that there is a very strong relationship between profit-sharing and respondents' ratings of recent profitability across the sample as a whole. There are weaker, but still statistically significant, links to respondents' assessments of the relative productivity and service quality of the organization. However, these associations are apparent only for a very few particular countries when the sample is broken down, although most of the country samples remain large. Moreover, it is possible that the findings express the relevance of sector, which is not controlled for, for both financial participation and performance.

These findings indicate the general fragility of the research evidence on financial participation and performance. Moreover, it is very plausible that organizations with better performance are likely to introduce financial participation rather than such participation promoting performance – as D'Art and Turner (2004) note such 'reverse causation' is particularly likely with regard to profitability and profit-sharing. Indeed, Wolf and Zwick's (2002) exemplary study of people management and establishment level productivity in Germany found that financial participation does not result in greater productivity, but rather results *from it*. This underscores the limits of the evidence available on the impact of financial participation *per se* on organizational performance.

Could it be that whilst financial participation does not have any general effect on organizational performance, it does in certain organizational circumstances which may occur internationally? Sesil (2006) finds, using conventional objective financial performance data for UK manufacturing establishments, that financial participation in the form of either ESOPs or profit sharing has no link to better financial performance, but that in combination with direct employee involvement or participation then financial participation is strongly and robustly associated with it. This suggests that the implications of financial participation are contingent upon the extent of employee involvement allowed by the organization of work. A 'reverse causation' interpretation of these findings would hold that superior financial performance coupled to greater employee involvement would give rise to greater financial participation, whilst superior financial performance allied to little employee involvement would not. This is rather implausible, implying that these findings reflect a real contingency in the impact of financial participation on performance.

In many respects these findings link to the international findings of Antoni *et al.* (2005). They consider the performance improvements from delegation to groups of non-managerial employees in 1,300 organizations in 10 European Union countries, focusing on the implications of what they term 'modern forms of variable pay' (collective PfP such as team/department performance, profit-sharing schemes or ESOPs) in these contexts. Companies with such pay systems report significantly better outcomes from group delegation, with greater reductions in management and increases in output. Where delegation is particularly advanced, such pay systems are also associated with reductions in costs and in throughput times. The effects are particularly strong in organizations lacking a systematic product innovation strategy, suggesting that the alignment of group delegation and reward for front-line employees corrects for shortcomings in the larger organization.

What then can we conclude regarding evidence based best practice? The first point of note emerging from the available evidence is that organizations should be all the more wary of pursuing individualized incentives if they operate internationally. Moreover, it is clear from the research evidence that steep pay hierarchies offering incentives via the pay structure do not in general promote better organizational performance. On the positive side, the most promising contender for generic best practice appears to be a marriage of delegation of tasks to groups of front-line employees with real autonomy *and* some form of collective reward.

May not organizations set aside any notion of best practice and simply look to similarly placed competitors for a guide? Given the international evidence on the business performance benefits of broad based group incentives where front-line employees have more autonomy, one might expect that organizations delegating more tasks to front-line employees would be the ones making most use of such group incentives. Yet, intriguingly, Poutsma *et al.* (2006) find at best very weak evidence of any links between either the existence or coverage of financial participation extending beyond executives or senior managers and direct employee participation or involvement. Antoni *et al.*'s (2005) work for 10 European countries shows some evidence that the use of 'modern forms of variable pay' does in general tend to be related across their sample as a whole to greater delegation of activities to groups – more reassuring for those with faith in the general wisdom of management hierarchies. However, this relationship is almost entirely due to such a link at organizations which have an identifiable product innovation strategy. In the majority of organizations which do not have such a product innovation strategy, there is no link between such group incentives and management delegation to groups of employees, echoing Poutsma *et al.* (2006). Yet, as noted earlier, Antoni *et al.* (2005) find that it is precisely organizations which lack a product innovation strategy which have more to gain from coupling delegation to groups with collective PfP for front-line staff. It thus seems that organizations' approach to reward is often at odds with the emerging international research evidence on what delivers better business performance.

To an extent this must express the conflicts and micro-politics which inhabit the strategic space allowed within management hierarchies. A more serious recourse by HR and/or other managers to research evidence, and to the analysis and monitoring of the impact of compensation, appears a precondition for the containment of such conflicts. Certainly, organizations must be prepared to forge their own path, as the research evidence suggests that organizations often make choices inappropriate for promoting performance.

Conclusions

As we have seen, there are dramatic differences across national environments in approaches to reward. To an extent, these reflect the constraints on the management of reward introduced by forces outside the management hierarchy – matters of national culture and more particularly national institutions. These forces mark the confines of what we can usefully think of as a 'strategic space' for reward. However, within these confines there remains much room for management activity – and management politicking and contestation. This is expressed in the different approaches to reward which emerge from within the management hierarchies of organizations, and most starkly in the often differing approaches of MNCs operating in the same host environments, even sometimes when these MNCs also share the same country of origin.

The pattern of MNC approaches also suggests that there is still room for MNCs to be more considered in their approach to reward. There seems rather too much of a bifurcation of approaches, with some MNCs pursuing a wholesale standardization of reward practice across their countries of operations based on an ethnocentric extension of what they do in their country of origin, and some adapting wholesale to the approaches they find in their various countries of operation. The ultimate external constraint on multinationals is the perceived legitimacy of pay arrangements (and the mechanism by which they are arrived at) in the eyes of the employees concerned. Care must be exercised with regard to the psychological contract, and it is clear that there are dangers for MNCs in pursuing a standardization or integration approach to reward. However, this does not mean that MNCs should simply adapt, or differentiate. Strategic international reward must involve a course between Scylla and Charybdis.

The research evidence on reward and organizational performance is as yet limited – particularly in international context – but does provide some useful pointers in steering a more considered course. Given the credence given such approaches in many management circles, it is noteworthy that all the indications are that an approach to international reward which centres on a general application of individualized performance incentives and/or steep pay hierarchies is not typically promising. The evidence suggests that some marrying of a delegation of tasks to teams of front-line employees with much autonomy and some form of group or collective reward is very much more likely to deliver superior performance. This still leaves room for sensitivity in local application – though the evidence also cautions against simply following other organizations' approaches.

What then of the rate for the job, or pay for post – the linking of pay to the role in which an employee is engaged via detailed job evaluation – and of the clear job hierarchies and career structures with which this is usually associated? Though much-slighted in many management discussions, such arrangements are often highly prized by employees. Indeed, an enormous international survey of more than 100,000 employees of a multinational hotel chain (McPhail and Fisher 2008) showed that elements of an internal labour market (job security, training opportunities and promotion opportunities) are critical to front-line employees' job satisfaction and organizational commitment. This should at least caution against a blinkered focus on pay-for-performance.

All this suggests that there is much space for international HR functions to fulfil a valuable role in identifying – with careful reference to existing evidence – promising ways forward in the realm of international reward. This attention to evidence may not only be significant in fashioning approaches which might, if implemented, actually improve performance, but also in the containing and perhaps even sometimes cutting through disputation and contestation around reward within the management hierarchy. This can only improve the prospects for the realization of these approaches. Of course, in any particular organizational context, evaluation of the outcomes of any new departure, even if this is based on more general evidence, is crucial. Yet this provides a further opportunity for international HR to display its analytical strengths. Indeed, international reward may provide an opportunity for international HR to reach that elusive fusion of a distinctively HR perspective with a focus on performance.

Review questions

1 What sort of differences exist between advanced industrialized nations in reward practice?
2 How have MNCs responded to the different national conditions that they find?
3 What seems to define the space available for reward strategy?
4 What may we say of 'best practice' in international reward?
5 In what respects is there potential in international reward strategy?

Further reading

1 Björkman, I. and Furu, P. (2000) 'Determinants of variable pay for top managers of foreign subsidiaries in Finland', *International Journal of Human Resource Management*, 11(4), 698–713.

This is a careful statistical/econometric study of the influences on the pay systems deployed for subsidiary managers.

2 Bloom, M., Milkovich, G. and Mitra, A. (2003) 'International compensation: learning from how managers respond to variations in local host contexts', *International Journal of Human Resource Management*, 14(8), 1350–67.

This article considers the often neglected issue of the variation present in institutions and, most particularly, cultures and practices even within single nations.

3 Newman, K. and Nollen, S. (1996) 'Culture and congruence: the fit between management practices and national culture', *Journal of International Business Studies*, 27(4), 753–78.

This article provides the seminal statistical contribution on the issue of the importance to the bottom line of cultural sensitivity in reward.

References

Antoni, C. *et al.* (2005). *Wages and Working Conditions in the European Union,* Dublin: European Foundation of the Improvement of Living and Working Conditions.

Bartlett, C. and Ghoshal, S. (1998) *Managing Across Borders: The Transnational Solution,* Boston: Harvard Business School Press.

Belanger, J., Berggren, C., Bjorkman, T. and Kohler, C. (1999) *Being Local Worldwide: ABB and the Challenge of Global Management,* Ithaca, NY: Cornell University Press.

Berggren, C. (1994) *The Volvo Experience,* London: Macmillan.

Björkman, I. and Furu, P. (2000) 'Determinants of variable pay for top managers of foreign subsidiaries in Finland', *International Journal of Human Resource Management*, 11(4), 698–713.

Bloom, M., Milkovich, G. and Mitra, A. (2003) 'International compensation: learning from how managers respond to variations in local host contexts', *International Journal of Human Resource Management*, 14(8), 1350–67.

Brewster, C., Sparrow, P. and Vernon, G. (2007) *International Human Resource Management,* London: CIPD.

Brown, M.P., Sturman, M.C. Simmering, M.J. (2003) 'Compensation policy and organizational performance', *Academy of Management Journal*, 46, 6, 752–62.

Coyle-Shapiro, J., Morrow, P.C., Richardson, R. and Dunn, S. (2002) 'Using profit-sharing to enhance employee attitudes', *Human Resource Management*, 41(4), 423–39.

D'Art, D. and Turner, T. (2004) 'Profit-sharing, firm performance and union influence in selected European countries', *Personnel Review*, 33(3), 335–50.

Dunn, B. (2004) 'One size does not fit all: global equity compensation in the New World', *Compensation and Benefits Review*, 36(4), 13–18.

Edwards, T. and Ferner, A. (2000) 'HRM Strategies of Multi-nationals: The Organisational Politics of "Reverse Diffusion"?', Paper presented at conference on 'Multinational Companies and Emerging Workplace Issues: Practice, Outcomes and Policy', Detroit: Wayne State University, 1–3 April.

Emans, B. *et al.* (2003) 'Pay for Performance in Europe: Prevalence and National Differences', Paper presented at European Congress on Work and Organizational Psychology, Lisbon, May.

Grund, C. (2005) 'The wage policy of firms: comparative evidence for the US and Germany from personnel data', *International Journal of Human Resource Management*, 16, 1.

Hassel, A. (1999) 'The erosion of the German system of industrial relations', *British Journal of Industrial Relations*, 37(3), 483–505.

Kalmi, P., A. Pendleton, E. Poutsma. (2005) 'Financial participation and performance in Europe', *Human Resource Management Journal*, 15(4), 54–67.

Kersley, B. *et al.* (2006) *Inside the Workplace*, London: Routledge.

Kessler, I. (2007) 'Reward Choices: Strategy and Equity', in J. Storey (ed.) *Human Resource Management: A Critical Text*, London: Thomson.

Kruse, D. L. (1993) *Profit-Sharing: Does it Make a Difference?* Kalamazoo, MI: W.E. Upjohn.

Kuvaas, B. (2003) 'Employee ownership and affective organizational commitment', *Scandinavian Journal of Management*, 19, 193–212.

Lazear, E. (2000) 'Performance pay and productivity', *American Economic Review*, 90, 1346–61.

Marsden, David. (1999). *A Theory of Employment Systems*. Oxford. OUP.

McPhail, R. and R. Fisher. (2008) 'Its more than wages: analysis of the impact of internal labour markets on the quality of jobs', *International Journal of Human Resource Management*, 19, 3.

Muller, M. (1998) 'Human resource and industrial relations practices of UK and US multinationals in Germany', *International Journal of Human Resource Management*, 9(4), 732–49.

Nergaard, K. *et al.* (2009) 'Engaging with variable pay: a comparative study of the metal industry', *European Journal of Industrial Relations*, 15(2), 125–46.

Newman, K. and Nollen, S. (1996) 'Culture and congruence: the fit between management practices and national culture', *Journal of International Business Studies*, 27(4), 753–78.

OECD (1998) 'Making the Most of the Minimum: Statutory Minimum Wages, Employment and poverty', *Employment Outlook*, Paris: OECD.

OECD (2001) Earnings dispersion database.

Pontusson, J., Rueda, D. and Way, C. (2002) 'Comparative political economy of wage distribution: the role of partisanship and labour market institutions', *British Journal of Political Science*, 32, April, 281–303.

Poutsma, E., Kalmi, P. and Pendleton, A. D. (2006) 'The relationship between financial participation and other forms of employee participation', *Economic and Industrial Democracy*, 27, 4, 637–67.

Rogers, M. and Vernon, G. (2003) 'Wage Inequality and Productivity Growth: Motivating Carrots and Crippling sticks', Economic and Social Research Council Research Centre on Skills, Knowledge and Organizational Performance, Warwick and Oxford, Working Paper No. 40, April.

Royle, T. (2000) *Working for McDonald's in Europe: The Unequal Struggle?* London: Routledge.

Royle, T. (2004) 'Employment practices of MNCs in the Spanish and German quick-food sectors: low road convergence?', *European Journal of Industrial Relations,* 10, 51–71.

Rueda, D. (2003) 'Government Partisanship, Policy and Inequality in the OECD', Presented at the Forum de Ciencia Politica at Pompeu Fabra, Barcelona, 15 Jan.

Rueda, D. and Pontusson, J. (2000) 'Wage inequality and varieties of capitalism', *World Politics,* 52, April, 350–83.

Schuler, R. and Rogovsky, N. (1998) 'Understanding compensation practice variations across firms: the impact of national culture', *Journal of International Business Studies,* 29(1), 159–77.

Sesil, J.C. (2006) 'Shared decision making and group incentives: the impact on performance', *Economic and Industrial Democracy,* 27(4), 587–607.

Shire, K. (1994) 'Bargaining Regimes and the Social Reorganization of Production: The Case of General Motors in Austria and Germany', in Bélanger, J., Edwards, P. and Haiven, L. (eds) *Workplace Industrial Relations and the Global Challenge.* Ithaca, NY: ILR Press.

Sisson, K. (1987) *The Management of Collective Bargaining,* Oxford. Blackwell.

Sliedregt *et al.* (2001) 'Job evaluation systems and pay grade structures: do they match?', *International Journal of Human Resource Management,* 12(8), 1313–24.

Stokke, T.A. (2008) 'The anatomy of two-tier bargaining models', *European Journal of Industrial Relations,* 14(1), 7–24.

Traxler, F., Blaschke, S. and Kittel, B. (2001) *National Labour Relations in Internationalized Markets,* Oxford: Oxford University Press.

Vernon, G. (2006) 'Does density matter? The significance of comparative historical variation in unionization', *European Journal of Industrial Relations,* 11(2), 189–209.

Vernon, G. *et al.* (2007) 'Unions, Employers' Associations and Collective Bargaining Over Pay', in Antoni, C. *et al.* (eds) *Shaping Pay in Europe: A Stakeholder Approach,* Oxford: PIE Peter Lang.

Vernon, G. (2010) 'Still accounting for difference? Comparative joint regulation and pay inequality', (Forthcoming) *Economic and Industrial Democracy.*

Wigham, R. (2003) 'Multinationals amend reward structures for global workers', *Personnel Today,* 16 Oct.

Wolf, E. and Zwick, T. (2002) 'Reassessing the Impact of High-Performance Workplaces', *ZEW Discussion Paper,* 02-07, Mannheim.

Wood, S. and Peccei, R. (1990) 'Preparing for 1992? business led vs. strategic human resource management', *Human Resource Management Journal,* 2(1), 94–109.

Chapter 12

International and comparative employee voice

Enda Hannon

Key aims

The aims of this chapter are to:

- introduce the concept of "employee voice" and discuss its relevance to International HRM;
- examine the nature of employee voice systems in different countries and regions around the world, and the significance of these for MNC managers;
- consider the impact of globalisation on national employee voice systems.

Introduction

The intensification of competition in the business environment over recent decades resulting from globalization and related processes has prompted managers across the world to examine ways of increasing firm productivity and performance. A common strategy adopted in this regard has been the introduction of various 'employee voice' policies and practices (for example suggestion schemes, quality circles or teamworking systems) aimed at increasing employee commitment and input into decision-making regarding their jobs and the issues that affect them at work. The rationale for the use of these practices has been twofold: firstly, employees possess a great depth of knowledge and expertise regarding what works and what doesn't work in their organisations and involving them in decision-making means that this can be tapped into and harnessed, resulting in improved business performance. Secondly, informing, consulting and getting the input of employees is seen to enhance their commitment and 'buy-in', which again may underpin an increase in productivity or performance improvement (Hyman and Mason 1995; Poole *et al.* 2001; Marchington and Wilkinson 2005).

The management of employee voice has as a consequence become a key concern for organizations in general and it is, therefore, of great importance for managers of multinational companies to carefully consider and implement policies and practices in this area. However, as will be discussed in detail in this chapter, designing and implementing employee voice policies is not a straightforward exercise for managers of multinational firms because there exists a great deal of diversity in approaches across the world.

The chapter begins by explaining and defining the term employee voice and the related concepts of 'employee participation' and 'employee involvement.' Next it considers the extent to which these processes are affected by international rules and regulations. Following this, the different types or groupings of employee voice systems that exist around the world are outlined and important trends and issues affecting them discussed. Firstly, the European Union will be examined as a possible example of a regional system of employee voice. Following this, the policies and practices adopted in individual European and other countries will be considered within the context of a discussion of employee voice in 'advanced industrialized nations'. This will be followed by a consideration of policy, practice and challenges arising for multinational companies in 'developing' or 'industrializing' countries. Finally, a conclusion will be provided.

Employee voice, employee participation and employee involvement

'Employee voice' is a general, overarching concept that refers to the various ways in which employees take part in decision-making in organisations and also the degree of influence they have over the same (Rollinson and Dundon 2007; Rose 2008). The essential focus is on what sort of input workers or employees have into decision-making in their organisations, how this is manifested and how strong or powerful it is.

'Employee participation' (EP) and 'employee involvement' (EI) are terms that have been developed to distinguish between different types of employee voice policies and practices. EP and EI practices are seen to be particular types of employee voice practice. Rollinson and Dundon (2007: 230) define employee participation as:

> The sharing of power between employees (or their representatives) and management, in the making of joint decisions.

In contrast, employee involvement is defined as:

> The soliciting of employee views, opinions and ideas to harness the talents and co-operation of employees, but without the sharing of power in an eventual decision-making outcome(2007: 230).

These definitions illustrate that the *objectives* or *focus* of employee involvement and participation practices are rather different. The central purpose of employee participation structures and practices, such as collective bargaining via trade unions or works councils, is to give employees decision-making power and authority. These processes therefore constrain management's freedom to make decisions. In contrast, the primary objective of employee involvement policies, such as suggestion schemes or quality circles, tends to be to improve organisational performance by tapping into the ideas and creativity of employees and gaining their commitment and enthusiasm. Here management's decision-making authority remains unaffected — they remain the final decision-maker.

These differences in essential focus or objectives both relate and lead to differences in the *content* of employee participation and involvement practices and processes. EI practices tend to be *task and performance centred* – for example it is common for suggestion schemes to ask employees how a particular job-related product or process might be adjusted so as to facilitate improved performance. In comparison, EP practices are typically concerned with fundamental organisational issues such as wage levels, working hours or the make-up of redundancy packages. They are therefore primarily *power-centred* – they involve workers challenging the decisions of managers.

Other related but important differences between EI and EP practices concern their *source* or *origin*, i.e. where they come from or who initiates them. Employee involvement practices generally originate from management decisions or initiatives – for example management in a company may make a decision to introduce a teamworking system. While employee participation practices may also be initiated by management, they more commonly have their origins in government legislation or worker actions or initiatives. In the former case, the legislative authority in a particular country may pass a law obliging management to set up structures which give employees influence in decision-making. In the latter, workers in a company or sector may through their trade unions be so powerful as to effectively compel management to share decision-making power with them.

Finally, there are commonly differences between EI and EP practices in the way in which employee input is manifested. Employee involvement systems are generally *direct* in nature, i.e. individual employees are directly involved in them. Examples of direct forms of employee involvement are attitude surveys or suggestion schemes – both these practices directly involve individual employees. In contrast, employee participation practices are generally *indirect,* with individual employees not participating directly but rather doing so indirectly through elected or appointed representatives. For example, a 'shop steward', trade union official or works council representative will negotiate with an employer on behalf of a number of employees.

Table 12.1 Key characteristics of employee involvement and employee participation practices

	Employee involvement	Employee participation
Core focus	Gaining/enhancing the commitment of employees to organizational goals	Providing employees with opportunities to influence and take part in decision-making
Content	Task/performance centred	Power centred; work tasks but also more fundamental organizational decisions
Origin	Management discretion	Legislation; worker organization and power
Authority	Resides with management	Joint/shared
Mode of involvement	Direct/individual or workgroup	Indirect/collective, via representatives
Examples	Staff surveys Suggestion schemes Teamworking systems Quality circles Staff forums	Collective bargaining Works councils Joint consultative committees

Sources: Salamon (2000: chapter 10); Lewis *et al.* (2003: 259)

This overview highlights that employee participation tends to be a stronger form of employee voice than employee involvement; EP practices typically give employees greater power and influence than EI practices. Table 12.1 below outlines the key differences between employee participation and involvement summarised above. It is important to note, however, that it may not always be clear under which category a particular practice falls, and that there may be significant overlap between EI and EP practices. Nevertheless, dividing employee voice practices into these two broad categories is useful in that it enables us to analyse trends and activities in this area in particular organizations or countries.

International regulation of employee voice

A recognition and commitment to the right of workers to combine together and form trade unions and, relatedley, to be represented by the latter in collective bargaining with employers, is one of the founding principles of the International Labour Organization (ILO). ILO Convention 87 on Freedom of Association and Protection of the Right to Organize (1948), sets out the right for workers to establish and join trade unions and the obligation on ILO member states that have ratified the convention to protect this right to organize. Convention 98 on the Right to Organise and Collective Bargaining (1949) prohibits anti-union discrimination and interference and requires signatory states to take measures to promote voluntary negotiation and collective agreements between trade unions and employers. The Collective Bargaining Convention (C154, 1981) also requires the promotion of collective bargaining between trade unions and employers. Finally, the Workers' Representatives Convention (C135, 1971) stipulates that worker representatives, whether union or non-union, should be protected against prejudicial treatment and provided with facilities to enable them to carry out their functions promptly and efficiently.

These ILO conventions have established some international laws and standards with regard to the exercise of employee voice. They provide important support to trade unions and employee participation in deciding terms and conditions of employment through the process of collective bargaining between trade unions and employers. However they do not make it compulsory for employers to engage in collective bargaining or for employee representatives to be provided with rights to participate more broadly in decision-making in the management of the firm. There is some other ILO legislation which deals with the latter issue, but this is in the form of non-binding recommendations. Recommendation 94 on Co-operation at the Level of the Undertaking (1952) states that ratifying states should take appropriate steps to:

> …promote consultation and co-operation between employers and workers at the level of the undertaking on matters of mutual concern not within the scope of collective bargaining machinery, or not normally dealt with by other machinery concerned with the determination of terms and conditions of employment.

Such consultation and co-operation should be facilitated by the encouragement of voluntary agreements between the parties, by laws or regulations or by both voluntary agreements and regulations, depending on each country's customs and traditions.

In addition, Recommendation 129 on Communications within the Undertaking (1967) states that managers should provide workers and their representative organizations with comprehensive information on relevant issues in a timely fashion, and apply 'an effective policy of communication' with workers and their representatives. The recommendation outlines that the latter should ensure that information is provided and consultation takes place before decisions on matters of major interest are taken, in so far as this would not cause damage to either management or workers.

Communication systems should ensure genuine and regular two-way communication between management and workers and between management and trade union or other representatives, who according to national law or practice or collective agreements have the job of representing the interests of workers. The information to be given by management to workers or their representatives should as far as possible include all matters of interest to the workers relating to the operation and future prospects of the enterprise and to the present and future situation of the workers. The recommendation lists specific topics which should be communicated about, such as general conditions of employment, job descriptions, working conditions, health and safety and training.

The ILO conventions on freedom of association, the right to organise and collective bargaining have been ratified by a large number of ILO member states (for example 150 countries had ratified convention 87, and 160 convention 98, as at February 2010). Although there continue to be very significant breaches of these conventions and problems in their implementation (ILO 2008), they have been influential in enabling workers in countries around the world to join trade unions and through them engage in collective bargaining with employers. This means that employee participation in determining terms and conditions of employment through the process of trade union-based collective bargaining is a relatively common feature of national employment relations systems.

However, due to their non-binding nature, recommendations 94 and 129 on co-operation and communication within the undertaking have not had the same practical impact in promoting the exercise of employee voice more broadly in the management of the firm. As a consequence, there continue to be great differences between individual countries in the way in which the latter process is regulated and controlled.

The focus of this chapter is therefore on examining the different approaches to the exercise of employee voice in the management of the firm that are identifiable internationally, possible changes in the same resulting from processes of globalization, and the issues and challenges facing managers of multinational companies in attempting to manage employee voice in diverse cultural and institutional contexts.

The European Union as a regional system of employee voice

As outlined above, international or transnational regulation of employee voice practices and processes is rather limited. However there is in fact notable international regulation of these issues at a regional level in the form of the European Union's growing body of legislation on employee participation. As Dicken (2007) explains, the European Union (EU) constitutes a relatively developed form of regional economic co-operation. For example, while NAFTA, the North American Free Trade Association involving the US, Canada and Mexico, is a mere 'free trade area', the European Union is an 'economic union' wherein economic policies are harmonised and subject to supra-national control. The various member states of the European Union have given the institutions of the EU the power to make laws binding on them in areas such as competition policy, product safety and environmental protection. European Union law also has supremacy in a significant number of employment related areas. The EU is therefore permitted to pass binding legislation on information and consultation of employees, provided that a majority of member states support a particular proposal (Barnard 2000). The EU has exercised this power by passing directives which make it compulsory for employers across the EU to involve their employees in organizational decision–making. The key provisions of the primary directives in this regard are summarised in Box 12.1, below.

BOX 12.1

European Union legislation on employee voice

- **Directive on Collective Redundancies 1998 (Directive 98/59/EC)**: this obliges employers in the EU to consult with employee representatives 'in good time with a view to agreement' on ways of avoiding, reducing the number or mitigating the effects of collective redundancies (e.g. where 20+ employees are to be made redundant over a period of 90 days). Employers must provide worker representatives with 'all relevant information' such as the reasons for the redundancies, the number and categories of workers affected and the period over which the planned redundancies are to take place, during the course of the consultations.

- **Directive on Transfers of Undertakings 2001 (Directive 2001/23/EC):** the purpose of this directive is to protect employees whose companies or undertakings are sold to or merge with another firm. It requires both the 'transferor' and 'transferee' to inform employees affected by the transfer, or their representatives, in good time about the date of the proposed transfer, the reasons for it, the legal, social and economic implications, and any measures envisaged in relation to the employees. Where measures are envisaged (for example, company restructuring), employee representatives must be consulted in good time 'with a view to reaching agreement' about them.

- **Health and Safety Framework Directive 1989 (89/391/EEC):** requires workers in the EU and/or their representatives to be provided with information on health and safety risks, measures taken to address them and inspection agency investigations. Workers or worker representatives with specific responsibility for health and safety should also be consulted on various issues including measures which may substantially affect health and safety and the planning of health and safety training. Representatives have the right to ask employers to take measures to remove or reduce hazards and to submit observations to health & safety inspectors.

- **European Works Council Directive 2009 (2009/38/EC):** creates obligations for multi-national companies operating in the EU to establish a system for the information and consultation of employees regarding issues of concern to employees at a transnational level. The directive applies to all companies with 1000+ employees and at least 150 in two or more EU member states, even if they originate from a country outside the EU. Relevant companies may be required to establish a 'European Works Council' (EWC) made up of representatives of employees from the various countries of operation which must operate according to a standard set of rules. These provide EWCs with a right to an annual meeting with management and also to be informed and to request a meeting where are 'exceptional circumstances or decisions affecting employees' interests'. Management is obliged to inform the EWC on the economic position of the company and business developments, and to inform and consult about investment plans and changes impacting on work organisation and employment.

- **Directive on Information & Consultation 2002 (2002/14/EC):** this established general, minimum requirements for the information and consultation of employees which are applicable throughout the EU as a whole (Weiss 2004). It applies to either all 'undertakings' with 50 employees or more or all 'establishments' with twenty employees or more (EU member states decide on this themselves). Employers covered by the directive are required to inform and consult employee representatives as follows:

  - *Information* should be provided on the organisation's business or operating situation and activities and likely developments in the same

  - Employee representatives should be *informed and consulted* on levels and nature of employment and any measures envisaged in that regard
  - Representatives should also be *informed and consulted* on decisions likely to lead to substantial changes in work organisation or in contractual relations

- Information must be provided at such time and in such a way as to enable employee representatives to conduct an adequate study and prepare for consultation. Consultation processes should enable employee representatives to meet with the employer and obtain a response to any opinion they might formulate. Consultation must take place 'with a view to reaching an agreement.'

In addition to setting out rights and obligations, these directives oblige EU member states to ensure that their provisions can be enforced via judicial or administrative institutions and procedures.

▶ Impact of European Union legislation on employee voice

Box 12.1, above, demonstrates how European Union regulation of employee voice has developed from the directives on collective redundancies and transfers of undertakings covering specific situations, to the general, framework directive on information and consultation. Two questions that arise from this are, firstly, whether these directives have resulted in a distinctive, common approach to employee voice being adopted across the EU, and secondly, whether their impact has been to provide employees in the EU with effective rights to participate in decision-making in practice.

It is certainly the case that the various directives mean that particular common, minimum standards regarding employee participation in decision–making now exist throughout the EU. There is also evidence to suggest that these directives have been quite effective in providing employees with input into and influence over decision–making in practice in EU member states where this has historically been absent (see for example Hall and Edwards' (1999) study on the implementation of the collective redundancy directive in the UK). However, a common approach providing employees and their representatives with strong participation rights has not resulted from these directives for a number of reasons.

Firstly, the purpose of EU directives is to create *minimum standards,* with member states free to enact more demanding legislation at national level. Therefore, at a general level these directives are not likely to lead to a harmonization of employee voice policies and practices across the EU. Secondly, there are very significant differences in the views and approaches of the various EU member states to the exercise of employee voice. As will be discussed further below, while some European countries such as Germany, Denmark and Austria strongly support employee participation in decision–making, others such as the UK and Ireland have historically been either ambivalent or opposed to this idea.

An effect of these national differences has been to weaken the content of EU legislation on employee voice. Because it is necessary for a majority of countries to agree for a directive to be passed, the existence of opposing views among member states tends to place limits on the potential content of new legislation. As Hall (2005) outlines, objections by the UK and other governments resulted in the final text of the Information and Consultation Directive being weaker in a number of respects than the European Commission's original proposal. For example, the Commission's proposal that company restructuring decisions taken by employers in breach of their obligations to inform and consult would not be given legal effect was not included in the final text, arguably making the directive less powerful from an employee perspective. European trade unionists have also criticised the definition of 'consultation' in the directive – 'the exchange of views and establishment of dialogue between the employees' representatives and the employer' – stating that this provides employee representatives with little power and influence in practice.

These differences in views and approaches to employee voice between countries also mean that the manner in which relevant directives have been implemented at national level has operated to limit their potential impact in a number of cases. Although the core provisions and obligations contained in EU directives are binding, member states need to bring these into force by implementing national legislation, and are provided with flexibility regarding how this is done. For example, article 1(2) of the Information and Consultation Directive states that 'the practical arrangements for information and consultation shall be defined and implemented in accordance with national law and industrial relations practices in individual Member States in such a way as to ensure their effectiveness'. Notably in this regard, the UK regulations implementing this directive stipulate that UK employers are only obliged to establish a procedure for the information and consultation of employees when they receive a written request from 10 per cent of the workforce in a relevant establishment. This is a so-called 'trigger mechanism' – the obligations in the directive are only triggered when employers receive this written request. However, commentators have highlighted the practical difficulties involved for employees and/or their representatives in attempting to collect signatures from this proportion of employees in a relevant undertaking (Hall 2005).

The UK regulations also provide that employers are entitled to use *direct* rather than indirect methods of information and consultation, provided these arrangements are agreed with their employees. This means that UK employers may not need to appoint employee representatives; it can be sufficient for them to communicate directly with their employees. Critics have noted that in such cases this means that employees are not in fact provided with representation, contrary to the spirit of the directive (Hall 2005). These examples illustrate how differences in national approaches to implementation can weaken the practical impact of EU directives and militate against the establishment of a common approach to employee participation across the Union.

While the discussion so far has focused on how European legislation impacts on national systems of employee voice, research evidence also highlights the limited nature of employee participation structures established in multinational firms operating across the EU in order to comply with the European Works Council Directive. Recent research identified approximately 820 EWCs active across Europe, covering 14.5 million employees. However, despite these impressive figures, EWCs have only been set up in 36 per cent of eligible undertakings (European Commission 2008: 2). In addition, the explanatory memorandum to the European Commission's recent proposal for a revised EWC directive notes that 'the right to transnational information and consultation lacks effectiveness, as the European Works Council is not sufficiently informed and consulted in the case of restructuring' (2008: 2).

This view is supported by the findings from a recent analysis of the operation of EWCs in practice (European Foundation 2008a). This review reported research findings highlighting how a majority of EWCs are typically provided with information either at the point at which decisions on transnational business issues are taken by management or afterwards. Consultation in good time is rare, with the consultation process typically concerning the *implementation* of decisions rather than the content of the original decisions themselves. The report does note that in a number of companies such as Volkswagen and General Motors, EWCs are engaged more fully in decision-making and negotiate outcomes with management (see also Banyuls *et al.* 2008), but these account for only a small minority of firms.

Concerns regarding the weakness of the EWC directive have recently prompted a formal revision of it, with a recast directive being adopted in May 2009. This strengthens the original 1994 directive in a number of ways, for example with a definition of what constitutes 'information' and a revised, stronger definition of 'consultation' included in the new text. The impact of these changes remains to be seen, however it is arguably unlikely that the revised directive will give EWCs significantly more power and influence in practice. For example, like the original, the revised directive states that while the EWC has the right to meet management where there are exceptional circumstances affecting employees' interests, this meeting 'shall not affect the prerogatives of central management'. This implies that management's decision-making power is to remain unaffected.

Overall, therefore, while the various directives have created certain minimum rules and standards regarding employee participation which member states are obliged to comply with, they have not led to a common approach to employee voice being adopted throughout the European Union. This means that it remains important to consider how individual countries approach this issue, and the remainder of this chapter is concerned with examining this.

National systems of employee voice

As outlined in Chapter 3, the human resource management policies and practices adopted in particular countries are strongly affected by cultural and institutional influences. Such influences also condition the way in which employee voice is exercised and expressed. As will be outlined below, in some countries legislation has been passed by national parliaments, which requires employers to allow employees to participate in decision–making regarding the management of the firm. Such legislation often establishes institutional structures or mechanisms (for example works councils) through which employee participation is to take place. Aside from legislation and dedicated institutional structures, the principles, morals and philosophical beliefs underpinning a particular culture or society generate certain understandings and expectations regarding how employee voice is exercised, which has important practical implications (Kessler et al. 2004). Although institutional and cultural influences are significant in every country, the latter are arguably of particular importance in developing or industrializing countries which may lack strong institutions and which may be characterized by very different cultural values than those that pertain in the West (Jackson 2002).

The fact that the practice of employee involvement and participation is so strongly determined by country specific institutional and cultural influences means that in general terms there is great diversity in national systems of employee participation. Nevertheless, it is possible to identify certain groups of countries with common features and characteristics (Biagi 2001). The sub-sections below provide an overview of identifiable groupings of countries among so called 'advanced industrialised economies'. Following this, the question of employee participation in 'developing' or 'industrializing' economies is addressed, with China used as a case study example in that regard.

Employee voice in 'advanced industrialized economies'

In advanced, industrialized economies it is possible to distinguish between countries which have predominantly 'voluntarist' systems of employee voice and those with predominantly 'mandatory' systems. In the former employers are generally in a position to freely decide what employee voice practices to implement, with governments tending not to intervene in this area or to force them to adopt particular systems or practices. In contrast, in the latter employers are generally obliged, typically by legislation enacted by national parliaments, to establish institutions or mechanisms through which employees can participate in decisions about the management of the firm.

It is not suggested that these groupings are watertight or comprehensive and it is recognised that some countries (e.g. Japan) may not fit within either. Nevertheless, they are seen to reflect quite distinct approaches to employee voice which effectively describe policy and practice across a sizeable number of countries. The essential characteristics of each group are, therefore, now discussed in some detail.

▶ Voluntarist systems

Countries whose legal systems are based on British 'common law' principles and whose economic policies tend to favour the free operation of market forces are most obviously those which have voluntarist employee voice systems. They include the UK, US, Australia, Ireland, Canada and New Zealand. In these countries there tends to be only limited legal regulation of the exercise of employee voice in decisions regarding the management of the firm, with the nature and extent of employee voice exercised in particular companies primarily determined by the policies and preferences of management (hence, the 'voluntarist' description – the practice of employee voice is something which management tends to *voluntarily* decide upon) (Roche and Geary 2000; Poole *et al.* 2001; Godard 2003; Gollan and Hamberger 2003; Rasmussen and Lind 2003; Katz and Wheeler 2004; Lansbury and Wailes 2004). European Union legislation and, in particular, the recent directive on Information and Consultation summarized above, has changed this situation somewhat for the UK and Ireland, although in practice employees in these countries continue to have only limited influence in decision-making, with management still the dominant actor.

Where employee voice is exercised in voluntarist system countries, it tends to be in the form of 'employee involvement' as opposed to 'employee participation' practices. Management are willing and eager to involve employees in decision-making so as to improve their performance and commitment to the organization, but are reluctant to cede control over decision-making to employees and their representatives. Outside the firm in the labour market and broader society, there tends to be no strong or pervasive culture in favour of employee participation in organizational decision-making (Rasmussen and Lind 2003; Gollan and Hamberger 2003). Employee participation is, therefore, limited in extent and scope.

For example, a recent survey of employee relations in Great Britain, the 2004 Workplace Employee Relations Survey (Kersley, *et al.*), identified quite extensive use by British employers of employee involvement practices. In 2004, 79 per cent of workplaces surveyed held meetings between senior management and the whole workforce, while at 71 per cent team briefings took place. Forty two per cent of workplaces had conducted a formal survey of employees in the preceding two years, with 30 per cent making use of suggestion schemes. Three-quarters of workplaces used notice boards to communicate with staff and 45 per cent regular newsletters. The available information from the survey illustrated that the use of such direct communication practices had increased since the previous survey in 1998 (Kersley *et al.* 2006: 134–43). In contrast, forms of representative participation such as joint consultative committees (JCCs) were limited in coverage, with their use having declined since 1998. JCCs were present at only 14 per cent of workplaces in 2004 compared with a fifth in 1998, with the proportion of all employees working in an establishment with such a committee declining from 46 per cent in 1998 to 42 per cent in 2004 (2006: 126–7).

▶ Mandatory systems

While in a number of countries, then, the exercise of employee voice is predominantly determined by management prerogative, in other advanced industrialized nations management is *obliged* to allow employee voice to be expressed and exercised. Legislation has been passed in many European countries including Germany, Austria, the Netherlands, France and Spain, which provides for the mandatory establishment and operation of institutions for the exercise of employee voice at workplace and/or company level (Slomp

1995). In other countries – for example Denmark and Italy – collective agreements between trade unions and employers make it compulsory for similar employee voice systems to be implemented (Carley *et al.* 2004).

These countries with such mandatory employee voice systems tend to have a long history of promoting employee participation in organisational decision–making, often operating alongside but separate to collective bargaining between trade unions and management over terms and conditions of employment. In addition to the laws and institutions regulating the exercise of employee voice, the wider culture of organizations and the broader society also tends to be strongly supportive of employee participation in organizational decision-making (Wever 1994). In practical terms, therefore, while decision-making power in these countries continues to rest mainly in the hands of management, substantial autonomy and control is ceded to employee representatives. The German system is often seen to be the exemplar of this sort of approach to employee voice and the key features of this system are therefore outlined in Box 12.2, below.

BOX 12.2

The German system of employee voice

Legislation passed by the federal parliament has created compulsory rules and regulations for German companies to follow regarding employee participation in the management of the firm:

- The **Works Constitution Act 2001** obliges German employers to set up employee only 'works councils' in workplaces with five or more employees, where requested by the employees. The purpose of works councils is to represent and promote the interests of employees, but they are also expected to consider the needs of the enterprise. Works councils and management are obliged to co-operate in 'a spirit of mutual trust for the good of employees and the establishment'.
- Works Council representatives are elected by a secret ballot of all employees aged 18 and over. The number of representatives can range from one to over 35 depending on the size of the workplace. They are entitled to paid time off from work to carry out their duties and in workplaces of 200+ employees, full-time representatives should be appointed. Employers and works councils are required by law to meet at least once a month.

- Employers are also required to establish a *company level* works council where more than one workplace works council is in operation.
- Works Councils have a *right to information* on financial and general business matters (e.g. company strategy or investment plans).
- They have *information and consultation rights* regarding company policies on jobs, levels of employment and work organization, and also on specific plans to close, reduce or amalgamate operations or change working methods and processes.
- They have *codetermination rights* regarding personnel policy matters such as working time and holiday arrangements, payment methods and principles, rules governing teamworking systems and health and safety. Codetermination rights also exist regarding the development of guidelines for recruitment, transfer, regrading and dismissal and the implementation of the same. In addition, they apply to the drawing up of a 'social compensation plan' to alleviate the negative social effects arising from restructuring or the implementation of redundancies. In these situations management is obliged to

seek the agreement of the works council and the works council is entitled to make its own suggestions. If agreement is not possible then the issue in question is adjudicated on by a 'conciliation committee' with a neutral chair. The right of codetermination is generally exercised through the signing of binding 'works agreements' with management.

- German law also provides for mandatory representation of employee interests in the 'supervisory boards' of companies above a certain size:

  - **'Third Part Act 2004':** companies with 500-2000 employees – 1/3 of the members of the supervisory board must be employee representatives

  - **Co-Determination Act 1976:** companies with more than 2000 employees – equal representation of employee and shareholder representatives; the chair of the supervisory board (usually appointed by shareholders) has the final say in the event of a tied vote

- Supervisory boards appoint and oversee the activities of the management board, which is responsible for the day-to-day running of companies

- Employee representatives directly elected by the workforce; many are works councillors and trade union members; trade unions entitled to appoint a number of representatives in larger companies

Sources: German Federal Ministry of Economics and Technology, www.bmwi.de; Page (2006)

▶ Impact of globalization on mandatory systems of employee voice

As outlined in previous chapters, the impact of globalization on human resource management or employee relations practices is a matter of great interest for students of international HRM and, therefore, a central focus of this book. Examining trends and developments in mandatory systems of employee voice provides an ideal opportunity to explore the practical impact of globalization. If 'strong globalization' theories are correct and national employment systems increasingly converging to one common model, then we might expect country-specific mandatory systems of employee participation to be under intense pressure and to be weakening. This is arguably particularly likely if, as highlighted by many commentators, the American approach to management and HRM is becoming progressively more dominant. As outlined above, American managers have a preference for employee involvement over employee participation, so we would therefore expect American MNCs operating in countries such as Germany, France and Spain to strongly challenge the mandatory systems of employee voice existing in those countries.

Before considering the policies and practices of US and other multinationals in these countries, we can use the example of German works councils to analyse how the general trends and pressures resulting from globalization are impacting on mandatory systems of employee voice.

The impact of globalization on German works councils

The evidence from Germany suggests that economic trends influenced by globalization, such as a growing shift from manufacturing to services in the advanced industrialized economies and a general intensification of competitive pressures, are impacting significantly on mandatory systems of employee voice. However, these trends appear to be having rather contradictory effects.

On the one hand, some survey evidence shows that globalization influenced economic trends are leading to a decline in the proportion of private sector companies and employees covered by works councils (Hassel 1999; Grahl and Teague 2004). Hassel (1999: 488) outlines that while in 1981, 52 per cent of private sector employees in Germany were covered by a works council, by 1994 only 42 per cent were covered. A survey conducted ten years later, in 2004, found that in that year 47 per cent of employees in private sector workplaces in West Germany were covered by a works council, but only 38 per cent of workers in East Germany were so covered (EIRO online 2005). Coverage was relatively high in the manufacturing sector, at 68 per cent (in West Germany), but substantially lower in services at only 33 per cent. A more recent survey found that only 11 per cent of companies (as opposed to employees or workplaces) had a works council in 2007. However, these figures disguise very significant differences between companies of varying sizes. While only 3 per cent of companies with 5–50 workers had a works council, 60 per cent of companies with 101–199 workers and 72 per cent with 501 or more workers had one (EIRO online 2007).

Important reasons for the decline in the number of German companies and employees affected by works councils include the growing importance of small firms in the German economy and the substantial increase in total employment in the private services sector over recent years (Hassel 1999). As indicated in the above figures, small firms and those in the services sector are less likely to have works councils than others (Grahl and Teague 2004). Trade unions find it particularly difficult to establish works councils in small 'new economy' firms such as those in the IT or biotechnology fields. These changes in the structure of the economy, influenced by processes of globalization, therefore, have served to undermine Germany's mandatory system of employee voice.

The increasing competition faced by German businesses as a consequence of globalization has also challenged the power and authority of works councils (Grahl and Teague 2004). As in other countries, managers in German companies have come under intense pressure to reduce costs and increase productivity, and these pressures and dynamics have led to widespread conflict and disagreement with works councils over issues such as relocation, outsourcing, employment levels and working arrangements (Hassel 1999; EIRO online 2008a). Raess and Burgoon's (2006) research demonstrates how works councils at German factories exposed to processes of foreign direct investment and trade have had to offer management substantial concessions in order to secure jobs, for example greater flexibility in work practices. Raess and Burgoon (2006: 304) conclude that 'greater openness, especially FDI openness, tends to increase concessions by works councils.' Similarly, research by Doellgast and Greer (2007) in the telecommunications and automotive sectors illustrates how the power and influence of works councils in those sectors has been substantially undermined by firms' strategies of outsourcing production and making greater use of temporary agency workers.

While the intensification of competition facing German firms has to a significant extent, therefore, operated to undermine the power of works councils, in other ways these difficult competitive conditions have served to make them more important and influential than before. This is because there is a growing trend in Germany for working conditions and employment practices to be negotiated at company or plant level instead of the historically dominant sector level, in recognition of the competitive pressures faced by individual firms (Behrens and Jacoby 2004; Whittall 2005; Gumbrell-McCormick and Hyman 2006). Works councils are playing a central role in these negotiations and the implementation of resulting agreements. For example, in recent years many collective agreements between unions and employers in Germany have provided trade unions and works councils the freedom to agree company-specific arrangements regarding working time with management, and this has in practice been a widespread occurrence (Keller 2004; Haipeter and Lehndorff 2005; Seifert and Massa-Wirth 2005). It can be noted, however, that while works councils may therefore be enjoying a greater role and involvement in decision–making at firm level than before, this typically involves them in the implementation of largely negative changes from a worker perspective, designed to reduce costs or increase productivity (for example, agreements to increase working time).

Impact of MNC policies on mandatory employee voice systems

Turning to the more specific question of the practices of multinational firms in countries with mandatory employee voice systems, the survey evidence on this is limited and what is available is rather mixed. Schmitt (2003) conducted a survey of a representative sample of indigenous German and foreign–owned companies employing 70 or more employees. He found that the foreign–owned firms in his sample were as least as likely to have works councils as indigenous German firms, with nearly 60 per cent of the personnel managers surveyed at the foreign firms placing a high importance on works councils as a means of management-employee communication. In contrast, a survey by Looise and Drucker (2002) found that works councils in the subsidiaries of Dutch and foreign-owned multinationals operating in the Netherlands had less influence on strategic and operational decision-making than works councils in firms based in the Netherlands alone.

While survey evidence is therefore arguably inconclusive, there have been quite a large number of case study based examinations of the practices of MNCs in mandatory systems. Royle (2002) examined the employee representation policies of the American fast food giant McDonald's in four European countries. He found that McDonald's did not comply with the compulsory rules on employee participation in Germany, France and Spain. Management in the company deliberately set out to prevent the establishment of employee participation structures and institutions and was largely successful in this strategy.

While this is quite an extreme case, other case study evidence also shows how MNCs operating in such countries can avoid complying with mandatory rules on employee participation. Muller (1998) conducted case studies at nine US and four UK-owned MNC subsidiaries in the German banking and chemical sectors, which he compared with twelve comparable German companies. He found that while all the indigenous and British owned firms complied with German legislation on employee participation, six of the nine US firms either did not comply at all or only partially complied. Four of these did not have any works councils at all while the two others did not have councils at major workplaces. Although this evidence suggests that globalization is a serious threat to the German employee participation system, Muller notes that the small size of a number of the US firms studied can explain why they were able to operate without a works council. In addition, he outlines how in order to prevent a works council from being established, these firms were in practice required to provide their employees with good terms and conditions as well as alternative communication mechanisms.

Findings similar to those of Muller (1998) emerge from a study focusing on the collective representation and participation practices of US multinationals operating in Germany, Spain, the UK and Ireland (Colling *et al.* 2006). This found that while the case study firms, which were large MNCs based across a range of sectors, generally established works councils in their German and Spanish subsidiaries as required by law, in practice management made strong efforts to limit the role and influence of works councils on organizational decision-making.

A more recent example of a foreign MNC challenging national rules on employee participation is the decision by the mobile phone company Nokia to close its manufacturing site at Bochum in western Germany. The decision to close the plant, which was announced in early 2008, was made on the basis that labour costs at the Bochum site were excessively high. However, the closure was announced without prior notice being given to the site's works council (as required by law), which caused great anger on the part of German workers, trade unionists and politicians (EIRO online 2008b). Although the closure went ahead, the works council was nevertheless able to negotiate a 'social plan' for the workers affected worth €200 million.

Summary

The above evidence demonstrates how processes of globalization are impacting heavily on employee participation practices in countries with mandatory voice systems. Economic trends associated with globalization mean that these systems are becoming less common across these countries as a whole, while in sectors in which they remain in place the intense competitive pressures faced by businesses are impairing the effectiveness of EP systems in representing and protecting workers. However, the economic and competitive environment resulting from globalization has also prompted change in the role of employee participation institutions, with bodies such as works councils becoming more involved in the negotiation of working conditions and employment practices. Globalization also affects mandatory employee voice systems more directly, through the policies and practices of multinational firms. Although what limited survey evidence exists does not suggest a clear pattern, a wide range of case studies highlight how many foreign-owned MNCs deliberately flout the rules and regulations regarding employee participation existing in mandatory system countries.

Managing employee voice in 'industrializing' or 'developing' economies

Due to the very large number of developing or industrializing economies and the great differences between them in economic conditions, culture and institutions, undertaking a comprehensive analysis of the practice of employee voice across these countries is clearly beyond the scope of this chapter. Instead a number of general observations will be outlined regarding these countries before the example of China is examined in some detail.

Common features of many developing or industrializing countries include a transition from closed to open economic systems based heavily on trade with other countries and regions and, related to this, a desire to attract inward foreign direct investment by multinational firms. These features have, for example, been strongly characteristic of the experience of China, India and the former member states of the Soviet Union in recent times. Like their advanced or developed counterparts, some developing countries have mandatory employee voice systems based on government legislation. However, the comparatively underdeveloped nature of economic and social institutions in these countries often means that binding rules on employee participation are not implemented fully in practice (see, for example, European Foundation (2008b) for a discussion of this issue in relation to some of the Central and Eastern European countries). In addition, because of the extent to which investment by MNCs is prized and desired, the latter tend to be in a strong position in deciding what sort of employee voice system to introduce in host developing countries. In general terms, therefore, the primary challenge facing expatriate managers implementing employee voice systems in industrializing countries may be to address and overcome cultural differences and issues, with the need to comply with legislation creating and regulating employee participation institutions being less important.

◗ Employee voice in China

MNC managers in China are faced with a complex working environment. This is because Chinese managers and workers' orientations and preferences regarding the exercise of employee voice are shaped by a wide range of cultural, social and institutional influences.

The ancient philosophical system of Confucianism forms a key foundation stone upon which contemporary Chinese society is built (Wang *et al.* 2005; Warner 2009). As Wang *et al.* (2005) outline, Confucianism is based on a number of fundamental principles, including hierarchy and harmony, group orientation, the development of close relationships (*guanxi*) and the preservation and promotion of reputation or 'face' (*mianzi*). The principles of Confucianism dictate that employees respect the position and authority of managers, while the latter should treat their subordinates in a humane and considerate manner. Social stability and harmony are greatly valued, while there is also a strong sense of collectivism, with group involvement and identity being of central importance. Work groups or organisations may be seen as equivalent to family environments, with the principles of egalitarianism and distributive fairness emphasized.

Wang *et al.* (2005) highlight how this Confucian cultural context has important implications for decision-making processes within Chinese firms. They note that while on the one hand, the strong sense of collectivism and group identity may be conducive to the successful adoption of team-working principles and systems, on the other hand, the same characteristics arguably militate against individual employees being held accountable for their work. Similarly, while the emphasis on hierarchy and harmony is likely to promote good working relationships between managers and employees, it may also lead to low levels of employee participation and autonomous working (Huo and Von Glinow 1995; Chen *et al.* 2000; Hirst *et al.* 2008). Wang *et al.* (2005) note how recent and current changes taking place in China are strongly challenging the influence of Confucian principles, but nevertheless maintain that it remains important for managers to be aware of these when implementing management practices (Warner 2009).

While Confucianism continues to underpin Chinese society today, it has over the last century been superimposed with other important belief systems, ideologies and institutions emanating from the political sphere. The Chinese Communist Party (CCP) came to power in 1949 and since then has transformed the country's society and economy. A central pillar of the CCP's early economic policy was the establishment of hundreds of thousands of state-owned-enterprises (SOEs). These are commonly seen to have been bureaucratic and paternalistic organisations, which adopted common structures and management practices (Warner 2008). While still important, the opening of the Chinese economy to world trade and the forces of globalization since 1979 has meant that SOEs have become less influential. Privately owned and multinational firms have grown in importance. Over the last two decades MNCs from a large number of countries have invested in China, establishing joint ventures with previously state-owned companies or their own wholly–owned Chinese subsidiaries (Warner 2008).

Despite the high importance ascribed to workers in China's social and political system, the Communist approach to economic management is seen to have historically provided little support for employee voice in decision-making (Taylor *et al.* 2003). The dominant state-owned enterprises were typically characterised by rigid and bureaucratic management structures, which strongly emphasised hierarchy and provided little autonomy or voice to workers (Cooke 2005; Warner 2008). This resulted in demotivated and uninvolved employees. While by law every state-owned enterprise should have a trade union guided workers' representatives congress with formal powers to participate in decision–making, in practice where they have existed these structures have been quite marginal, having little influence or impact (Cooke 2005; Taylor *et al.* 2003; Nichols and Zhao 2010).

Although there is a rapidly expanding body of research on human resource management in China, thus far few studies have examined the exercise of employee voice in contemporary China in much detail. Lewis (2002) conducted research at a large SOE, which manufactured consumer electronics products, in 2000 and 2001. He found employee involvement at the company to be very limited indeed. There was minimal direct communication between managers and employees. Communication was hindered by 'the almost obsessive concern for maintenance of status' on the part of staff at all levels (2002: 55–6). Lewis (2002) also found that the traditional structures and management practices in the company impacted negatively on employee morale and in particular on that of enthusiastic young graduates whose expectations and ambitions were stifled by the prevailing working environment.

In contrast, Gamble (2003) examined the HRM practices adopted at two Chinese stores of a British–owned DIY multinational. Previous research has illustrated the difficulties faced by Western firms in attempting to transfer non-hierarchical management structures to China (Ilari and La Grange 1999), but Gamble's research provides an example of an MNC where this appears to have been possible. The main findings are outlined in Box 12.3, below.

Employee involvement at a British multinational in China

Gamble (2003) conducted interviews with 70 employees at two DIY stores owned by a UK multi-national in Shanghai in 1999 and 2000. A focus of his research was on communication and representation systems and organizational structures.

The British parent company, 'StoreCo', expressly attempted to transfer important elements of its organizational model to these Chinese stores, including formal employee communication mechanisms, a flat organizational structure and an emphasis on close, informal interpersonal relationships between management and staff. Two British expatriate managers played a hands-on role in implementing these structures and practices.

The Chinese employees reacted very positively to these policies. They greatly enjoyed the extensive informal communication they had with management. They felt that the expatriate managers cared about them and treated them as important members of the organization, which contrasted strongly with their previous experience of impersonal and hierarchical management practices in working at state-owned enterprises. Gamble (2003: 384) notes how the management systems at the company had 'tapped into an egalitarian ideal' which the employees possessed and which was seen to be linked to past policies and ideals espoused by the Communist Party. The British managers noted that as a consequence of the policies adopted the Chinese employees were gradually becoming more willing to question those above them. Gamble explains how the suitable personalities and strong abilities of the two expatriate managers were key to the successful implementation of the parent company's operating policies.

Source: Gamble (2003)

Gamble subsequently undertook additional research at another store owned by the same company as well as at a branch of a comparable state-owned retailer (Gamble 2006). Drawing on interviews and questionnaire surveys, he outlines how employees at the UK–owned multinational reported higher levels of management consultation, closer supervisor-worker relationships and a more positive employee relations climate than their counterparts at the state-owned retailer; with the distinctive approach to communication, employee involvement and participation at the British MNC seen to be key in accounting for these differences.

The research by Gamble is of great interest. It highlights both the opportunities and challenges for MNC managers attempting to introduce employee voice practices in China. The findings demonstrate that the Chinese context in many ways provides fertile ground for the implementation of such practices, but that this process needs to be undertaken with care and sensitivity and a strong awareness of social and cultural issues. Of particular concern is the need to establish close, respectful relationships between managers and staff, which is something that Gamble has also highlighted in more recent research (Gamble and Huang 2008; see also Wang 2008).

Conclusions

This chapter has provided an overview and discussion of employee voice from an international and comparative perspective. The concepts of employee voice, employee involvement and employee participation were explained before relevant international regulations and the nature of regional and national models of employee voice were examined in some detail. This showed there to be minimal international legal regulation of the exercise of employee voice in organisational decision–making, with the European Union the only regional international entity with some common rules and regulations in this area. The diverse nature of European Union member states, alongside the flexibility provided to them in implementing relevant legislation, was however found to be preventing the emergence of a common approach to employee voice across the EU.

The examination of national models identified two broad groupings of countries among the advanced industrialized economies: those with 'mandatory' employee voice systems and those with 'voluntarist' systems. While the former have developed binding rules and regulations regarding employee participation for employers to follow, the latter generally give managers the freedom to implement whatever employee voice policies and practices they see fit to adopt. A central focus of the discussion in this section was the impact of globalization on mandatory system countries. The example of Germany illustrated how processes of globalization in general, and the activities of multinational companies in particular, strongly challenge and to a significant extent undermine mandatory employee voice systems.

The final section of the chapter addressed the practice of employee voice in developing or industrializing countries. It was noted that while there is great diversity between these countries, in general terms addressing cultural rather than institutional influences and considerations can be seen to constitute the primary challenge for managers of multinational firms operating in such contexts. Cultural considerations were found to heavily influence employee voice practices in China, the developing country chosen to be the focus of this section. Here the ancient philosophical system of Confucianism was found to constitute an important influence on contemporary organisational life, emphasising hierarchy and status but at the same time a sense of common identity and paternalistic relationships between managers and employees. Alongside this, the pervasive structures and policies established by the Communist Party over recent decades were also noted to be highly significant. In particular, the state-owned-enterprises set up by the Chinese government were found to have greatly inhibited the exercise of employee voice in organizational decision–making due to their rigid, bureaucratic and hierarchical management structures and approaches. While combined these elements of the Chinese context make the adoption of employee voice policies and practices very challenging for multinational managers, Gamble's research from the retail sector demonstrated how it may be possible for MNCs to implement such polices in China, provided that this process is managed carefully.

Review Questions

1 What is 'employee voice', what forms does it take, and why is it of importance to managers of multinational firms?

2 What different types of employee voice system are evident around the world? What are the possible implications of these differences for decision-making in MNCs?

3 How might 'developed' and 'developing' countries differ in the nature of employee voice systems they possess, and what are the implications of this for MNCs? Give examples.

4 How are processes of globalisation impacting on national employee voice systems? Is there a tendency towards convergence or divergence of the same?

References

Barnard, C. (2000) *EC Employment Law* (2nd edition), Oxford: Oxford University Press.

Banyuls, J., Haipeter, T. and Neumann, L. (2008) 'European Works Council at General Motors Europe: bargaining efficiency in regime competition?', *Industrial Relations Journal,* 39(6): 532–47.

Behrens, M. and Jacoby, W. (2004) 'The rise of experimentalism in German collective bargaining', *British Journal of Industrial Relations,* 42(1), 95–123.

Biagi, M. (2001) 'Forms of Employee Representational Participation', in Blanpain, R. and Engels, C. (eds), *Comparative Labour Law and Industrial Relations in Industrialized Market Economies* (7th edition), The Hague: Kluwer Law International, 483–524.

Carley, M., Baradel, A. and Welz, C. (2004) *EIRO Thematic Feature: Works Councils – Workplace Representation and Participation Structures,* European Industrial Relations Observatory Online, www.eurofound.europa.eu/eiro.

Chen, X., Bishop, J. and Scott, K. (2000) 'Teamwork in China: where reality challenges theory and practice', in Li, J., Tsui, A. and Weldon, E. (eds), *Management and Organizations in the Chinese Context,* New York: St. Martin's Press, 269–82.

Colling, T., Gunnigle, P., Quintanilla, J. and Tempel, A. (2006) 'Collective Representation and Participation', in Almond, P. and Ferner, A. (eds), *American Multinationals in Europe: Managing Employment Relations Across National Borders,* Oxford: Oxford University Press, 95–118.

Cooke, F.L. (2005) *HRM, Work and Employment in China,* London: Routledge.

Dicken, P. (2007): *Global Shift: Mapping the Changing Contours of the World Economy,* (5th edition), London: Sage.

Doellgast, V. and Greer, I. (2007) 'Vertical disintegration and the disorganization of German industrial relations', *British Journal of Industrial Relations,* 45(1), 55–76.

EIRO online (2005) *New Data on Coverage of Collective Agreements and Works Councils,* European Foundation for the Improvement of Living and Working Conditions, www.eiro.eurofound.eu.int/2005/09/feature/de0509205f.html

EIRO online (2007) *Impact of Codetermination at Company Level',* European Foundation for the Improvement of Living and Working Conditions, www.eurofound.europa.eu/eiro/2007/07/articles/de0707049i.htm.

EIRO online (2008a) *Survey Examines Extent of Relocation and Outsourcing,* European Foundation for the Improvement of Living and Working Conditions, www.eurofound.europa.eu/eiro/2008/10/articles/de0810029i.htm

EIRO online (2008b) *Social Plan for Redundant Workers Agreed at Nokia Plant in Bochum*, European Foundation for the Improvement of Living and Working Conditions, www.eurofound.europa.eu/eiro/2008/05/articles/de0805019i.htm.

European Commission (2008): *Proposal for a European Parliament and Council Directive on the Establishment of a European Works Council or a Procedure in Community-Scale Undertakings and Community-Scale Groups of Undertakings for the Purposes of Informing and Consulting Employees*, Commission of the European Communities, Brussels, 2 July, COM (2008) 419 final, 2008/0141 (COD).

European Foundation (2008a) *European Works Councils in Practice: Key Research Findings. Background Paper*, Dublin: European Foundation for the Improvement of Living and Working Conditions.

European Foundation (2008b) *Impact of the Information and Consultation Directive on Industrial Relations*, Dublin: European Foundation for the Improvement of Living and Working Conditions.

Gamble, J. (2003) 'Transferring human resource practices from the United Kingdom to China: the limits and potential for convergence', *International Journal of Human Resource Management* 14(3), 369–88.

Gamble, J. (2006) 'Introducing Western-style HRM practices to China: shopfloor perceptions in a British multinational', *Journal of World Business*, 41, 328–43.

Gamble, J. and Huang, Q. (2008) 'Organizational commitment of Chinese employees in foreign-invested firms', *International Journal of Human Resource Management*, 19(5), 896–915.

Godard, J. (2003) 'Labour unions, workplace rights, and Canadian public policy', *Canadian Public Policy*, 29(4), 449–67.

Gollan, P. and Hamberger, J. (2003) 'Employer strategies and future options towards enterprise based employee representation in Australia', *New Zealand Journal of Industrial Relations*, 28(1), 45–57.

Grahl, J. and Teague, P. (2004) 'The German model in danger', *Industrial Relations Journal*, 35(6), 557–73.

Gumbrell-McCormick, R. and Hyman, R. (2006) 'Embedded collectivism? Workplace representation in France and Germany', *Industrial Relations Journal*, 37(5), 473–91.

Haipeter, T. and Lehndorff, S. (2005) 'Decentralised bargaining of working time in the German automotive industry', *Industrial Relations Journal*, 36(2), 140–56.

Hall, M. (2005) 'Assessing the information and consultation of employees regulations', *Industrial Law Journal*, 34(2), 103–26.

Hall, M. and Edwards, P. (1999) 'Reforming the statutory redundancy procedure', *Industrial Law Journal*, 28(4), 299–318.

Hassel, A. (1999) 'The erosion of the German system of industrial relations', *British Journal of Industrial Relations*, 37(3), 483–506.

Hirst, G., Budhwar, P., Cooper, B., West, M., Long, C., Chongyuan, X. and Shipton, H. (2008) 'Cross-cultural variations in climate for autonomy, stress and organizational productivity relationships: a comparison of Chinese and UK manufacturing organizations', *Journal of International Business Studies*, 39, 1343–58.

Huo, Y. and Von Glinow, M. (1995) 'On transplanting human resource practices to China: a culture-driven approach', *International Journal of Manpower*, 16(9), 3–15.

Hyman, J. and Mason, B. (1995) *Managing Employee Involvement and Participation*, London: Sage.

Ilari, S. and La Grange, A. (1999) 'Transferring ownership-specific advantages to a joint venture in China', *Asia Pacific Business Review*, 5(3/4), 119–46.

ILO (2008) *Freedom of Association in Practice: Lessons Learned*, Geneva: International Labour Organisation.

Jackson (2002) 'The management of people across cultures: valuing people differently', *Human Resource Management,* 41(4), 455–75.

Katz, H. and Wheeler, H. (2004) 'Employment Relations in the United States of America', in Bamber, G., Lansbury, R. and Wailes, N. (eds), *International and Comparative Employment Relations* (4th edition), London: Sage, 67–90.

Keller, B. (2004) 'Employment Relations in Germany', in Bamber, G., Lansbury, R. and Wailes, N. (eds), *International and Comparative Employment Relations* (4th edition), London: Sage, 211–53.

Kersley, B., Alpin, C., Forth, J., Bryson, A., Bewley, H., Dix, G. and Oxenbridge, S. (2006) *Inside the Workplace: Findings from the 2004 Workplace Employment Relations Survey,* London: Routledge.

Kessler, I., Undy, R. and Heron, P. (2004) 'Employee perspectives on communication and consultation: findings from a cross-national survey', *International Journal of Human Resource Management,* 15(3), 512–32.

Lansbury, R. and Wailes, N. (2004) 'Employment relations in Australia', in Bamber, G., Lansbury, R. and Wailes, N. (eds), *International and Comparative Employment Relations* (4th edition), London: Sage, 119–45.

Lewis, P. (2002) 'New China – old ways? A case study of the prospects for implementing human resource management practices in a Chinese state-owned enterprise', *Employee Relations,* 25(1), 42–60.

Lewis, P., Thornhill, A. and Saunders, M. (2003) *Employee Relations: Understanding the Employment Relationship,* Harlow: Pearson Education.

Looise, J. and Drucker, M. (2002) 'Employee participation in multinational enterprises: the effects of globalisation on Dutch works councils', *Employee Relations,* 24(1/2), 29–52.

Marchington, M. and Wilkinson, A. (2005) 'Participation and Involvement', in Bach, S. (ed.), *Managing Human Resources: Personnel Management in Transition* (4th edition), Oxford: Blackwell.

Muller, M. (1998) 'Human resource and industrial relations practices of UK and US multinationals in Germany', *International Journal of Human Resource Management,* 9(4), 732–49.

Nichols, T. and Zhao, W. (2010) 'Disaffection with trade unions in China: some evidence from SOEs in the auto industry', *Industrial Relations Journal,* 41(1), 19–33.

Page, R. (2006) 'Co-determination in Germany – A Beginner's Guide', Arbeitspapier No. 33, Revised edition, Düsseldorf: Hans-Böckler-Stiftung, March.

Poole, M., Lansbury, R. and Wailes, N. (2001) 'A comparative analysis of developments in industrial democracy', *Industrial Relations,* 40(3), 490–525.

Raess, D. and Burgoon, B. (2006) 'The dogs that sometimes bark: globalization and works council bargaining in Germany', *European Journal of Industrial Relations,* 12(3), 287–309.

Rasmussen, E. and Lind, J. (2003) 'Productive employment relationships', *New Zealand Journal of Industrial Relations,* 28(2), 158–69.

Roche, W.K. and Geary, J. F. (2000) '?"Collaborative production" and the Irish boom: work organisation, partnership and direct involvement in Irish workplaces', *The Economic and Social Review,* 31(1), 1–36.

Rollinson, D. and Dundon, T. (2007) *Understanding Employment Relations,* Maidenhead: McGraw-Hill.

Rose, E. (2008) *Employment Relations* (3rd edition), Harlow: Pearson Education.

Royle, T. (2002) 'Just vote no! Union-busting in the European fast-food industry: the case of McDonald's', *Industrial Relations Journal,* 33(3), 262–78

Salamon, M. (2000) *Industrial Relations: Theory and Practice* (4th edition), Harlow: FT Prentice Hall/Pearson Education.

Schmitt, M. (2003) 'Deregulation of the German industrial relations system via foreign direct investment: are the subsidiaries of Anglo-Saxon MNCS a threat for the institutions of industrial democracy in Germany?', *Economic and industrial Democracy,* 24(3), 349–78.

Seifert, H. and Massa-Wirth, H. (2005) 'Pacts for employment and competitiveness in Germany', *Industrial Relations Journal,* 36(3), 217–40.

Slomp, H. (1995) 'National variations in worker participation', pp. 291–317 in Harzing, A.-W. and van Ruysseveldt, J. (eds) *International Human Resource Management: an integrated approach* (1st edition), London: Sage.

Taylor, B., Kai, C. and Qi, L. (2003) *Industrial Relations in China,* Cheltenham: Edward Elgar.

Wang, J., Wang, G., Ruona, W.E., and Rojewski, J.W. (2005) 'Confucian values and the implications for international HRD', *Human Resource Development International,* (8)3, 311–26.

Wang, Y. (2008) 'Emotional bonds with supervisors and co-workers: relationship to organizational commitment in China's foreign-invested companies', *International Journal of Human Resource Management,* 19(5), 916–31.

Warner, M. (2008) 'Reassessing human resource management "with Chinese characteristics": an overview', *International Journal of Human Resource Management,* 19(5), 771–801.

Warner, M. (2009) '"Making sense" of HRM in China: setting the scene', *International Journal of Human Resource Management,* 20(11), 2169–93.

Weiss, M. (2004) 'The Future of Workers' Participation in the EU', in Barnard, C. and Deakin, S. (eds), *The Future of Labour Law,* Oxford: Hart, 229–52.

Wever, K. (1994) 'Learning from works councils: five unspectacular cases from Germany', *Industrial Relations,* 33(4), 467–81.

Whittall, M. (2005) 'Modell Deutschland under pressure: the growing tensions between works councils and trade unions', *Economic and Industrial Democracy,* 26(4): 569–92.

Chapter 13

International corporate social responsibility and HRM

Sanjiv Sachdev

Key aims

The aims of this chapter are to:

- understand the concept of CSR and its application at the international level;
- appreciate the role of HR in developing CSR programmes;
- become familiar with the consequences of CSR, particularly the limitations to actual practice living up its formal aims;
- understand the role of national context in shaping CSR.

Introduction

Issues of corporate social responsibility (CSR) often have a high public profile, regularly featuring in the news, sometimes involving some of the world's leading firms. Setting up CSR codes is, of course, an attempt by senior managers to alter the public image of companies that have encountered bad publicity. Thus, Shell has faced allegations of (long-standing) human rights abuses and environmental abuses (Macalister 2009; Pilkington 2009). The food retailer Tesco, which in 2009 recorded record profits of £3 billion, has been criticized for not improving the pay and working conditions of the South Africa fruit pickers who work for its suppliers (Smithers and Smith 2009; House of Commons 2007). The fashion chain Primark axed three longstanding suppliers in India for using child labour (Finch 2008). The fashion retailer Banana Republic (owned by the retailer Gap) faced allegations that workers in India who made its clothes were being forced to work more than 70 hours a week for as little as 15p an hour (Smithers and Ramesh 2008) and of workers not being paid for overtime (Ramesh 2008). In 2007, Gap itself withdrew a line of children's wear following allegations of forced child labour at Indian subcontractors; the second largest US oil company, Chevron, agreed to a $30 million settlement after acknowledging bribes were paid for oil it obtained (Morris 2007). In 2006 Nike sacked its main manufacturer of hand-stitched balls amid concerns that they may have been stitched by children (Clark 2006). All are vivid instances of the issues that businesses can face in an international climate where there is a widespread view that the responsibilities of businesses extend beyond the maximization of profits within the confines of adherence to the law.

Since the mid-1990s, CSR has rapidly risen up the hierarchy of issues that businesses seek to address. In the wake of the Enron crisis, corporate behaviour and governance was subject to unprecedented attention. In 2001 the UK stock exchange, following the example of Dow Jones sustainability index in 1999, launched the 'ethical index' FTSE4Good (similar indices operate in Japan, France, Italy and Belgium). The UK has appointed a minister for corporate responsibility and established a website giving examples of good practice and seeking views on the future direction of policy on corporate behaviour. Company reports and corporate websites routinely include sections on CSR, detailing the organization's work on issues such as the environment, human rights and fair trade.

More recently, amid evidence of excessive risk-taking, inadequate regulation and disproportionate bonus and pension payments awarded to leading executives by banks such as Citigroup, Merrill Lynch, Goldman Sachs and the Royal Bank of Scotland and insurance companies such as AIG, have attracted widespread criticism and calls for greater transparency (one US congressman declared that AIG had come to stand for 'Arrogance, Incompetence and Greed') (Lanchester 2009; Farrell 2009). Concern over corporate behaviour is particularly heightened in times when there are concerns about the future of capitalism and the legitimacy of markets are weakened (Wolf 2009) and when the conduct of leading financial corporations appears to leave much to be desired. Conversely, pressures to behave responsibly may however weaken as shoppers look for cheaper goods and as investors focus on short-term returns.

Running parallel to the growth of CSR has been the related growth of Socially Responsible Investment (SRI). In Europe it rose to a high of € 2,600 billion at the end of 2007 – more than twice the level of two years earlier (Brewster 2009). While there is no robust evidence that the performance of SRI funds is better than non-SRI funds, the growth of SRI funds is expected to rise further (Brewster 2009; Grene 2008). Since July 2000, British pension fund trustees have been required to report on whether they take account of social and environmental matters.[1] In 2001, Germany introduced a similar measure. French law now requires companies to take into account, in their annual reports, the 'social and environmental consequences' of their activity. Belgium has a national 'kitemarking' scheme so that consumers can identify companies that follow CSR principles. The Netherlands, Denmark and Norway have long-standing environmental disclosure requirements. One dollar in every eight invested in the US is invested in ethical funds (Heertz 2001). In 2004, the United Nations issued the draft 'UN Norms' which bring together a range of international human rights instruments in a single code and envisages ways of enforcing them (Maitland 2004). By 2007, the 'Fair-trade' brand globally accounted for € 2.3 billion – a 48 per cent increase on the previous year (www.fairtrade.org). Evidently, there is an international trend towards companies and public authorities becoming more interested in 'ethical' and 'socially responsible' corporate behaviour.

---

[1] Although the impact of this measure would appear to be very limited (see Cicutti 2002).

Three-quarters of the UK companies surveyed in 2000 had a code of conduct, while 62 per cent of respondents from the FTSE 350 or equivalent sized unquoted companies claimed that ethical policies were a priority; in contrast, in 1993 barely a third of leading companies either had or were developing a code (Carmichael 2001). Social responsibility appears to have become a generally accepted principle that applies to a growing variety of business partnerships involving multinational and local enterprises in both developed and developing economies. To some extent, therefore, CSR may be seen as one sign of the globalization of economic activity, resulting in converging approaches by firms across borders. However, as we will see, the extent and nature of CSR varies by country, and even in MNCs the continuing embeddedness in their original national bases shapes their approach.

Conceptual confusion

CSR is 'poorly defined' (Murray 2002). It is said to involve 'identifying every aspect of society on which a company has an impact, through its non-core as well as core activities' (Joseph 2001). The range of issues embraced by the term can be extensive; Table 13.1 outlines some of them.

Distinctions have been developed between fair trade and ethical trade; the former focuses on the trading terms for producers, while the emphasis of ethical trade is on the conditions of production; fair trade seeks to change unequal relationships into partnerships which benefit producers; ethical trade seeks to improve the welfare of producers in the workplace (and is thus more likely to be used for multinational brands and retailers and for complex production processes) (Smith and Barrientos 2005).

CSR is far from being uncontroversial. Advocates of CSR argue that it has many benefits for employers. Some advocates emphasize the defensive aspects of CSR in protecting reputation, profits and share price. Others adopt a more ambitious proactive stance, seeing a CSR role in redefining the corporate mission, protecting reputation, offering a distinctive positioning, building credibility and trust with employees and customers, assisting recruitment and retention and fostering dialogue with interest groups (CIPD

Table 13.1 **Issues covered by CSR**

Environmental	Concern for human rights
Fair trade	Philanthropic history
Organic produce	Co-operative principles
Not tested on animals	Support for education
Community involvement	Participates in local business initiatives
Cause related marketing	Supports national business initiatives
Charitable giving	Commitment to reporting
Religious foundation	Employee schemes
Support for social causes	Refusal to trade in certain markets

Source: Howard and Willmott (2001)

2002: 8). Some commentators see it as a corporate fig leaf to enhance reputations (Klein 2000; Christian Aid 2004), others as a wasteful distraction from the proper activities of firms (Henderson 2001; Wolf 2002); as Milton Friedman (1973) famously stated – 'there is one and only one social responsibility of business – to use its resources and engage in activities designed to increase its profits so long as it stays within the rules of the game...'.[2] Most businesses see CSR/'ethics' as a niche issue, but in some cases, for example the Co-op bank and retailer, ethical issues have become mainstream by being applied to existing product lines rather than niche alternatives (Buckley 2002). Some businesses appear to be hostile to the concept altogether; the former chairman and chief executive of ExxonMobil, Lee Raymond, declared the 'we don't invest to make social statements at the expense of shareholder return' (cited in McNulty 2003). Henderson (2001) contends that 'It is probably in relation to terms and conditions of employment, and "human resources" policies generally, that CSR, and the ways of thinking that are linked to it, have the greatest potential for doing harm.'

HRM and CSR

Labour issues are frequently at the heart of 'ethical' disputes and these often fall under the remit of HR departments. Issues of discrimination, working conditions, health and safety, harassment, pay, child labour, forced labour, 'whistleblowing', freedom of association and collective bargaining – all employment relations matters – are prominent in debates around CSR. Thus Gap's 2005/6 CSR report (www.gapinc.com/public/documents/CSR_Report_05_06.pdf) devotes considerable attention to employee rights, working conditions, health and safety, diversity and wages and benefits. Since January 2007, the FTSE4Good index requires companies exposed to supply chain risks to demonstrate polices on labour standards such as non-discrimination, forced labour, child labour and worker representation. The International Labour Organization (ILO) is notable in these debates and international trade union confederations are active within them (Ann Elliot and Freeman 2003). HRM departments are often either heavily involved or have lead responsibility in CSR issues; one survey found the HR department was second only to the legal department in devising a company code of ethics (cited in CIPD 2002). Gap employs more than 80 people around the world whose sole responsibility was to ensure factories compliance with ethical sourcing criteria and Nike has quadrupled the number of employees dealing with labour practices (Murray 2002). Moreover, the employment practices of some leading transnationals, such as Coca Cola (Thomas 2008; War on Want 2006), Nike (Clark 2006; Murray 2005; Skapinker 2002; McCawley 2000; Klein 2000) and McDonald's (Vidal 1997; Royle 2000; Schlosser 2001; Maitland 2002a) have come under close scrutiny. Some commentators have emphasized the ethical dimension of HR issues such as recruitment (Spence 2000), flexible working (Stanworth 2000) and human resource development (Woodall and Douglas 2000). Others studies have included redeployment and redundancy strategies as CSR issues (Baxter 2009; Segal *et al.* 2003).

---

[2] According to Friedman, those who advocated the 'social responsibilities of business' were preaching 'pure and unadulterated socialism'.

It is also argued that a poor public reputation of companies impairs the recruitment and retention of staff. According to Heertz (2001), directors of both BP and Shell reported being overwhelmed by the large number of concerned e-mails they received from staff following adverse TV and press coverage of their operations in Colombia and Nigeria. This echoes the experience of Nike staff who, in the wake of various scandals surrounding the firm, according to a Nike official, 'were going to barbecues and people would say: "How can you work for Nike?"...I don't know if we were losing employees but it sure as hell didn't help in attracting them' (Skapinker 2002). The CIPD survey of graduate workplace attitudes in 2001 found that for two-thirds of graduates a company's ethical reputation would influence their decision whether or not to apply for a specific job.

Some companies use HR practices to encourage responsible behaviour by their staff. The bank Standard Chartered uses a social networking site called 'Greenstorming' to promote staff engagement in environmental activities; staff propose ideas and ask other staff to join their campaigns (Murray 2009b). Pay and appraisal systems can also be affected; thus the chief executive of Statoil, Norway's largest oil company, has his bonus payments partly dependent on the outcomes of indicators on health and safety, the environment and employee satisfaction (Maitland 2003). The human resources department of Adidas has made performance in human rights a factor in calculating annual bonuses for country managers (Crawford 2000). As we see below, HR considerations are also central to most codes of conduct. Labour regulation in international trade is also important. It is certainly claimed that the good reputation of firms attracts 'top-class graduates', improves retention rates and morale and increases productivity (see, for example, PricewaterhouseCoopers in Save the Children 2000: 34). It has been argued that 'if employees don't see the point of CSR initiatives, or understand the message, initiatives are unlikely to be effective' (CIPD 2002: 7). Moreover, the CIPD (the professional body representing HR in the UK) sees CSR as being intrinsic to being a 'good' employer, the skills of HR being key to communicating and engaging employees for an effective implementation of a broader CSR strategy.

CASE STUDY

Cadbury's – CSR in action

A company, founded by Quakers who wanted to provide drinking chocolate and tea as a substitute for alcohol, continues to have an ethical strand running through its activities. It has also had its share of controversy – in 1999 and 2000 the company was accused of buying cocoa produced by slaves in Africa. Partly in response to these accusations, in 2001 the company created a formal board for corporate social responsibility; by 2003

the company's strategic plan included corporate social responsibility among its five goals. Business unit leaders report to the chief executive on a monthly basis as to their progress in attaining CSR programmes. This includes actions such as the sponsorship of an orphanage in Mexico and an after school programme in Brazil.

Ethical sourcing of raw materials such as cocoa, sugar and nuts has involved managers throughout

the supply chain. Non-governmental organizations, such as the Fairtrade Foundation, play a
role in its pursuit of sustainable cocoa sourcing in
Ghana, India, Indonesia and the Caribbean
through the Cadbury Cocoa partnership. In
March 2009, Cadbury's announced a deal with
the Fairtrade Foundation estimated to be worth
some £200 million to certify its Cadbury Dairy
Milk chocolate bars. It is also seeking to reduce by
almost 20 per cent its consumption of water in
regions where water is scarce. Cadbury's endorsement of Fairtrade may in part also arise from
seeking to secure long term supplies; the former
buys nearly two-thirds of its cocoa from Ghana;
Fairtrade farms appear to be much more productive and better run than non-Fairtrade ones.

Sources: Murray (2009b); Skapinker (2009); Blowfield and
Murray (2008)

Question

In firms like Cadbury's how can those in the HR
function use CSR initiatives to their advantage?

The rise of corporate social responsibility

Ethical pressures on businesses to behave responsibly are far from new (Blowfield and
Murray 2008). The specific issues have shifted, but issues such as the protection of
workers, environmentalism and consumer protection are long standing. A striking
example is that of slavery; few considered this lucrative trade immoral until the second
half of the eighteenth century. Yet, within 30 years the practice in the UK was out-
lawed. Quaker-led campaigns, beginning with the first important anti-slavery petitions
to parliament in 1783, eventually led to the abolition of the slave trade with the
colonies (1807) and the end of slavery in the Caribbean plantations (1834). The efforts
of abolitionists to encourage the purchase of sugar from non-slave owning countries
strongly mirror the activities of organisations like the Fairtrade Foundation today. In
the nineteenth century industrialists like Hershey, Cadbury, Fry and Rowntree (Quakers
all) sought to humanize capitalism, creating better living conditions for workers. Robert
Owen had similarly attempted to use enlightened methods at his textile mill in New
Lanark (Thompson 1968). Reformers like John Ruskin (1862) made a clear distinction
'between well-gotten and ill-gotten wealth'.

Towards the end of the twentieth century, with the end of the cold war a profound
shift towards an aggressive capitalism was evident, unrestrained by an available alternative (Marquand 1997). This witnessed the faltering of traditional social democracy
(Sassoon 1996), the retreat of the state (Kuttner 1997; Hutton 1995) and a new ascen-
dancy of corporate power (Korten 1995; Luttwak 1996; Lloyd 2000; Klein 2000;
Monbiot 2000). Capitalism was both resurgent and triumphant. A character in Don
DeLillo's *Underworld* captures this well:

> Many things that were anchored to the balance of power and the balance of terror
> seem to be undone, unstuck. Things have no limits now. Money has no
> limits…Money is undone.(1998: 76)

However, it was this that led to particular concerns as to the nature of capitalism
increasing. The triumph of capitalism and the creation of a civilization in which business values 'are seen as central has paradoxically generated a public which demands
that business behaves better' (Hutton 2000:13). It is argued that the new centrality of

business in contemporary life means that business must acknowledge that it too has citizenship responsibilities; its ideological 'victory' means that paradoxically it has greater pressures upon it to act with integrity and accountability, paying attention to wider social purposes. As Sen argues (1996), 'critiques of capitalism have to a considerable extent, become more widely shared after their dissociation from the particular institutional remedies traditionally championed by socialists'. Concerns as to the conduct of capitalism grew as its role became more prominent, intensifying in the wake of the global recession and evidence of corporate financial misconduct (Lanchester 2009).

Several concerns were evident; the particular model of globalization that was being promoted, the greater inequality that arose from it and the role and (lack of) accountability of corporate power as well as the power and employment practices of transnationals. As the state began to withdraw from key economic activities, business was asked to fill the gaps, playing a substantially greater role in providing products and services that were once the domain of the state. The spread of globalization was said to have altered the position of multinationals in a fundamental manner. It is argued that it has weakened the political institutions of the nation state and elevated the role of multinationals (Korten 1995). Accordingly, there has been a concentration of economic power; the 12 most important global industries, such as textiles and the media, are each more than 40 per cent controlled by five or fewer corporations (cited in McIntosh *et al.* 1998; see also Fairtrade Foundation 2000, 2002).

Concerns about these developments lie behind the emergence of the so-called 'anti-globalization movement'. The anti-globalization movement coheres around a shared disillusionment rather than specific concerns or proffered solutions. It is in Lloyd's phrase, 'the critique without the antidote' (2001: 25). Some within its ranks call for globalisation to be reshaped, others for it to be resisted. More radical voices still question the entire basis of economic organization, predicting environmental disaster unless a profound shift in direction takes place; 'the profitable exchange of goods within the ship is a less urgent matter than how to keep the whole ship above water' (Midgley 2001: 97; Levett 2001). The internet, part of the communications revolution aspect of globalization, has significantly amplified the speed and potential power of consumer protests. For example, in 2001 a student, Jonah Perretti, at the Massachusetts Institute

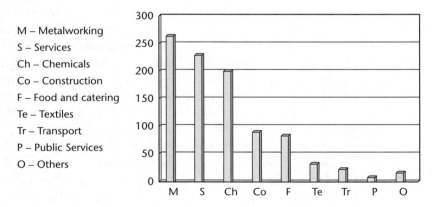

Figure 13.1 MNCs with European Works Councils by sector

of Technology responded to Nike's offer to personalize customers' trainers by asking for the word 'sweatshop' to be printed on the side. When Nike refused, Mr Perritti e-mailed the company saying: 'Thank you for the time and energy you have spent on my request. Could you please send me a color snapshot of the 10 year old Vietnamese girl who makes my shoes?' His e-mail exchange with Nike was flashed around the world. CSR is the means by which some businesses engage and connect with these movements and concerns.

To some extent the incentives that MNCs have to develop a CSR code are shaped by the incentives the financial benefits that accrue. Moreover, the recession has strengthened the case for resource efficiency where the savings can be substantial – thus, Coca Cola's goal of achieving a 20 per cent improvement in water efficiency by 2012 would, if met, allow the company to avoid $150 million in water acquisition, treatment and discharge costs between 2008 and 2011 (Murray 2009a). As well as cutting carbon emissions, greener forms of service delivery can also reduce costs; from cutting down on the wasteful use of energy to economizing with other materials. Thus, Kimberly-Clark found it could cut costs by redesigning its toilet tissue, Andrex; the company put 50 per cent more sheets on each roll and trimmed the packaging from its packs, saving about 83,000 kg of plastic a year and cutting transport costs (Harvey 2008). At the bank HSBC, energy efficiency measures across its branch and office network saved $7.3 million in 2008 (Murray 2009a). Similarly, between 2005 and 2008, the US retailer Wal-Mart cut its fuel consumption by 25 per cent, which it estimates generated savings of more than $40 m a year (Murray 2009).

However, the incentives that firms have to develop CSR codes are variable, shaped in part by the degree to which they rely on a brand. For many multinationals, their key asset is the reputation of their brands; when Ford bought Jaguar, it was estimated that the physical assets were only 16 per cent of the value (Bunting 2001). Accordingly, the *Economist* (2001a) argues, 'The more companies promote the value of their brands, the more they will need to be seen as ethically robust and environmentally pure'. For example, when Heineken pulled out of Burma in 1996, the CEO said: 'Public opinion and issues surrounding this market have changed to a degree that could have an adverse effect on our brand and corporate reputation' (cited in Klein 2000: 424). Another example concerned the 'toycott' organized against Toys 'R' Us in the 1990s to protest against the use of child labour in China – the company subsequently endorsed a code prohibiting the use of child or slave labour by its contractors (Cavanaugh 1997).

The limits to this form of pressure upon corporations are well known. As Klein notes 'the most significant limitation of brand-based campaigns (is that) they can be powerless in the face of corporations that opt out of the branding game' (Klein 2000: 424). This has been one factor in the growth of non-governmental actors (NGOs), some of whom are also global actors (notably the International Red Cross, Greenpeace International and Amnesty International) and who can apply pressure on business to make policy socially and environmentally responsible. The growth in the size, number and influence of NGOs is striking. Parkin (2001) states that NGOs worldwide have a GDP of $1.1 trillion. NGOs themselves are characterized by high levels of diversity in size, aims and nature (the term embraces the National Rifle Association as well as Save the Children).

It is argued that NGOs have emerged as a result 'of the frustrations brought about by existing institutional structures' (McIntosh *et al.* 2003: 69). Thus, they can persuade transnational corporations to become better global citizens – mobilizing consumers to act as a potentially powerful check upon the actions of transnationals 'shaping the rules and norms of business behaviour' (McIntosh *et al.* 2003). A key role that some NGOs are playing is in the development, administration and promotion of standards, codes and certifications. NGOs have played a major role in development and monitoring of many codes including the influential SA8000, the Apparel Industry Partnership and the Fair Labor Association in the US and the Fairtrade Foundation and Ethical Trading Initiative in Britain (House of Commons 2007; Tsogas 2001). Similarly, the code on child labour drafted by Unicef, the ILO and an association of Pakistani manufacturers was signed by all the major soccer-ball manufacturers; it provides for outside monitoring as well as education and rehabilitation for the child labourers (Klein 2000: 432). NGOs like Amnesty International have also been involved in the training of senior staff in multinationals (Finch 2002). Partnerships between NGOs and business have seen the New York based Rainforest Alliance (RA) provide CSR information for and on Chiquita Brands International, as well as verifying whether the latter's 115 farms meet RA standards (Silver 2004); interestingly, the cost of bringing the farms up to RA standards ($20 m) has already been more than repaid by cost savings on lower pesticide spending, recycling and a lower investment risk rating. It is this issue of the auditing of CSR codes that is the subject of the next section.

Codes of conduct in MNCs: management initiatives, the role of audit and negotiated agreements

There is a range of sources of evidence concerning the prevalence of CSR codes in MNCs. For instance, survey evidence of multinationals in Britain revealed that 72 per cent of the UK operations of MNCs are covered by a CSR code. The vast majority of these codes (86 per cent) were part of a wider international code within the multinational (Edwards *et al.* 2007). Two of the key debates concerning the issue of CSR are the content of the codes of conduct and the issue of how such codes are monitored and enforced. Often developed in response to particular crises in supply chains across countries, codes of conduct are written statements of principle or policy intended to serve as the expression of a commitment to particular business conduct. Most of the codes which have propelled the topic to the spotlight are operational codes; that is, codes that enterprises apply to themselves and their business partners to set out commitments to a specific conduct (Hepple 2005; Diller 1999). They can be distinguished from model codes that are generic statements issued by a body such as an international agency or NGO that forms the basis for firms to devise their own codes.

There are good grounds for expecting these aspects of codes in MNCs to be shaped by the national origins of the MNCs. A number of studies of CSR have pointed to the ways in which national institutions shape their character (e.g. Chapple and Moon 2005; Matten and Moon 2008). One distinction we might use is that introduced at the beginning of the book between companies from liberal market economies (LMEs) and coordinated market economies (CMEs). It will be recalled that firms in LMEs are those where the primary pressure on management is to deliver enhanced returns to share-holders, while firms in CMEs balance this concern with greater emphasis on the rights of other stakeholders, particularly employees. Edwards *et al.*'s (2007) analysis of CSR in MNCs demonstrated that these codes were much more prevalent in companies from LMEs, particularly those from the US, than in those from CMEs. This finding was explained in terms of managers in US and UK MNCs being keen to use CSR as a way of countering the perception that they were prepared to exploit their workers or the envi-ronment in order to deliver returns to shareholders; in contrast, MNCs originating in CME countries, particularly those in mainland Europe, already possessed institution-alised ways of expressing their social responsibility through, for example, having employee representatives on the boards of the company.

Turning to the issue of the content of the codes, it is clear that this varies markedly across firms. An ILO review of 215 codes, focusing on the coverage of labour practices, found 'significant discrepancies' in content and operation between them. Occupational health and safety was the most cited labour issue appearing in three-quarters of the codes reviewed. Discrimination in hiring/terms and conditions was addressed in two thirds of the codes. The elimination of child labour (including refusing to use it or deal with companies that used it) appeared in 45 per cent of the codes, and the level of wages appeared in 40 per cent. Refusal to use forced labour appeared in only 25 per cent of the codes and the principles of freedom of association and collective bargaining appeared in only 15 per cent (Diller 1999).

According to Diller, 'the content of codes often appears to be largely decided in non-transparent and non participatory processes, which may be conducted within executive boardrooms or through ad hoc negotiations between parties with varying degrees of access to information and bargaining power'. Furthermore, most 'codes and labelling programmes tend to reflect their drafters' own definitions of what the desired improve-ments in labour practices should be' (Diller 1999). Some codes, for example those of Caterpillar and Sara Lee Knit Products, favour the elimination of trade union activities.[3] In Britain the clothing retailer C&A left the ETI, 'finding the commitment to freedom of association collective bargaining in contradiction with its own antiunion practice' (Tsogas 2001: 72). Few codes reiterated all internationally recognised grounds of dis-crimination and child labour.[4] These instances of American and British firms may also reflect national influences in the sense that we might expect an opposition to organ-ized labour to be a feature of firms from LMEs compared with their CME counterparts. Accordingly, Bondy *et al.*'s (2004) study of CSR in different countries showed how one

---

[3] The code for Sara Lee Knit Products reads: 'The company believes in a union-free environment except where the laws and cultures require [it] to do otherwise...[and] believes that employees themselves are best able to voice their concerns directly to management'.

[4] ILO convention 138, ratified by 89 countries, sets the minimum age for work in developed countries at 15 for full time employment and 13 for light work and 14 and 12 as optional limits for some developing countries. It is one of the ILO's core conventions and widely used in codes of conduct to define child labour (Save the Children 2000).

source of variation in the content of CSR codes is the corporate governance requirements of the country of origin.

As noted above, the content, distribution and purpose of these codes have been widely criticised. Hepple (2005) found the choice of labour issues highly selective and that
codes were made unilaterally without the involvement of trade unions, implementation
and monitoring were poor and that sanctions for non-compliance were weak. The monitoring of codes is by large accounting firms has been particularly controversial, especially after the Enron crisis, because of perceived conflict of interest problems; similar concerns are expressed on internal monitoring (Hepple 2005; Klein 2002; Kolk and van
Tulder 2002; Tsogas 2001). Thus, in their examination of the sporting goods industry,
van Tulder and Kolk (2001) found under-developed compliance mechanisms among
some major firms and the sanctions for non-observance of codes were generally not
made clear. Research (cited in Doane, 2002) found that while 79 of the FTSE 100 published some social information on their website, only 16 companies used any qualitative
performance data to support their policy assertions. Few reports – the accountants
KPMG (in 1999) estimated that one in six – were checked by third parties for accuracy
and 'where they are it tends to be the data collection processes rather than the end
results that are audited' (Joseph 2002). According to Doane (2002), 'while some companies utilize the accounting sector to provide a statement of verification for the contents
of a report, these loose statements do little to provide assurance that the report is accurate. For example, it is common practice for a verification statement to ignore what has
not been included in the report'.[5] Moreover, a survey by PricewaterhouseCoopers found
that nearly 30 per cent of chief executives tend to agree that CSR is mainly a public relations issue (cited in CIPD 2002). Doane (2002) argues: 'the market does not provide
sufficient incentives for companies to report no their social and environmental impacts
on a voluntary basis' and calls, with others (for example, Henriques 1999; Christian
Aid 2004) for a shift to a more mandatory basis to surmount the difficulties currently
experienced.

There are some sources of mandatory codes through the legislative provisions that
already exist. The United States has statutory provisions banning the import of goods
manufactured by prison labour and by indentured (bonded) child labour (Hepple 2005).
The US also has procedures under its amended Section 301 of the 1974 Trade Act
whereby it can impose import restrictions on countries failing to respect internationally
recognised workers rights (although its deployment has been used to further foreign
policy aims, as against Nicaragua, rather than enhance labour reforms). The governments of EU countries have a power of whole or partial withdrawal of trading, exercis-
able only in relation to forced or prison labour, and currently deployed against
Myanmar (Burma) (Hepple 2005). There are also some instances of NGOs providing
protocols that, while evidently not mandatory, do establish some pressure on companies to comply. For instance, the SA8000 code is an effort to introduce some consistency

---

[5] This in turn raises the wider issue of whether interested parties have a formal method of redress
if they believe the published information to be a misrepresentation.

and rigour into codes. This was drafted by the Council on Economic Priorities Accreditation Agency (CEPAA), a consumer watchdog in New York, along with several large corporations, NGOs and trade unions. The CEPAA code would inspect factories for adherence to a set of standards covering key issues such as health, safety, overtime, child labour, and so on. Under this model, brand-name multinationals like Avon and Toys 'R' Us, rather than trying to enforce their own codes around the world (these include core ILO codes and 'a living wage'), simply place their orders with factories that have been found in compliance with the code.

Then, the factories are monitored by a private auditing company, which certifies factories that meet the code as 'SA8000' (SA stands for social accountability) (Tsogas 2001). Van Tulder and Kolk's (2001) study of sportswear manufacturers showed that such 'model' codes were influential on the development of corporate codes in US firms, particularly in the form of the 'Apparel Industry Partnership'; in contrast, German firms were keener to arrive at a code in concert with their competitors rather than a company-specific code.

The sceptical nature of much of the discussion of CSR has led to considerable attention being placed on those codes that are negotiated with employee representatives. These are of particular interest because the monitoring body is internal to the firm; trade union representatives and works councillors have inside knowledge of how the firm actually operates and also have some power to protest and conceivably take industrial action if the agreements are not honoured. Such agreements at the international level in MNCs are in their infancy, but are perhaps not as rare as we might have anticipated. Edwards *et al.*'s (2007) study shows that of those MNCs that have a CSR code, just under one in five is negotiated with an international union federation or European Works Council. This, too, appears to be shaped by the national origins of the firm; MNCs from Germany and the Nordic area are significantly more likely to have a negotiated CSR code than are those from the US, a finding that reflects the tradition of co-management in Northern Europe and hostility to organized labour in the US.

CASE STUDY

Nike

Perhaps more than any other multinational, Nike has been the subject of enormous controversy surrounding its employment practices. Many observers have contrasted the firm's payments to stars who endorse the products with the wages earned by those engaged in the production of them. For example, the basketball player Michael Jordan earned more ($20 million) in 1992 for endorsing Nike's running shoes than Nike's entire 30,000 strong Indonesian workforce for making them (Ross 1997). The company has also been severely embarrassed by the publication of images such as a young Pakistani boy sewing together a Nike football and of reports claiming that workers in one of its contracted factories in Vietnam were being exposed to toxic fumes at up to 177 times the Vietnamese legal limit (Wazir 2001).

Dogged by allegations of this sort, in May 1998 Nike's CEO, Phillip Knight, told an audience that 'Nike has become synonymous with slave wages, forced overtime and arbitrary abuse' (cited in McCawley 2000). Knight committed the company to act in a responsible manner and made a number of specific promises concerning the treatment of workers in the subcontracted production operations, mainly in south-east Asia. These commitments became part of the firm's code of conduct which states that:

Nike is committed to being a responsible corporate citizen. We work strenuously to improve the lives and working conditions of all workers. We don't own these factories, but we take pride in our relationships with them.

Among the specific promises that it makes are that:

- The minimum age would be raised to 18 for workers in Nike shoe factories and 16 those in for clothing factories.
- The contractor provides each employee at least the minimum wage, or the prevailing industry wage, whichever is higher, and does not deduct from employee pay for disciplinary infractions.
- The contractor complies with legally mandated work hours, provides for one day off in seven and requires no more than 60 hours of work per week on a regularly scheduled basis (or complies with local limits if they are lower).
- Nike would include non-governmental organisations in factory monitoring, and the company would make inspection results public.

Moreover, some commentators contend that Nike's code of conduct ensures that workers are not exploited, especially when one considers that many of those employed in 'sweatshops' have left even harder, lower-paying jobs in agriculture to move to garment factories. This argument is often used to make the case against boycotts of Nike and other MNCs; it is argued that such boycotts will only force the employees into less favourable forms of work, prostitution or poverty. The defenders of Nike also make the point that a consumer can have no idea about the conditions in the production of unbranded goods and thus the brand is a safeguard that can be used to check the company's actions. Others are less convinced of the impact of the firm's code of conduct in particular or the benefits it brings to local communities in general. For instance, a report entitled *Still Waiting For Nike To Do It*, published by the San Francisco-based Global Exchange, argues that the code of conduct has been of 'little benefit to Nike workers' or 'have helped only a tiny minority, or else have no relevance to Nike factories at all' (quoted in Wazir 2001). The study also indicates that in many Nike factories the employees are still being coerced into working up to 70 hours per week and are being humiliated in front of other workers or threatened with dismissal if they refuse to do the extra work. 'During the last three years, Nike has continued to treat the sweatshop issue as a public relations inconvenience rather than as a serious human rights matter', said Leila Salazar, corporate accountability director for Global Exchange (Wazir 2001).

In 2005, Nike published its entire list of contract manufacturers to diffuse criticism (Skapiner 2005) and to be relatively open and transparent to its critics. It argues that it sees corporate responsibility as a way of improving its performance rather than just protecting its reputation. Nike provides a vivid example of where 'an activists campaign that attracts public support can do huge damage to a company' (Skapinker 2005).

Question

What is the potential for the HR function in organizations like Nike to play a part in the company's desire to be seen as a good corporate citizen?

Conclusions

CSR is a nascent, evolving, disputed but influential concept. Although a definitive definition remains elusive, a common element is an awareness that businesses operate in a wider community and that its future interests are bound up with that community. It is also a concept that has rapidly acquired a high public profile, partly in the wake of trends such as globalization, greater corporate power (and the issues this raises) and concern about its misuse. In a wider climate of corporate distrust, CSR is a useful tool in engaging with the concerns of employees, customers and interest groups. This is especially important for 'brands' whose reputation can be tarnished by consumer boycotts or NGO campaigns. HRM plays a key, sometimes central, role in issues raised by CSR, as many CSR issues having a strong employment relations aspect. Labour issues are important to most codes of conduct. HRM skills can also be crucial to the implementation of CSR strategies, and thus to wider corporate legitimacy and accountability.

The actual practice of CSR is distinctly uneven. Criticisms of 'corporate gloss' or public relations are often well founded. In part, this may be because CSR is still in its infancy. Although codes of conduct and other forms of voluntary regulation have proliferated, the limits and weaknesses of such regulation have led in turn to calls for an extension of mandatory regulation. However, while it seems unlikely that such calls will have anything more than a piecemeal international impact, within specific countries and/or regions the potential of such measures is much more significant. Moreover, some leading firms have integrated CSR practices into their operational behaviour and arguably established broader and higher standards of behaviour in their supply chains.

This discussion has highlighted two of the key themes of the book. The first is that it captures the dialectic between globalisation and embeddedness. To some extent the pressures on companies to have a CSR code stem from the process of globalization itself in that it is concern about exploitation of unprotected workforces in developing nations that is one of the drivers of CSR. However, the extent to which companies use CSR codes, and the way in which they develop them, are deeply influenced by the national context in which the firm operates. The second is that it clearly demonstrates how international HRM is hotly contested both internally within the firm and externally. The fact that national economies differ in the extent and nature of regulation is of course one of the attractions for many companies of operating at the international level, yet we have seen that there are significant, if variable, constraints on the ability of firms to take advantage of these differences. CSR has been a management response to achieve legitimacy in the international environment, but one that is challenged by pressures from outside pressure groups and also employee representatives within firms.

Review questions

1 What are the main areas of a firm's business that 'corporate social responsibility' can cover?

2 How can the HR function use the interest on the part of senior management in corporate social responsibility to its advantage?

3 What is distinctive about the international dimension to corporate social responsibility initiatives?

4 On balance, what does the experience of companies that have engaged with corporate social responsibility tell us about how much difference it makes to the behaviour of firms?

Further reading

1 Kolk, A. and van Tulder, R. (2002) 'The effectiveness of self-regulation: corporate codes of conduct and child labour', *European Management Journal* 20(3), 260–71

This article is a case study examining how some leading multinationals deal with the complex and emotive issue of child labour through codes of conduct and the issues raised by their approaches.

2 Christian Aid (2004) 'Behind the mask: the real face of corporate social responsibility' accessible at www.christian-aid.org.uk/news/media

A vigorous critique of the actual practice of CSR. Several case studies are used to argue that the claims made by some firms mask inaction or limited action. It attacks the voluntary approach calling for mandatory regulation of transnationals.

3 Ann Elliot, K. and Freeman, R. B. (2003) *Can Labor Standards Improve Under Globalization?* Washington, DC: Institute for International Economics

A broad examination of a range of issues around labour standards, including the role of codes of conduct and the ILO. Detailed case studies are examined.

4 Hepple, B. (2005) 'Privatising Regulation: Codes, Agreements and Guidelines', in Labour Law and Global Trade

A succinct, insightful account of the growth, character and implications of codes of conduct and ways they can be reformed.

References

Ann Elliot K. and Freeman, R. B. (2003) *Can Labor Standards Improve Under Globalization?* Washington, DC: Institute for International Economics.

Baxter, A. (2002) 'Flexibility works both ways', *Financial Times,* 10 June.

Benjamin, A. (2002) 'Still less than half per cent' in The Giving List, *Guardian* supplement, 25 Nov.

Blowfield, M. and Murray, A. (2008) *Corporate Social Responsibility – A Critical Introduction,* Oxford: OUP.

Bondy, K., Matten, D. and Moon, J. (2004) 'The adoption of voluntary codes of conduct in MNCs: a three-country comparative study', *Business and Society Review,* 109, 4, 449–77.

Brewster, D. (2009) 'Institutions lead the way in investments', *Financial Times,* 4 June.

Buckley, S. (2002) 'All sweetness and light at the Co-op', *Financial Times,* 26 Nov.

Bunting M. (2001) 'The new gods', *Guardian,* 9 July.

Cafod (2004) *The Rough Guide to Labour Standards,* www.cafod.org.uk

Carmichael S. (2001) 'Accounting for ethical business', in Bentley, T. and Stedman, D. (eds) *The Moral Universe,* Winter, London: Demos.

Cavanaugh J. (1997) 'The global resistance to sweatshops' in Ross, A. (ed.) No Sweat: fashion, free trade and the rights of garment workers, London: Verso.

Chapple, W. and Moon, J. (2005) 'Corporate social responsibility: a seven country study of CSR website reporting', *Business and Society,* 44(4), 415–41.

Chartered Institute of Personnel and Development (2002) *Corporate Social Responsibility,* Autumn, London: CIPD.

Christian Aid (2004) *'Behind the Mask: The Real Face of Corporate Social Responsibility',* www. christian-aid.org.uk/news/media.

Cicutti, N. (2002) 'Pension funds fail to invest ethically', *Financial Times,* 15 July.

Delillo, D. (1998) *Underworld,* London: Picador.

Clark, A. (2000) 'Church is dumping GKN', *Guardian,* 21 Nov.

Clark, A. (2006) 'Nike sacks Premiership ball maker over labour fears', *Guardian,* 6 Nov.

Crawford, R. (2000) 'Adidas' s human rights policy back on track', *Financial Times,* 21 Dec.

Dickens, C. (1995[1854]) *Hard Times,* London: Penguin Books.

Diller, J. (1999) 'A social conscience in the global marketplace? Labour dimensions of codes of conduct, social labelling and investor initiatives', *International Labour Review,* Vol. 138, No. 2.

Doane, D. (2002) *Market Failure: the Case for Mandatory Social and Environmental Reporting,* London: IPPR.

Economist, The (2001) 'The case for brands', 8 Sep.

Economist, The (2001) 'Who's wearing the trousers', 8 Sep.

Edwards, T., Marginson, P., Edwards, P., Ferner, A. and Tregaskis, O. (2007) 'Corporate Social Responsibility in Multinational Companies: Management Initiatives or Negotiated Agreements?', IILS Discussion Paper, Geneva.

Fairtrade Foundation (2000) *Unpeeling the Banana Trade,* London, www.fairtrade.org.uk.

Fairtrade Foundation (2002) *Spilling the Beans on the Coffee Trade,* London, www.fairtrade.org.uk

Farrell, G. (2009) 'Bail-outs and bonuses transform once-respected brand', *Financial Times,* 19 March.

Finch, J. (2002) 'Norsk Hydro makes rights its business', *Guardian,* 20?

Finch, J. (2008) 'Primark sacks three Indian suppliers for using child labour', *Guardian,* 17 June.

Friedman, M. (1973) 'The Social Responsibility of Business is to Increase its Profits', reprinted in Chryssides, G. D. and Kaler, J.H. (eds) *An Introduction to Business Ethics* (1993), London: International Thomson Business Press.

Grene, S. (2008) 'SRI funds not outperforming', *Financial Times,* 15 Dec.

Harvey, F. (2008) 'Save energy – the less painful way to cut costs', *Financial Times,* Special Report, 9 Oct.

Heertz, N. (2001) *The Silent Takeover,* London: Heinemann.

Henderson, D. (2001) *Misguided Virtue, False Notions of Corporate Social Responsibility,* London: Institute of Economic Affairs.

Henriques, A. (1999) 'Opening up for business: the logic of legislation' in McIntosh, M. (ed.)

Visions of Ethical Business, London: Financial Times: Prentice Hall.

Hepple, B. (2005) *Labour Laws and Global Trade,* Oxford: Hart Publishing.

House of Commons International Development Committee (2007) *Fair Trade and Development,* 14 June, HC 356-1.

Howard, M. and Willmot, M. (2001) 'Ethical Consumption in the 21st century' in T. Bentley and D. Stedman Jones (eds) *The Moral Universe*, London Demos.

Hutton, W. (1995) *The State We're In,* London: Jonathan Cape.

Hutton, W. (2000) *Society Bites Back: The Good Enterprise, the Purposeful Consumer and the Just Workplace,* London: Industrial Society.

Joseph, E. (2001) 'Corporate social responsibility – delivering the new agenda', *New Economy,* 121–3.

Joseph, E. (2002) 'Promoting corporate social responsibility', *New Economy,* 96–101.

Kolk, A. and van Tulder, R. (2002) 'The effectiveness of self-regulation: corporate codes of conduct and child labour', *European Management Journal,* 20(3), 260–71.

Korten, D. C. (1995) *When Corporations Rule the World,* London: Earthscan.

Klein, N. (2000) *No Logo,* London: Flamingo.

Klein, N. (2002) *Fence and Windows,* London: Flamingo.

Lanchester, J. (2009) 'It's Finished', *London Review of Books,* 28 May.

Levett, R. (2001) 'Sustainable development and capitalism', *Renewal,* 59–72, Vol. 9, No. 2/3.

Lloyd, J. (2001) *The Protest Ethic,* London: Demos.

Lloyd, J. (2000) 'Cultivating the world', *Financial Times,* 20 Sept.

Macalister, T. (2009) 'Tide turns against Shell as durable chief executive gives up his crown', *Guardian,* 27 May.

Maitland, A. (2002a) 'McDonald's responds to anti-capitalist calling', *Financial Times,* 15 April.

Maitland, A. (2002b) 'The hearts are won but not the minds', *Financial Times,* 18 June.

Maitland, A. (2003) 'Tools to build a reputation', *Financial Times,* 20 Jan.

Maitland, A. (2004) 'Problem that is gaining higher political profile', *Financial Times,* 29 Nov.

Marquand, D. (1997) *The New Reckoning; Capitalism, States and Citizens,* Oxford: Polity Press.

Matten, D. and Moon, J. (2008) 'Implicit and explicit CSR: a conceptual framework for a comparative understanding of corporate social responsibility', *Academy of Management Review,* 33(2), 404–24.

McCawley, T. (2000) 'Racing to improve its reputation', *Financial Times,* 21 Dec.

McIntosh, M., Leipzieger, D., Jones J. and Coleman, G. (1998) *Corporate Citizenship,* Harlow: Financial Times/Pitman.

McIntosh, M., Thomas, R., Leipzieger, D. and Coleman, G. (2003) *Living Corporate Citizenship,* Harlow: Financial Times/Prentice Hall.

McNulty S. (2003) 'The oil company the greens love to hate', *Financial Times,* 11 June.

McVidal, J. (2003) 'Fair Trade', *Guardian,* 8 Sept.

Midgley, M. (2001) 'Individualism and the concept of Gaia', in Bentley, T. and Stedman, D. (eds) *The Moral Universe,* Winter, London: Demos.

Monbiot, G. (2000) *Captive State: The Corporate Takeover of Britain,* London: Macmillan.

Morris, H. (2007) 'Chevron pays in Iraq bribes case', *Financial Times,* 15 Nov.

Murray, S. (2002) 'The rapid rise of a new responsibility', *Financial Times,* 11 June.

Murray, S. (2005) 'Nike makes the step to transparency', *Financial Times,* 13 April.

Murray, S. (2009a) 'It's an ill wind that blows no good', *Financial Times,* 10 June.

Murray, S. (2009b) 'Ethical sourcing highlights Cadbury's commitment', *Financial Times,* 10 June.

Murray, S. (2009c) 'Leading banks reap benefit of environmental agendas', *Financial Times,* 4 June.

Murray, S. (2009d) 'Credentials that make the money men happy', *Financial Times,* 16 March.

Parkin, S. (2001) 'Thirst for justice', *Guardian,* 11 July.

Pickard, J. (2002) 'B&Q attacked over charity project adverts', *Financial Times,* 9 March.

Pilkington, E. (2009) '14 years on, family seeks justice for Ken Saro-Wiwa in New York Court', *Guardian,* 27 May.

Ramesh, R. (2008) 'When the foreigners come, we know to tell them we only do two hours a day overtime', *Guardian,* 20 March.

Ross, A. (1997) 'Introduction' in Ross, A. (ed.) *No Sweat: Fashion, Free Trade and the Rights of Garment Workers,* London: Verso.

Royle, T. (2000) *Working for McDonald's in Europe,* London: Routledge.

Ruskin, J. ([1862] 2000) *Unto This Last,* Nelson: Hendon Publishing Co.

Sessoon, D. (1996) *One Hundred Years of Socialism.* London: IB Tauris; in Kutner, R. (1997) *Everything for sale*, New York: Alfred A. Knopf; Luttwak, E. (1996) Turbo-Capitalism; Texere Publishing.

Save the Children (2000) *Big Business, Small Hands,* London: Save the Children.

Schlosser, E. (2001) *Fast Food Nation,* London: Allen Lane.

Segal, P, Sobczak, A. and Triomphe, C.E. (2003) *Corporate Social Responsibility and Working Conditions,* Dublin: European Foundation for the Improvement of Living and Working Conditions.

Sen, A. (1996) 'Social Commitment and Democracy: the Demands of Equity and Financial Conservatism', in Barker, P. (ed.) *Living as Equals,* Oxford: OUP.

Skapinker, M. (2002) 'Why Nike has broken into a sweat', *Financial Times,* 7 March.

Skapinker, M. (2005) 'Nike Ushers in draw age of corporate responsibility' *Financial Times,* 20 April.

Skapinker, M. (2009) 'Fairtrade and a new ingredient for Business', *Financial Times* 10 March.

Silver, S. (2004) 'How to grow a good name in green bananas', *Financial Times,* 26 Nov.

Smith, S. and Barrientos, S. (2005) 'Fair trade and ethical trade: are there moves towards convergence?', *Sustainable Development,* 13, 190–8.

Smithers, R. and Ramesh, R. (2008) 'Charity planning Banana Republic protest over employees' plight', *Guardian,* 20 March.

Smithers, R. and Smith, D. (2009) 'Tesco's record annual profits: #3 bn. South African fruit picker's wages: #98 a month', *Guardian,* 16 May.

Spence, L. (2000) 'What ethics in the employment interview?' in Winstanley, D. and Woodall, J. (eds) *Ethical Issues in Contemporary Human Resource Management,* London: Macmillan.

Stanworth, C. (2000) 'Flexible working patterns', in Winstanley, D. and Woodall, J. (eds) *Ethical Issues in Contemporary Human Resource Management,* London: Macmillan.

Thomas, M. (2008) *Belching Out the Devil – Global Adventures with Coca Cola,* London: Ebury Press.

Thompson, E.P (1968) *The Making of the English Working Class,* London: Pelican.

Tsogas, G. (2001) *Labor Regulation in a Global Economy,* New York: M.E. Sharpe.

Tulder, R. and Kolk, A. (2001) 'Multinationality and corporate ethics: codes of conduct in the sporting goods industry', *Journal of International Business Studies,* 32(2), 267–83.

Vidal, J. (1997) *McLibel: Burger Culture on Trial,* London: Pan.

War on Want (2006) *Coca-Cola – The Alternative Report,* London: War on Want.

Wazir, B. (2001) 'Nike accused of tolerating sweatshops', *Observer*, 20 May.

Wolf, M. (2002) 'Response to confronting the critics', Papers for the IPPR debate, 18 Jan.

Wolf, M. (2009) 'Seeds of its own destruction', *Financial Times*, 12 May.

Woodall, J. and Douglas, D. (2000) 'Winning hearts and minds: ethical issues in human resource development', in Winstanley, D. and Woodall, J. (eds) *Ethical Issues in Contemporary Human Resource Management*, London: Macmillan.

Chapter 14

Migration and international HRM

Stephen Bach

Key aims

The aims of this chapter are to:
- examine trends in international migration and the links to analysis of globalization;
- familiarize readers with the main debates about the causes of migration;
- explore the main winners and losers of international migration;
- assess the human resource management challenges that arise from employing a more diverse workforce.

Introduction

Within the human resource management literature most analysis of globalization has concentrated on the movement of capital. As other chapters in this book indicate, it is the role of multinationals that dominate the analysis of international human resource management (IHRM) because of their size and their pivotal role in diffusing innovative HR practice. It is only in recent years that the mobility of labour has received more consideration as migration has become a controversial issue with significant HR consequences. A great deal of attention has focused on the movement of Polish and other east European citizens to the UK which increased dramatically after 2004, when the European Union expanded eastwards. The process of European integration led to the largest movement of population within Europe since the end of the Second World War.

Migration, of course, is not a new phenomenon. There have been previous waves, as people have sought to escape religious persecution and famine. It was migrants from Ireland that constructed the railways in Britain and those from China that made a major contribution in building the railroad in the US. Influential commentators suggest that the current era differs because we are in an 'age of migration' (Castles and Miller 2003: 4), underpinned by structural inequalities in wealth between the global North and the global South, and reinforced by the falling cost of transportation and communication technologies. Governments and employers, however, are not passive onlookers and are seeking to *manage* migration much more actively; using immigration to enhance national competitiveness. For employers, migrants play a vital role in addressing labour shortages, especially in sectors like construction, agriculture, hospitality and healthcare. Indeed, employers often express a preference for migrant workers because of their strong work ethic and readiness to be flexible; often a euphemism for a willingness to accept low wages. Migrants are not confined to the lower skilled and make an essential contribution in the finance, health and education sectors. Those countries that encourage, or at least tolerate their citizens working abroad, usually termed source countries, benefit from the large flows of financial resources that return to the country and migration often acts as a safety valve reducing unemployment and political dissent.

In receiving countries, however, the native-born population is often wary of immigration. They are often concerned that labour market competition will increase and that migrants may be willing to work for lower wages, placing downward pressure on pay and benefits. These concerns are invariably heightened in periods of sluggish economic growth and rising unemployment. This situation gives rise to what Hollifield (2007) terms the 'liberal paradox' in which the economic demand for labour points to an open approach to immigration, but there is political pressure from citizens to limit it. Political pressure that leads to restrictions on immigration, especially for the lower skilled, has unintended consequences, encouraging more clandestine immigration. It is often these unauthorised migrants that are most vulnerable to employer exploitation.

Trade unions also have to reconcile these political and economic tensions. They need to be sensitive to their existing members that may be suspicious of new arrivals, but seek to recruit and organise migrants both to limit exploitation and maintain wage levels for their existing members drawing on a large and vibrant source of potential trade union members. These dilemmas were illustrated during 2009 in a series of unofficial strikes in power stations, which originated at Total's oil refinery in Lincolnshire over the use of subcontracted labour from Italy and Portugal. Underpinning these disputes has been a concern that the EU posted workers directive and associated judgements favourable to employers in the Laval and Viking cases enable contractors to hire foreign workers from their own country and post them to work in another country. Crucially, contractors only need pay these workers the UK statutory minimum wage and not the agreed pay rate that prevails in the UK for this work, undermining negotiated terms and conditions of pay (Davies 2008; Gennard 2008).

International migration: dimensions and trends

Migration is not a single phenomenon and there are many different categories of migrant that have diverse motives for leaving the country of their birth. In some cases migrants are seeking permanent settlement whilst for others only a temporary stay is envisaged. A relatively small proportion of migrants are escaping political or religious persecution, whilst larger numbers move to be reunited with family members and many move to work. It is not straightforward to know with any precision the number of migrants globally because there are shortcomings in the data. Countries are usually more systematic in documenting when migrants arrive but keep less detailed records of when people leave the country. In addition many migrants are undocumented, moving across borders without the authorization of the country they are entering. Unauthorized migration has risen sharply in recent decades (Castles and Miller 2003). The best known case is of the USA which has proved a magnet for workers from Mexico but also other Latin American countries since the 1970s. Large segments of the US economy could not function without the estimated 11.6 million unauthorised migrants (Terrazas *et al.* 2007). Policy makers and employers are not only interested in the number of migrants and the skills they possess, they also use immigration policy to signal if migrants are viewed as a temporary or more long-term feature of the labour market. Government's often conceive of migrants as a temporary labour source that will return home after the end of their contract or if labour market conditions change, but the experience of guest workers in Germany recruited from the mid-1950s demonstrates that such expectations are often confounded as migrant communities develop and become embedded in the host society (Castles and Miller 2003).

A migrant is defined as an individual that has lived outside of the country of their birth for more than one year. Official United Nations estimates, based on census data, suggest that in 2005 there were 191 million migrants worldwide, comprising 3.0 per cent of the world population. An estimated 86 million people are working in a country other than their country of birth (International Organization of Migration [IOM] 2008).The number of migrants more than doubled between 1975 and 2000, from 82 million to 175 million but as the world's population increased from 3.5 to 6 billion in this period migrants' share of the population only crept up by less than one per cent. A great deal of this change in migrant population is accounted for by the break up of the Soviet Union and related border changes in Eastern Europe, which resulted in millions of people living in different countries than had previously been the case (Legrain 2007). These figures do not seem to indicate a transformation in the scale of migration as is frequently implied or merit the degree of controversy that the subject often engenders, so why the fierce debate?

These global figures disguise the degree of concentration in a relatively small number of countries with 75 per cent of all migrants located in only 28 countries. One out of every four migrants lives in the USA and one in three lives in Europe. A critical challenge facing advanced capitalist countries is their rapidly ageing workforce and the sharp decline in the proportion of the population that is of working age. These trends are encouraging workers from the global South, with younger population structures, to move in search of better lives to the global North. The number of migrants in the advanced capitalist countries has increased substantially and their share of the population nearly doubled from 4.3 per cent to 8.3 per cent between 1975 and 2000 (IOM 2005). As Table 14.1 indicates, the United States hosts the largest number of migrants at close to 40 million, 12.5 per cent of the population, a substantial increase from the 1970 level of 10 million (just under 5 per cent of the population).

In Europe, the creation of the single market in 1992 entitled any citizen from any member state to live and work in any other member state (apart from temporary restrictions on flows from the former communist states). In Britain, as in other EU member states, recent debate about migration has been dominated by the impact of the accession of eight former communist countries (termed A8 countries) into EU membership in May 2004 with a particular focus on the mobility of Polish nationals. The UK government was one of only three EU member states (out of 15) that placed few restrictions on labour market access for A8 nationals, although registration under the Worker Registration Scheme (WRS) was necessary for those who wished to work for more than

Table 14.1 **Countries hosting the largest number of
international migrants in 2005 in millions**

United States	38.4
Russian Federation	12.1
Germany	10.1
Ukraine	6.8
France	6.5
Saudi Arabia	6.4
Canada	6.1
India	5.7
United Kingdom	5.4
Spain	4.8

Source: International Geneva: Organization for Migration

a month and income-related benefits could not be accessed until a year's continuous employment had been gained. By contrast, in January 2007 when Romania and Bulgaria became members of the EU, restrictions were placed on labour market access for citizens of these countries. The outcome of this policy is evident from Table 14.2. The UK has long been a destination for immigrants from Ireland and the Indian sub-continent and this is reflected in the stock of immigrants in the UK. EU expansion has altered the picture substantially with more than a quarter of the 970,000 working age immigrants who arrived in the UK between 2005–7 born in Poland. Immigrants from within the enlarged EU comprise around a quarter of the stock of immigrants but account for over half of new entrants in 2005. The flipside is that exit from Poland and other new member states is creating skill shortages and pay disputes in the home country (EIROnline 2007).

It is not only the scale of recent migration that is important but these trends are more pronounced because migrants are not evenly spread throughout the economy but are concentrated in particular sectors, occupations and regions. Migrants often gravitate to larger conurbations where ethnic enclaves exist and the dominance of migrants within agriculture and food processing, accounts for their geographical concentration in Eastern England, and in the US in California. Migrants are often found in jobs that local workers shun because they are dirty, demeaning, dangerous or of a seasonal character which accounts for a high proportion working in agriculture, care homes, hospitality and construction. Migrants, however, are by no means confined to the bottom of the labour market. Work permits which are allocated to employers to bring in skilled labour provide an indication of the more highly skilled jobs that employers are seeking to fill. In 2007, 23,700 work permits (27 per cent) out of a total of 88,000 work permits were granted to one industry, computer services, to bring in managers and professionals in information technology. Financial services, education and health services were the other dominant industries with between 7 to 10,000 work permits granted in 2007 (Migration Advisory Committee [MAC] 2008). These industry and occupational patterns also impact on nationality. A8 nationals have tended to be concentrated in lower skilled jobs such as in hospitality and care work, and temporary agricultural work is

Table 14.2 **Stock of immigrants by country of birth in the UK, 2007**

	All immigrants			*New entrants (2005–7)*	
Country	*000s*	*% of all immigrants*	*Country*	*000s*	*% of all new entrants*
India	430	8.6	Poland	260	26.9
Poland	380	7.6	India	90	9.4
Pakistan	330	6.6	Pakistan	34	3.5
Ireland	230	4.6	China	31	3.2
Germany	200	4.1	Slovakia	30	3.0
Other	3,120	68.5	Other	530	54.0
Total	**4,690**	**100.0**	**Total**	**975**	**100.0**

Source: LFS (2007), cited in MAC (2008: 30)

currently restricted to nationals from Romania and Bulgaria. India is associated with information technology and computer programmers, whilst the growth of Philippine nationals in the UK has been boosted strongly by the demand for nurses, in which the Philippines is a dominant sending country (Kingma 2006).

Two other features of contemporary migration experience are notable. First, women account for almost half of all migrants but it is only recently that the important role that gender plays in international migration has been recognized. The majority of women migrating to Australia, New Zealand, Europe and North America still do so for family reunification reasons, but there is also a growing trend towards so called mail-order or internet brides as well as other forms of arranged marriage which can also act as a front for the trafficking of women that end up working in the sex industries of many countries (United Nations Population Fund [UNPF] 2006). In Asia, the majority of women migrate alone to work in neighbouring countries and the Middle East mainly as domestic workers, leaving women vulnerable to physical and sexual abuse in the isolation of the employer's home. The migration of women reinforces what Hochschild (2000: 131) has termed global care chains: 'a series of personal links between people across the globe based on the paid or unpaid work of caring'. Leaving one's family to provide care for an employer's child or elderly relative, in return for earnings to improve the quality of life of their own children, places a huge psychological strain on these families (Parrenas 2005).

Second, policy makers are increasingly concerned with skilled migration and focusing on attracting talent to enhance economic competitiveness. The OECD (2008) has noted intensifying competition between countries for knowledge workers where shortages are projected to worsen over the next 20 years. In 2007, The European Commission President proposed an EU blue card scheme to signal that 'highly skilled migrants are welcome in the EU' (Barroso 2007). This was developed into an EU-wide immigration pact during 2008. Finally, it is important to recognise the increased significance of student mobility which represents a potential source of highly skilled migrants. Over the period of 2000–5, the number of international students increased by about 50 per cent with many countries such as New Zealand, the Czech Republic and Japan experiencing strong growth. The US is dominant with 583,000 international students enrolled in 2006–7, whilst the UK enrolled 350,000. In both countries students from China and India comprise the largest number of enrolments (OECD 2008).

These trends indicate that migration, whilst certainly not novel, is becoming a more prominent feature of the global economy. Nonetheless labour remains far less mobile. Some countries, notably the USA, have been more receptive to immigrants suggesting that government policy has been an important consideration in explaining patterns of labour mobility.

What shapes migration?

Migration has been analysed from a variety of disciplinary perspectives with limited consensus about its causes and consequences (Massey *et al.* 1998). Without a clear understanding of why migration occurs, governments and employers cannot be confident that they are using the appropriate immigration and labour market interventions to maximize the benefits of immigration. A very widespread view is that migration is an inevitable component of globalization (Castles and Miller 2003). As economic activity becomes more integrated and trade barriers decline so it is assumed that a global labour market is emerging in which all factors of production move around the world in search of the best returns and this is encouraging a 'war for talent'. The war for talent metaphor (Michaels *et al.* 2001) assumes that there is as a fixed supply of talent, but most countries are upskilling their workforce. Moreover, it assumes that workers around the world compete for the same jobs, but in reality migrants often fill particular niches in the labour market. While it might appear that the 'age of migration' and the 'war for talent' mean that labour is increasingly globalized, in practice significant constraints remain on mobility.

More convincingly, the current preoccupation with migration as a defining feature of globalization has its origins in the historical-structural tradition within migration studies. This approach suggests that migration arises from the insertion of countries into an international division of labour in which cheap labour from source countries is mobilized to advance the interests of employers in industrialised destination countries. Sassen (1988, 2001) in her influential global cities hypothesis emphasizes the importance of global cities, such as London, New York and Tokyo in which great wealth is concentrated, creating strong demand for an array of low-paid service workers such as cleaners and nannies which encourages a dramatic increase in migration. Related developments are addressed by Richard Freeman (2005) in what he terms the 'great doubling'. This refers to the entry of India and China into the global labour market, doubling the global supply of labour from approximately 1.46 billion to 2.92 billion. Freeman predicts that this will lead to downward pressure on wages and conditions in the North. The difficulty of these accounts is their emphasis on the *inevitability* of global mobility as a structural feature of the world economy with little consideration of the extent to which other stakeholders, migrants themselves, employers and the nation state have an influence on the extent and types of mobility. For example, it is evident that London is reliant on low-paid migrant labour but this is not driven solely by the needs of global elites. Instead, the outcome has been actively created by the nation state that has encouraged immigration, privatized public services thereby eroding pay and conditions, and limited migrants access to welfare benefits, cajoling migrants to accept low wage work (May *et al.* 2007).

In contrast to the emphasis on structural factors, many migration specialists focus on the individual *agency* of the potential migrant to explain migration; in other words, the emphasis is on the choices that individuals make. Neoclassical economic analysis suggests that migration flows stem from the existence of geographical wage differentials which are governed by the laws of supply and demand. Individuals undertake cost-benefit analysis, comparing the relative costs and benefits of remaining in their current country compared to the anticipated wage returns in moving to a new country. The decision to migrate is therefore an investment, intended to boost the individual's human capital in a similar fashion to investing in further education. This theory's underlying approach is often abbreviated to focus on the push and pull factors that influence an individual's decision to migrate. Push factors encourage people to leave their country of origin and pull factors attract individuals to particular countries. With its intuitive appeal that migration can be explained by the location and intensity of push-pull factors, especially disparities in wage levels between source and destination countries, push-pull models underpinned by neoclassical assumptions about individual behaviour have exerted a powerful influence over research and policy making concerned with migration.

Sociologists and more institutionally orientated labour economists have always had doubts about the neoclassical approach. Although not ignoring the relevance of wage differentials in influencing migrant behaviour, the empirical evidence does not correspond closely to the predictions of neoclassical theory (McGovern 2007). Only 3 per cent of the world's population are migrants, but if wage differentials were the main influence on behaviour this proportion would be much higher because of the vast differences in wage differentials between countries. Of course, migration is a costly and difficult process that requires considerable personal drive and financial resources. This helps explain the observation by Portes and Rumbaut (1990) that major labour flows often arise from countries at intermediate levels of development rather than from the poorest to the richest countries (as neoclassical theory implies) and it is rarely the poorest in a society that migrate. A further limitation of the neoclassical approach is that by focusing solely on the aspirations of the individual migrant, a range of other actors and constraints that influence migrant behaviour are ignored. In the terms of this book, individuals do indeed make choices, but these are heavily constrained by the context in which they operate. In particular, restrictive admissions policies reflect the extent to which governments actively select potential migrants on the basis of specific traits, such as skill levels. These policies have a substantial influence on the type and volume of migration flows. Consequently an authoritative analysis concludes that a wage gap has some influence on behaviour, but 'the existence of a wage differential still does not guarantee international movement, nor does its absence preclude it' (Massey *et al.* 1998).

Instead of focusing exclusively on the individual, much migration research highlights the extent to which migration represents a household or community strategy to maximize income, with different roles allocated to household members. As Ball (2004) notes in her study of nurses from the Philippines, women are often encouraged to become nurses to gain employment abroad, spreading risk and bolstering household income.

Migration specialists also recognize that migration is facilitated by networks. The network is often characterised loosely as a web of relationships and acquaintances, not confined to immediate kin, which link potential migrants in source countries with existing migrants in destination countries. These networks provide potential migrants with information about employment opportunities, housing and visa requirements, although they are not always benign as new arrivals are vulnerable to exploitation. The network is conceived, therefore, as an important mechanism for reducing the risks of migration and over time, as networks become embedded within destination countries, it enables community formation. Migration becomes self-sustaining as the network continues to replenish its labour supply irrespective of the conditions that initiated migration (Massey *et al.* 1987). Employers often make use of these informal networks to recruit labour.

These perspectives provide a more sophisticated understanding of labour migration, however, they still only focus on labour supply, neglecting the central role of employers in creating demand for migrant labour. In contrast to these supply-side accounts, Piore (1979) in an influential study suggested that migration stems from the structural demand for migrant labour within advanced industrial economies and it is only when employer demand stimulates migration that such flows occur. Piore argued that the use of migrant labour has specific advantages for employers that arise primarily from the attributes of jobs that migrants fill, rather than solely the wages that they are paid.

First, migrants often fill jobs that are dirty, difficult, dangerous and demeaning. These jobs are not always low-paid but they usually denote low status with few opportunities for advancement. These jobs are frequently spurned by native-born workers because of their low status and the stigma attached to undertaking particular jobs, as in the case of care work (Cangiano *et al.* 2009; McGregor 2007). Even in higher status professions like medicine there are certain unpopular specialties or particular grades that lie outside the main career structure that are hard to fill (British Medical Association 2007). Consequently, some jobs that are unattractive to native-born workers are taken up by migrants, who are less influenced by social status and more concerned with economic security, an orientation reinforced by the opportunities available to them.

Second, employers respond to labour shortages by using migrant labour and increasingly use employment agencies to fill these vacancies (McDowell *et al.* 2008). Employers are reluctant to raise wages to alleviate shortages because of the impact on the wage structure with higher paid workers seeking to restore wage differentials. As Piore (1979: 33) argues, 'the hospital administrator cannot envisage paying more to orderlies without paying more to nurses'. Moreover, migrants' wage expectations are framed by the labour market in their country of origin, reducing their wage expectations, especially if they envisage a temporary stay abroad. Finally, Piore draws on dual labour market theory to argue that the labour market is segmented with good secure jobs located within the primary labour market and bad jobs with worse terms and conditions located in the secondary labour market; migrants are concentrated in this secondary labour market. In addition to their influence on labour demand, employers also have a significant influence on immigration policy because they have a strong common interest in maintaining an open immigration regime and expend resources to lobby for such policies. By contrast, opponents of immigration policy have diverse interests and may be influenced by immigration in diffuse and intangible ways, limiting effective opposition.

As well as employers, the nation state has an important influence on migration with governments more actively managing migration to enhance its benefits. The Philippines occupies a pivotal role in the political economy of migration and highlights the impact of proactive state policy over many years. Since the 1970s facilitating emigration has been central to political and economic policy, designed to alleviate high levels of unemployment and to generate economic growth from the remittances sent back by those employed abroad. Each year out of a population of around 88 million, more than one million citizens leave to work abroad contributing to an estimated 8 million migrant workers deployed in more than 200 countries across numerous industries. Filipinos dominate the sea faring industry whilst women are employed as domestic helpers, entertainers and nurses. Institutionalization has occurred by the government licensing Philippines-based agencies to recruit labour for employers in Saudi Arabia and other countries. The government also established the agency that became the Philippines Overseas Employment Administration (POEA), which provides contract labor directly to foreign employers, maritime agencies, and governments and which has a regulatory role, for example arranging mandatory pre-orientation training. This policy generates around $8 billion dollars a year in remittances but is not without its critics because of concerns about the impact on the economic and social fabric of society (Martin *et al.* 2004; Parrenas 2005).

State intervention in UK immigration policy has been framed by its role as a destination country, even though the UK experiences high levels of emigration by its own citizens. Since the late 1990s, strong economic growth and the expansion of public services encouraged the UK government to relax immigration policy and issue more work permits. In 2007, an estimated 577,000 people came to live in the UK for more than a year (340,000 emigrated), a reduction on the 2006 level of 591,000 (ONS 2008). In 2005, the government announced plans to move towards a points-based system (PBS) for labour migration, modelled loosely on the Australian system, divided between five tiers and implemented from 2008. The government used the discourse of global competition to argue that a new PBS would target skilled migrants that were essential to the UK's position in the world economy. The system is explicitly linked to economic requirements, with different degrees of eligibility to enter the UK based on a skill hierarchy. The most highly skilled are able to enter the UK and settle without a job offer, those with slightly lower skills are able to enter with a job offer if the job is regarded as a shortage occupation, and the least skilled are excluded except in very specific circumstances. Underpinning the system, the government established an independent Migration Advisory Committee (MAC) to identify labour market shortages amongst skilled occupations and to recommend where it is sensible to fill that shortage via immigration from outside the European Economic Area. The MAC recommended its first list of shortage occupations in September 2008 (MAC 2008). Although the PBS is only just being implemented, it demonstrates that state policy can actively seek to attract or discourage immigration and it is predicted that the implementation of the PBS will ensure a sharp decline in non-EEA nationals entering the UK.

What are the implications of these different approaches? First, the role of wage differentials as a key driver of migration provides an insufficient basis to understand why migration occurs. Second, although global economic integration is important, to assume that globalization fosters an inevitable increase in migration and that governments and employers are powerless to intervene to shape migration flows and outcomes is wide of the mark. Institutions matter as much in the realm of migration as in other aspects of international HRM.

The impact of migration

A great deal of debate about migration concentrates on its effects on the economy. Most economists support the free movement of labour in the same way as they support free trade because it enables workers to be allocated in the most efficient manner. The argument can be simply stated. When migrants move to industrialized countries with higher productivity, arising from higher levels of capital investment, these workers are more productive, generating higher levels of productivity than in their home country. This outcome not only benefits the migrants themselves but enhances economic performance in the destination country, encouraging governments to upskill the indigenous workforce to enable them to take up higher skilled, more productive jobs. Consequently, there is considerable consensus that immigration creates significant economic benefits. In the UK, immigration has helped to boost growth above its long-term trend and helped dampen down inflationary wage pressures by increasing the supply of labour relative to demand (Blanchflower *et al.* 2007). The UK government estimated that immigration added half a per cent to trend output growth between 2001 and 2006, equivalent to £6 billion in 2006 (Home Office 2008). These benefits may be higher because of cluster or 'spillover' effects which are hard to measure. For example, the finance sector based in London has been able to attract a diverse workforce with knowledge and networks from around the world which has been critical to the growth of the sector.

These type of spillover effects have been investigated in detail by Saxenian (2008) in her work on Silicon Valley. She identifies the contribution of US educated, but foreign-born engineers as a crucial component of its success. By 2000, over half of scientists and engineers working in Silicon Valley were foreign-born and those from China (Taiwan and the mainland) and India alone comprised more than a quarter of those employed. These staff not only made a direct contribution to Silicon Valley, but Saxenian extends the argument demonstrating that transnational networks of US educated Chinese engineers transferred the Silicon Valley model of venture capital back to Taiwan. In this way she argues that the expertise and capital of expatriate professionals stimulates investment and entrepreneurial activity in the home country and a potentially damaging form of brain drain is converted into a beneficial form of brain circulation. The other main benefit to source countries relates to the income that migrants remit to their families back home. The World Bank estimates that remittances to developing countries amounted to $283 billion dollars in 2008, a figure that far exceeds overseas development aid. The largest recipient countries - India, China and Mexico – each received between $20–30 billion dollars in 2008 in remittances (Ratha *et al.* 2008).

◗ Wages and employment

These macroeconomic benefits tell us little about the consequences for individual work-ers with most debate concentrated on the effects on wages and employment. A common argument is that immigration by increasing labour supply, with no change in labour demand, will have a negative effect on wage levels in the short run until supply and demand factors bring wages back into equilibrium. But even in this simplified version of the operation of the labour market the relationship between immigration and wages is not straightforward because wages depend on the availability of capital as well as labour. Immigration may reduce wages by increasing labour supply but this in turn will increase the return to employers of investing in new productive facilities, boosting the demand and hence the wages of the workforce. The degree to which this capital adjustment effect is included in the analysis can have a crucial bearing on the conclusions drawn. Another important consideration is the degree to which the skills of migrants are viewed as complementary or a substitute for those possessed by the resident population. Resident workers that have skills which are most like recent migrants are most likely to lose out. Consequently, many studies not only consider average wages but focus on those considered to be most affected by immigration–low skilled resident workers.

In the US, Borjas (2003) has argued that immigration has a negative effect on the wages of unskilled native-born workers, but more recent studies have challenged these results (see Dustmann *et al.* 2008). Woolfson (2008) documents the situation in Latvia, a new member state, in which very poor pay and working conditions has encouraged exit to other EU countries, but this has created a secondary process of migration into Latvia in which workers from other former soviet countries are willing to work for even lower wages than their Latvian counterparts.

These results are influenced by the degree of labour market regulation. Crucially, US studies are based on lightly regulated US labour markets with a very low federal minimum wage and these studies are less applicable to more regulated labour market contexts. In general, UK studies have found very modest effects on wages as a result of immigration. Research for the Low Pay Commission examined the effects of the inflow of migrants to the UK between 1997 and 2005 (Dustmann *et al.* 2007). It found that there was, on aver-age, a slightly positive effect on wage growth, but there were some very small negative effects at the lower end of the wage distribution. It is not straightforward to interpret the evidence but a degree of consensus is emerging. Some witnesses in the House of Lords (2008) inquiry suggested that low-skilled immigration reduced wage growth at the bottom of the labour market because of substitution and increased competition, leading some workers to fear that they may face unemployment if they didn't accept low wages. At the middle and upper ends of the earnings hierarchy immigration appears to boost wages because immigrants provide complementary skills to higher earners.

An important explanation as to why immigration has only had a modest effect on wage growth in the UK is because of the impact of the national minimum wage (NMW), which from October 2009 was set at £5.80 per hour for those over 22. The NMW has protected many low-paid workers from the potentially adverse effects of immigration by placing a legal floor on wages. The protection provided by the NMW, however, does have limitations. Many employers whilst appearing to pay the national minimum wage make deductions for accommodation or transport and make false declarations about the number of hours worked or the number of employees, reducing wage levels below the NMW. A study of the employment practices in the ethnic restaurant and textile sectors reported that the informality of employment practices in the sector and limited enforcement ensured evasion of the minimum wage was relatively straightforward. These consequences were attributed to low levels of profitability, intense competition and the collusion of workers, albeit reluctantly, in accepting low wages (Ram *et al.* 2007).

A related issue is the impact of immigration on employment with concerns linked to the lump of labour fallacy; the assumption that there is a fixed amount of employment in an economy and therefore if migrants gain employment, other, native-born workers must be displaced generating unemployment. The experience of the labour market does not bear out the assumption that there are only a certain amount of jobs in the economy. The influx of A8 immigrants after 2004 provides a good test of whether increased immigration is associated with raised levels of unemployment. Dustmann *et al* (2006) noted that the claimant count did increase during 2004–5, but after examining the numbers and geographical location of A8 workers on the Workers Registration Scheme, concluded that there was no discernable statistical evidence that linked increased unemployment to the arrival of A8 workers. Whilst accepting the overall conclusion, the Trade Union Congress (TUC 2006) acknowledged that there might be particular problems for the most disadvantaged workers and that in specific sectors such as construction immigration may have caused some job losses.

An investigation by the House of Lords (2008: 32) on the effects of immigration raised similar concerns, concluding that:

> In the short term, immigration creates winners and losers in economic terms. The biggest winners include immigrants and their employers in the UK. Consumers may also benefit from immigration through lower prices. The losers are likely to include those employed in low-paid jobs and directly competing with new immigrant workers. This group includes some ethnic minorities and a significant share of immigrants already working in the UK.

Despite this note of scepticism, the overwhelming majority of studies do not point to negative effects of immigration on wages and employment in the long run and there remains a high level of consensus amongst government, employers and unions that immigration has been beneficial (Dustmann *et al.* 2008).

HR implications

A great deal of the analysis of international migration has focused on the economic effects, but what have been the consequences for employers and workers of the expansion of migrant workers across many countries in recent years? Employers are seen as one of the main beneficiaries and key advocates of an open immigration policy. Employers have always drawn on migrant labour to address labour shortages, relying on them to fill jobs in low wage sectors such as agriculture, construction, hospitality, care work and food processing. Until the recession which began in 2008, the UK labour market was very tight and unemployment had been low. As Table 14.3 indicates, the

Table 14.3 Distribution of employment across occupations, 2007 (and percentage of working-age population)

Men		Women	
UK-born (% of total)	Immigrant (% of total)	UK-born (% of total)	Immigrant (% of total)
Works managers (2.4)	Chefs (3)	Sales assistants (5.6)	Nurses (5.8)
Sales managers (2.4)	Warehouse workers (2.7)	Office clerks (4.2)	Care assistants (5.2)
Heavy goods drivers (2.3)	Taxi drivers (2.6)	Care assistants (4.1)	Cleaners (4.8)
Warehouse workers (2.1)	Software professionals (2.3)	Nurses (3.5)	Sales assistants (3.9)
Sales assistants (2.0)	Medical practitioners (2.1)	Educational assistants (3.4)	Kitchen assistants (2.9)

Note. Population of working age, excluding those who do not record an occupation and students. Occupations are ranked in order of the working population share. For example, nurses account for 5.8 per cent of employment among immigrant women.

Source: LFS (Sept.–Dec. 2007), cited in MAC (2008: 32)

distribution of immigrants in the UK labour market differs from that of the UK born population. Amongst men, chefs are the occupation with the highest proportion of immigrants, reflecting their key contribution to ethnic restaurants, and amongst women nurses are the largest occupational group (see case study discussion).

In some sectors the variation in demand for labour over the year has encouraged a reliance on migrant labour. In agriculture, the average UK farm employs 134 workers in peak season and 29 workers in low season. During the 2008 peak season, a staggering 84 per cent of all agricultural workers comprised migrant labour, compared to around 1 per cent in the 1970s (Scott *et al.* 2008). This massive shift in employer reliance on migrant labour cannot simply be attributed to the seasonal character of the work. As Scott points out, the supply chain in agriculture has become dominated by the power of the large supermarket chains that have placed downward pressure on food prices, which has depressed farm workers' wages. This has reinforced the view amongst native-born workers that agriculture comprises low paid, dead-end jobs.

Employers not only view migrants as cost effective, but they also bring attributes to the workplace that are absent in native-born workers and which better serve the needs of clients. In schools in East London, the employment of teaching assistants from the local Bangladeshi community provided an important channel of communication between predominantly white teachers and Bangladeshi parents who spoke little English. Pupils also interacted in a more informal manner with the teaching assistants, compared to their teachers (Bach *et al.* 2006). In hospitality, part of the customer's expectations of an ethnic restaurant is that they will be served by someone from that country (Lucas and Mansfield 2008). These arguments have many similarities to the 'business case' for managing diversity.

In the UK, as in many other countries, migrants are generally better educated than the native-born population, but occupy low paid jobs. This reflects the fact that migrants often experience downward occupational mobility. They often have difficulty gaining proper recognition for their qualifications, have less familiarity with the operation of the labour market and are frequently anxious to gain employment rapidly ensuring that they do not maximize, at least initially, their earnings potential. This ensures that employers gain a more qualified employee than they would otherwise recruit. This is evident from the experience of the UK construction industry which has benefited from highly skilled East European migrants that have often served five-year apprenticeships that used to exist in the UK (Blackman 2007). The irony is that a relatively liberal UK immigration policy has facilitated migration which is necessary because the same *laissez faire* policies have failed to institutionalize training, creating skill shortages within construction and other sectors. A less benign interpretation of employer demand for migrant labour is that their availability discourages employers from investing in the training of the native-born workforce or raising wages to more attractive levels.

It is not only technical skills that may lead employers to express a preference for migrant labour but also the availability of 'soft skills' such as customer service skills. In this sense, immigration enables employers to differentiate within their workforces by occupational group and ethnicity. Waldinger and Lichter (2003) in their research in California suggest that employers have a cognitive map, which they term 'a hiring queue' in which they rank job candidates according to ethnic and racial origins which intersects with issues of nationality. Employers often have strong preferences for particular ethnic groups because of their perceived attitude to work and Latinos were favoured because they were seen as hard working. Interviews in the hospitality sector in Brighton, indicated that employers had particular preferences for certain nationalities in specific roles, for example, they favoured Australians and South Africans for bar work. As one hotel manager explained:

> The Polish in my mind are very hard workers — they could work all day and not really complain, whereas the Spanish are a bit more fiery. But that just goes with the culture I suppose. Italians, I've found to be the most professional, and the Greeks are very good as well — very, very professional, very proud of what they do. (cited in Matthews and Ruhs 2007: 30)

These positive views of migrants are frequently matched by negative views of resident workers who are characterised as demanding, inflexible and possessing the wrong work ethic. Amongst farmers, the domestic population was viewed as unreliable and viewed as reluctant to start work at 8.00 a.m. or to work at weekends (Scott *et al.* 2008). Many commentators point out, however, that although these stereotypes are widespread, they are often utilized to disguise other advantages of migrant labour, not least being compliant and accepting poor terms and conditions (Anderson *et al.* 2006), themes identified by Piore (1979) 30 years ago.

For employers, the use of migrant labour is often associated with greater control over labour deployment, enhancing flexibility. The dependence of migrant workers on their employers is reinforced by their precarious status in the labour market, in which they are often not accorded the same employment and welfare rights as other workers. In some cases a migrant worker is tied to an employer because his or her work permit is granted on the basis of remaining with the existing employer, increasing dependence on the migrant's current employer. In the hospitality sector, employees are expected to be flexible in terms of hours worked and to cover for sickness absence. This flexibility is facilitated by the fact that almost half of migrant workers have accommodation provided for them by their employer, often at their place of work. This ensures that they are available 24 hours a day (Lucas and Mansfield 2008). In many cases migrant workers depend also on their employers for transportation to their place of work.

These strategies can extend beyond the individual to comprise whole industries. Champlin and Hake (2006) document the evolution of the American meatpacking industry which comprises physically demanding, unpleasant and frequently hazardous work. The industry which is dominated by a small number of large corporations has become increasingly reliant on non-unionized immigrant labour and this process was brought about by shifting plants from urban areas to more rural areas in the South and mid-West and actively recruiting workers from Mexico, that were often undocumented workers making them especially vulnerable to exploitation. Since this article was published, there has been a clamp down on unauthorised migrants and employers have replaced many Latino workers with Somalis that are in the US legally as political refugees and have been recruited to work in meatpacking plants in large towns such as Grand Island, Nebraska. This has created tensions between co-workers with Somali workers requesting special breaks for prayers (Semple 2008).

Employers also confront considerable challenges in employing migrant workers that stem from the complexities of employment and immigration law. In the UK, recent changes in immigration law have placed far greater responsibilities on employers to ensure that they are complying with immigration law and have introduced much higher levels of fines (up to £10,000 per undocumented worker). Many employers may not have the requisite expertise or HR systems to be certain that all their employees are lawfully employed. Employers also face the challenge of ensuring that migrant workers are effectively inducted and integrated into the organization and that they do not face discrimination from their co-workers and service users. Employers have taken steps to provide mentors to new staff and developed welcome packs providing a wide range of information about working in the UK. In some cases employers have provided support in English for Speakers of Other Languages (ESOL) courses and trade unions have also facilitated access to English-language tuition (Heyes 2009).

▶ Worker and trade union responses

Considering the variation in the jobs occupied by migrant workers, it is difficult to generalize about their experience of employment. Nonetheless, a number of issues frequently arise indicating the experience of employment can differ in important ways for migrant workers. Some of the advantages of employing migrant labour for employers such as low wages and the flexibility that arises from being accommodated by the employer are identified as disadvantages by migrant workers. Three factors have an important influence on their experience of employment.

First, their unfamiliarity with the labour market and employment rights increases their vulnerability in the labour market. In some cases this can relate to their treatment by their supervisors and co-workers with under-utilization of their skills a common complaint. Workers in Stoke-on-Trent raised concerns that they were allocated harder tasks by their team leaders than indigenous workers making it very difficult for them to achieve their targets. When concerns were raised on this matter and related concerns such as requesting a pay slip and national insurance number, contracts were terminated or workers relocated to distant geographical locations (French and Mohrke 2006). In general, the informality and lack of transparency about pay rates, deductions made for housing and transport, long working hours and unpaid hours are the most commonly reported difficulties (Anderson *et al.* 2006). Health and safety problems also arise from language differences and inadequate training and information (McKay *et al.* 2006).

Second, the degree to which migrants are protected by employment law, which is itself influenced by their immigration status, has an important bearing on their vulnerability in the workplace. If an individual is working without authorization i.e. illegally, workers are deprived of their employment rights. This situation extends far beyond people entering and working in the UK on a clandestine basis (see Pai 2008) but also includes overseas students working more hours than permitted, asylum seekers and overstayers (Ryan 2005). A related issue concerns bogus self-employment in sectors like construction which enables workers to lower their tax liabilities, but allows employers to terminate employment at will and avoids payment of sick pay and holiday pay. For many workers the fear of being reported to the immigration authorities ensures compliance and this can enable employers to take advantage of vulnerable workers, for example, by removing their passports preventing them from leaving their employer. Ryan (2005: 59–60) notes several cases in which trade union attempts to organise migrant workers and take industrial action were made more difficult by employer threats to check the immigration papers of workers and to call in immigration officers if necessary.

A third influence on the experience of employment stems from the recruitment channels used in the employment of migrants. Migrants often gain access to the labour market by drawing on networks or what are sometimes termed ethnic enclaves to gain employment. Employers often have a preference for these informal word-of-mouth recruitment practices because these networks provide access to a reliable source of labour in a an inexpensive way. Some of the responsibility for managing the workforce is transferred to the workers themselves, who will cover for each other in the event of sickness absence. Although informal networks also have certain advantages for migrants in terms of gaining employment, they are often a strategy of necessity rather than choice with new migrants exposed to wage skimming and blackmail by earlier arrivals that act as intermediaries with employers (Pai 2008; Shelley 2007). Not only is a job search costly and difficult in an unfamiliar environment, it is frequently the absence of adequate language skills that makes many migrant workers dependent on recruitment agencies. A study for the UK Home Office (Dench 2006: 61) noted 'although there are many good agencies, this is also an area where a considerable amount of exploitation can occur'. The deaths by drowning of 23 Chinese cockle pickers in Morecombe Bay during 2004 illustrates the degree to which 'gangmasters' were prepared to exploit undocumented workers, leading to the establishment in 2005 of the Gangmasters Licensing Authority to provide some regulation of these labour practices.

Trade unions have sought to safeguard the interests of migrant workers. This is not straightforward as existing trade union members are not always supportive of migrant workers because of concerns that migrants may erode wages and conditions. Trade unions, however, increasingly view migration as an integral component of globalization and that the best means to protect labour standards is to campaign for the regularization of unauthorized migrants and to draw migrants into union membership. Trade unions have worked with unions in the source country, seconding or employing officials of the same nationality, to organize migrant workers. These links have also encouraged agreements enabling trade union membership to be transferred to the destination country, intended to ensure that migrant workers achieve pay and working conditions that are equivalent to local workers. The agreement between the UK TUC and the largest Bulgarian union organizations is illustrative of these trends (Dimitrova 2008). Trade unions have established new structures that are more open and welcoming to migrant workers, including working with other social movements and faith groups. In Scotland, the Overseas Nurses Network was established with Unison's endorsement, enabling nurses and other care workers to network and to exchange information and support.

Overall, however, British trade unions have made limited headway in organizing migrant workers, which stems from their continuing decline and limited resource base but also broader shortcomings in the structure and strategy of British unions. The trade union movement's own inquiry into vulnerable workers described the union record as 'patchy' (TUC 2008).

This record is often contrasted with the experience of the trade union movement in the United States in which migrant workers have become a key element of trade union revitalization (Givan 2007). The most prominent case concerns the Justice for Janitors campaign in which a local union branch won a major contract from one of Los Angeles major building contractors after an intensive union recruitment campaign amongst Latino workers. As Milkman (2006) explains, the success of these forms of organizing stem from their focus on organizing immigrants across an industry rather than in a single workplace. In addition a number of facilitating conditions existed which included the dense networks of immigrants which were often replicated in the workplace, the class consciousness and sense of stigmatisation amongst migrant workers, and the perception that the risks for migrants workers whilst not insignificant were less extreme than the risks attached to being union activists in countries such as El Salvador (Milkman 2006).

CASE STUDY

Nursing

Few patients in hospital cannot fail to have noticed the increased contribution to their care made by staff that have migrated from an increasing array of countries. Many European Union countries as well as the USA, Canada and Australia have become increasingly reliant on internationally recruited health professionals, especially nurses. The scale of nurse migration is unprecedented and this movement highlights the feminisation of migration. It also has significant consequences for the home country. Poland has experienced a wave of migration to other EU countries and this has worsened the shortages of nurses and other skilled workers and led to widespread pay disputes.

The recent experience of the UK health sector throws much light on the causes and consequences of nurse migration. This phenomenon is not entirely new as nurses and doctors have transportable skills and in the 1950s and 1960s came to the UK to train and stayed on to work in the National Health Service (NHS). What is different about recent experience has been the extent to which governments in source and destination countries have actively encouraged nurse mobility. When the Labour government came into office in 1997 it committed itself to improving the NHS and it decided an important way to do this was to expand staffing levels. In 2000, the Labour government established a target for England to recruit an additional 20,000 nurses and midwives by 2004 and the target was subsequently increased to 35,000 by 2008. Taking account of existing staff shortages and the three years that it takes to train a nurse, international recruitment was identified as the preferred strategy to ensure rapid workforce growth.

The Department of Health established an institutional infrastructure to promote recruitment activity. An NHS Director of International Recruitment was appointed supported by International Recruitment Co-ordinators and the number of staff recruited internationally comprised a key performance target for these co-ordinators. Financial assistance was made available by the government to enable managers to travel to the Philippines in particular, to recruit batches of 50–100 nurses at a time. The Department of Health actively marketed the NHS to potential recruits and entered into bilateral agreements with countries such as Spain to get over the message that the NHS was welcoming nurses to the UK. Between 1999 and 2004, 68,000 additional nurses were recruited by the NHS in England, a significant proportion were overseas nurses recruited to work in less popular specialties and geographical locations.

The NHS and independent care homes have relied heavily on nurses recruited from the Philippines to address its nurse shortage. Strong demand for Filipino nurses stemmed from its US colonial past which ensured proficiency in English and a US orientated nurse education system that dovetailed with the requirements of overseas employers. Nursing schools have played an important part in ensuring a growing supply of nurses to feed international demand. Although nursing schools in the Philippines are privately owned, the government has sponsored their growth and this has encouraged nursing as a career because of the opportunities it presents to work abroad. By contrast, low levels of health expenditure and poor wages encourage exit overseas.

The experience of overseas nurses working in the UK has varied. Nurses often make use of recruitment agents that charge high fees to place nurses in employment and sometimes provide misleading information about the type of work and the geographical location of the workplace. All nurses have to be registered with the UK professional nursing organization before they can be employed as registered nurses and it can be difficult to gain the relevant placements and experience, resulting in qualified nurses working as health care assistants for much lower wages. In general, nurses employed in the NHS have a much more positive experience of employment with formal induction and mentoring. This contrasts with nurses working in independent sector nursing homes that frequently confront issues of deskilling as their qualifications are not utilized and their experience discounted. Internationally recruited nurses want to be treated with respect by patients and other staff and not allocated poor shift patterns or provided with few training and promotion opportunities. There are also important consequences for the home country.

Question

Does the experience of nurses coming to the UK from other countries suggest that constraints on migration are falling?

Conclusions

International migration has become an increasingly important element of international HRM. In a context of labour shortages and ageing populations, governments and employers have looked to migrant labour to undertake jobs that the indigenous population are unwilling to undertake and to use high skilled migration to boost competitiveness. As in other areas of human resource management, it is deceptively simple to view international migration as an inevitable outcome of global economic and political developments. A number of actors, migrants themselves and their representatives, employers and governments are actively seeking to shape the migration process and its consequences. This is evident from the UK's government points-based system of managed migration and the European Commission's emphasis on attracting highly skilled workers to boost EU competitiveness.

International migration has created winners and losers. Employers are a key beneficiary, ensuring that they recruit to hard-to-fill posts, gain a relatively compliant and hard-working workforce, and often benefit from a more highly qualified workforce at lower cost than would otherwise be the case. Nonetheless the integration of a more diverse workforce, the need to get to grips with complex immigration regulations, and the response of co-workers and customers to the migrant workforce all raise new challenges for employers. For migrants themselves, the decision to migrate is frequently a constrained choice reflecting dismal employment prospects in the source country. Consequently, although lower skilled workers in particular are vulnerable in the labour market and are often employed on poor terms and conditions of employment, there are still considerable personal and family benefits that accrue from migration. It seems certain that international migration will remain a prominent HR concern for many years to come.

Review questions

1 Why do you think Castles and Miller (2003) suggest that we are in 'an age of migration'?

2 How important is globalization in explaining why international migration occurs?

3 What are the advantages and disadvantages for employers of employing migrants? Do these differ from the native-born population?

4 Why are migrants viewed as vulnerable to exploitation in the labour market. What remedies would you suggest to safeguard their employment rights?

Further reading

1 LeGrain, P. (2007) *Immigrants: Your Country Needs Them.* London: Little Brown.

A highly accessible and readable account of the main trends and arguments within the immigration debate.

2 May, J., Wills, J., Datta, K., Evans, Y., Herbert, J. and McIlwaine, C. (2007) 'Keeping London working: global cities, the British state and London's new migrant division of labour', *Transactions of Institute British Geographical Society*, 32, 151–67.

This research examines the role of migrants in low-paid jobs in London and explores their pay and conditions. It argues that the policies of the British state are integral to understanding the emergence of a new migrant division of labour.

3 McDowell, L., Batnitzky, A. and Dyer, S. (2008) 'Internationalization and the spaces of temporary labour: the global assembly of a local workforce', *British Journal of Industrial Relations*, 46(4), 750–70.

This study examines the role of employment agencies in sourcing migrant labour for employers, drawing on case studies of a hospital and hotel, and examines employer preferences for migrant labour.

4 McGovern, P. (2007) 'Immigration, labour markets and employment relations: problems and prospects', *British Journal of Industrial Relations,* 45(2), 217–35.

This review article provides a good overview of the main theories of immigration and draws out the consequences of immigration for key stakeholders.

References

Anderson, B., Clark, N. and Parutis, V. (2006) *New EU Members? Migrant Workers' Challenges and Opportunities to UK Trades Unions: a Polish and Lithuanian Case Study,* www.tuc.org.uk/extras/migrantchallenges.pdf.

Anderson, B., Ruhs, M., Rogaly, B. and Spencer, S. (2006) *Fair Enough? Central and East European Migrants in Low-wage employment in the UK,* www.compas.ox.ac.uk/changingstatus.

Bach, S., Kessler, I. and Heron, P. (2006). 'Changing job boundaries and workforce reform: the case of teaching assistants', *Industrial Relations Journal,* 37(1), 2–21.

Ball, R. (2004). 'Divergent development, racialised rights: globalised labour markets and the trade of nurses — The case of the Philippines', *Women's Studies International Forum,* 27: 119–133.

Barroso, J.-M. (2007) '*Making Europe more attractive to highly skilled migrants and increasing the protection of lawfully residing and working migrants*', Press Release, IP/07/1575, Brussels, 23 Oct.

Blackman, B. (2007) 'Regulating the situation for migrants in the British construction industry', *CLR News,* 4, 12–17.

Blanchflower, D., Saleheen, J. and Shadforth, C. (2007) *The Impact of Recent Migration from Eastern Europe on the UK Economy,* London: Bank of England, www.bankofengland.co.uk/publications/speeches/2007/speech297.pdf.

Borjas, G. (2003) The Labor Demand Curve *Is* Downward Sloping: Reexamining the Impact of Immigration on the Labor Market, *Quarterly Journal of Economics,* 118(4) 1335–1374.

British Medical Association (2007) *Memorandum by the British Medical Association.* Evidence to the House of Lords Select Committee on Economic Affairs. The economic impact of immigration, HL paper 82-I. London: The Stationery Office.

Cangiano, A. Shutes, I. Spencer, S. and Leeson, G. (2009) *Migrant Care Workers in Ageing Societies: Research Findings in the United Kingdom.* Oxford: Compas.

Castles, S. and Miller, M. (2003) *The Age of Migration: International Population Movements in the Modern World,* Basingstoke: Palgrave Macmillan.

Champlin, D. and Hake, E. (2006) 'Immigration as industrial straetgy in American meatpacking', *Review of Political Economy,* 18(1), 49–69.

Davies, A. (2008) 'One step forward, two steps back? The Viking and Laval cases in the ECJ', *Industrial Law Journal,* 37(2), 126–48.

Dench, S., Hurstfield, J., Hill, D. and Akroyd, K. (2006) *Employers' Use of Migrant Labour: Main Report.* London: Home Office.

Dimitrova, S. (2008) '*Bulgarian and UK Trade Unions Cooperate to Support Migrant Workers*', http://www.eurofound.europa.eu/eiro/2008/05/articles/bg0805019i.htm.

Dustmann, C., Glitz, A and Vogel, T. (2006) *Employment, Wages and the Economic Cycle: Differences between Immigrants and Natives* CReAM Discussion Paper Series 09/06. London: University College London.

Dustmann, C., Frattini, T. and Preston, I. (2007) *A Study of Migrant Workers and the National Minimum Wage and Enforcement Issues that Arise,* www.econ.ucl.ac.uk/cream/pages/LPC.pdf.

Dustmann, C., Glitz, A. and Frattini, T. (2008) *'The Labour Market Impact of Immigration'*, Centre for Research and Analysis of Migration, Discussion Paper, 11, London: University College London.

EIROnline (2007) *Poland–Pay Disputes in the Health Sector Escalate,* www.eurofound.europa.eu/eiro/2007/07/articles/pl0707019i.htm.

Freeman, R. (2005) 'What really ails Europe (and America): the doubling of the global workforce', *The Globalist,* 3 June, www.theglobalist.com.

French, S. and Mohrke, J. (2006). *The Impact of 'New Arrivals' Upon the North Staffordshire Labour Market,* www.lowpay.gov.uk/lowpay/research/pdf/t0Z96GK3.pdf.

Gennard, J. (2008) 'Vaxholm/Laval case: its implementations for trade unions', *Employee Relations,* 30(5), 473–78.

Givan, R. (2007). 'Side by side we battle onward? Representing workers in contemporary America', *British Journal of Industrial Relations,* 45(4), 829–55.

Heyes, J. (2009) 'Recruiting and organising migrant workers through education and training: a comparison of Community and the GMB', *Industrial Relations Journal,* 40(3), 182–97.

Hochschild, A. (2000) 'Global Care Chains and Emotional Surplus Value' in Hutton, W. and Giddens, A. (eds) On the Edge: Living with Global Capitalism. London: Jonathan Cape, pp. 130–146

Hollifield, J. (2007) 'The Emerging Migration State', in Portes, A. and DeWind, J. (eds) *Rethinking Immigration: New Theoretical and Empirical Perspectives*. New York: Berghahn.

Home Office (2006) *A Points-Based System: Making Migration Work for Britain,* Cm 6741. London: Home Office.

Home Office (2008) *The Economic Impact of Immigration*. Cm 7414. London: Home Office.

House of Lords (2008) *Select Committee on Economic Affairs 1st Report of Session 2007–08: The Economic Impact of Immigration,* HL paper 82-I. London: The Stationery Office.

International Organization for Migration (2005) *World Migration Report,* Geneva : International Organization for Migration.

International Organization for Migration (2008) *IOM and Labour Migration,* www.iom.int/jahia/Jahia/cache/offonce/pid/1674?entryId=17414.

Kingma, M. (2006) *Nurses on the Move: Migration and the Global Health Care Economy*. Ithaca: Cornell University Press.

Legrain, P. (2007) *Immigrants Your Country Needs Them*. London: Little Brown.

Lucas, R. and Mansfield, S. (2008) Staff shortages and Immigration in Hospitality, www.ukba.home office.gov.uk/sitecontent/documents/aboutus/workingwithus/mac/lucasandmansfield2008.

Martin, P., Abella, M. and Midgley, E. (2004) 'Best practice to manage migration: the Philippines', *International Migration Review,* 38(4), 1544–59.

Massey, D., Alarcon, R., Durand, J. and Gonzalez, H. (1987). *Return to Aztlan*. Berkeley: University of California Press.

Matthews, G. and Ruhs, M. (2007) 'Are you Being Served? Employer Demand for Migrant Labour in the UK's Hospitality Sector, *COMPAS Working Paper,* 51, Oxford: Oxford University.

May, J., Wills, J., Datta, K., Evans, Y., Herbert, J. and McIlwaine, C. (2007) 'Keeping London working: global cities, the British state and London's new migrant divison of labour', *Transactions of Institute British Geographical Society* 32, 151–67.

McDowell, L., Batnitzky, A. and Dyer, S. (2008) 'Internationalization and the spaces of temporary labour: the global assembly of a local workforce', *British Journal of Industrial Realtions,* 46(4), 750–70.

McGovern, P. (2007) 'Immigration, labour markets and employment relations: problems and prospects', *British Journal of Industrial Relations,* 45(2), 217–35.

McGregor, J. (2007) 'Joining the BBC (british bottom cleaners): Zimbabwean migrants and the UK care industry', *Journal of Ethnic and Migration Studies,* 33(5), 801–24.

McKay, S., Craw, M. and Chopra, D. (2006) *Migrant Workers in England and Wales: An Assessment of Migrant Worker Health and Safety Risks.* HSE Research Report 502.

Michaels, E., Handfield-Jones, H. and Axelrod, B. (2001) *The War for Talent.* Harvard: Harvard Business School Press.

Migration Advisory Committee (2008) *Skilled, Shortage, Sensible: the Recommended Shortage Lists for the UK and Scotland,* London: Migration Advisory Committee.

Milkman, R. (2006) L.A. story: Immigrant Workers and the Future of the US Labor Movement. New York: Russell Sage Foundation.

OECD (2008) *International Migration Outlook SOPEMI– 2008 Edition,* Paris: OECD.

ONS (2008) *International Migration First Release Calendar Year 2007,* London: Office for National Statistics.

Pai, H.-H. (2008) *Chinese Whispers: The True Story Behind Britain's Hidden Army of Labour.* London: Penguin.

Parrenas, R. (2005) *Children of Global Migration: Transnational Families and Gendered Woes.* Stanford: Stanford University Press.

Piore, M. (1979) *Birds of Passage: Migrant Labor and Industrial Societies.* Cambridge: Cambridge University Press.

Portes, A. and Rumbaut, R. (1990). *Immigrant America: A Portrait. Berkeley:* University of California Press.

Ram, M., Edwards., P. and Jones, T. (2007) 'Staying underground: informal work, small firms and employment regulation', *Work and Occupations,* 34(3), 318–44.

Ratha, D., Mohapatra, S. and Xu, Z. (2008) *Outlook for Remittance Flows 2008–2010.* Migration and Development Brief, http://worldbank.org/prospects/migrationandremittances.

Ryan, B. (2005) *Labour Migration and Employment Rights.* London: Institute of Employment Rights.

Ruhs, M. and Martin, P. (2008) 'Numbers vs. rights: trade-offs and guest worker programs', *International Migration Review,* 42(1), 249–65.

Sassen, S. (1988). *The Mobility of Labour and Capital.* Cambridge: Cambridge University Press.

Saxenian, A. (2008) 'The International Mobility of Entrepreneurs and Regional Upgrading in India and China', in Solimano, A. (ed.) *The International Mobility of Talent.* Oxford: Oxford University Press.

Scott, S., McCormick, A. and Zaloznik, M. (2008) *Staff shortages and Immigration in Agriculture,* www.ukba.homeoffice.gov.uk/mac.

Semple, K. (2008) 'Among immigrants a clash of cultures, *New York Times,* 15 October.

Shelley, T. (2007) *Exploited: Migrant Labour in the New Global Economy.* London: Zed.

Terrazas, A., Batalova, J. and Fan, V. (2007) 'Frequently Requested Statistics on Immigrants in the United States', *Migration Information Source,* www.migrationinformation.org/USfocus/display.cfm?id=649.

Trade Union Congress (TUC) (2007) *The Economics of Migration: Managing the Impacts.* London: TUC.

TUC (2008) *Commission on Vulnerable Employment: Hard Work: Hidden Lives,* www.vulnerableworkers.org.uk/2008/05/full-report-of-the-commission-released/.

United Nations Population Fund (UNPF) (2006) *State of World Population 2006. A Passage to Hope: Women and International Migration,* www.unfpa.org/swp/2006/english/print/introduction.html.

Waldinger, R. and Lichter, M. (2003), *How the Other Half Works: Immigration and the Social Organisation of Labor.* California: University of California Press.

Woolfson, C. (2008) 'Labour standards and migration in the new Europe: post-Communist legacies and perspectives', *European Journal of Industrial Relations,* 13(2), 199–218.

Chapter 15

Outsourcing and international HRM

Virginia Doellgast and Howard Gospel

Key aims

The aims of this chapter are to:

- identify the forms that outsourcing can take and its relationship with offshoring;
- examine the institutional context in which outsourcing takes place;
- reflect on the dilemmas that managers face in coordinating HRM practices in outsourcing;
- examine ways in which aspects of the HR function itself are outsourced.

Introduction

Outsourcing of various kinds has always existed, as firms put out work to suppliers, contractors, and intermediaries to organize the production of goods and services. In recent years, however, outsourcing has increased in both scale (the volume of outsourcing) and scope (the number of activities outsourced). This has several related causes. First, the advent of new transportation systems, such as the growth of container shipping, and the advent of new information and communications technologies (ICTs) have facilitated ordering, monitoring, and delivery of products and services. Second, as markets have extended and become more competitive, firms increasingly seek to save costs through focusing on their core value-maximizing activities, handing others over to suppliers. Third, management fashion has played an important role in popularizing networked production models, as firms watch and imitate their competitors. Finally, the relaxation of trade barriers, emergence of new markets, and expansion of a more highly skilled labour force in Asia have increased the ease and cost savings of outsourcing to these regions. (IMF 2007; OECD 2007a, 2007b).

These trends have implications for the management of human resources across firms' increasingly fragmented (and often international) supply chains. Managers face choices concerning how to help employees adjust during worker transfer or downsizing following the decision to outsource work. Networked relationships across core firms and their subcontractors introduce new demands as firms seek to co-ordinate practices and incentives across organizations. In addition, the human resource management function itself is increasingly being outsourced to specialist organizations, often involving substantial restructuring and rationalization.

In this chapter, we first provide background on outsourcing trends and then discuss the HRM issues and choices associated with outsourcing. Throughout, we examine the ways in which national institutions affect the costs and benefits of different strategic choices by firms, as well as the particular challenges multinationals face as they seek to manage outsourcing contracts across national borders. The discussion addresses many of the themes of the book. We show that outsourcing is both driven by and used to facilitate globalization. However, outsourcing strategies and their impact on different stakeholder groups continue to be embedded in distinct national settings.

Conceptualizing outsourcing

The decision to outsource work has several distinct dimensions. First, outsourcing involves the decision to carry out certain activities inside or outside the boundaries of the firm. Economists have described this in terms of the use of the visible hand of management or the invisible hand of the market, the use of internal or external methods of co-ordination, or decisions to make something oneself or to buy it in from others (Coase 1937; Williamson 1975). More recently, scholars have begun to refer to the 'vanishing hand', as highly integrated businesses are reducing co-ordination via internal mechanisms and are increasing coordination via market mechanism (Langlois 2003). In practice, firms typically use a combination of internal and external arrangements, shifting the balance between in-house and outsourced production Some activities may lie in an area between the firm and the market, e.g. where a company contracts with a supplier or subcontractor that it partly owns or with an association of which it is a member. For the sake of clarity, this first aspect of outsourcing can be seen in terms of a simple horizontal spectrum from internal to external, or in-sourcing to outsourcing.

Second, firms face decisions concerning what to outsource. Here a distinction may be made between people and activities. The firm can outsource workers who have previously been employed within the firm, transferring them to another firm on a permanent basis. The firm can also outsource activities, which can be further categorized as primary and support activities (Porter 1985). Primary activities are those that are integral to the firm's value chain, such as components in a manufacturing company or accounts processing in a service organization. Support activities are those processes that facilitate the firm's value chain, such as IT, advertising, accounting and HRM.

Third, firms must decide on the location of outsourced operations, or to which regions, countries, or continents outsourcing will occur. Historically, outsourcing was largely domestic, to other firms or organizations in the near vicinity of the outsourcing firm. As communications improved, transportation developed, and markets expanded, the geographical scope of outsourcing extended to the national level. More recently, with further improvements in ICTs, outsourcing has come to cross national boundaries and even continents, with increased outsourcing by firms in developed countries to developing countries. Where transactions take place across international boundaries, the term *offshoring* is used. We can distinguish further between *near-shoring,* in which work is moved to a neighbouring country (such as when a German firm shifts production

Geographical location		Internal v. external	
		Internal	External
	Domestic	In-house production	Domestic outsourcing
	Overseas	In-house off-shoring	Off-shore outsourcing

Figure 15.1 **Outsourcing and offshoring**

to Poland) and *far-shoring,* in which work is moved over a greater geographical distance (such as when a UK firm shifts production to China).

The main distinctions made so far are shown diagrammatically in Figure 15.1. The two boxes on the right hand side cover outsourcing. The bottom top boxes cover off-shoring. In this chapter, we are primarily concerned with the two boxes to the right, or outsourcing domestically and internationally.

Below we examine particular implications of outsourcing for the management of human resources. We focus on three themes: employment restructuring associated with outsourcing, especially where this involves transfers and/or redundancy of workers; the challenges of coordinating HRM across organizational boundaries after outsourcing has occurred; and the particular case of the outsourcing of the HRM function itself.

Employment restructuring and the outsourcing decision

One set of HRM challenges associated with outsourcing concerns the transfer or dismissal of current employees following the decision to move the activities that they perform out of the core organization. Companies typically choose among several organizational forms for a new outsourced operation, including:

- establishing a subsidiary that remains under their direct control;
- shifting work to a third-party subcontractor;
- initiating a joint venture with a third-party subcontractor.

Managers then face the decision either to:

- dismiss the workforce performing the outsourced functions; or
- transfer a portion or all workers to the new organization.

The decision to adopt a particular organizational and staffing strategy has important HRM implications. The retention of staff during outsourcing may be useful in transferring firm-specific knowledge, particularly for complex business processes such as IT, research and development, or HRM. It avoids costs associated with layoffs and new recruitment.

However, the transfer of existing workers may conflict with plans to implement new working practices or reduce direct labour costs and is impractical when outsourcing is undertaken with the intention of shifting work to another country or region.

From an employee's perspective, the opportunity to transfer to a new employer is generally preferable to layoffs. There may be additional positive aspects of moving to a more specialist organization, such as new opportunities for career development (Kessler *et al.* 1999). However, employees also often experience disruption associated with broken career ladders and changes in management practices and style, which may negatively affect motivation and commitment. In the terms used in this book, outsourcing is often a contested process. The decision to adopt a more intermediate organizational form such as a wholly owned subsidiary or joint venture can create more continuity in management and reduce disruption to employees, while allowing the core firm to retain additional control during the outsourcing process.

While employers face similar challenges in managing employee transfer or downsizing regardless of location, national context may influence the costs and benefits of different strategic choices. Two institutions at the national level are particularly important in this respect: transfer of undertakings legislation and industrial relations systems.

▶ Transfer of undertakings

Laws concerning employee rights during the transfer of undertakings affect the ease with which management can downsize the workforce or alter employment contracts when outsourcing work (see Chapter 8 on international M&As). In the European Union (EU), the Acquired Rights Directive seeks to safeguard employees' rights in the transfer of ownership of a business or part of a business, defined to include the transfer of employees between organizations. The directive specifies that the terms and conditions in a collective agreement must be observed until the agreement expires, the transfer of ownership does not constitute justifiable reason for dismissals, and the status of existing employee representatives should be preserved (i.e. the new employer must continue to recognize and negotiate with existing unions or works councils). In addition, these representatives are entitled to be consulted as to the 'likely or planned economic and social implications of the transfer' 'in good time' before the transfer (Eurofound 2007). The European Court of Justice has broadly interpreted this to apply to the transfer of work associated with outsourcing, even when a contract is shifted from one outsourced firm to another and involves no transfer of 'tangible or intangible assets' (Justice 2002). Thus, the directive covers cases where services are outsourced, insourced or assigned to a new contractor.

These rules mean that staff transfers or downsizing associated with outsourcing are more strongly regulated in Europe compared to North America or Asia. For example, In the US, employment contracts are 'at will' unless otherwise agreed through individual contracts or collective bargaining agreements, meaning the employer can terminate the contract at any time without giving cause. There is thus no legal protection of contracts following the transfer of work through outsourcing, either to a third party or a subsidiary. In Japan the Labour Contract Succession Law was passed in 2000, giving the parent company the right to transfer its existing workforce employed in a line of business to a separate company (Sako 2006). Existing employment contracts and collective agreements are automatically transferred to a spin-off. However, this does not apply to transfer of undertakings associated with outsourcing to a third party (Araki 2005).

Despite overall stronger employment protections in Europe, there is also significant variation between EU member states in the terms of national regulations. In the UK, the Transfer of Undertakings Protection of Employment (TUPE) legislation safeguards to a degree the terms and conditions of employees affected by outsourcing (see also Chapter 8). For instance, the 'transferee' (the firm taking in the outsourced staff) takes on the liability for the key aspects of the contract of employment and while the 'transferror' (the firm losing the outsourced staff) is obliged to undertake a 'full and meaningful' consultation process as early as is practical. However, some aspects of terms and conditions, such as pensions, are not fully protected in the transfer and the consultation process does not oblige management to negotiate.

Consultation requirements are substantially stronger in continental Europe. For example, in the Netherlands, management must inform works council and union representatives of the decision to transfer part of the business, provide information on the likely impact and justification of its decision, and show that it has taken account of workers' interests. If works councils challenge the proposals, they must be postponed for a month, and the works council can subsequently go to labour court to formally contest the decision. In addition, once the process of outsourcing has begun, the employer must consult with the works council on any contract changes with the subcontractor (Caprile and Llorens 2000). France, Italy, and Spain also have additional regulations that make it difficult for employers to use subcontracting arrangements that do not involve the transfer of staff to terminate employment contracts or change working conditions, and that establish joint responsibility by the client and subcontractor for observing employment rights (Caprile and Llorens 2000). These different regulations affect the extent to which workers are able to have a say in the restructuring process, as well as the cost advantages of different organizational forms to employers.

▶ Industrial relations

A second set of national-level institutions that can influence outsourcing decisions is the national industrial relations system. First, negotiation and consultation rights affect employees' ability to participate substantively in restructuring decisions – and thus may shape both the form that outsourcing takes as well as outcomes for employees. These rights can be important for the implementation of transfer of undertakings rules. In many continental European countries, employees have additional representation rights on corporate boards which allow them to have prior knowledge and to be consulted on restructuring decisions.

Second, the bargaining power of trade unions can influence their ability to negotiate job security provisions, which make it difficult or costly to lay off workers, or to oppose outsourcing through strikes or other forms of industrial action. In countries where unions are weak, with lower bargaining coverage, membership density, and participation rights such as the US and UK, workers are less likely to have these forms of leverage. For example, under the UK's TUPE regulations, an employer can dismiss workers if it can be demonstrated that they were undertaken for economic, technical, or organizational reasons; and employment contracts can be changed with the approval of individual employees. These conditions can be easy to meet, in the absence of strong unions or works councils to inform workers of their legal rights or to contest decisions. A study by Cooke *et al.* (2004), based on a series of UK case studies, showed that employers had broad discretion in reducing staff numbers and altering working practices following the transfer of workers, for example through dismissing employees for economic reasons and then re-hiring them under less favourable contracts.

Third, variation in bargaining coverage, or the number of workplaces covered by central collective agreements, may influence employers' ability to use outsourcing to reduce labour costs through varying employment terms and conditions. Companies may seek to use new organizational forms to escape or renegotiate strong collective agreements. This means that the ease of renegotiating agreements can influence employers' cost-benefit calculations.

For example, in France, the government typically extends agreements negotiated between the major employers' association and trade unions in a sector to all firms, while in Germany employers must agree to such an extension (which rarely occurs). Today, France has sectoral collective agreements that cover all firms and subsidiaries in major industries like telecommunications and banking, as well as for the contractors that service these industries (Doellgast *et al.* 2009). In Germany, many subcontractors do not have agreements, and firms often form subsidiaries to move work out of stronger sectoral or company agreements (Doellgast and Greer 2007). German banks have set up 'direct banks' for their call centres in order to transfer work to new companies not covered by the sectoral banking agreement. This has largely been uncontested following one unsuccessful strike by workers at Citibank facing redundancy (Holtgrewe 2001). Inclusive sectoral or national bargaining has also been maintained in Austria, Denmark, and Spain, among other countries, which may affect firms' ability to vary working conditions across their 'production chain' (Shire *et al.* 2009; Sorensen and Weinkopf 2009).

Finally, differences in union strategies may also affect outsourcing decisions. Worker representatives have distinct interests in keeping work in-house or maintaining a coherent framework of collective bargaining. Sako (2006: 4) argues that unions themselves choose to extend or contract their boundaries, and these decisions then can affect management's choice of a corporate structure. As representation rights regarding outsourcing are often weak, unions may draw on distinct forms of bargaining power in other areas to try to influence employment restructuring decisions. For example, in a comparison of call centre outsourcing strategies, Doellgast (2008) finds that US unions adopted strategic campaigns and strike tactics to extend agreements to new organizations and protect the working conditions of members, while German unions relied more on the co-determination rights of works councillors.

▶ Institutions and strategic choice

A key question the above discussion raises is to what extent these national differences in institutions influence the strategic choices of firms concerning staff transfer and layoffs, as well as the organizational form adopted. The results of a survey by Kakabadse and Kakabadse (2002) suggest that the cross-national differences in outsourcing strategies between the more 'liberal' US and the more 'social' Europe may not be as substantial as we might expect. They found that staff were transferred to a supplier following outsourcing in 38 per cent of US and 39 per cent of European companies surveyed; post-transfer redundancies occurred in 28 per cent of US and 24 per cent of European companies; while managers adopted new terms of employment for redeployed workers in 13 per cent of US and 10 per cent of European cases. Although the extent of employment change associated with outsourcing appears to be somewhat higher in the US, with more firms pursuing redundancies or changing HRM practices, these differences are relatively small.

Other studies find more substantial differences in outsourcing decisions within Europe. Barthelemy and Geyer (2001) conducted a survey of firms undertaking IT outsourcing and found that 69 per cent of these decisions involved personnel transfers and layoffs in France compared to 42 per cent in Germany. They argue this is explained by the greater power of German trade unions, which allows employees to oppose measures disruptive to employees. Grimshaw and Miozzo (2006) conducted a similar study of IT outsourcing in Germany and the UK, based on in-depth case studies of 13 outsourcing contracts. They show that all of these contracts involved some staff transfer through direct outsourcing, joint venture, or a captive market subsidiary. However, national differences in consultation rights and the period of protection against dismissal affected how the transfer was managed in each country. In Germany, management typically conducted six months of communications and negotiations with works councils, and demonstrated a stronger determination to win the 'hearts and minds' of IT workers through designing a restructuring process that allowed staff to adjust to changes. In the UK, they found minimal consultation, little labour influence over the transfer, and, subsequently, substantial resistance – in one case resulting in a strike. These procedural differences also resulted in different organizational strategies: the German firms initially adopted joint ventures between client and supplier to transition workers to the subcontractor, because this was viewed as better for employees; while the UK firms all relied on direct outsourcing, with an immediate shift from in-house to externalized provision.

Together, this research shows that institutional factors which vary across countries, including legal systems and industrial relations arrangements, can influence employment restructuring decisions associated with outsourcing. Stronger laws protecting employee rights during the transfer of assets or people and more inclusive bargaining systems create constraints on strategic choice, encouraging consultation and discouraging the renegotiation of employment contracts at a lower level. While these constraints may represent short-term costs for firms, they also can have long-term advantages, in terms of higher levels of employee commitment and co-operation with restructuring plans. The Grimshaw and Miozzo (2006) study cited above found that German client firms were more satisfied with HR practices and service quality of new supplier firms than those in the UK, which they attribute to the more extensive process of consultation in Germany.

Co-ordination of HRM across organizational boundaries

A further set of HRM challenges associated with outsourcing concerns the coordination of management decisions and processes between organizations. Here we refer to the firm that outsources work as the *client* and the firm that performs the outsourced work as the *subcontractor*. The following areas of HRM tend to be the focus of co-ordination efforts.

- *Employee selection and skill development.* Clients may seek to establish a common set of standards for employee qualifications and training across their subcontractors. This may be particularly important for higher skilled jobs or services in which the subcontractors' workers are interacting with the clients' customers.

- *Performance management.* Clients may seek to harmonize incentives to promote shared goals, such as meeting sales or performance targets. Monitoring practices that track individual and group performance are often important for ensuring that standards are met.

- *Work design.* Clients may seek to encourage shared principles of work design, such as use of teams, participation or suggestion initiatives, and the use of shared procedures. This may be most important where employees work with each other across organizations, or in cases where a firm is strongly committed to particular principles of work organization (such as lean production historically in Japan).

- *Scheduling and staffing.* Clients often demand a certain level of flexibility from subcontractors in adjusting the volume of goods or service production at short notice. This can have a direct effect on scheduling practices, with higher requirements for employees to be flexible with their own schedules, more use of part-time or temporary contracts, and lower job security.

Below we consider the conditions under which client firms are more likely to seek to influence or jointly manage subcontractors' HRM practices. We then discuss the challenges of co-ordinating HRM across organizational boundaries. Again, we show that national context can have an important influence on management strategy and outcomes, affecting the costs and benefits associated with co-ordination. In addition, the international character of many outsourcing contracts – and the internationalization of subcontractors themselves – create distinct co-ordination challenges.

▶ The decision to co-ordinate or differentiate HRM practices

It is not obvious that a client should seek to intervene in the HRM decisions of subcontractors, or to co-ordinate these decisions in some way. Companies often outsource certain functions to reduce costs, concentrate on their core competencies, or rely on a specialist organization's expertise – with the option of terminating the contract or switching providers if quality does not meet expectations. In other words, one of the attractions of outsourcing might be to increasingly differentiate HRM between occupational groups. However, there are certain conditions under which a client may have more of an interest in its subcontractors' HRM practices, depending on the nature of the contracted product or service, the extent of joint production carried out across organizations, and the national (or international) context of the contracting relationship.

First, where the product or service is more intangible or complex, contracting firms may take more interest in management practices used at the point of production. In settings such as business services or call centres, services are simultaneously produced and consumed, and thus the client is typically unable to rely on quality control mechanisms used in manufacturing at the point of delivery to prevent 'defective' products from getting to the customer. The reasons for outsourcing this work may also play a role: clients pursuing a business strategy focused on quality rather than cost reduction may be particularly concerned with ensuring that successful practices used in-house are extended to subcontractors, or that workers in the subcontracted firm develop a shared organizational identity with the client firm.

Second, where the outsourcing contract involves substantial collaboration or joint production with in-house staff, the client may encourage the co-ordination of practices to facilitate cooperation and harmonize incentives. Under so-called 'relational contracting', managers seek to encourage the development of social capital or collective goals across organizations (Dyer and Singh 1998). However, even in more transactional or mixed settings, there can be incentives for developing shared procedures and skills. For example, Rubery *et al.* (2003) show in a case study of 'multi-agency' subcontracting relationships in the airline industry that a high level of interdependence between staff from different organizations meant that employees were subject to 'multiple sources of control and evaluation' as 'organizations attempted to control staff employed by other organizations and through actions to encourage these staff members to increase identity with and commitment to the goals of the client organization' (2003: 285).

Third, national context can influence strategy concerning HRM co-ordination. Geographical or cultural distance between the client and subcontractor(s) may have contradictory influences on the extent and goals of coordination. On the one hand, a client may be more likely to allow its subcontractors to adopt HRM practices that are consistent with the local conditions and business environment. Companies may also be more likely to offshore the production of products or services that are relatively standardized or easily codifiable, allowing them to engage in more arms-length contracting. On the other hand, cultural distance may increase uncertainty, leading firms to seek tighter control over HRM. In addition, firms with subcontractors in developing countries are increasingly concerned with the negative effects on their image associated with labour standards violations, and thus may establish codes of conduct with monitoring mechanisms to ensure that suppliers meet minimum terms and conditions (see Chapter 13 on CSR).

National institutions such as corporate governance, industrial relations, or traditions of corporate organization may also influence the extent and nature of HRM co-ordination. For example, Japanese firms traditionally developed close, trust-based relational contracting with suppliers, based on the *keiretsu* form of business organization. Core firms sought to influence the promotion, training, and work design practices of their subcontractors, even moving employees across firms to adjust to changing demand in different areas of the business. In Germany, strong industry-based unions have coordinated HRM to some extent across core firms and suppliers through sectoral agreements, while strong business associations serve to diffuse best practices and establish shared rules and acceptable behaviour of members. In contrast, US and UK firms have pursued more arms-length contracting relationships, explained in part by weaker organization of employers, distinct traditions of law, and more decentralized or disorganized industrial relations institutions (Helper 1991; Lane and Bachmann 1997).

▶ Challenges of HRM co-ordination

In cases where firms do seek to co-ordinate HRM across organizational boundaries, a further set of issues concerns the particular challenges clients, subcontractors, and employee representatives face in managing co-ordination and how these may be overcome.

First, client firms face high costs of enforcement or monitoring when seeking to promote a shared set of standards or practices across subcontractors, as they do not have direct control over management. They thus often develop complex systems for ensuring compliance with contract terms; for example, through assigning special account managers to meet regularly with subcontractors or requiring detailed information on success in meeting training goals or quality targets. Third-party certification through consultants also plays an increasingly important role, with the growing popularity of both general certifications such as ISO 9000 and more targeted certification for particular industries or types of work.

A second set of challenges is faced by the subcontractors themselves, as they seek to adapt internal HRM practices to the demands of multiple clients. Contracts with different customers or clients may have widely varying terms concerning quality specifications and flexibility in adjusting the volume of goods or service production at short notice. This, in turn, affects the subcontractor's ability to invest in training or to offer its employees predictable schedules and long-term contracts. In addition, clients may provide different variable incentives or offer contract terms that allow vendors to pay certain employees at a higher level. These difficulties are particularly pronounced in service settings, such as call centres or technical support, in which different groups of employees are 'dedicated' to a particular client. Under these conditions, managers face the potential problem of managing widely varying HRM practices within the firm (and often in one location), as well as dealing with possible negative effects on employee motivation of this internal variation.

Third, worker representatives such as unions and works councils face a new set of challenges as they seek to coordinate collective bargaining across organizational boundaries. In many countries, HRM practices are regulated by collective agreements at the industry, firm, or establishment level. However, these structures are typically organized around traditional industry or firm boundaries, which may not fit the 'networked firm' model characteristic of outsourcing relationships. Different unions may be responsible for in-house and outsourced firms whose workers carry out similar functions; or, as discussed above, were formerly employed in the same organization. Improving bargaining co-ordination between these unions and works councils at different organizations can be quite difficult due to conflicting interests and increased variation in pay and working conditions across in-house and outsourced firms (Doellgast and Greer 2007).

These co-ordination issues usually have an important international dimension. Multinationals face particular challenges in coordinating HRM across international borders (see Chapters 6 and 7). This can be exacerbated by the fragmented ownership structures associated with subcontracting. Performance management and monitoring practices may be particularly important in helping to facilitate co-ordination, and thus there may be more focus on standardization in a multinational setting. For example, Indian call centres have received a lot of attention in the media in recent years for their intensive monitoring practices, with workers' calls often listened to by both internal managers and a series of additional quality control managers from client firms seeking to harmonize standards across subcontractors (Taylor and Bain 2004). A study by Batt *et al.* (2006) showed that subcontracted call centres in the US were more heavily monitored than in-house centres, but that monitoring was even more intensive in offshore settings such as India. In addition, subcontractors themselves are often multinationals, possibly serving other multinational clients. This poses multiple coordination issues as firms seek to provide a standardized service across national boundaries. The case study, below, illustrates some of the challenges faced by a multinational, call-centre subcontractor along these lines, and how it sought to resolve them.

This additional focus on co-ordination and harmonization may be positive, in terms of ensuring a standardized product, but may also have costs as local managers are constrained from adapting to local conditions. For example, the study by Batt *et al.* (2006) cited above found that higher monitoring rates were associated with high employee turnover, indicating possible negative implications in terms of employees satisfaction and commitment of attempts to control performance management too closely.

CASE STUDY

'Vendotel'* – co-ordinating HRM in a multinational, call-centre vendor

Vendotel is a multinational call-centre vendor based in the US, with call centres in over 10 countries across North America, Europe, and Asia. It prided itself on its ability to keep labour costs low through locating in countries such as India and Indonesia, while adopting lean scheduling and intensive performance monitoring practices in higher wage countries. Vendotel had no collective bargaining agreements in most locations. The one exception was France, where it was obligated to follow the terms of the sectoral agreement for third-party services.

Vendotel expanded into Germany, France, and the UK in the late 1990s. Managers in US headquarters had misgivings about the expense of operating call centres in Europe, where they were often forced to modify their 'best practice' HRM practices to fit local labour laws:

The biggest one is the employment agreement we have to enter into with employees there...In the US, it is employment at will, and so if an employee doesn't work out, we can fire him or her. There, we have to take on a lot of responsibility for the employee once we hire them on a permanent basis, so we need to find ways around these rules...Otherwise, it's like a contract for life, and

you put yourself at risk, because in this business there are major fluctuations: what if you lose a client, and then you're stuck with all of those employees?' (Interview, HR manager (HQ), July 2003)

The company also faced challenges in harmonizing its practices across employee groups, as many of its European locations had been acquired and the existing workforce retained their former contracts under transfer of undertakings rules. For example, the previous workforce had more frequent breaks and more flexibility over when they took them, and these workers refused to negotiate new individual contracts when the new management tightened scheduling. This led to some resentment between groups of employees, and managers complained that Germany's 'rigid' regulatory environment was preventing them from implementing a more consistent policy.

However, Vendotel had been successful in diffusing a common culture throughout the organization. Several layers of management were dedicated to coordinating strategies and 'aligning metrics' across the company's European call centres. At the same time, specific incentives and training were also driven by different client

---

*Vendotel is a pseudonym.

demands. Most of Vendotel's clients were multi-national firms that contracted with the vendor to service their customers in North America and Europe. This led to intensive benchmarking and communication across 'account groups'. Vendotel had also recently joined a quality certification program developed for the call centre industry, in which third-party monitors visited different locations to ensure they were meeting targets for reducing staff turnover, improving training quality, and meeting targets for improving agent performance. This was driving more standardization across the

European locations, and managers were convinced the certification process had contributed to improved quality.

For further details, see Doellgast (2006).

Questions

1 How did Vendotel's relationships with its clients influence the HRM practices it adopted?

2 How did managers seek to create consistency in HRM across locations, and what challenges did they encounter?

The outsourcing of the HR function

The outsourcing of HR departments and HR activities is one specific form of outsourcing and off-shoring that has direct effects on HRM. Here we refer to the firm that performs the outsourced work as a *service provider*, consistent with the terminology used in this industry. As we noted in the introduction, firms have long outsourced support services, including HR activities such as recruitment or executive salary and benefit comparisons. In some countries, such as Germany and the Scandinavian countries, firms have also handed over aspects of their dealings with trade unions to employers' organizations. Here, however, we are primarily concerned with the relatively recent phenomenon of the outsourcing of a significant part of HR departments and HR activities.

The growth of HR outsourcing has been facilitated by the development of ICT platforms, pressures to reduce support costs, and the growth of provider companies. Adler (2003) describes several recent trends that have been particularly important: HR departments have been the target of 'belt-tightening' as firms seek to focus on core activities; the HR legal environment has become increasingly complex, requiring subject matter experts (particularly for international firms); M&As create new challenges in managing the cross-border movement of employees; and improvements in HR information systems have made it easier to outsource information in areas such as payroll.

In response to these trends, several segments of HR service providers have developed. First, specialized consultants supply a particular service, such as recruitment support, pensions planning, or wage and benefit surveys and systems. Second, technology providers supply specialist technological support services such as customized HR software. Third, a growing number of very large providers (such as IBM, Accenture, Exult, and HP) provide a wide range of HR services and operate on a global scale. These often involve multi-billion pound deals lasting up to 10 years. Overall, it has been estimated that the global market for HR outsourcing is growing rapidly, and may rise from $30 billion in 2005 to $50 billion by 2010 (Sako and Tierney 2005).

The recent increase in the demand for such services started with a small number of large firms in the private sector in the US and UK. However, in more recent years demand has grown among smaller companies and public sector organizations across countries. National context again appears to have some affect on strategies: firms in countries such as Germany or Japan have preferred to keep more of their HR in-house, perhaps reflecting greater risk aversion and a willingness to continue to accept support services as a fixed cost. However, even in these countries firms have recently shown a greater willingness to outsource support services. Despite some reversions to in-sourcing, it is likely that the outsourcing of many aspects of HR will continue (Adler 2003; Gospel and Sako 2008).

Firms face a number of considerations in managing the outsourcing of HR processes. First, managers should evaluate the pros and cons of moving these activities to a provider. Advantages are similar to those of other forms of outsourcing, including lower costs through the reduction of overall headcount, the payment of lower salaries, the greater division of labour, and access to better ICT systems; higher quality work with fewer mistakes, especially in routine areas; and the freeing up of internal staff to concentrate on more important strategic or operational matters. Estimates suggest the average annual HR cost per supported employee is between $1,500 and $2,000 when carried out by an outsourced HR service provider, compared to $5,000 in-house (Sako and Tierney 2005). However, there are also disadvantages and risks, such as reduction in morale both among transferred and retained staff; the risk of losing core competencies and control over activities; and the costs of administering what are often very lengthy contracts. Because of the sensitive nature of these contracts and because they often run for between up to 10 years, there has to date been little research evaluating these costs and benefits.

Second, managers must decide which HR functions to outsource. For the most part, strategic and high value-added activities will be kept in-house. These usually include the management of senior managers, the development of HR strategy, and the development of HR policy. Sensitive issues such as dealings with works councils and trade unions will also typically be kept in-house. More transactional services are more often outsourced, including the running of HR information systems (including call centres), the administration of recruitment and exits, payroll processing, compensation and benefits, pensions administration, training administration, and expatriate and travel arrangements. Outsouring the 'transactional' and retaining the 'strategic' activities has been a way in which HR professionals working in different functions have sought to improve their profile within their organizations.

There are several borderline or 'grey' areas where the advantages of outsourcing are more ambiguous. For example, an employee at a manufacturing plant might have a complaint about his or her level of pay. This may seem to be a simple individual issue, for which the facts are easily ascertained and where, if necessary, corrective action can be taken by the service provider. However, several employees may start to make similar complaints, contributing to a collective grievance and possible trade union involvement in an industrial dispute. If payroll is outsourced, it may be unclear who should spot this escalating problem and who should intervene at what stage. Such contingencies are usually set out in the service contract with procedures for resolving disputes between the user and the provider about 'who does what'. For the most part, however, the parties prefer to deal with these issues through personal contact and trust rather than on a purely contractual basis – and this may become more difficult when one or more service providers are involved. Overall, in deciding what to keep in-house and what to outsource, firms have to think through what aspects of HR add value, based on their core competencies or strategies (Adler 2003; Gospel and Sako 2008).

Third, managers face the choice among different routes to outsourcing. One decision concerns whether to integrate and transform HR arrangements before handing them over to a provider or to first hand them over and let the provider transform systems (Sako and Tierney 2005). Large multinational companies typically have different HR arrangements that cover distinct product or service areas and geographical areas, which may be the legacy of mergers and acquisitions or a decentralized organizational structure. The decision to transform and integrate these HR systems before outsourcing may allow the firm to form a better opinion about what to outsource and what to keep in-house and to retain knowledge and capability in core areas. The firm will also pay a lower price for the service contract since much of the hard work of integrating and standardizing HR will have already been done.

An increasingly popular strategy for transforming HR systems is to create a shared services centre (SSC) that brings together business processes shared across units within a company. A recent survey of MNCs in the UK revealed that around one third of the companies operated an international SSC in the HR function (Edwards *et al.* 2007). A large multinational may establish a limited number of these centres in different parts of the world covering all its global activities. A related decision is then whether to outsource HR for a particular country or region or to do this worldwide. This latter decision will depend on factors that have been discussed elsewhere in this volume, such as how centralised the company already is and whether it has gone down the shared services route (Gospel and Sako 2008).

The next case study, below, provides an example of different approaches to outsourcing of shared services taken by two multinationals, P&G and Unilever.

A fourth consideration relates to the effects of outsourcing on HR professionals. Here two main groups should be considered. The first group are those who stay within the firm. On the one hand, these employees can be freed up from more routine matters and allowed to become 'business partners', where they may work as part of more value-adding line management teams. On the other hand, there may be a continuing need for some 'experts' who will have a more detailed knowledge of one particular area, such as the design of executive compensation plans. There will also be a need for a new class of managers whose job is to administer the contract with the service provider and deal with 'seam' issues when they arise. These include issues that are in grey areas, that have not been sufficiently thought through when the contract was negotiated, or that are new to the contract; for example, when an acquisition is made and new employee groups have to be integrated in the contract.

The second group are the HR managers who are transferred to or hired by the service provider. On the one hand, some of these employees will have to concentrate on rather narrow areas, losing their ability to perform generalist roles. On the other hand, they are able to move into an organization specializing in their area, rather than working in a department that is an adjunct to the primary activity of the firm. They, therefore, may feel that their careers have been enhanced (Gospel and Sako 2008; Ulrich 1997).

The outsourcing of HRM by P&G and Unilever

Procter & Gamble (P&G) and Unilever are two older, established companies; the former US, the latter Anglo-Dutch. Both firms grew from origins in soap and detergent manufacturing and moved into home and personal care, food processing, and other areas. They are two of the world's leading companies in the fast moving consumer goods industry and have long been rivals with one another throughout the world.

Both had expanded internationally from the interwar years onwards and now operate in most major countries in the world. Unilever has always been larger, operating in more countries and producing a wider range of products and brands. The two firms expanded through internal growth, but grew most significantly via M&As.

To manage their diverse activities, both companies developed international and product divisions and for a time managed their complexity through something like matrix structures. They gave significant autonomy to their subsidiary companies; and as a result, national, divisional, and subsidiary headquarters developed extensive managerial hierarchies in areas such as marketing, finance and accounting, procurement, IT and HRM.

Through the 1990s, pressure on both companies grew, as many of their brands matured and became subject to competition from other companies and from supermarket own-label products. They came to realise that there were economies of scale and scope to be gained from focusing on a smaller number of categories and brands. Hence, the two companies began substantial programmes of closure, divestiture, and reorganization, with a trend towards greater centralization.

P&G moved faster in this direction and reorganized itself in a more centralized manner, with greater oversight of activities by corporate headquarters. In parallel, it gave less emphasis to divisions and constituent companies. One aspect of this was the creation in 1999 of a worldwide shared services centre, defined as business processes shared across units within the company. This was called Global Business Services (GBS) and brought together support staff in various areas, including HRM, in three main centres throughout the world. In this way, the company felt it achieved better services at lower cost by leveraging economies of scale, standardizing processes, introducing the newest technology, and freeing higher level staff to concentrate on less routine personnel matters.

In 2003, P&G decided that it would outsource most of its GBS activities. After a long process, it outsourced many lower-level transactional and a middle-level HR services to IBM on a global basis. The service contract is for 10 years, is valued at $400 million, and covers 98,000 employees in over 80 countries.

Unilever, being more complex and less centralized, moved more slowly. But, from the early 2000s onwards, it also developed shared services centres, though mainly on a regional basis. In turn, it then had a set of decisions to make as to whether to develop shared services further or more directly to outsource certain activities. In 2006, it chose to leap-frog and outsource HR on a global basis. The resulting contract with Accenture is for seven years, is valued at €700 million, and covers 200,000 employees in 100 countries.

For further details, see: Gospel and Sako (2008).

Questions

1 Why did P&G and Unilever decide to outsource their HR activities?

2 How did the two companies' outsourcing strategies differ?

3 What are the advantages and disadvantages of these different approaches to outsourcing?

Conclusions

The management of outsourcing is increasingly important to the HRM strategies of both national and international firms. This chapter has presented a number of issues that managers face in deciding to outsource various aspects of production or service provision and in managing contracts with subcontractors. On the basis of this discussion, we can draw several broad conclusions concerning the role of national context and firm strategies in outsourcing decisions.

First, while management faces an increasing range of choices concerning the structure of outsourcing and activities outsourced, these choices are often influenced by distinctive institutional constraints. Transfer of undertakings rules, industrial relations institutions, and the strategies of trade unions and other worker representatives can affect the cost of outsourcing and its impact on employees. Continental Europe stands out as having stronger protections than those in most other parts of the world, including organized consultation mechanisms to ensure that employee interests are considered in outsourcing decisions.

However, second, firms may increasingly be able to by-pass or circumvent these constraints. Outsourcing may weaken collective bargaining institutions; for example, by moving work outside of establishments covered by collective agreements or disrupting co-ordinated bargaining across a firm's production network. The threat of outsourcing or offshoring may allow firms to gain concessions from worker representatives. The HR function itself within large multinationals is increasingly shifted to shared service centres, and then often transferred to outsourced providers. This drives standardization and benchmarking of practices across countries, creating pressure to adopt a common HRM strategy across organizations or regions.

Taken together, this suggests that outsourcing will remain a contentious (and contested) area of firm strategy. Consideration of this phenomenon has shed further light on the extent to which firms are embedded in distinct contexts, demonstrating that they have increasing scope to globalise their operations. We have also seen that as they do so they face competing incentives to differentiate the way that different occupational groups are managed but also to achieve a degree of integration across them. Managing the process of outsourcing and its long-term effects on employees will be an increasingly important area for international HRM practitioners.

Review questions

1 Why do firms outsource people, primary activities, and support activities? Why has the volume of work that is outsourced been growing in recent years?

2 How do legal and institutional arrangements affect the transfer of people and work and the subsequent coordination of activities across organizational boundaries?

3 What are the potential benefits and costs of outsourcing aspects of the HR function?

Further reading

1 Special Issue on European Call Centres (2009) *European Journal of Industrial Relations,* 15(4).

The articles in this special issue examine cross-national differences in management strategies and employee outcomes in European call centres, based on survey data and case studies from Austria, Denmark, France, Germany, the Netherlands and Spain. Findings show large variation in outsourcing strategies and their impacts.

2 Grimshaw, D. and Miozzo, M. (2006) 'Institutional effects on the IT outsourcing market: analysing clients, suppliers and staff transfer in Germany and the UK', *Organization Studies,* 27(9), 1229–59.

The authors compare case studies of IT outsourcing in the UK and Germany. They illustrate the ways in which deliberative institutions and contracting rules affect strategies for transferring staff and managing HRM post-transfer.

3 Sako, M. and Tierney, A. (2005) 'Sustainability of Business Service Outsourcing: The Case of Human Resource Outsourcing', *AIM Research Working Paper,* 19 June.

This paper provides a good overview of recent trends in human resource outsourcing.

References

Adler, P. S. (2003) 'Making the HR outsourcing decision', *MIT Sloan Management Review,* 45(1), 53–60.

Araki, T. (2005) 'Corporate Governance, Labour, and Employment Relations in Japan: The Future of the Stakeholder Model', in Gospel, H. and Pendleton, A. (eds) *Corporate Governance and Labour Management.* Oxford: Oxford University Press, 254–83.

Barthelemy, J. and Geyer, D. (2001) 'IT outsourcing: evidence from France and Germany', *European Management Journal,* 19(2), 195–202.

Batt, R., Doellgast, V. and Kwon, H. (2006) 'Service Management and Employment Systems in US and Indian Call Centers', in Collins, S. M. and Brainard, L. (eds), *Offshoring White-Collar Work.* Washington, DC: Brookings Institution Press.

Caprile, M. and Llorens, C. (2000) *Outsourcing and Industrial Relations in Motor Manufacturing* (cited February 2005), www.eiro.eurofound.eu.int/2000/08/study/tn0008201s.html.

Coase, R. H. (1937) 'The nature of the firm', *Economica,* 4, 386–405.

Cooke, F. L., Earnshaw, J., Marchington, M. and Rubery, J. (2004) 'For better and for worse: transfer of undertakings and the reshaping of employment relations', *International Journal of Human Resource Management,* 15(2): 276–94.

Doellgast, V. (2006) 'Negotiating Flexibility: The Politics of Call Center Restructuring in the US and Germany', Dissertation, School of Industrial and Labor Relations, Ithaca, NY: Cornell University.

Doellgast, V. (2008). 'National industrial relations and local bargaining power in the US and German telecommunications industries', *European Journal of Industrial Relations,* 14(3), 265–87.

Doellgast, V. and Greer, I. (2007) 'Vertical disintegration and the disorganization of German industrial relations', *British Journal of Industrial Relations,* 45(1), 55–76.

Doellgast, V., Nohara, H. and Tchobanian, R. (2009) 'Institutional change and the restructuring of service work in the French and German telecommunications industries', *European Journal of Industrial Relations,* 15(4).

Dyer, J. H. and Singh, H. (1998) 'The relational view: cooperative strategy and sources of interorganizational competitive advantage', *The Academy of Management Review,* 23(4), 660–79.

Edwards, P., Edwards, T., Ferner, A., Marginson, P. and Tregaskis, O. (2007) *Employment Practices of MNCs in Organisational Context: A Large Scale Survey,* Survey Report, www2.warwick.ac.uk/fac/soc/wbs/projects/mncemployment/.

Eurofound (2007) Acquired Rights Directive, Review of Reviewed Item, European Foundation for the Improvement of Living and Working Conditions, *European Industrial Relations Dictionary,* www.eurofound.europa.eu/areas/industrialrelations/dictionary/definitions/acquiredrightsdirective.htm.

Gospel, H. and Sako, M. (2008) 'The Unbundling of Corporate Functions: The Evolution of Shared Services and Outsourcing in Human Resource Management', Oxford: Said Business School, mimeo.

Grimshaw, D. and Miozzo, M. (2006) 'Institutional effects on the IT outsourcing market: analysing clients, suppliers and staff transfer in Germany and the UK', *Organization Studies,* 27(9), 1229–59.

Helper, S. (1991) 'How much has really changed between US automakers and their suppliers', *Sloan Management Review, Summer,* 15–28.

Holtgrewe, U. (2001) 'Recognition, intersubjectivity and service work: labour conflicts in call centres', *Industrielle Beziehungen,* 8(1), 37–54.

IMF (2007) *World Economic Outlook,* Washington: International Monetary Fund.

Justice, E.C. o. (2002) Temco Service Industries SA, Judgement of the Court (Sixth Chamber), Directive 77/187/EEC – Safeguarding of employees' rights in the event of transfers of undertakings, 24 Jan., Review of Reviewed Item, http://curia.europa.eu/jurisp/cgibin/gettext.pl?lang=en&num=79979875C19000051&doc=T&ouvert=T&seance=ARRET&where=().

Kakabadse, A. and Kakabadse, N. (2002) 'Trends in outsourcing: contrasting USA and Europe', *European Management Journal,* 20(2): 189–98.

Kessler, I., Coyle-Shapiro, J. and Purcell, J. (1999) 'Outsourcing and the employee perspective', *Human Resource Management Journal,* 9(2), 5–19.

Lane, C. and Bachmann, R. (1997) 'Co-operation in inter-firm relations in Britain and Germany: the role of social institutions', *British Journal of Sociology,* 48(2), 226–54.

Langlois, R. N. (2003) 'The vanishing hand: the changing dynamics of industrial capitalism', *Industrial and Corporate Change,* 12(2), 351–85.

OECD (2007a) *Economic Outlook,* Paris: Organization for Economic Cooperation and Development.

OECD (2007b) *Offshoring and Employment: Trends and Impacts,* Paris: Organization for Economic Cooperation and Development.

Porter, M. E. (1985) *Competitive Advantage: Creating and Sustaining Superior Performance.* New York: Free Press.

Rubery, J., Cooke, F.-L., Earnshaw, J. and Marchington, M. (2003) 'Inter-organizational relations and employment in a multi-employer environment', *British Journal of Industrial Relations,* 41(2), 265–89.

Sako, M. (2006) *Shifting Boundaries of the Firm: Japanese Company – Japanese Labour,* Oxford: Oxford University Press.

Sako, M. and Jackson, G. (2006) 'Strategy meets institutions: the transformation of labor relations at Deutsche Telekom and NTT', *Industrial and Labor Relations Review,* 59(3), 347–66.

Sako, M. and Tierney, A. (2005) 'Sustainability of Business Service Outsourcing: The Case of Human Resource Outsourcing', *AIM Research Working Paper, 19 June.*

Shire, K., Schönauer, A., Valverde, M. and Mottweiler H. (2009) 'Union bargaining and temporary contracts in call centre employment in Austria, Germany and Spain', *European Journal of Industrial Relations,* 15(4).

Sørensen, O. and Weinkopf, C. (2009) 'Pay and working conditions in finance and utility call centres in Denmark and Germany', *European Journal of Industrial Relations*, 15(4).

Taylor, P. and Bain, P. (2004) '"India calling to the far away towns': the call centre labour process and globalisation', *Work, Employment and Society*, 19(2): 261–82.

Ulrich, D. (1997) *Human Resource Champions*, Boston, MA: Harvard Business School Press.

Williamson, O. E. (1975) *Markets and Hierarchies: Analysis and Antitrust Implications*, New York: Free Press.

Index